Indigenizing Education

A volume in
Research for Social Justice: Personal~Passionate~Participatory Inquiry
Ming Fang He and JoAnn Phillion, *Series Editors*

Research for Social Justice:
Personal~Passionate~Participatory Inquiry

Ming Fang He and JoAnn Phillion, *Series Editor*

Indigenizing Education

Transformative Research, Theories, and Praxis

edited by

Jeremy Garcia
University of Arizona

Valerie Shirley
University of Arizona

Hollie Anderson Kulago
Penn State University

INFORMATION AGE PUBLISHING, INC.
Charlotte, NC • www.infoagepub.com

Library of Congress Cataloging-in-Publication Data

A CIP record for this book is available from the Library of Congress
http://www.loc.gov

ISBN: 978-1-64802-690-4 (Paperback)
       978-1-64802-691-1 (Hardcover)
       978-1-64802-692-8 (E-Book)

CONTENTS

SECTION I
INDIGENIZING CURRICULUM AND PEDAGOGIES

SECTION II

REVITALIZING AND SUSTAINING INDIGENOUS LANGUAGE

SECTION III

ENGAGING FAMILIES AND COMMUNITIES IN INDIGENOUS EDUCATION

SECTION IV

CLOSING SECTION: INDIGENIZING TEACHING AND TEACHER EDUCATION

LIST OF FIGURES

LIST OF TABLES

RESEARCH FOR SOCIAL JUSTICE

Personal~Passionate~Participatory Inquiry

Research for Social Justice: Personal~Passionate~Participatory Inquiry is a book series which features social justice research on life in schools, families, and communities. This work connects the personal with the political, the theoretical with the practical, and research with social and educational change. The inquiries demonstrate three distinct and interconnected qualities. Each is personal, compelled by values and experiences researchers bring to the work. Each is passionate, grounded in a commitment to social justice concerns of people and places under consideration. Each is participatory, built on long-term, heart-felt engagement, and shared efforts. The principal aspects of the inquiries that distinguish them from others are that researchers are not detached observers, nor putatively objective recorders, but active participants in schools, families, and communities. Researchers engaged in this form of inquiry have explicit research agendas that focus on equity, equality, and social justice. Rather than aiming solely at traditional educational research outcomes, positive social and educational change is the focal outcome of inquiry.

Indigenizing Education, pages xiii–xviii
Copyright © 2022 by Information Age Publishing
www.infoagepub.com
All rights of reproduction in any form reserved.

Researchers engaged in personal~passionate~participatory inquiry in this series are diverse and their inquiries are far ranging in terms of content, people, and geographic locations studied. Their studies reflect new and exciting ways of researching and representing experiences of disenfranchised, underrepresented, and invisible groups, and challenge stereotypical or deficit perspectives on these groups. It is our hope that this book series will inspire preservice and in-service teachers, educators, educational researchers, administrators, and educational policy makers to commit to the enactment of educational and social change that fosters equity, equality, and social justice.

The work in this book series draws on diverse research traditions which promote social justice (Ayers et al., 2009) and the "Democratic Ideal" (Dewey, 1916, pp. 86–88) in education and life. The work of Du Bois (1903/1994), Cooper (1892/1988), Woodson (1933/1977), Freire (1970), and Ayers (2006) has also influenced social justice work in terms of its emphasis on the emancipatory, participatory, and social activist aspects of research. This work builds upon narrative inquiry (Clandinin & Connelly, 2000; Schubert & Ayers, 1999), particularly cross-cultural and multicultural narrative inquiry (He, 2003; He & Phillion, 2008; Phillion, 2002; Phillion & He, 2008; Phillion et al., 2005) in response to recognition of the complexity of human experience in increasingly diversified societies. These researchers incorporate narrative, story, autobiography, memoir, fiction, oral history, documentary film, painting, and poetry into inquiries. One special quality of their inquiries that distinguish them from other forms of educational research lies in understanding experience in its own terms rather than categorizing experience according to predetermined structures and theories (Phillion, 1999). Their inquiries are "peopled" with characters, rather than filled with categories and labels. In some forms of traditional educational research, experience is seen, shaped, and written about by the researcher using theoretically derived forms; in effect the experience is determined by the theory. Experience is the starting point of these inquiries and is in the forefront at every stage of research. Their inquiries arise from experiences of researchers and participants, rather than being formulated as abstract research questions, and they proceed by continual reference to experience as field texts are collected, analyzed, and interpreted, and as meanings are crafted.

Researchers engaged in this form of inquiry also draw on critical race theory (Gutierrez-Jones, 2001; hooks, 1991; Ladson-Billings, 1998, 2003; Parker et al., 1999; Stovall, 2005, 2016) and use stories to disclose hidden and silenced narratives of suppressed and underrepresented groups to counter metanarratives that portray these groups as deficient and inferior. They ask themselves questions about what is missing from the *official story* that will make the problems of the oppressed more understandable. By telling counter stories, researchers recognize the importance of commitment to equity and social justice and their obligation to link inquiry to social and educational change. The explicit aim of democratic and social justice work is to engage with oppressed groups and individuals and empower them to take effective action toward more just and humane conditions.

Three distinct and interconnected qualities, *personal~passionate~particip atory*, permeate the process of these social justice inquiries. Researchers not only collect, but often live in the stories of people with whom they engage in inquiry. They position stories collected in historical, sociopolitical, economic, linguistic, and cultural contexts, and contextualize their inquiries within struggles of underrepresented individuals and groups. Stories are presented in life-like ways; readers vicariously experience complexities, contradictions, and dilemmas of people's lives. There is a sense of "being there" and a sense of urgency for change. The stories told challenge orthodoxy, awaken critical consciousness, and create possibilities for change.

The work featured in this book series, embedded in life in schools, communities, and societies on the one hand, and powerful ideas of being human with strong commitment to a just society on the other, are at the heart of social justice work. Researchers begin with conscious reflection on experience to challenge assumptions, "to raise embarrassing questions," and "to confront orthodoxy and dogma" (Ayers, 2006, p. 85). They listen to "issues that marginalized or disadvantaged people speak of with excitement, anger, fear, or hope" (Ayers, 2006, p. 88). They learn directly from individuals and communities about problems and obstacles they face and explore possible solutions by drawing upon the experience and knowledge of participants. Researchers demonstrate strong commitment to the plight of their participants and the injustice embedded in the larger society. This commitment permeates every aspect of life, begins with small changes, and expands to larger contexts.

Personal~passionate~participatory inquiry thrives on the researcher's passionate involvement, strong commitment, and unfaltering advocacy for disenfranchised, underrepresented, and invisible individuals and groups. This passion, commitment, and advocacy cannot be cultivated in isolation. Rather, it calls for researchers to work with allies in schools and communities, to take to heart the shared concerns of individuals and groups, to build a community to develop strategies for the enactment of educational and social change that fosters equity, equality, social justice, freedom, and human possibility. Such a community can only flourish when the efforts of researchers join with the efforts of all educational stakeholders—preservice and in-service teachers, educators, administrators, educational policy makers, students, parents, and community members. We hope that the inquiries featured in this series will help social justice researchers and workers of this community move beyond boundaries, transgress orthodoxies, and build a participatory movement to promote a more balanced, fair, and equitable human condition. An expanded community, such as this, embodies possibilities and creates hope for more fulfilling, more equitable, more humane lives in an increasingly diversifying world.

—**Ming Fang He**
JoAnn Phillion

REFERENCES

Ayers, W. C. (2006). Trudge toward freedom: Educational research in the public interest. In G. Ladson-Billings & W. F. Tate (Eds.), *Education research in the public interest: Social justice, action and policy* (pp. 81–97). Teachers College Press.

Ayers, W., Quinn, T., & Stovall, D. (2009). *Handbook of social justice in education.* Routledge.

Clandinin, D. J., & Connelly, F. M. (2000). *Narrative inquiry.* Jossey-Bass.

Cooper, A. (1988). *A voice from the South.* Oxford University Press. (Originally published in 1892)

Dewey, J. (1916). *Democracy and education: An introduction to the philosophy of education.* Free Press.

Du Bois, W. E. B. (1994). *The souls of Black folks.* Fine Creative Media. (Originally published in 1903)

Freire, P. (1970). *A pedagogy of the oppressed.* Seabury.

Gutierrez-Jones, C. (2001). *Critical race narratives: A study of race, rhetoric, and injury.* New York University Press.

He, M. F. (2003). *A river forever flowing: Cross-cultural lives and identities in the multicultural landscape.* Information Age Publishing.

He, M. F., & Phillion, J. (2008). Personal~passionate~participatory inquiry into social justice in education. In M. F. He & J. Phillion (Eds.), *Research for social justice: Personal~passionate~participatory inquiry* (pp. 1–22). Information Age Publishing.

hooks, b. (1991). Narratives of struggle. In P. Mariani (Ed.), *Critical fictions: The politics of imaginative writing* (pp. 53–61). Bay.

Ladson-Billings, G. (1998). Just what is critical race theory and what's it doing in a nice field like education? *International Journal of Qualitative Studies in Education, 11*(1), 7–24.

Ladson-Billings, G. (Eds.). (2003). *Critical race theory perspectives on the social studies: The profession, policies, and curriculum.* Information Age Publishing.

Parker, L., Deyhle, D., & Villenas, S. (1999). *Critical race theory and qualitative studies in education.* Westview.

Phillion, J. (1999). Narrative and formalistic approaches to the study of multiculturalism. *Curriculum Inquiry, 29*(1), 129–141.

Phillion, J. (2002). *Narrative inquiry in a multicultural landscape: Multicultural teaching and learning.* Ablex.

Phillion, J., & He, M. F. (2009). Multicultural and cross-cultural narrative inquiry in educational research. *Thresholds in Education, 34*(1 & 2), 2–12.

Phillion, J., He, M. F., & Connelly, F. M. (Eds.). (2005). *Narrative and experience in multicultural education.* SAGE Publications.

Schubert, W. H., & Ayers, W. C. (Eds.). (1999). *Teacher lore: Learning from our own experience.* Educators International Press.

Stovall, D. (2005). A challenge to traditional theory: Critical race theory, African-American community organizers, and education. *Discourse: Studies in the Cultural Politics of Education, 26*(1), 95–108.

Stovall, D. (2016). *Born out of struggle: Critical race theory, school creation, and the politics of interruption.* State University of New York.

Woodson, C. G. (1977). *The mis-education of the Negro.* Africa World Press. (Originally published in 1933)

INTRODUCTION

Over the course of our educational journeys, as editors, we shared stories of what it has meant to be Diné and Hopi/Tewa educators. Through this process we found ourselves reflecting on our own pathways of becoming teachers who would eventually serve various Native schools. Our reflections revealed that we have collectively endured moments of tension, disconnect, healing, and transformation as we grew into the process of becoming Indigenous educators, and now, faculty and advocates working with and on behalf of Indigenous communities. A critical challenge in this process of becoming educators serving Indigenous communities is reflected in the history of our educational experiences across all learning contexts—both within Western schooling systems and within our local Native communities. We recognize the depths of which our own experiences have been heavily shaped by settler colonial ideologies; yet, we also have come to terms with the complexities in sustaining our own indigeneity, which for us and many others, signifies the strength and sustainability of our Indigenous values and knowledge systems. As we have pushed forward in engaging with our own work as scholar-educators, we recognize the need to continue co-creating opportunities that are driven by Indigenous values and contribute to supporting our youth, families, and communities. Over time, we have come to see that our Indigenous communities continue to work through similar tensions and questions of what it means to enact curriculum, pedagogy, and language revitalization grounded in transformative possibilities for social change and advocacy for Indigenous communities while sustaining Indigenous values and knowledge systems.

Indigenizing Education, pages xix–xxxiv
Copyright © 2022 by Information Age Publishing
www.infoagepub.com
All rights of reproduction in any form reserved.

This edited book brings various scholars, educators, and community voices together in ways that reimagines and recenters a learning process that embodies notions of Indigenous education rooted in critical Indigenous studies and pedagogies (Brayboy, 2005; Cajete, 2015; Garcia, 2020; Grande, 2015; Lee & McCarty, 2017; Lomawaima & McCarty, 2006; Shirley, 2017). By reimagining Indigenous education, we suggest that it be rooted in opportunities for a deep analysis of the systemic processes, forces, and structures of colonialism, White supremacy, capitalism, and neoliberalism that have worked to defy and dismiss our right to engage an education that is critical, culturally sustaining, and centers Native nation-building. Thus, reimagining and recentering Indigenous education rooted in critical Indigenous studies and pedagogies becomes a process of activating a critical consciousness that renews and sustains Indigenous goals through and across decisions made regarding curriculum, pedagogy, policies, assessments, and other aspects of education. We are indebted to the Indigenous youth, families, and communities who have shared their interactions with education across the chapters and who provide pathways to reconceptualize the intersection between Indigenous education, research, theories, and praxis.

INDIGENOUS EDUCATION

We hold firmly that Indigenous epistemologies serve as the basis for healing and resistance—leaving us to reaffirm, draw on, and enact Indigenous knowledge as a humanizing pedagogy and as a pedagogy of resistance. The values and strength of Indigenous Peoples are reflected in specific knowledge, worldviews, and relations to natural elements and land which reaffirm our indigeneity. Education from this context is evident within everyday life activities, lessons, stories, and songs; as well as more formally, during ceremonies. Within these settings, Indigenous educators are our parents, grandparents, uncles, aunts, and clan relatives whose knowledge is not measured by state regulations but is measured by an Indigenous identity rooted in the values of accountability to community through reciprocity, generosity, care, and responsibility. We also affirm that Indigenous youth are our educators as they tell us not only what they desire to know, to revitalize, to disrupt, to protect, but they also call upon us to learn from them—to co-construct knowledge—as they navigate new spaces and opportunities that inform their own identities. In many respects, youth are deconstructing Western structures of colonialism as they examine capitalist systems of exploitation and extraction or demand opportunities to unpack issues of identity politics and stereotypes. They are calling upon all who are invested in Indigenous education to engage a renewed spirit of education that is critical and underscores our relations to sustaining our Indigenous values and knowledge systems to be the source of guidance.

That said, Indigenous teachings continue to thrive in many ways. We are, however, aware of the concern that access to such knowledge and language has shifted in classroom spaces and continues to take on new meaning over the course of time. It is without question that we can observe how centuries of Western schooling has been an ongoing space of contention when deciding whose knowledge and values guide the framework for defining education within Indigenous communities. Unfortunately, oppressive Westernized schooling systems have been internalized; therefore, a process of unlearning and unschooling must take place. More recently, we see the resurgence of Indigenous teachings reflected in movement spaces where actions to protect our sacred sites, water, and land are occurring. Education in movement spaces creates opportunities for Indigenous education to be "a site of resistance and hope that reflects collective solidarity, sustains our epistemologies, and humanizes our relations to our landscapes" (Garcia et al., 2019, p. 97). Framing education in this way reconceptualizes education for Indigenous students, educators, and communities (Eagle Shield et al., 2020; Garcia, 2021; Garcia & Shirley; 2012).

Indigenous Research and Theories

> Anchor your research in Indigenous teachings. If you need guidance in Indigenous methodologies, follow the teachings. Indigenous theory-principles (or teachings) in Indigenous methodologies ensures that your research is and feels Indigenous. (Kovach, 2018, p. 223)

Fundamental to Indigenous research is centering epistemology. It also situates self, includes story, is political, and promotes justice in Indigenous communities and across diverse contexts (Archibald, 2008; Archibald & Parent, 2019; Kovach, 2009; Smith, 2012). As co-editors, our work has been guided by critical Indigenous research methodologies which privileges the voices of Indigenous communities and centers decolonization in the inquiry and meaning making processes. Based on our experiences, we found that using Indigenous research methodologies offers opportunities to draw on Indigenous epistemologies, axiologies, and ontologies to confront social, political, cultural, and educational challenges. More than just the collection of data, Indigenous research is a humanizing process that confronts settler colonialism, and treats our Indigenous knowledge systems as living, complex, intricate, and innovative principles that form new theories of thought and promotes self-determination and Native nation-building for Indigenous Peoples.

When working with Indigenous communities, it is important to reflect on the problematic history of unethical research conducted in Indigenous communities. Uncovering this history demonstrates how Western research methods were used to colonize, exploit, extract, and misrepresent Indigenous Peoples and communities. As such, we value Maori scholar Linda Smith's (2012) questions that communities and Indigenous activists continue to pose:

> Whose research is it? Who owns it? Whose interests does it serve? Who will benefit from it? Who has designed its questions and framed its scope? Who will carry it out? Who will write it up? How will its results be disseminated? (p. 10)

These questions are important to consider because any work done with Indigenous Peoples must be done in a good way and with a good heart. It entails having a heartfelt connection to the communities and requires researchers to be accountable to the communities. Similar to the contributors of this book, we were fortunate to have drawn on a variety of Indigenous research methodologies and theories to guide the ways in which our research would give back—but most importantly, how we would ethically engage research with our communities.

Critical Indigenous research and theories have offered new ways of contextualizing what it means to engage educators serving Indigenous students, schools, and communities within the field of Indigenous education. These important theoretical orientations, such as critical Indigenous theories and pedagogies (Brayboy, 2005; Brayboy & McCarty, 2010; Cajete, 2008; Garcia, 2020; Garcia et al., 2021; Grande, 2015; Lee & McCarty, 2017; Lomawaima & McCarty, 2006; Shirley, 2017) and decolonization (Battiste, 2000; Garcia & Shirley, 2012; Smith, 2012), call for Indigenous Peoples to critically examine the ways in which settler colonial structures and processes have impacted Indigenous communities. Such theoretical orientations also move us to be intentional in privileging Indigenous values and knowledges to center education as a space of healing, revitalization, and resistance. As a result, this book is a quest to understand and learn from the ways in which Indigenous scholarship and theoretical orientations create opportunities for Indigenous youth, educators, and community members to engage in transformative praxis.

Transformative Praxis

We perceive transformative praxis to be critical to any movement toward self-determination, sovereignty, and Native nation-building as it is a dialectical process that includes self-reflection and analysis of oppressive systems. It is an intentional effort that challenges oppressive systems and applies actions to address and transform injustices that have long impacted Indigenous Peoples. Rooted in critical pedagogy, leading scholar Paulo Freire, conceptualized praxis as a form of *conscientization* where marginalized peoples develop a critical awareness of the specific instances by which they have been silenced, exploited, and oppressed. Freire (2002) expands on the notion of praxis by suggesting:

> It is only when the oppressed find the oppressor out and become involved in the organized struggle for their liberation that they begin to believe in themselves. This discovery cannot be purely intellectual but must involve action; nor can it be limited to mere activism, but must include serious reflection; only then will it be a praxis. (p. 65)

A critical component of praxis is the process of bringing to the conscious mind the analysis of how one's social, cultural, political, and economic circumstances are affected by external conditions. Praxis is a form of self-liberation and a form of humanization in which individuals consciously "reflect upon their world in order to transform it" (Freire, 2002, p. 79). Our positioning of praxis insists that Indigenous youth, educators, families, and communities actively engage in *dialectical* processes where they participate in dialogical methods that analyze colonial and settler colonial systems and structures impacting their education, political status, communities, and lifeways. Praxis also embodies transformative actions that are guided by and sustain Indigenous values and knowledge systems.

While we value the possibilities critical pedagogy and Freire's conceptualizations of developing a critical consciousness holds for education; we recognize this takes on a distinct meaning when applied to Indigenous Peoples. Quechua scholar Sandy Grande (2015) proposes a Red pedagogy which offers a significant critique of critical pedagogy's positioning in relation to Western concepts of democracy and social justice; and underscores the notion that Indigenous Peoples have, and continue to, strive for intellectual and spiritual sovereignty. She further suggests:

> Most of all, it is a hope that believes in the strength and resiliency of indigenous peoples and communities, recognizing that their struggles are not about inclusion and enfranchisement to the "new world order" but, rather are a part of the indigenous project of sovereignty and indigenization. (Grande, 2015, p. 32)

In addition, we find Diné scholar Tiffany Lee's (2006) notion of developing a *critical Indigenous consciousness* with Diné youth helpful in naming this distinct process for Indigenous Peoples. Lee (2006) states:

Critical pedagogy provides the means to restore [an] Indigenous educational philosophy by calling attention to the effects of colonization and by empowering students to become critically conscious and aware of their own worth. However, a critical Indigenous consciousness emphasizes the notion that one's own worth is tied to their connection and service to their community. (p. 7)

Of significance to this book, each of the contributors activated a critical Indigenous consciousness with diverse Indigenous youth, educators, families, and community members that led to transformative praxis. Across the chapters, you will observe dialogues between the scholar-educators as they enacted various theories, shared stories, indigenized various curriculum and teaching practices, and reflected on the process of engaging in critical dialogues that generates a (re)new(ed) spirit of hope and commitment to intellectual and spiritual sovereignty (Grande, 2015). We learned that the intersection of critical Indigenous consciousness and transformative praxis "remain[s] an inward—and outward—looking process, a process of re-enchantment, of ensoulment, that is both deeply spiritual and sincerely mindful" (Grande, 2015, p. 74). The beauty of the work gifted to us across the chapters reflect a humanizing commitment to centering Indigenous knowledge, values, and language revitalization efforts that lead to collective solidarity and Native nation-building.

AROUND THE FIREPLACE TEACHINGS: THE INTERSECTION OF RESEARCH, THEORIES, AND PRAXIS

As co-editors, we reflect on the deep processes of how research, theory, and praxis intersect to move Indigenous education forward. Within our own work, we each centered our own Diné and Hopi/Tewa cultural values and philosophies to guide our research, teaching, and praxis. As a result, these cultural values and philosophies have shaped how we conceptualize our efforts in developing Indigenous teacher education programs in our respective universities. Hollie was director of Elmira College's Empowering Relationships Teacher Project that served several students from Native communities primarily located in the north eastern region of the United States. Valerie and Jeremy are the founding co-directors of the Indigenous Teacher Education Program[1] (ITEP, Figure I.1) at the University of Arizona. In what follows, we highlight ITEP's efforts in exemplifying the intersection of theory, research, and praxis within preparing cohorts of Indigenous teachers. ITEP is designed around four key aspects that drive all efforts in Indigenous teaching and teacher education. They are: (a) teachers as Native nation builders, (b) Indigenous knowledges, values, languages, (c) critical Indigenous theories and pedagogies, and (d) justice-centered education (Garcia, 2021;

Figure I.1   ITEP logo designed by Hopi artist, Samuel Tenakhongva.

Garcia et al., 2021; Shirley, 2021). In this generative process of creating the ITEP conceptual framework, we found correlations to the premise of this book. During a conversation in the fall of 2020 with ITEP coordinator, IngriQue Salt (Diné) we discussed the creation of a visual that reflected the intersection of research, theory, and praxis with the ITEP framework at the center. The visual in Figure I.2 serves as a metaphor and symbolic representation that depicts the fundamental process in developing ITEP—and now, it is embedded in the collective work of Native nation-building across this book. The following is IngriQue's narration of her thought process as she designed

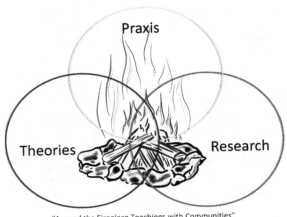

"Around the Fireplace Teachings with Communities"
by Lók'aad Dine'é | Ashį́į́hí | Bit'ąąnii | To'dích'íi'nii
IngriQue Salt and the teachings instilled by her mother, father, and grandparents

Figure I.2   Around the fireplace teachings with communities: Research, theories, and praxis. Visit ITEP website for color image.

the visual entitled *K'o nibaahgonaa Nanit'in: Around the Fireplace Teachings With Communities* based on Diné epistemology and ontology. She reflects:

> Embedded within the ITEP framework are the Blue, Yellow, White, and Red variations of colors that are associated with not only the four components of the theoretical framework, but also the teachings embedded in the various Indigenous communities in which the ITEP teacher candidates represent.[2]
>
> We all share a form of the fireplace (see Figure I.2) and we, as Indigenous Peoples, have specific teachings that are shared around the fireplace which brings community together in ceremony, for social gatherings, or for winter story sharing. For Diné, this is known as *ko biyaagi danitignigii* (under the fireplace knowledge where it is held). *K'ó*, the fireplace, has deep significance. *K'ó nibaahgonaa nanit'in* means "around the fireplace teachings" and has been with us since time immemorial. The philosophy of K'ó nibaahgonaa nanit'in nourishes us physically, emotionally, spiritually, and mentally. This nourishment is done through sharing *hané* (stories and teachings) around our creation, our way of life, and our oral histories passed down from our Ancestors. These fireplace teachings bring together our *K'é*, known as "all our relations."
>
> From the hottest source of the fire are blue flames which are at the center and represent our theories/philosophies rising up. This energy represents the thermodynamics for community to internalize the teachings that inform research, theory, and practice to sustain our communities. Next, the red flames represent research. Through research, we are learning, planning, identifying ways of healing, problem-solving, and solution-building. The theories instilled in the land and the universe have influenced us to be Indigenous researchers since time immemorial. Finally, the yellow flames signify *Nilch'i* (our air/oxygen), which represents praxis. Collectively, the flames rise high because of oxygen generated by our *Nanit'in* (teachings), our *Jei* (heart), our *Iiná* (life), our *Naat'aanii Naat'a* (hope). It is what brings life and energy to us. Here we practice, privilege, and promote our Indigenous knowledge, values, and languages. This can be done through *Sa'ah Naagháí Bik'eh Hozhóón* which is the corn pollen path of life. These teachings form the basis of Diné theories and praxis.
>
> We, as Indigenous Peoples, have teachings that have been shared by the researchers, scientists, theorists, philosophers, and educators in our communities. These teachings form the basis of our theories. We have to be able to strategically think about why things fail, why we succeed, and understand how to move forward with what we are given. Just like *Tó* (water), we must know how the waters move across various terrains, how it is absorbed by the land and sun. Learning from the water, we have to be mindful of how we move with care in our planning and learning because our theories can be destructive, but also so beautiful because they are natural laws that bring our healing. When we center ourselves back to the fireplace teachings, we are valuing the voices, stories, and theories; we are valuing the planning process for moving forward in life with a good heart, mind, and body. (personal communication, August 2020)

As we engaged in dialogue, IngriQue shared her ideas of around the fireplace teachings where the flames symbolize the *energy needed to activate Native nation-building*. In essence all elements of the fire represent the energy needed to sustain, revitalize, and (re)center our communities. Through the fireplace teachings, the emergence of this energy has always been with us and this energy radiating through the flames fuels our responsibility, respect, reverence, and reciprocity (Archibald, 2008; Archibald & Parent, 2019) to Indigenous communities. These values and responsibilities are the jei (heart), íína (life), nanit'in (teachings), and naat'aaníí naat'a (hope) that drive the Native nation-building work embedded in each of the chapters reflected in this book. We see that the intersection of research, theories, and praxis are profoundly evident across the landscapes of the good work occurring across Indigenous education, communities, and Native nations. We trust this visual will continue to contextualize the deeper layers of what Indigenous research and education mean for and with Indigenous Peoples. We are indebted to IngriQue for her deep engagement in generating a visual that represents the core of how each of the chapters have been conceptualized. It is an indigenizing process that gives life and breath to all that we are accountable to in our respective Indigenous nations.

Indigenous Education as Native Nation-Building

Native nation-building is intimately linked to the learning contexts of our Indigenous theories that move Indigenous youth and communities to enact respect, responsibility, reverence, and reciprocity in their daily thoughts and actions. Native nation-building is an essential process that speaks to developing and sustaining a consciousness around how Indigenous communities collectively privilege traditional knowledge, culture, and language as sources of reasoning to advance agency, social change, advocacy, and leadership in Indigenous communities. We suggest drawing on critical Indigenous theories in learning contexts to activate a critical consciousness that leads to Native nation-building. Having the analytical tools for deconstructing educational choices from critical Indigenous theoretical orientations, educators and researchers are rethinking the process and purpose of education in ways that are transformative and sustainable in Indigenous communities. However, it is important to note that, "Indigenous nations cannot successfully engage in nation building projects that are driven by sovereignty and self-determination unless they develop independence of the mind by taking action to restore pride in their traditions, languages, and knowledge" (Brayboy et al., 2012, p. 15). As such, the intention of this book is to bring forth the ways in which researchers, educators, and Indigenous communities are co-constructing transformative efforts that draw on Indigenous theories to intentionally

Indigenize learning contexts. Specifically, highlighting the on-the-ground work occurring in Indigenous communities.

CENTERING SCHOLAR-EDUCATOR RELATIONS

This book highlights the importance of dialogues and the strength in relationships necessary for Indigenizing learning contexts; therefore, faculty affiliated with higher education institutions in affiliation with Indigenous educators share their experiences in promoting Indigenous knowledge, values, and languages in their collaborative efforts. The book includes authors who are Indigenous parents, community members, knowledge holders, and/or educators who work within preK–20 institutions. We feel this is a powerful collaboration to highlight the ways in which critical and culturally sustaining Indigenous theories intersect with research to influence praxis (spaces of practice, reflection, action); thus, we asked faculty associated with various projects to contribute to this book in partnership with Indigenous teachers, Elders, or community members who are engaged with their respective projects. Each scholar-educator wrote their own chapters in relation to one another. The chapters written by faculty describe the theoretical orientations and research methodologies. The partnering *transformative praxis* chapters are shorter in length, are self-reflective, and are written as stories that capture the process, impacts, and outcomes of engaging critical Indigenous theories and research. Some of the scholar-educators chose to re-story their work together rather than within separate chapters. Across the chapters, the scholar-educators identify prominent Indigenous theoretical frameworks that shaped their research and scholarship while engaging Indigenous youth, educators, and communities in developing a critical Indigenous consciousness. We asked the contributors to consider the questions: (a) "What is the intersection of critical Indigenous theory, research, and learning spaces (schools/nonschool settings)?"; (b) "How does Indigenous knowledge, culture, and language lead to empowerment and Native nation-building?"; and (c) "How are transformative possibilities and outcomes reflected in projects and dialectical relationships between the scholar-educators?"

We are pleased to have contributions from diverse educational contexts spanning across early childhood education, elementary education, secondary education, and tribal colleges and universities (TCUs). The following sections that shape the premise of this book are: "Indigenizing Curriculum and Pedagogies," "Revitalizing and Sustaining Indigenous Languages," and "Engaging Families and Communities in Indigenous Education."

Section I: Indigenizing Curriculum and Pedagogies

This section focuses on critical Indigenous theories and pedagogies that center Indigenous knowledges, culture, and identity. The scholar-educators within this section address notions of Indigenous education as culturally and linguistically sustaining, revitalizing, humanizing, transformative, decolonizing and/or social justice oriented. Each chapter examines and problematizes the process of activating Native nation-building through education. We begin this journey with scholar-educators Valerie Shirley (Chapter 1) and Samuel Tenakhongva (Chapter 2). Valerie creates pathways for the theoretical orientation of Indigenous social justice pedagogy as a critical and heart-felt engagement. While Samuel's transformative narrative illuminates the ways Indigenous social justice pedagogy was enacted in the classroom with Hopi students in Arizona. Next, Timothy San Pedro and Andrea Box (Chapter 3) engage us in a collaborative sharing and a re-storying of lessons learned from a Native American literature class within an urban setting in the southwest region of what is now known as the United States. In the closing chapters for this section, we journey to the islands of Hawaii. Walter Kahumoku III (Chapter 4) introduces the Hawaiian Culture Based Education (HCBE) movement that emerged as a grounding framework for Kamehameha Schools and Native Hawaiian education. The complementary HBCE chapter by Monica Kaʻimipono Kaiwi (Chapter 5) is a transformative narrative that describes her process of analyzing selected curriculum and engaging a decolonizing pedagogy in her English literature class.

Section II: Revitalizing and Sustaining Indigenous Languages

Of great significance to Indigenous Peoples is sustaining and revitalizing Indigenous languages. They are vital to and inseparable from educational approaches that ensure "cultural continuity and community sustainability because it embodies both every day and sacred knowledge essential to ceremonial practices" (McCarty & Lee, 2014, p. 109). Additionally, Indigenous languages are linked to the epistemologies that guide the identity formations of Indigenous Peoples and are the means by which values, philosophies, principles, theories, and an entire worldview are conveyed. The contributions to this section center Indigenous knowledge, language, and identity formations that facilitate the process by which youth, community educators, teachers, and schools understand their roles and responsibilities to their families, community, and people. We begin with Tiffany Lee (Chapter 6) who reflects on her partnership with the Native American Community Academy (NACA) where she describes a pedagogy of relationships to achieve a state of *hózhó* and *wólakȟota* that supports learning Indigenous languages through relationships with each other and through cultural values and protocols. Anpaoduta Flying Earth's (Chapter 7) transformative narrative expands on sharing his experiences of sustaining relationships and language revitalization efforts as a leader of NACA. Kari Chew (Chapter 8) and Michelle Scaggs Cooke (Chapter 9) share efforts to engage in the revitalization of the Chickasaw language. Michelle's transformative narrative draws upon key successes and impacts of community Indigenous language teachers in classrooms. Next, the late Ataugg'aq Grant Kashatok and Leisy Wyman's co-authored chapter (Chapter 10) is rooted in *Yuuyaraq* (the way of the human being) to guide educational leadership by asserting rhetorical sovereignty in supporting Yup'ik youth development and linguistic survivance while addressing climate change. We close the section by looking to transformative possibilities for the "the making of an Indigenous language teacher." Through personal narratives, co-authors Bernita Duwahoyeoma, Ada Curtis, and Sheilah Nicholas (Chapter 11) provide pathways to sustain opportunities for Indigenous language teachers to promote self-determination and Native nation-building.

Section III: Engaging Families and Communities in Indigenous Education

The final section illuminates the values of family–community–education partnerships that mobilize a collective effort to engage with and inform Indigenous education. Spanning across early childhood education, Indigenous teacher education, and Tribal community colleges, this section focuses on how Indigenous knowledges are identified as a foundation to systematically build and sustain social-educational environments that align with those of Indigenous communities. They collectively contribute to newly envisioned approaches to emphasize ways family–community–educators collaborate to support Indigenous students; particularly in ways that are grounded in sustaining relationships, embodying reciprocity, and contributing to cultural sustainability through curriculum development. Centering on Diné and Haudenosaunee contexts, co-authors Hollie Anderson Kulago and Tsiehente Herne (Chapter 12) open this section by storying their experiences in reflecting on the power of community and the ways certain concepts taught through ceremonies can guide Indigenous family and community engagement. Danielle Lansing (Chapter 13) describes the process of engaging Native families in co-creating meaningful early childhood education (ECE) curriculum through a photovoice project. Vibeka Mitchell's transformative narrative (Chapter 14) expands on her experiences of working with Danielle as she navigated the curriculum development process.

Also rooted in ECE, Nahrin Aziz-Parson presents experiences of developing a Coast Salish place-based education curriculum with families and communities (Chapter 15). Cynthia Wilson's transformative narrative (Chapter 16) further contextualizes her contributions as a representative of the Lummi Sche'lang'en department and community member who supported the process of developing the Coast Salish place-based curriculum. We close this section with Christine Stanton (Chapter 17) who contextualizes a unique community-centered digital storywork project to support the revitalization of Indigenous knowledges in partnership with the Blackfeet Nation. The transformative narrative shared by Brad Hall, Cinda Burd-Ironmaker, and Eric Cox (Chapter 18) share their insights on the process of co-creating Piikani digital histories with the Blackfeet Nation in relation to the theoretical concepts of community-centered digital storywork.

Closing Section: Indigenizing Teaching and Teacher Education

The closing chapter centers Indigenous teaching and teacher education as a space of hope in advancing Native nation-building. Indigenizing teacher education "is a call to action, a journey to REgenerate our languages, cultures, and traditions. It is time to REthink our current practices and REclaim our traditional wisdom and practices from within which Native pedagogy and practice have always existed" (Kawai'ae'a, 2008, p. 42). Indigenizing teacher education from this lens is essential as teacher education programs tend to "perpetuate mainstream systems of thought and practices" (Lansing, 2014, p. 26) rather than prepare teachers to be accountable to the unique social, cultural, and political contexts of Indigenous communities. In the concluding chapter, Keiki Kawai'ae'a, Jeremy Garcia, renee holt, Ac'aralek Lolly Carpluk, and Valerie Shirley bring forward a call to action that moves critical Indigenous theories to practice and action within the field of Indigenous teaching and teacher education.

PATHWAYS TO SOLIDARITY AND NATIVE NATION-BUILDING

Each scholar-educator woven across the chapters embodies the drive to center and (re)conceptualize the intellectual and spiritual sovereignty (Grande, 2015) of Indigenous Peoples and communities. We are indebted to the scholar-educators and Indigenous children, youth, families, educators, and communities who have shared their personal narratives that speak to the strength of critical and culturally sustaining pathways. These are transformative moments grounded in critical Indigenous theories, research, and praxis that inform the next generation of Indigenous educators who sustain Indigeneity and promote Native nation-building.

Before moving forward, and in recognition of the dialogical nature of the scholar-educators, we turn to Indigenous scholars Jo-ann Archibald and Amy Parent's (2019) recollections of the late First Nation Elder, Dr. Vincent Stogan, who gifted them with the Indigenous teaching of "Hands Back, Hands Forward." They write:

> In our gatherings, he often asked us to form a circle in order to share some good words and thoughts to establish a comfortable environment before beginning our work together. In the circle, we extend our left palm upwards, to symbolize reaching back to receive teachings (knowledge and values) from the Ancestors and those who have traveled before us. We are given the challenge and opportunity to put these teachings into our everyday lives. We then have a responsibility to pass those teachings to others, especially the younger generation, which is shown when we put our right palm downwards. In the circle we join hands in respect, reverence, responsibility and reciprocity. Elder Stogan's teaching also exemplifies inter-generational learning. (p. 4)

As you engage with the Indigenous communities reflected in the following chapters, we invite you to extend your *left palm upwards* in ways that allow you to receive the teachings of not only your own Indigenous knowledge and values; but also the lessons inherent in this book on Indigenizing education through transformative research, theories, and praxis. As you hold your *right palm downwards*, we hope the work offered here will continue to be shared with the next generation of Indigenous scholar-educators, youth, families, and communities in ways that lead to collective solidarity and Native nation-building in Indigenous communities.

— **Jeremy Garcia**
Valerie Shirley

NOTES

1. See University of Arizona Indigenous Teacher Education Program website at http://itep.coe.arizona.edu/
2. See ITEP website http://itep.coe.arizona.edu

REFERENCES

Archibald, J. A. (2008). *Indigenous storywork: Educating the heart, mind, body, and spirit.* University of British Columbia Press.

Archibald, J., & Parent, A. (2019). Hands back, hands forward for Indigenous storywork as methodology. In S. Windchief & T. San Pedro (Eds.), *Applying Indigenous research methods: Peoples and communities* (pp. 3–20). Routledge

Battiste, M. (2000). *Reclaiming indigenous voice and vision.* UBC Press.

Brayboy, B. (2005). Toward a tribal critical race theory in education. *The Urban Review, 37*(5), 425–446.

Brayboy, B., Fann, A., Castagno, A., & Solyom, J. (2012). *Postsecondary education for American Indian and Alaska Natives: Higher education for nation building and self-determination.* In K. Ward & L. Wolf-Wendel (Eds.), ASHE Higher Education Report, *37*(5).

Brayboy, B. J., & McCarty, T. L. (2010). Indigenous knowledges and social justice pedagogy. In T. K. Chapman & N. Hobbel (Eds.), *Social justice pedagogy across the curriculum: The practice of freedom* (pp. 184–200). Routledge.

Cajete, G. (2008). Seven orientations for the development of Indigenous science education. In N.

K. Denzin, Y. S. Lincoln, & L. T. Smith (Eds.), *Handbook of critical and Indigenous methodologies* (pp. 487–496). SAGE Publications.

Cajete, G. A. (2015). *Indigenous community: Rekindling the teachings of The Seventh Fire.* Living Justice Press.

Eagle Shield, A., Paris, D., Paris R., & San Pedro, T. (2020). *Education in movement spaces: From Standing Rock to Chicago freedom square.* Routledge.

Freire, P. (2002). *Pedagogy of the oppressed.* Continuum.

Garcia, J. (2021). Decolonial praxis: Hopi/Tewa educators engage critical Indigenous theories and pedagogy. In J. Tippeconnic & M. J. Tippeconnic Fox (Eds.), *On Indian ground: The southwest* (pp. 131–148). Information Age Publishing.

Garcia, J. (2020). Critical Indigenous pedagogies of resistance: The call for critical Indigenous educators. In S. Steinberg & B. Down (Eds.), *The SAGE handbook of critical pedagogies* (Vol. 3; pp. 574–586). SAGE Publications.

Garcia, J., & Shirley, V. (2012). Performing decolonization: Lessons learned from Indigenous youth, teachers and leaders' engagement with critical Indigenous pedagogy. *Journal of Curriculum Theorizing, 28*(2), 76–91.

Garcia, J., Shirley, V., & Grande, S. (2021). Grounding Indigenous teacher education through red praxis. *Oxford research encyclopedia of education.* https://oxfordre .com/education/view/10.1093/acrefore/9780190264093.001.0001/ acrefore-9780190264093-e-1112.

Garcia, J., Shirley, V., Windchief, S., & San Pedro, T. (2019). Pedagogy of solidarity: Hope and promise in Indigenous movement spaces. In D. Paris, A., Eagleshield, R. Paris, & T. San Pedro (Eds.), *Education in movement spaces: From Standing Rock to Chicago freedom square* (pp. 87–98). Routledge.

Grande, S. (2015). *Red pedagogy: Native American social and political thought* (10th anniversary ed.). Rowman & Littlefield.

Kawai'ae'a, K. (2008). "Ho'I hou I ke kumu!" Teachers as nation builders. In M. Benham (Ed.), *Indigenous educational models for contemporary practice: In our mother's voice volume II* (pp. 41–45). Routledge.

Kovach, M. (2009). *Indigenous methodologies: Characteristics, conversations, and contexts.* University of Toronto Press.

Kovach, M. (2018). Doing Indigenous methodologies: A letter to a research class. In N. K. Denzin & Y. S. Lincoln (Eds.), *The SAGE handbook of qualitative research* (5th ed.; pp. 214–234). SAGE Publications.

Lansing, D. R. (2014). Preparing teachers to contribute to educational change in Native communities: Navigating safety zones in praxis. *Journal of American Indian Education, 53*(3), 25–41.

Lee, T. S. (2006). 'I came here to learn how to be a leader': An intersection of critical pedagogy and Indigenous education. *InterActions: UCLA Journal of Education and Information Studies,* 2(1). http://escholarship.org/uc/item/92m798m0

Lee, T. S., & McCarty, T. L. (2017). Upholding Indigenous education sovereignty through critical culturally sustaining/revitalizing pedagogy. In D. Paris & S. H. Alim (Eds.), *Culturally sustaining pedagogies: Teaching and learning for justice in a changing world* (pp. 61–82). Teachers College Press.

Lomawaima, K. T., & McCarty, T. L. (2006). *"To remain an Indian" Lessons in democracy from a century of Native American education.* Teachers College Press.

McCarty, T. L., & Lee, T. S. (2014). Critical culturally sustaining/revitalizing pedagogy and Indigenous education sovereignty. *Harvard Educational Review, 84*(1), 101–124.

Shirley, V. J. (2021). Finding face, finding heart, and finding foundation: The making of an Indigenous teacher. In J. Tippeconnic & M. J. Tippeconnic-Fox (Eds.), *On Indian ground: The southwest* (pp. 97–113). Information Age Publishing.

Shirley, V. J. (2017). Indigenous social justice pedagogy: Teaching into the risks and cultivating the heart. *Critical Questions in Education, 8*(2), 163–177.

Smith, L. T. (2012). *Decolonizing methodologies* (2nd ed.). St. Martin's Press.

ACKNOWLEDGMENTS

As members of the Diné Nation (Valerie Shirley and Hollie Anderson Ku-lago) and the Hopi/Tewa Nation (Jeremy Garcia), we appreciate all who have guided us along this journey. The strength of this work comes from the love and care for our Indigenous Peoples, communities, languages, and knowledge systems that have guided us long before this publication. We continue to be guided by the teachings and visions of our Ancestors, fami-lies, communities, and children. Essential to this process is the continued engagement with our respective cultural practices which sustains our indi-geneity. Thus, we are indebted to our community Elders, knowledge keep-ers, and speakers of Indigenous languages who continue to share knowl-edge and engage in ceremonial processes that define our epistemological and ontological worldviews as Indigenous Peoples.

We thank JoAnn Phillion and Ming Fang He for selecting this book to be represented as part of their series, *Research for Social Justice, Personal~ Passionate~Participatory Inquiry*. The scholars, educators, and communities captured within this book unquestionably speak to notions of social justice. Each chapter is grounded in unique personal, passionate, and participatory inquiry that contributes to advancing the field of Indigenous education. We each offer special recognition to JoAnn, our former dissertation chair at Purdue University, for her guidance and support. Her mentorship has allowed us to grow professionally and personally in necessary ways that un-doubtedly informed our work.

To the contributors of this book. We appreciate your patience as this project took longer than anticipated. Your work has moved us in so many

Indigenizing Education, pages xxxv–xxxviii
Copyright © 2022 by Information Age Publishing
www.infoagepub.com
All rights of reproduction in any form reserved.

ways. We are privileged to have been the first to have learned with and from your work. We thank you and your communities for sharing the work you do to ensure the continuance of our existence as Indigenous Peoples, communities, and sovereign nations. We know that behind each chapter comes devoted careers and immeasurable networks of relationships created to better the educational opportunities for our children. None of us are alone in this work and the collaboration between universities, Tribal colleges and universities, and community educators straightens solidarity with boundless possibilities. We appreciate the work that each contributor put into the harmonious preservation of these relationships. You collectively embody deep levels of reciprocity and accountability to Indigenous children, youth, families, Elders, and communities.

As editors, we want to offer a special acknowledgment of the late Ataugg'aq Grant Kashatok who has since journeyed on to be with his Ancestors. Grant's contributions to this book, his community, and the field of Indigenous education are received with much gratitude. We are blessed to have been informed by his long standing leadership and advocacy for Yup'ik and Indigenous Peoples. Grant's legacy will leave footprints that will continue to guide Indigenous youth, families, and communities for generations to come.

We give special thanks to the contributing Indigenous artist who created the visuals and symbols that give this work deep meaning and intentionality in centering our Indigenous worldviews. Mavasta Bryant Honyouti (Hopi), we thank you for creating the cover to the book. We also value the symbols that were designed for the Indigenous Teacher Education Program (ITEP) at the University of Arizona and were utilized at the introduction of each section in this book. To, IngriQue Salt (Diné), we value your immense contributions in building ITEP as program coordinator. Your ITEP design representing the *Fireplace Teachings Across Indigenous Communities* has become part of the conceptual framework of the book.

To our families, we appreciate the patience as we navigated a new process of co-editing a book. Valerie Shirley and Jeremy Garcia give special thanks to their daughters Sonwai and Talasmoenom Garcia for their unwavering support and patience. Hollie Anderson Kulago would like to thank her son Hunter and daughter Haylee. Our children have informed our thinking along the way as we strive to understand and respond to evolving conceptualizations of Indigenous education. We give deep gratitude to our parents and clan relatives who continue to offer stories of emergence and commitment to our cultural epistemologies and ontologies—you are the foundation that grounds our Indigeneity.

Throughout the course of co-editing this book, we were also directing Indigenous teacher education projects at our respective institutions. Valerie and Jeremy are co-founding directors of the ITEP at the University of

Arizona. Prior to her joining Penn State University, Hollie was director of the Empowering Relationships Project at Elmira College. We would like to recognize our Indigenous teacher candidates who have accepted the responsibility to be caretakers of the next generation of learners. Your willingness to engage in reconceptualizing curriculum and pedagogy on behalf of your respective Native nations is evident. Through examining your own identities and engaging with notions of Indigenizing pedagogies, decolonization, and critical Indigenous studies, we know our Indigenous students, youth, families, and communities are in good hands.

Finally, to our Ancestors who endured challenges that have impacted our lifeways as Indigenous Peoples, we honor you for embodying the strength needed to ensure the next generations continue to speak our Indigenous languages and remain committed to being guided by Indigenous knowledges and values. As we complete this project, we give thanks to our Elders and holders of knowledge who share(d) the knowledge needed to understand and reach this celebratory moment. Our collective resiliency is a keen reminder that we must continue to strive for an education that is intergenerational and grounded in our Indigenous values, knowledge, and languages.

—**Ahxe'hee** (Dine)/**Kwakwhá** (Hopi)

SECTION I

INDIGENIZING CURRICULUM AND PEDAGOGIES

CHAPTER 1

NATIVE INTELLECTUALISM THROUGH INDIGENOUS SOCIAL JUSTICE PEDAGOGY

Learning as a Critical and Heartfelt Engagement

Valerie Shirley

Nibi [water] is who we are and what we are made of. Our first teaching of water begins in our mother's womb. We all have this teaching. We can't live in our mother's womb without water. All of you would not be sitting here today if it was not for water. It makes me sad every time I think about the water. I'm sad because our waters are sick. Not just here in Canada but all over the world. I worry that we will be facing the same situation in our neighbor country where pipelines have burst and contaminated the land and water. I'm not standing here for fun. I'm here to make a serious statement. I don't want to come back when I am seventy and nothing has been done. Mother Earth was in existence for billions of years and she doesn't need us; we need her. It is time for humanity to stop terrorizing Mother Earth and give her time to heal. This land is not for sale or profit. We need to come together for our water (APTN News, 2016).

Indigenizing Education, pages 3–20
Copyright © 2022 by Information Age Publishing
www.infoagepub.com
All rights of reproduction in any form reserved.

The opening words are from 12-year old Autumn Peltier who spoke at the United Nations Summit in December 2016. Autumn is Anishinaabe-kwe and a member of the Wiikwemkoong First Nation which is in northern Ontario, Canada. The work of being a water protector and activist for her started at the age of 12 when she began to question why people could not drink the water on Ontario Indigenous lands. She shared that the strength and inspiration to do this activist work emerged from two women in her life—her mother who continues to ensure her girls are raised with a deep sense of identity through Anishinaabe teachings (Peltier, 2016) and her great aunt, Josephine Mandamin, also known as "Grandmother Josephine" (Peltier, 2019). Grandmother Josephine was founder of the Mother Earth Water Walks which is a water walk movement that began in 2003. Josephine was a "tireless advocate and Water Walker [who] dedicated her life to the protection of the Great Lakes and surrounding waters while raising awareness that water is not only sacred but also our lifeline" (Indigenous Goddess Gang, 2019). Josephine walked 10,900 miles around each of the Great Lakes and helped establish the Great Lakes Protection Act (Indigenous Goddess Gang, 2019). Grandma Josephine passed on in 2019 and Autumn has continued to carry the work of her great aunt Josephine in taking care of the water. Autumn is now 16 years old and has continued her advocacy through large venues such as the United Nations Global Landscapes Forum in 2019. In another poignant address, she stated:

> We need to have more Elders and youth sitting at the decision table when people make decisions about the lands and waters. We need to protect the inhabitants around all waters across the world. We need to remember that our Ancestors' prayers are still protecting this land and that we are our Ancestors' hope. One day I will be an Ancestor and I want my descendants to know I used my voice so that they can have a future. (CBC News, 2019)

The deep sense of responsibility in protecting the water stems from Anishinaabekwe teachings that women are caretakers of the water (Indigenous Goddess Gang, 2019). Through Autumn's story, it is evident that Indigenous youth have a significant role in sustaining Indigenous lifeways and communities. Embodying this role and responsibility requires a critical Indigenous consciousness (Lee, 2006) about the spiritual and cultural significance of and connection to land and water in addition to an awareness of the exploitation and extraction of land from corporations who see land and natural resources as profit. More than ever, cultivating and sustaining collective agency among youth, Elders, and community members are needed in protecting Indigenous futures. Though Autumn had become critically aware of the contamination and pollution of the water in her community through her own life and family experiences, other Indigenous youth can, and do, have similar experiences of developing critical awareness of such environmental and social justice issues within the classroom context as well.

Educators of Indigenous youth are in ideal settings to engage youth in thinking critically and purposefully about the contexts of their people and land. In this chapter, I provide an overview of, and expand on, a decolonial framework for teaching and learning that I call "Indigenous social justice pedagogy" (ISJP). The framework of ISJP evolved from a research study I conducted with Indigenous Diné (Navajo) youth in which I drew on social justice principles of transformation, decolonization, healing, and mobilization to examine identity with Diné youth (Shirley, 2017). When Autumn started her work as a water protector, she was the same age (12 years old) as some of the Diné youth in my research study (Shirley, 2011).

RESEARCH CONTEXT: DINÉ YOUTH (DE)CONSTRUCT IDENTITY

In a classroom located on the Diné Nation in Arizona, I[1] taught a variety of lessons connected to settler colonialism, White supremacy, assimilation, and Diné *hané* (Diné philosophies and origin stories) within a critical Indigenous qualitative research study. Over the course of 4 months, I experimented with teaching these topics to Diné students (ages 12–14) because I was interested in learning more about how youth would respond to engaging with the process of decolonization that included the advancement of a critical Indigenous consciousness, healing, and transformative action. The overarching question that guided this study was: How do Diné youth produce and make meaning of their identities when they are exposed to a process of critically examining Diné history and contemporary issues while simultaneously learning Diné stories, values, and philosophy? The youth were taken through a preliminary process of decolonization that allowed them to self-reflect on their own identities and examine how they were being influenced by surrounding social forces. Specifically, they engaged in critical dialogues around the history of colonialism through the Diné Long Walk period and the Treaty of 1868; the history of boarding school experiences and the policies toward civilization and assimilation; and the contemporary influences of popular culture, the media and technology. I also included a component that emphasized Diné hané (stories and teachings) embedded in Sa'ah Naagháí Bik'eh Hozhóón (Diné epistemology that translates into living a long, balanced and harmonious life). By the end of the study, the students spoke about ways they could actively make changes within themselves and their people (Shirley, 2011).

Mobilizing Native youth to critically engage in examining colonial history and present-day realities of their Indigenous communities were at the core of my research journey. My ideas and pedagogical approaches were influenced by my own personal experiences of being both a student and a teacher on the Diné Nation, as well as critical Indigenous theoretical frameworks in the fields of critical Indigenous studies and education. I also made it a point to first center my pedagogical approach on the Diné epistemology and then make connections to the critical scholarship on colonization and decolonization.

INDIGENOUS SOCIAL JUSTICE PEDAGOGY: INDIGENOUS TEACHERS AS NATIVE INTELLECTUALS

Indigenous social justice pedagogy is a pedagogical framework for reconceptualizing curriculum in schools serving Indigenous students and relies heavily on the role of Native educators cultivating a political, spiritual, and critical consciousness in Indigenous youth. Native educators have a decision to make in the classroom: whether they will continue to reinforce the standard schooling processes centered on Western structures and ideologies or whether they will embody intellectual sovereignty through their curriculum and pedagogy to reinforce Indigenous lifeways. In making such a decision, it is important for Native educators to see themselves as Native intellectuals and to think critically about the knowledge and stories that make up curriculum. One is encouraged to reflect on the types of curricula within schools by asking such questions: Whose knowledge and stories are told and whose are left out? Who is represented in the curriculum and who is not? What theories guide the curriculum development process? I turn to Dakota scholar Elizabeth Cook-Lynn (2008) who posed the following questions on conceptualizing Native intellectualism:

> Is anyone doing the intellectual work in and about Indian communities that will help us understand our future?...What is Native Intellectualism? Who are the intellectuals? Are they presenting ideas, moving through those ideas and beyond? Are they the ones who recapture the past and preserve it? Are they thinkers capable of supplying principles that may be used to develop further ideas? Are they capable of the critical analysis of cause and effect? (p. 343)

Cook-Lynn (2008) drew attention to the ways individuals might reflect on their roles and responsibilities "to change the world, to know it, and make it better by knowing how to seek appropriate solutions to human problems" (p. 341). In such roles and responsibilities, she pointed out that intellectuals would need "to be at the forefront of theory" (p. 340). In this respect, it is important to note that within Indigenous contexts, our theories are intricately connected to origin stories (Archibald, 2008; Begay, 2002; Benally, 1994), life-experience stories (Archibald, 2008), and survivance stories (Vizenor, 2007). In connecting theory and stories, Cook-Lynn (2008) drew specific attention to identity and how storytelling assists in understanding and defining what it means to be "Indigenous." Origin stories are grounded in Indigenous epistemologies that describe our relationships to land, values, ceremony, and many cultural contexts in which we are immersed; therefore, these stories are the foundation of one's Indigenous identity (Begay, 2002; Benally, 1994; Cook-Lynn, 2008). Tanana Athabaskan scholar Dian Million (2014) posited that Indigenous Peoples "have always had theories about their worlds and their lives and their communities...These Indigenous concepts of how the world works, and how it came to be, can never be summarily dismissed. They work differently...Story *is* Indigenous theory" (p. 35). Similarly, in "Land as Pedagogy," Leanne Simpson (2012) expanded on theory within Nishnaabeg context as stories embedded in the land:

> A "theory" in its simplest form is an explanation of a phenomenon, and Nishnaabeg stories in this way form the theoretical basis of our intelligence. But theory also works a little differently within Nishnaabeg thought. "Theory" is generated and regenerated continually through embodied practice and within each family, community and generations of people. "Theory" isn't just an intellectual pursuit—it is woven within kinetics, spiritual presence and emotion, it is contextual and relational. It is intimate and personal, with individuals themselves holding the responsibilities for finding and generating meaning within their own lives. Most importantly, "theory" isn't just for academics; it's for everyone." (p. 7)

Theories are infused with energy and strength to generate meaning within our lives. Cook-Lynn suggests the idea that Native intellectuals should embody and ground such theories in relation to their work. There are, however, various types of stories and theories to consider. For example, life-experience stories are personal stories learned through one's life's journey and recounting life-experience stories informs teaching and learning (Archibald, 2008). In addition, survivance stories are stories of one's interactions with oppressive situations and systems that also exemplify the courage and strength in resisting the effects and impacts of colonial violence. Survivance stories frame the ways in which Indigenous Peoples continue to take action in promoting well-being in Indigenous communities collectively (Vizenor, 2007). Origin stories, life-experience stories, and survivance stories are theoretical framings that guide the ways we make sense of our world; the ways we engage a critical analysis of how and what we might change in our world to create a better future for our communities. In addition to drawing on stories, one must also center political notions of tribal sovereignty and self-determination within one's role as a Native intellectual.

Native intellectualism reinforces theories that "produce forms of analysis that take up political issues in ways that have important consequences for communities of every sort" (Simpson & Smith, 2014, p. 7). Teaching is not only an intellectual act, but also a political one. Teachers of Indigenous youth are in ideal positions to embody Native intellectualism and move theory to practical action, specifically through curriculum and pedagogy. In essence, they become Native intellectuals who move theory to action in the classroom. Through their curriculum and pedagogy, they awaken a level of critique of numerous oppressive forces and (re)align the consciousness of the students with *k'é*—relations to land, culture, people, and the universe—which embody Indigenous notions of praxis.

Native intellectuals draw on critical Indigenous theories to inform curriculum and pedagogy. Critical Indigenous theoretical frameworks critique and disrupt the impacts of colonial structures and systems and foregrounds Indigenous perspectives, contexts, and knowledge systems to bring about change and transformative outcomes in Indigenous communities. A pedagogical framework I propose to guide this endeavor is ISJP. ISJP informs the curriculum development process in examining issues of oppression, marginalization, and settler colonialism in historical and present-day contexts to promote transformative outcomes in Indigenous communities. Settler colonial systems have worked to disconnect Indigenous Peoples from their worldviews which result in disrupting connections to Indigenous knowledges, values, and languages; therefore, we must collectively, and intentionally, work to reconnect ourselves and the next generations to Indigenous epistemologies, ontologies, and axiologies. Particularly within the classroom, ISJP influences educators to be intentional in creating curriculum and pedagogical experiences that (a) mobilize decolonization; (b) promote, revitalize, and protect Indigenous languages, values, and knowledge systems; and (c) inspire youth to advance collective solidarity and sustainability in seeking solutions to contemporary issues by bringing about tranformative outcomes, balance, and well-being within their communities. Such a pedagogical approach to teaching and learning ultimately contributes to Indigenous nation-building. Embedded in ISJP are three components: decolonization, Indigenous epistemologies and ontologies, and Native nation-building. Each of the ISJP components are described in the following sections.

Decolonization: Mobilizing Decolonial Praxis

Every school is either a site of reproduction or a site of change. In other words, education can be liberating, or it can domesticate and maintain domination. It can sustain colonization in neo-colonial ways, or it can decolonize. (Battiste, 2013, p. 175)

Any discussion about (re)visioning schools as sites of change that are liberating and decolonizing for Indigenous students must be accompanied by an examination of settler colonialism characterized by White supremacy, racism, land dispossession, and cultural genocide. It is no question that the roots of schooling structures are shaped in relation to these ideologies and fundamentally worked to promote an education for colonization, Christianization, and assimilation. In her work on the history of American Indian education, Mvskoke/Creek scholar K. Tsianina Lomawaima (1999) exposed such colonial ideologies and tactics of "civilization." She explained "that civilization required Christian conversion; that civilization required subordination of Native communities, frequently achieved through re-settlement efforts; and that Native people had mental, moral, physical, or cultural deficiencies that made certain pedagogical methods necessary for their education" (p. 3). Without a critical awareness of this history and ideologies, Native educators risk reinforcing these ideologies; therefore, it is incredibly important for Native educators to have ideological clarity in understanding how schools are structurally rooted in the ideological forces of White supremacy, patriarchy, racism, and capitalism. As such, a decolonial examination of such structures in Indigenous communities should ultimately be "informed by critical theories of education" (Grande, 2008, p. 250). Robert Allen Warrior (1995) and Donna Deyhle and Karen Swisher (1997) critiqued the early conceptualizations of culturally responsive teaching approaches within the field of "Indian education" in the 1990s. They revealed, "American Indian scholars have largely resisted engagement with critical educational theory, concentrating instead on the production of historical monographs, ethnographic studies, tribally centered curriculums, and site-based research" (in Grande, 2004, p. 1). Critical theories of education—such as Red pedagogy (Grande, 2015); Tribal critical race theory (Brayboy, 2005); critical Indigenous pedagogy (Garcia & Shirley, 2012); land as pedagogy (Simpson, 2012); critical culturally sustaining/revitalizing pedagogy (Lee & McCarty, 2017); among many others—critique and disrupt colonial and Westernized schooling structures and its impacts on Indigenous Peoples and communities; and recognize Indigenous epistemologies and ontologies as sources of strength and power to activate transformative possibilities in Indigenous education and communities. Such critical Indigenous theories of education engage the process of decolonization by uncovering the historical and present-day infiltration of colonial structures, policies, practices, and ideologies that are entrenched in schools serving Indigenous students and communities. Critical Indigenous theories assist in reconceptualizing and restructuring schools rooted in Indigenous knowledges, languages, and values.

Decolonization is an essential component in ISJP. Winona Wheeler was influential in informing my initial ideas on decolonization which has guided the pedagogical process of conducting my research study with Diné youth. She stated:

> A large part of decolonization entails developing a critical consciousness about the cause(s) of our oppression, the distortion of history, our own collaboration, and the degrees to which we have internalized colonialist ideas and practices. Decolonization requires auto-criticism, self-reflection, and a rejection of victimage. Decolonization is about empowerment—a belief that situations can be transformed, a belief and trust in our own peoples' values and abilities, and a willingness to make change. It is about transforming...reactionary energy into the...rebuilding energy needed in our communities. (as cited in Wilson, 2004, p. 71)

Wheeler's conceptualization of decolonization influenced my thoughts on thinking deeply about developing a critical consciousness in the Diné youth through my curriculum planning and implementation process. Based on my personal experiences as a student and former teacher in Diné schools, I knew Indigenous histories and present-day contexts were silenced and/or excluded in the curriculum; and if they were included, it was a whitewashed version. As a student, I recall reading short paragraphs about the Navajo Long Walk and the Trail of Tears in textbooks—each excluded perspectives from Diné and Cherokee people and did not problematize settler narratives about Manifest Destiny, land acquisition/theft, or racism. For these reasons, I needed to engage the Diné youth in truth-telling of our histories. Truth-telling is a practice that brings in the narratives and perspectives that are intentionally excluded in curriculum documents. Examples of these are survivance stories that depict the violence, trauma, injustices, and atrocities prompted by racism/White supremacy, patriarchy, and capitalism/greed/profit as well as the stories that illustrate Indigenous Peoples' courage and strength in resisting such colonial violence (Shirley, 2017). Truth-telling advances a critical Indigenous consciousness (Lee, 2006). I included truth-telling narratives which activated a critical Indigenous consciousness with Diné youth about the history of Hwéeldi (the Diné Long Walk period) and the early boarding schools. The dialogues that followed each historical event were both critical and emotionally moving.

Truth-Telling as a Pedagogical Practice: Teaching Into the Risks

Students need to know that historical accounts are selective and are based on an interpretation that is determined by someone who decides how to tell a story. As Levstik and Barton (2005) explain, "Whenever history is told as a narrative, someone has to decide when the story begins and ends, what is included or left out, and which events appear as problems or solutions" (p. 6). This history involves a retelling from a certain person's interpretation. However, as storytellers determine what to include and not include, we may miss out on the perspectives of other people and groups deeply involved in the historical event. We need to help our students recognize that this is the way history is written and show them how to find additional stories. (Agarwal-Rangnath, 2013, p. 40)

Teachers are storytellers who decide what to include in their curriculum. One of the sessions in my research focused on examining the assimilative "Erase-Replace" policies and practices (Lomawaima & McCarty, 2006) within early boarding schools through truth-telling. I used photo analysis to explicitly analyze the process of transformation through assimilation in Native students at different boarding and missionary schools. I showed the students PowerPoint slides which included photos of Native children from Carlisle Indian School, Sherman Indian School, and other boarding schools in the early 20th century to provide the context of "to kill the Indian and save the man" within school policies and practices. During the presentation of slides, the students silently observed the images and examined details of each photo. At various points, they responded with, "wow" and "hmm" as they vicariously imagined what the Native children their age may have felt and experienced during that period. When I opened space for dialogue, the overall reactions and responses were first emotional. After expressing their initial feelings of sadness, anger, and shock, the students made personal connections to their own lives and recognized that their identities were certainly impacted by this process of forced assimilation their Ancestors had undergone. The students connected this process of assimilation to the present-day cultural and linguistic decline occurring in their community contexts. One student shared that her grandmother was punished for speaking the language. She stated:

My grandmother was whipped with a horsewhip when she spoke the language and now she doesn't really speak Navajo that much because of what they did to her and how they treated her. So now all of my cousins and I, we hardly know Navajo because of everything that happened to her.

This grandmother's life-experience stories informed her granddaughter's critical analysis of how historical events shaped the current contexts of the linguistic decline in community contexts.

In another session about the Diné Long Walk period and Hweéldi (known by Diné as "The place of great suffering" which was the concentration camp where Diné were held captive by the U.S. government), the stories were from a book called *Navajo Stories of the Long Walk Period* (Roessel, 1973). The book reinforced Diné perspectives and each chapter was a narrative retold by a Diné individual who heard the story from his or her grandparent/great-grandparent about their experiences with the extreme cruelty and harsh conditions before, during, and after their imprisonment at Hweéldi. The students were assigned a story to read and share with the group. One story was about a Diné woman who was pregnant and struggled to walk the 450-mile trek to Fort Sumner in New Mexico. Fatigued and exhausted, she and her family pleaded with the U.S. Army soldiers to let her rest. The student shared her thoughts:

> It was really sad to see that she got shot just because she couldn't keep up. And she tried to say we could wait until I had it [the baby] and maybe I could keep up, but [the soldiers] didn't want to do that. I was sad because a lot of us died during the Long Walk. I was mad at the same time too. Pissed off, angry. I still feel mad about it. I mean in our culture we just have to protect our people.

In response to how the events were driven by U.S. policies rooted in imperialism, White supremacy, and a desire for material gain, one student shared that he was angered by how our people were kept inside a fence and treated like animals and suffered from sicknesses due to lack of food, water, and shelter.

Truth-telling is emotionally intense and will leave students exhausted due to the violence. When I read stories from the book *Reclaiming Diné History: The Legacies of Navajo Chief Manuelito and Juanita* (Denetdale, 2007), one student shared that she previously read the book and appreciated how Diné scholar Jennifer Denetdale described the Long Walk experiences because "some of the other books told by non-Navajos would tell lies." While students are ready to engage this history through survivance stories, it is critical for teachers to consider the age and developmental level of students and remain committed to telling the truthful histories, including such survivance stories. Pedagogically, teachers must cautiously navigate the emotional responses and reactions of students who need assistance in reasoning through their emotions and should, therefore, intentionally draw on Indigenous epistemologies and ontologies to move students toward healing, resistance, and transformative outcomes. The "heart knowledge" within Indigenous epistemologies and ontologies (Archibald, 2008) soothe emotions and reinforce students' identities. Within such heart knowledge, Beth Cuthand clarified, "There is something more than information being transmitted: there's energy, there's strength being transmitted from the storyteller to the listener and that is what's important in teaching young people about their identity" (as cited in Archibald, 2008, pp. 84–85). ISJP assists teachers in mobilizing the decolonization process and infuses Indigenous epistemologies and ontologies into the classroom by not only guiding the curriculum development process, but by also cultivating Indigenous identities. Considering that the deconstruction of colonialism engenders feelings of anger, sadness, and frustration when truth-telling reveals stories of injustice and violence, I propose educators draw on Indigenous epistemologies to cultivate the heart toward healing and empowerment.

Cultivating the Heart: Indigenous Epistemologies

Cultivating the heart through Indigenous epistemology is fundamental for nurturing and guiding students through the process of critically examining "the root harm" (McCaslin & Breton, 2008, p. 512) of the social, political, and environmental issues occurring in Indigenous communities caused by the impacts of colonialism, oppression, and injustice on students' lives and communities. Indigenous epistemologies and nihí o'ol'íí (our ways of life through our worldview) fundamentally contributes to the healing of our community members and promotes empowerment. Indigenous stories have power because they are infused with Indigenous philosophies, values, language, songs, histories, and worldviews. Stories of origin and creation "are always treated as treasured and precious teachings, they not only contain valuable knowledge about the environment but are fundamental to our identity—[traditional stories] provide and inform the uniqueness of us as groups of people" (Pihama, 2019, p. 140). In Diné, these stories are known as hané and are the sources of healing and empowerment. Engaging youth in such decolonizing and Indigenizing experiences provide them with real opportunities to "reject victimage" and begin working for social change and Native nation-building in their communities. Hawaiian scholar Manu Aluli Meyer (2008) affirms that the goal is to rely on "ancient agency [our Indigenous epistemology] so we can accurately respond to what is right before our very eyes" (p. 217). ISJP encourages educators to integrate unique ways for ensuring Indigenous epistemologies are reflected in both the curriculum and in the overall classroom community that fosters relationships based on Indigenous values of respect, reciprocity, reverence, and responsibility (Archibald, 2008).

The Diné epistemology of Sa'ah Naagháí Bik'eh Hozhóón, for example, is an entire system grounded in Diné spiritual teachings and traditional wisdom that constitutes the basis where one finds strength and stability (Benally, 1994). This holistic knowledge system and foundation explain how we gain teachings and learn from the experiences in which we engage (Benally, 1994; Haskie, 2002). We place the concept of hozhó (harmony and balance) at the center of our consciousness as we reason through our daily decisions in life. Hozhó is the last word in Sa'ah Naagháí Bik'eh Hozhóón and is an important concept (of many) that we continuously strive to achieve at all times. I connected the teachings of Sa'ah Naagháí Bik'eh Hozhóón to the overall design of my research with Diné youth because hozhó is intricately connected to emotions. As an adult, I personally experienced the feelings of anger, frustration, and grief as I deeply examined the impacts of colonialism in Indigenous contexts in graduate school. I, therefore, wanted to ensure hozhó was restored within each of the students at each phase of the research process. It is important to note that maintaining hozhó and living Sa'ah Naagháí Bik'eh Hozhóón are activated through the Indigenous theory principles of Nitsáhákees (thinking), Nahat'á (planning), Iiná (implementing), and Siih Hasin (assessing)—this is our process of praxis (Shirley & Angulo, 2019). Emotions are central in each of these principles and guide the meaning making and learning processes toward hozhó.

Guided by the teachings within Diné philosophy of life and learning in my research, I was intentional in considering the emotions of students during each session and discussion; particularly considering the emotions that would be prompted by truth-telling and moving them toward the state of hozhó activating healing, empowerment, and motivation. Collectively, the Diné youth expressed similar sentiments I experienced when introduced to the topics within the curriculum stating, "the process got me thinking a lot" and it "was good because we spoke to each other and talked a lot about how we felt about things that we were learning in the discussions." As educators, it is our job to nourish the learning spirit (Battiste, 2013) and pedagogically elicit spaces of learning that purposefully and carefully activate the mind and emotions within students. Meyer (2008) described the power of emotions within the learning process through the notion of embodied knowing: "Our thinking body is not separated from our feeling mind. *Our mind is our body.* And both connect to the spiritual act of knowledge acquisition" (p. 223). The pedagogical tools used to generate these spaces of learning in my research study were critical dialogues and critical self-reflections. As a result of the interactive exchange of thoughts and feelings within these learning spaces, the emotional and critical responses led to contradictions, tensions and "a-ha moments" within the students' conceptualizations of their situations and identities.

Other studies conducted on Diné education focused on the larger rationale of including Diné Indigenous knowledge in the classrooms for the purpose of maintaining and sustaining a strong Diné cultural identity to promote intellectual sovereignty. In a study entitled *Awakened Belonging: Utilizing Traditional Stories to Enhance Self-Perception of Diné Children*, Diné scholar Lula Begay (2002) examined Diné students' experiences of hearing traditional Hózhóójí[2] stories in the classroom and found that the spiritual stories affected their self-perception and enhanced their identity as Diné. Begay's work pointed out that the students were highly interested in hearing more stories because the stories reflected their history, their heritage, their language, their culture, and their ancestral way of life in the past. When Begay integrated traditional stories into the classroom, the students made such comments as:

> I like the Navajo [stories] Ms. Begay told us today. I felt [proud] of myself and I just wanted to hear more and could not wait [until] Monday again. And I told my [whole] family. And my grandma [told] us all about her mom and

the way she told her [stories]. And we always sit in front of her and she would tell us all about things. I [learned] that I need to be strong and be on my own rainbow road. (p. 78)

Traditional Diné stories are the foundation for stabilizing one's identity, and this study showed that strengthening one's identity enhanced students' self-perception and contributed to academic success in school. Similar comments were made by other students in her research as they demonstrated their pride in being Diné. Begay (2002) concluded:

> It is important that teachers provide a foundation for both the cultural and educational growth for the Diné children by utilizing the traditional Diné stories in the classrooms. Perhaps as a result of this intervention, in spite of the continued Western education, Diné society will be able to retain its unique Diné identity. (p. 108)

Another study that integrated Diné cultural knowledge is *"Our Songs are Alive": Traditional Diné Leaders and a Pedagogy of Possibility for Diné Education* by Elizabeth McCauley (2004). McCauley collaborated with traditional Diné leaders (healers, *hataalii*) to inform a "pedagogy of possibility" in classrooms. One traditional Diné leader problematized how Western schooling structures limit (or completely eliminate) the use of Diné knowledge systems in schools and shared:

> The only way to get our young Diné children to learn again is to teach them about their identity as Diné. Teach them about how they are related to everything, how to care for all life and understand all that goes on in life. The children have to be here to see, feel, and experience what we understand about life. The fire in the Hogan is a grandmother to us. The children need to live it daily to learn it. (as cited in McCauley, 2004, p. 10)

Cultivating the heart though Indigenous epistemologies is an intentional form of education to critically examine community circumstances and situations to mobilize transformative outcomes in Indigenous communities. It is critical for teachers to create a space in the classroom for Indigenous youth to dialogue and engage critical analyses around various environmental and sociopolitical issues impacting their communities. This pedagogical approach encourages teachers to consider the ways in which their classroom can be "a sacred landscape which is a sacred space of engagement shaped by Indigenous knowledge systems, values, languages, prayer, and unity" (Garcia, 2020, p. 577). The stories we tell as Native people in our communities are stories that "contain the affective legacy of our experiences. They are felt knowledge that accumulates and becomes a force that empowers stories that are otherwise separate to become a focus, a potential for movement" (Million, 2014, p. 32). ISJP assists teachers in mobilizing the decolonization process through truth-telling and infuses Indigenous epistemologies and ontologies as "heart knowledge" to move Indigenous youth towards liberatory outcomes within their communities.

Native Nation-Building: Indigenous Teachers as Native Intellectuals

Teaching is a political process that not only challenges hegemonic schooling structures, but also deliberately promotes the goals of intellectual sovereignty (Grande, 2015) and self-determination in the classroom. Envisioning schools as sites of change must connect to these political ideals through Native nation-building. As a theoretical and political construct that problematizes and expands on Tribal sovereignty, Native nation-building fundamentally situates Indigenous knowledge, values, and language as *the foundation* for reclaiming, restructuring, and guiding Indigenous Nations. Native Nations, according to the Native Nations Institute, "are moving to assert their own governing authority. They are reclaiming the right to make decisions for themselves on their lands and in their communities" (Native Nations Institute, 2020). However, contemporary structures of sovereignty in Indigenous communities require an "unmapping" of its relationship to settler colonial logics, processes, and discourses (Grande, 2015). For example, tracing the modern-day tribal government systems to the Indian Reorganization Act of 1934 (IRA) exposes what Hopi elder, Vernon Masayesva, calls "a neocolonial form of government" (personal communication, May, 21, 2020), and relates to the forced democracy that Sandy Grande interrogates in *Red Pedagogy*—Indigenous Nations were forced "to adopt Western-style constitutions, to form and elect tribal councils, and to implement a variety of economic development plans" (Grande, 2015, p. 61). The IRA had fundamentally restructured traditional governing systems and replaced them with Western constructs of sovereignty so that corporations, in partnership with the federal government, could attempt to gain access to resources on Indigenous lands. Native nation-building requires an unmapping of such Westernized notions of tribal sovereignty and instead calls for Indigenous communities to infuse and ground their governing structures in Indigenous epistemologies, such as the Diné Nation drawing on their epistemological foundations of Sa'ah Naagháí Bik'eh Hozhóón.

Native nation-building entails "generations of Indigenous Peoples to grow up intimately and strongly connected to our homelands, immersed in our languages and spiritualities and embodying our traditions of agency, leadership, and decision making" (Simpson, 2014, p. 1). What is needed is a generation of Indigenous youth, like Autumn Peltier, as well as the Native intellectuals in our communities to collectively work toward protecting, sustaining, and transmitting our knowledges through our traditions, landscapes, languages, and spiritualities. By taking control of the education systems, Indigenous educators can then enact intellectual sovereignty and restructure the schools that serve Indigenous students to become immersed in Indigenous philosophies while simultaneously critiquing the continual impacts of settler colonialism surrounding us—this process mobilizes Indigenous youth toward transformative outcomes. Within the Diné epistemology, the phrase t'áá hwó ájít'éégo (it's up to you) is embedded in the nanit'in (teachings) of Sa'ah Naagháí Bik'eh Hozhóón. This concept embodies empowerment, responsibility, self-determination, and agency to advance self-motivation, self-confidence, critical thinking, planning, and personal responsibility for family and humanity. Native intellectuals strategically draw upon this energy to foster and guide the youth toward Native nation-building.

Hopi teacher Samuel Tenakhongva, in the following chapter, shares his reflections on using ISJP to develop curriculum and guide his teaching with Hopi students. Sam was a student in the Hopi cohort who completed their elementary education program at Northern Arizona University, and I was the instructor of the social studies methods course for this cohort. Embedded in his reflections are the ways in which he embodies Native intellectualism.

CONCLUSION

The pathway to decolonization requires a fundamental epistemological shift away from Western theory. Indigenous epistemologies, Deloria Jr. concludes, will provide the foundation for Indigenous liberation. (Simpson & Smith, 2014, p. 4)

When conceptualizing the transformative possibilities in teaching and learning within Indigenous education, the ethical responsibility of educators is to liberate curriculum and pedagogy from Westernized schooling structures. Settler-colonial ideologies and structures through the schooling processes worked to disconnect Indigenous Peoples from their cultural traditions; therefore, Indigenous educators must find ways to *reconnect and relearn* their Indigenous languages, knowledge systems, values, and stories. In this regard, teachers are encouraged to be conscious of how their philosophy shapes their work in the classroom and be deliberate in choosing what to teach and how to teach. Educators of Indigenous students are encouraged to integrate Indigenous origin stories, life-experiences stories, and survivance stories in the classroom to initiate the processes of decolonization, healing, and action in their pedagogical approaches. With this constant presence of settler structures and logics impacting Indigenous communities, there is an urgent need for future generations to think critically about their contemporary issues and struggles facing their communities. It is then vital for teachers to provide analytical tools for Indigenous youth to critically examine colonial structures and become aware of themselves and the community's concerns so that they can address certain struggles and respond to future issues. Again, this can be accomplished if teachers find the best ways to move toward a possibility of hope and action in our education systems. ISJP through decolonization, Indigenous epistemologies, and Native nation-building sustains Indigenous communities; this approach to teaching will strengthen us—*ei béé nihidziil doléét.*

NOTES

1. I am a member of the Diné Nation. I resided on the Diné Nation from birth through high school. I am faculty in the College of Education at the University of Arizona, and I continue to return "home" to Ganado, Arizona.
2. Begay (2002) defined hózhóójí as, "The word made of the verb stem, '-zhó,' meaning 'beauty or happiness' and 'hó-,' meaning 'whole locality.' Hózhóójí, then may be interpreted as positive surroundings, or The Beauty Way of Life, Harmony Way of Life, or Good Way of Life that Diné people, accordingly, have lived by" (p. 5).

REFERENCES

Agarwal-Rangnath, R. (2013). *Social studies, literacy, and social justice in the common core classroom: A guide for teachers.* Teachers College.

APTN News. (2016, December 8). *Autumn Peltier talks pipelines* [Video]. YouTube. https://www.youtube.com/watch?v=wEDqbzLFOlc

Archibald, J. A. (2008). *Indigenous storywork: Educating the heart, mind, body, and spirit.* University of British Columbia Press.

Battiste, M. (2013). *Decolonizing education: Nourishing the learning spirit.* Purich Publishing.

Begay, L. (2002). *Awakened belonging: Utilizing traditional stories to enhance self-perception of Diné children* [Unpublished doctoral dissertation]. Fielding Graduate Institute.

Benally, H. (1994). Navajo philosophy of learning and pedagogy. *Journal of Navajo Education, 12*(1), 23–31.

Brayboy, B. (2005). Toward a tribal critical race theory in education. *The Urban Review, 37*(5), 425–446.

CBC News. (2019, September 28). Water protector Autumn Peltier speaks at UN [Video]. YouTube. https://https://www.youtube.com/watch?v=OusN4mWmDKQ

Cook-Lynn, E. (2008). History, myth, and identity in the new Indian story. In N. Denzin, Y. Lincoln, & L. Smith (Eds.), *Handbook of critical and Indigenous methodologies* (pp. 329–346). SAGE Publications.

Denetdale, J. N. (2007). *Reclaiming Diné history: The legacies of Navajo Chief Manuelito and Juanita.* University of Arizona Press.

Garcia, J. (2020). Critical Indigenous pedagogies of resistance: The call for critical Indigenous educators. In S. Steinberg & B. Down (Eds.), *The SAGE handbook of critical pedagogies* (Vol. 3; pp. 574–586). SAGE Publications.

Garcia, J., & Shirley, V. (2012). Performing decolonization: Lessons learned from Indigenous youth, teachers and leaders' engagement with critical Indigenous pedagogy. *Journal of Curriculum Theorizing, 28*(2), 76–91.

Grande, S. (2004). *Red pedagogy: Native American social and political thought.* Rowman & Littlefield Publishers.

Grande, S. (2008). Red pedagogy: The un-methodology. In N. K. Denzin, Y. S. Lincoln, & L. T. Smith (Eds.), *Handbook of critical and Indigenous methodologies,* (pp. 233–254). SAGE Publications.

Grande, S. (2015). *Red pedagogy: Native American social and political thought* (10th anniversary edition). Rowman & Littlefield Publishers.

Haskie, M. (2002). *Preserving a culture: Practicing the Navajo principles of hozhó d00 k'é* [Unpublished doctoral dissertation]. Fielding Graduate Institute.

Indigenous Goddess Gang. (2019, April 1). *Josephine Mandamin.* https://www .indigenousgoddessgang.com/matriarch-monday/2019/4/1/josephine -mandamin

Lee, T. S. (2006). 'I came here to learn how to be a leader': An intersection of critical pedagogy and Indigenous education. *InterActions: UCLA Journal of Education and Information Studies, 2*(1). http://escholarship.org/uc/item/92m798m0

Lee, T. S., & McCarty, T. L. (2017). Upholding Indigenous education sovereignty through critical culturally sustaining/revitalizing pedagogy. In D. Paris & H. S. Alim (Eds.), *Culturally sustaining pedagogies: Teaching and learning for justice in a changing world* (pp. 61–82). Teachers College Press.

Lomawaima, K. T. (1999). The unnatural history of American Indian education. In K. Swisher & J. Tippeconnic III (Eds.), *Next steps: Research and practice to advance Indian education* (pp. 1–32). ERIC Clearinghouse on Rural Education and Small Schools.

Lomawaima, K. T., & McCarty, T. (2006). *To remain an Indian: Lessons in democracy from a century of Native American education.* Teachers College Press

McCaslin, W., & Breton, D. (2008). Justice as healing: Going outside the colonizers' cage. In N. Denzin, Y. Lincoln & L. T. Smith (Eds.), *Handbook of critical and Indigenous methodologies* (pp. 511–531). SAGE Publications.

McCauley, E. (2004). *"Our songs are alive": Traditional Diné leaders and a pedagogy of possibility for Diné education* [Unpublished doctoral dissertation]. Northern Arizona University.

Meyer, M. (2008). Indigenous and authentic: Hawaiian epistemology and the triangulation of meaning. In N. Denzin, Y. Lincoln, & L. T. Smith (Eds.), *Handbook of critical and Indigenous methodologies* (pp. 217–232). SAGE Publications.

Million, D. (2014). The river is in me: Theory from life. In A. Simpson & A. Smith (Eds.), *Theorizing native studies* (pp. 31–42). Duke University Press.

Native Nations Institute. (2020, January 20). *What is native nation-building?* https://nni.arizona.edu/

Pihama, L. (2019). Whanau storytelling as Indigenous pedagogy: tiakina te pa harakeke [To nurture the harakeke plant]. In J. Archibald, J. Lee-Morgan, & J. De Santolo (Eds.), *Decolonizing research: Indigenous storywork as methodology* (pp. 137–150). Zed Books.

Roessel, R. (1973). *Diné Stories of the Long Walk Period.* Navajo Community College Press.

Shirley, V. (2011). *Indigenous subjectivities: Diné youth (de)construct identity* [Unpublished doctoral dissertation]. Purdue University.

Shirley, V. (2017). Indigenous social justice pedagogy: Teaching into the risks and cultivating the heart. *Critical Questions in Education, 8*(2), 163–177.

Shirley, V., & Angulo, D. (2019). Enacting Indigenous research methods: Centering Diné epistemology to guide the process. In S. Windchief & T. San Pedro (Eds.), *Applying Indigenous research methods: Storying with peoples and communities* (pp. 57–75). Routledge.

Simpson, A., & Smith, A. (2014). Introduction. *Theorizing Native studies* (pp. 1–30). Duke University Press.

Simpson, L. (2012). Land as pedagogy: Nishaabeg intelligence and rebellious transformation. *Decolonization: Indigeneity, Education & Society, 3*(3), 1–25.

Vizenor, G. (1994). *Manifest manners: PostIndian warriors of survivance.* Wesleyan University Press.

Wilson, W. A. (2004). Reclaiming our humanity: Decolonization and the recovery of Indigenous knowledge. In D. A. Mihesua & A. C. Wilson (Eds.), *Indigenizing the academy* (pp. 69–87). University of Nebraska Press.

CHAPTER 2

TRANSFORMATIVE PRAXIS

I Have 180 Days With These Kids . . . the Community Has Them for Life

Samuel Tenakhongva

Nu Taawma yan Hopi maatsiwa, Nu Katsinwungwa niikyangw nu Sistomon-gaqw. Greetings, my name is Samuel Tenakhongva and my Hopi name is Taawma (To Sing). I come from the Katsina clan from the Hopi village of Sitsomovi.[1] I am a fourth-grade teacher in a Hopi elementary school. Each day on my walk to classroom, I speak these words, "Kwakwhá itaana taawa pew öoki," along with a few other words thanking our father Sun for the opportunity to spend a day with Hopi students. For me, I have to start my day first as a Hopi, then as a teacher. I am grateful that I have life experiences rooted in my home community and culture. Growing up on the Ancestral homelands of the Hopi people has provided me with a unique lens that continues to shape my values and worldview. Elsewhere, I shared my personal identity which I would like to share here:

> Any Indigenous person at some point has asked themselves the question, "Who am I, where do I come from?" most often in times of reflection or in times where meaning of self-value is being explored. Throughout my life I

Indigenizing Education, pages 21–28
Copyright © 2022 by Information Age Publishing
www.infoagepub.com

have often asked this question of myself in relation to the roles I have been vested with and the required responsibilities I would have to carry out. Long before deciding to become an educator, I was being prepared for a cultural role that few are privileged to hold, and in some instances would be hesitant to embrace. I would no longer be responsible for my own decisions, but for those of the community as well. Rather than view this task as a burden, I welcomed it. Within many Indigenous communities, in the case of Hopi, clans are vested with responsibilities as leaders and caretakers—I was given the responsibility of being a ceremonial leader. As a result, my perspective on life changed from an inward view to one of reciprocity and how I can help to fulfill the greater needs of my people and community. I now became not only a ceremonial leader, but also a parental figure to a whole community. In addition, I became an educator due the observations of "my" children's thirst for knowledge both in the context of Hopi language and culture and the Western ideological frameworks. (Garcia et al., 2019, p. 111)

Oftentimes in our Hopi households and villages, youth hear the message of, "Take the best of the *Pahana*[2] education and our Hopi values, go out, and learn as much as you can. Come back to help and teach our people." Similarly, this was advice given to me by my late *Taha* (uncle) at the age of 7–8 years old. At that time I did not know the true value of these words, but as with Hopi custom, I absorbed and held it within myself in respect to my Taha as that is an uncle's role: advising, disciplining, and helping to guide their nieces and nephews. These words still echo in the back of my mind as I help to guide, mentor, and support 8–10-year-old students sustain their Indigenous Hopi identities as a teacher and ceremonial leader. Oftentimes, I find myself trying to find balance between the Hopi culture and values that dates thousands of years back with a Western education that is designed to encourage students to be "college and career ready." Though there are distinctions between these knowledge systems, I take pride in knowing that my lived experiences and identity as a Hopi benefits both my students and I within the classroom—I am able to infuse my cultural knowledge and experiences to support my students in understanding various concepts from a Hopi perspective.

For instance, one day I was teaching a science unit about the process of transpiration. Throughout the lesson I could see that students were having difficulty processing and imagining the information. As the teacher, I was trying to think on the spur of the moment what I could do to help them. I pondered, "Did I have a YouTube video, did I need to figure out how to develop a science project?" The clock was ticking, and I was thinking, "What can I do?" Again, being fortunate to grow up and teach on my homelands, I looked out the classroom window and saw my clan father's cornfield in the distance. "Aha! I have it!" I had my students close their science books and I transformed into a storyteller, singer, and historian all at the same time. I asked them to revisit being in a cornfield early in the morning and to recall what they saw, what they smelled and what they felt. I then started singing a Hopi song and asked them if they ever heard this particular song. Many of them responded with a resounding, "Yes" and a smile. At that point I shared with them the Hopi oral traditions related to songs, history, and *Naavoti* (sharing and attaining knowledge). I let them know that long before we had a science book, long before we had a school or classroom, Hopis had a word to describe the early morning dew that is on our corn plants. I explained that Hopis were and continue to be scientists as we recognize the relationships between the natural processes we observed in our daily lives and that this song was referring to what is scientifically known as "transpiration." I was thinking and teaching as a Hopi.

My experiences of adjusting to be a culturally responsive educator continues to grow; however, my teaching has also shifted in certain ways as I continue to be exposed to new critical theories in Indigenous education. In this chapter, I share and discuss how I have utilized Indigenous social justice pedagogy (ISJP) practices in curriculum development and instruction to support and help Hopi elementary students build pride in their Indigenous identities, understand social constructs, and connect to modern day issues while considering and privileging their Indigenous belief systems. Additionally, through the lens of ISJP, I share examples of students being challenged to develop critical thinking skills, hypotheses, and alternative solutions to problems. Through these examples, I provide experiences on what it means to think Indigenous while developing and implementing curricula.

BECOMING AN INDIGENOUS SOCIAL JUSTICE EDUCATOR

During the final semester of my program to earn an elementary education degree at Northern Arizona University, I was fortunate to take a social studies course with Dr. Valerie Shirley. Within this course, I was introduced to the theoretical concept and process of engaging ISJP. As teacher candidates, this class provided us the opportunity to create a justice-centered curriculum that drew on the frameworks of critical Indigenous pedagogy (CIP) and ISJP—each of these frameworks focus on privileging Hopi values, culture, and thought processes. At the time, creating curriculum from a social justice or critical lens was daunting as each of us did not feel empowered or ready to tackle such a task, but despite these feelings we forged forward. Unlike other units we had planned, we agreed that this unit would most likely be one of the most important units we would create as Hopi educators because it required us to "Think Hopi." By thinking Hopi, we relied upon our cultural knowledge, language, history, and values with one end goal in mind—to leave our future Hopi students feeling empowered to call themselves Hopi.

Developed with co-creators, Kiara Pahovama and Cheyenne Harding, the unit we developed was entitled, "Who Am I, Where Do I Come From," and it relied heavily on cultural knowledge based on familial ties, history, and clanships. Through this unit, we would lead students on a journey of self-discovery and learning not only about their personal family histories, but also about Hopi cultural knowledge focused on tribal history, language, and stories. The unit was guided by the following focus questions: "What is the problem when you only learn about one perspective of history?"; "What is the difference between historical fact and opinion?"; "What influences do historical events have on our lives today?"; and "What influence will knowing my personal history have on me?" One essential process we understood was that in order to be educators who wanted to engage our students in critical issues and to encourage them to be change agents by addressing injustices, we needed to ensure we built a classroom community before entering critical dialogues. This unit was intended for that purpose. I was fortunate to have co-developed this unit with Hopi colleagues as I continue to use this community building process with my students. In providing context to this activity, the students would stand in a large circle and a ball of yarn would be tossed from one student to another based on clan relationships until all students participated. When implementing this activity, I always include myself as I know it is important that my students see me as an active practitioner who values and integrates Hopi cultural knowledge. Told in another context, I provide a brief description that captures this process and expands on the activity within the unit:

> In the unit, students are tasked with completing a family tree based on clan kinships on both maternal and paternal sides. Following the return of the family tree activity, I rely upon my cultural knowledge of clan (matrilineal and paternal) and develop connections students may not be aware of. From this we then hold a class activity that starts with each person holding a string in which we are first connected as members of a class. That is followed by creating clan connections based upon matrilineal ties, and lastly connections based on patrilineal ties. The result is a visual that students can readily see that they are not an individual, or just a member of the class, but rather they are connected culturally and are a brother, sister, aunt, uncle, father, mother or grandparent to their fellow class-mates. We become a family and I am now able to share values we hold in esteem as a Hopi, including kyaapsti (respect), suminangwa (working for the greater good), and naminangwa (selfless giving), and how they support our newly discovered relationships in day-to-day interactions as well as during ceremonial functions. (Garcia et al., 2019, p. 112)

In doing this activity, I found that a web of relations is formed and soon enough, nearly every student is, in some way, connected to one another. In some cases, students are often unaware of ties they have to other individuals; and when I explain the clan obligations, most of the students gain an awareness of clan responsibilities of their fellow classmates. The outcome of this classroom and community building process is that students not only develop knowledge of their roles and responsibilities based on clanship, but they also establish trust in one another, and respect is shared. This activity in establishing trust and respect is essential as it allows me to provide opportunities to engage in critical and justice centered dialogues and to remind them of why we need to learn and think about critical issues that impact our community.

Embodying ISJP as a Hopi Teacher

I learned that establishing this type of classroom community was essential for me as I start to share and educate students on topics that others would see as hot button issues, such as the Pueblo Revolt of 1680, American Indian boarding school history, Christopher Columbus and his "discovery," westward invasion, and manifest destiny. Often when faced with modern day issues or historical events, the perspectives and narratives are typically from a Western viewpoint. I ask myself the following questions: How can I engage my students in a process where they question the viewpoint presented in textbooks? Do I stay safe and allow the textbook to guide my teaching? Lastly, what opportunities for learning will my students miss out on if I choose to ignore essential issues reflected in their community and society? In fact, one of my 9-year old students stated, "How am I supposed to know these other viewpoints if they're not in the book?"

Such comments move me to begin actively seeking out additional resources that would offer an array of perspectives. I look to social media, Native news outlets, and other sources to find current issues happening in Native communities to connect, compare, and contrast the viewpoints. I also revisit historical events to pose questions that are intentionally designed to have the students think critically, question history, and develop ideas on how they believe the issue or topic could have been handled from a Native perspective. It is important to include multiple perspectives as this is part of the truth telling and empowering process, in that, I, as the educator, must allow the students to make their own decisions, provide space for them to share their own viewpoints, and go through the thinking process of critically examining issues and topics. With the access to social media and online resources, it is now easier as an educator to research and utilize sources where Native voices are shared or heard, and most importantly written from and with Native perspectives. Such social media and online resources are integral in my teaching because Native perspectives tend to be excluded in school textbooks.

In addition to seeking alternative sources to inform my curriculum, I also turn to my students' questions and comments around the issues we examine. These moments are important as it informs me on how they are interacting with and responding to issues they see in both the local community and within society overall. I find these moments to be informative as I see how their own Hopi identity is evolving in relation to the history of their community, their cultural experiences, and contemporary issues in society. As an example of drawing on their comments, I turn to sharing a curriculum unit I designed in order to help them see the relationship to the history of why we live on reservations. This was informed by students' comments saying, "I am from the rez," and observations of them accepting that once they cross into a local border town, they are no longer on their homelands. I felt they needed to see that our relations to the land exceeds settler colonial imposed boundaries and that it was, in fact, a form of colonization and land dispossession.

Deconstructing "the Rez" and Reclaiming Relations to Land

In the creation of "Who Am I, Where Do I Come From," one section of the unit focused on deconstructing imposed governmental boundaries of what is referred to as "the Rez" and in most cases for Indigenous People, "home." Within ISJP as well as CIP, a core instructional tenet that teachers have to consider is positionality as it influences the decisions we make in the classroom: from the lens of Western ideology versus Indigenous worldviews. From this stance, I developed a lesson titled "Hopi Tutskwa and Name Places" that centered on Hopi Ancestral boundaries and homelands which are vital and important to our identity as our relationships to these spaces intertwine language, ceremony, history, and our positionality in relating to and protecting the natural environment.

In this lesson, students were given modern-day maps that included a template of map boundaries of the southwestern United States, Arizona, and the Hopi reservation. On these maps were specific identified locations that have historical and cultural significance to Hopi as they mark settlements, migration routes, or places of spiritual and religious importance. Each student was tasked with taking the maps home and completing them as a family project with the instructions to label the Hopi and English names for the identified points, and complete as much as possible. The only resource I provided to the students was a reference list which included the Hopi names of the locations. Outcomes varied from student to student as the full completion of the assignment relied upon knowledge from a family member who knew of the place names in the Hopi language, could translate them, and also knew the general location on the map. When the assignments were returned, many of the students and families were not able to 100% fully complete the whole assignment, with one offering an apology, "I'm Hopi but I'm sorry, I don't know any of this and am at a complete loss as to how to answer these. I wish I had someone here to help us," while another family who completed it shared, "Without our grandfather here, we would have never been able to finish this. We spent almost 4 hours going over all the names and why they are important. History was shared with us, even some of our own clan history and we want to thank you for doing this. This reminded us that we need to know these things and why they are important, and that we need to teach this in our homes."

When we visited these responses in class, more students shared their experiences of either not knowing or being able to learn more through their family members' stories. For those who weren't able to complete the lesson, I shared cultural knowledge and history by projecting the answer key and singing Hopi songs that named some of the locations. I also explained their significance to Hopi culture, clans, migration, and history. Through the use of technology, I was able to take these students to some of these places virtually. As I closed the lesson, I also shared digital maps of what was considered Indigenous homelands prior to Western contact and students were then able to see a picture that extended off "the Rez" and into urban centers and metropolitan areas that most didn't consider as part of their identity. As we reflected on the assignment, students shared that they "wished we could get all our land back." One student said, "I want to take a field trip to these places, now I know why they are important, and we should protect them." While another shared, "Even if we don't get the land back, it's still Hopi because our katsinas and Ancestors still live there." Through this lesson, their positionality was further framed in relation and connection to the land and their physical environment. They understood that lines, maps, and boundaries that are defined by the federal government do not define us; and therefore, understood why we must always protect and (re)claim our relationship to land.

CONCLUSION

I will be remiss to say that although it sounds easy, I often find myself emotionally immersed and engaged deeply in my teaching as well as the students' emotional responses to the truth telling narratives. For example, I heard comments such as: "They should just leave; it's not their land anyway!"; "I would want to fight them!"; "Why did they just bring diseases and try to make us slaves?"; and "Can we make signs to protest Columbus?" These are all quotes that students have made to highlight how emotionally vested they were when learning about topics covered in the classroom. As a practitioner, time and experience do help as feelings of anger, resentment, and sadness are often shared; however, cultivating the heart through integrating Hopi stories is important as I want my students to also feel empowered in this process. To facilitate this, I start to question students on how they feel about a topic, what they think could be done differently, or what they would have done if given the opportunity to be involved. I draw upon my Hopi values to handle concepts such as land dispossession and ownership and historical injustices. I ask students to think critically and pose the questions, "Has anything changed? If not, what can you do about it?" Through this process, I take students on a journey of self-discovery and learning, and I must allow them to start forming their own conclusions. Hopefully, they take their newfound voices to their homes, their communities, and beyond. In writing this chapter, I hope the reader will find their voice, and most importantly, remind themselves that it is okay to THINK INDIGENOUS. Lastly, without my students, I would never be able to share these experiences, and I'll leave with a quote from another 9-year-old student who I had for 180 days, "I'm proud to be Hopi. I'm glad my Ancestors kept our traditions alive! I know I'll always be Hopi wherever I go!" That's empowerment... *Kwakwhá* (thank you)!

NOTES

1. Within the Hopi tribe, there are 12 different villages. They are Walpi, Sitsomovi, Shongopavi, Mishongnovi, Sipaulovi, Hotevilla, Bacavi, Moencopi, Kykotsmovi, Orayvi. There is one additional non-Hopi village whose members identify as *Tewa*.
2. This is a Hopi term often used to refer to White people or Western forms of education.

REFERENCES

Garcia, J., Tenakhongva, S., & Honyouti, B. (2019). Indigenous teachers: At the cross-roads of applying Indigenous research methodologies. In S. Windchief & T. San Pedro (Eds.), *Applying Indigenous research methods: Storying with peoples and communities* (pp. 103–121). Routledge.

CHAPTER 3

RESTORYING LESSONS LEARNED FROM A HIGH SCHOOL NATIVE AMERICAN LITERATURE CLASSROOM

Timothy San Pedro
Andrea Box

DEDICATION

We (Timothy and Andrea) dedicate this conversation/chapter to the students and young activists who helped us become better educators, better scholars, better people.[1] To Elijah, Danelle, Kyle, Nizhoni, Allyson, Nichelle, Brissaneira, and Elissa, thank you for continuing to co-construct new spaces to share our stories.

> *By reducing the space between things, we are strengthening the relationship that they share. And this bringing things together so that they share the same space is what ceremony is about."*
> —Shawn Wilson[2]

Indigenizing Education, pages 29–51
Copyright © 2022 by Information Age Publishing
www.infoagepub.com
All rights of reproduction in any form reserved.

In this chapter, we (Timothy and Andrea) argue for the use of critical asset-based pedagogies to (a) move beyond the western knowledge systems and norms in U.S. schools and (b) center Indigenous and community-based knowledges and paradigms. This move is intentional since Indigenous youth continue to be harmed by assimilative schooling systems that silence, ignore, and/or erase their Indigenous values and stories[3] as part of the continued settler colonial project. Patrick Wolf[4] states that in order for settlers to legitimize their claim on Native lands, there must be an elimination of the Native body and mind. Since Indigenous bodies have survived, schooling practices have focused, instead, on the elimination of the mind such as practices that "kill the Indian and save the man" (an infamous quote by Carlisle Indian School founder, Richard H. Pratt). To combat the erasure of indigeneity, we discuss the ways one unique classroom pushed against assimilative schooling practices by creating opportunities for Indigenous youth to deepen their tribal and community knowledges and to be supported in their discoveries of what it means to be Indigenous and to enact their indigeneity.

Relatedly, we believe critical asset-based pedagogical practices that advance what students bring with them to school—their tribal, community, and home-based knowledges—ought to be centered in the successful co-construction of learning spaces. While there are a number of pedagogical theories forwarding asset-based pedagogies, we rely on the intersections of decolonizing and critical Indigenous pedagogy[5] and culturally sustaining and revitalizing pedagogies.[6] Critical Indigenous pedagogy (CIP) works to disrupt social inequities by developing lessons and teaching strategies that provide opportunities for students to empower themselves, their families, and their communities by first reflecting on their realities and then developing strategies to disrupt settler colonial systems. Similarly, culturally sustaining and revitalizing pedagogy (CSRP) calls out inequities and access in education, and seeks to refuse schooling systems as an extension of settler colonialism by creating spaces to "explore, honor, [and] extend . . . heritage and community practices,"[7] which leads to greater opportunities to "critique regressive practices . . . and raise critical consciousness."[8] The intersection of these pedagogical contributions challenge and push traditional understandings of asset-based pedagogies by viewing cultural practices within communities and Tribal nations not as something trapped and locked in the past (in an attempt to recreate in the present), but as something that is evolving and constantly in motion based on the lived realities and experiences of contemporary life.

In an effort to "show" critical asset-based pedagogies in action—specifically the intersections of CIP and CSRP—we re-story a retrospective dialogue in which we came back together to discuss the impacts a 12th-grade, English elective course titled Native American literature taught by Andrea had upon each other and upon students. We used dialogue, self-reflection, critical thinking, and praxis as we considered, through storied memories, the impact this course had upon us and students. Jo-Ann Archibald's Indigenous storywork (ISW) methodology provided the needed guidance in order to frame our work and our relationship. ISW is a synergistic and dialogic interaction between listener and storyteller whereby "respect, responsibility, reciprocity, reverence, holism, interrelatedness, and synergy"[9] are developed and nurtured through sustained relationship building over time. Through our retelling using the main tenets of ISW, we attempt to answer the central question of this chapter: What does it look like and what are the implications of a classroom that centers students' community and tribal knowledges using critical asset-based pedagogies? To answer this question, we begin by sharing the genesis of our relationship.

. . .

In the Fall of 2010, having never met before, Andrea Box (or Ms. Boxy as many of her students have fondly called her) welcomed Timothy San Pedro, a first-year PhD student at Arizona State University, into her Native American literature classroom. Their only connections were shared friendships with ASU professors Jim Blasingame and Simon Ortiz. Timothy and Andrea felt such strong relations with Jim and Simon because of a common goal—to engage in work that benefited students whose histories, stories, literacies, and lives have historically been excluded from "official" academic spaces.

Long before Timothy and Andrea's friendship began, Native American students and their parents who attended Desert View High School,[10] where Andrea teaches, voiced their frustration and outrage with the school's administration. The parents' concern: For a school district that bordered a Native American reservation and had the highest population of Native students (in an off-reservation school), the curricula was void of their tribal stories and Indigenous knowledges (apart from the problematic mention of them as historic beings, long gone from the United States or savage groups of people unworthy of cultivating and living upon this land). These parents fought for a more accurate representation of their lives in the curricula and—with the help of the school district's diversity specialist (a position that has since been removed) who reached out to Drs. Blasingame and Ortiz—approved a course that recentered students' Indigenous perspectives, languages, and histories in one classroom space.

Immediately, Jim and Simon reached out to Andrea, a veteran teacher who taught multicultural education for 11 years prior to teaching this class. She always desired a more in-depth opportunity for students to engage with Native American histories and stories beyond the few weeks spent in her multicultural classroom. This desire was (and continues to be) rooted in her need to reconnect with her Indigenous identity that, through erasure, has been stripped from her family. However, she knows that students might question that passion when they first see her—a "White girl" standing in front of them. But after she shares her story, students begin to realize that she is on a voyage of remembering and revitalizing her Opata and Mayan identity that, through painful processes of settler colonialism, have undergone attempted erasure.

She says, "I've always been raised to be proud of my Native American heritage, but it was never formally taught to me, so I'm still learning about it."

Much of her learning and discovering has been concurrent with teaching this class, which, she says, has done two things: One, helped her to gain greater connections to her Indigenous roots, and two, spurred similar realizations for students who have also come to understand the erasures happening in their own lives.

Creating a classroom space to share in such discoveries, however, was a long time in the making as Drs. Ortiz and Blasingame helped others see the importance and legitimacy of this course. Blasingame said he based this importance on two points: "One, Native American students are being harmed when none of the curricula reflects their culture, their heritage, or their identity and two, the other (non-Native) students are not getting the true picture when they're studying American literature devoid of any Native authors in North America."

Ortiz built upon these two points stating: Indigenous knowledge, the historical events which have been erased and replaced in schools in this area have been "missing since the very beginning [and needs to be] recognized in the public school...because teaching knowledge is primary and fundamental to any society and nation."

From 2010–2012, Andrea taught more than 90 multi-tribal and multicultural students. During that time, Timothy worked closely with 16 focal students in this course, reading their written work, listening to their conversations in small- and whole-group settings, interacting with them in hallways and in the library, and engaging in dialogic interviews whereby they both asked and answered questions to share their lives, histories, and stories.[11]

. . .

Four years later, in the Summer of 2016, Timothy and Andrea reconnected by collaborating on a retrospective study whereby participants (including Andrea) discussed what they remembered learning, feeling, thinking from this course that was previously taught. Rushing from shadow to shadow to protect themselves from the suffocating summer heat, Timothy and Andrea made their way to the air-conditioned room to share memories. Two friends embraced in a long-overdue hug, exchanging updates on their lives

both within the ethnic studies classroom they shared from 2010–2012 and beyond it, sharing their joy and excitement in seeing each other after quite some time. They sat on two couches that were angled toward one other. An audio recorder was placed upon a coffee table; a red dot indicating it was recording. In their exchange, they considered the lessons learned, the impacts felt, the missed moments, and the hopes for what classes like this could be and should be.

A NOTE ON LITERARY TECHNIQUE

Before entering into this shared storied space,[12] we pause to explain how we are playing with time to make conversations connect with students who impacted them and are part of their storied memories. Because technologies (audio recorders, field notebooks, photocopies) preserved classroom conversations, interviews, writings, and interactions during that time, we chose to share some conversations as "flashbacks" to related prior interactions with students as they remember them in their current conversation. For example, Andrea remembered and shared a specific written reflection Elijah wrote on the last day of the semester in 2010. Since Timothy still had those reflections stored, he brought Elijah's exact written words into their current conversation as a "flashback" to classroom interactions from 2010–2012.

. . .

To signify a flashback, we use italic font, which represents prior classroom interactions and conversations they are remembering. The text is separated by centered ellipses (. . .) as it is now, to help readers move between past interactions and the current conversation (not italicized).

. . .

Timothy begins: "Alright, so I've told you a little bit about this project. It's an opportunity to come back and hear from students who were in your class and reconnect with them. The purpose of these discussions is to talk with them about what they remember from the class. At the time, all the students I worked with found your course deeply impactful, but in thinking 4 or 5 years after they took this course, what is still resonating with them? What stories are still with them? What impact did it or does it have on their lives now? What lessons, what activities, what readings connected with them? And how did the significant shift in the curriculum that recentered Indigenous histories and literacies impact them. So, a good place to start our conversation is with the question: Just thinking back to those early semesters that you taught this course (2010–2012), what were you thinking about? How were you preparing, and what did you envision for that classroom space?"

Andrea: "I just remember being so insecure. I just felt like a fish out of water. But I had to come across as acting like I knew what I was doing. But I mean even to this day, I remember, I think it was Elijah's final reflection essay that he said the one thing he appreciated most about the class was that it was organic."

. . .

Elijah: *As we learned about our Native heritage, we were forced to examine the way we learn, the way we know, the way we see, OUR discriminations and prejudices. We learned about ourselves, but more importantly, we learned about each other. We learned about how humans with all their flaws can love each other for simply being, where classmates can share their concerns and not-understandings, and teaching can truly happen. It is not just repetition and copying but genuine learning. It's ORGANIC.*[13] *(2010)*

. . .

Andrea: "I still teach this course to this day, and I think that it's still evolving, and I still try to keep it organic. It's always been. I want the students, from all backgrounds, Native American or African American or White or Latino, Latina, I want them to be proud of the culture and their heritage and who they are. And I want the class to be meaningful so that, hopefully when they look back, 10 years from now, they will still remember lessons or ideas or concepts, or even just feelings from the class; being validated, knowing that their voice matters, knowing that their story matters. That's always been the forefront of my curriculum, no matter what I teach. I want the kids to know that they matter. I just feel like it's so important, especially for the Native American students, to document their stories and to keep that going for their own children and their grandchildren. But there were things that I know I could've done differently, but you know as any good teacher does, they self-reflect and say what worked or didn't work."

. . .

Ms. Boxy asks students to fill out a questionnaire that asks about their schooling experiences. After reading and processing their answers, she says, "I appreciate your honesty and your candidness. Many of you, I would say more than about 65% of the class, said that you had not heard your culture represented in English classes or even in history classes."

She shuffles through their questionnaires and reads directly from one student's response: "It makes me feel like the education system doesn't feel like we're important."

She looks up from the paper and says to the class, "That really hurts my heart. I want you all to feel validated, to feel that your culture, your stories, they matter in here."

. . .

Andrea (then asks Timothy): "How about you? I know that you were just beginning your PhD program and learning what it meant to be a scholar and researcher. What do you remember from those first few semesters of being in this class?"

Timothy smiles as he remembers how Andrea and the participants he learned with never allowed the interviews or discussions to be one-sided, where one person is asking someone to reveal their stories without asking and having those stories returned in a dialogic way.[14]

He answers her question, saying: "I remember feeling uneasy as I learned in my research courses that if we were to remain 'objective' and 'neutral' in order to find some sort of 'truth,' we had to remove our stories; we had to ignore that meaningful relationships were being developed. It felt cold, wrong. That was one of the first lessons you taught me and that the students taught me: If I am asking others to reveal their lives and realities in the stories they share with me, the human thing to do is to reveal my own stories and answer questions that are asked of me. Sharing stories in a dialogic way rather than in one direction provided multiple opportunities to develop trust with each other and to develop meaningful relationships with them."

. . .

During an interview, Charlotte (Diné) asked Tim: "Are you Native?"

"No, I'm not," Tim replied.

"You're not? What are you?" she asked.

"I'm Filipino-American. I grew up on the Flathead Indian Reservation, which is right here in Montana," he said while standing to point to a map of U.S. reservations on the wall. "A lot of my friends and friends' families from the Salish, Kootenai, and Pend d'Oreille tribal nations welcomed me into that culture, which is why I'm here. It's kind of a strange situation, umm . . . yeah."

"So do you know about Native stuff or what?" she says with a cautious laugh.

"Mmm-hmmm, I do."

"You do. Then you're good to go."

From this point, Tim turned off the digital recorder he was using, and had a conversation about Native knowledge that they both knew should not be recorded. That conversation will always remain between Charlotte and Tim. (2010)

. . .

Timothy continues: "I remember seeing the impact sharing stories had upon students when you did that first activity, the one where you had them create artistic expressions of themselves and then write a poem or essay about how that art work represented who they were."

Andrea: "Yes! I've always loved that first activity where they get to not only talk about themselves,[15] but creatively describe themselves through art, you know what I mean? Every time I teach this class the kids always say they were actually angry and upset that we started with their stories because they're like: 'it's so personal; we just got to know each other.' But then after they showed their art piece and read their stuff out loud, they're like: 'that was the coolest activity. That was the ice breaker for us.' And they're just like: 'we were so nervous the first time, but when we started getting the feedback from each other, we became this family.' And so that activity has always been, for me, the most impactful one the entire semester. So I definitely keep that one."

. . .

It was Nisha's turn to share her art piece and her story (Figure 3.1). There was much hesitancy before she began speaking, but after 5 seconds, she held up her symbol and talked about the large crack that separates the circle. On one side of the circle is the border of one of her reservations, Zuni, and on the other is her other reservation, Jicarilla Apache. She says the crack represents the split her family has had to endure

Figure 3.1 Nisha's work/shield.

and how this splitting has severed her two worlds. Her eyes look only to the back of the paper; they don't try to find anyone else's. After everyone has shared their stories, Ms. Boxy hands out folded thank you cards and asks students to write letters to students whose stories impacted them. They begin handing them to each other. Nisha's desk is filled with thank you cards. (2012)

. . .

Timothy: "So what is it about the stories or the symbols and the sharing of those stories that students have said is impactful for them to where they can feel like they're family."

Andrea: "I think just that they know that there's absolutely no putting down of anyone's stories, and they can actually be honest. And I think, unlike their other English classes, instead of getting stuff back knowing it's going to be corrected for grammar and spelling and formatting, they get these 'Thank You' letters back acknowledging that we've listened to each other. It just inherently brings about trust and listening to each other. And again just that validation, because they're like: 'wow, we're not going to write a 5-paragraph essay right off the bat' or 'we're not going to write about some issue that we don't care about.' They're always like: 'it's about us, and we can be as creative as we want with it.' So I think, again, it's the validating of who they are and not what they know or don't know. It's a much deeper level."

Timothy: "I'm wondering, students often referred to the classroom space as feeling like family, what do you have to do prior to that in order to create such an environment?"

Andrea: "I think once they realize that I'm human and that I love to laugh, and even going over class rules on the first day, I will interweave stories into the class rules. They're not just funny stories, but they're also sad stories. Stories about my daughter with special needs. It's about stories where I was disrespected in class. But just so that the students understand, these are the rules in place, and this is why I have the rules. And so by the time we get to the actual writing piece, I have hopefully established that this is a comfortable place for them; this is a safe place for them. But we have boundaries, and so hopefully just within those first 5 days of school we've kind of already started to establish that sense of comfort and level of trust. I want them to know that I'm a safe person to come to not just for writing but just if they need to talk, if they need a safe place and someone to listen, I'm here."

Timothy: "That feeling of safety is so important, but you and I both know that as this course was being developed, the Arizona legislature passed house Bill 2281[16] that essentially made the teaching of ethnic studies illegal. Students expressed worry that this course, even though it was protected by federal law, might also be taken from them."

. . .

The ethnic studies ban and the man who fought to pass it, Tom Horne, have come up in classroom conversations.

One student asked, "Now whatever happened to Tom Horne?"

Ms. Boxy replied, "He's the one that banned ethnic studies because he thought it was teaching students to hate the government. They can't touch this class though [because of federal legislation protecting the teaching of such courses to Native American students]."

Still, despite Ms. Boxy's saying so, in conversations between the two of us, we realize that this classroom is not immune to the political workings in the state and in the country. (2011)

. . .

Timothy: "Within such a political climate, I wonder, was there ever any pushback from either students or from administrators, or from teachers about this Native American literature class?"

Andrea: "No I didn't, nope. But that is because it is a voluntary class, so they know what they're coming into. And I make no bones about it. From day one I say, 'I am not anti-White, but you are going to be learning stuff in this class that you have never been taught before, and a lot of it has to do with the government and with European Americans and what they have done to our Native tribes. So come into this class knowing that there will be discomfort.'"

. . .

Ms. Boxy introduces the contents of the class in the first week of the semester: "By nature, this class will be controversial. I had a White student who came up to me the last day of class and say, 'This is a White hating, White bashing classroom. He took it very personally. And my other students stood up for me and they said, 'It's not bashing or hating, but coming to understand the history of us.'" (2011)

. . .

Andrea: "But I let them know, 'Let's understand the past so that we can define the present and be hopeful and make a better future for our kids. Don't just sit there and be angry, but what are we going to do? How are we going to channel what we're learning so that it's productive? So that the learning can be a springboard for something better, for all cultures.' That's so important to me, to just establish the intentions of this class upfront."

Timothy: "So as a 12th grade English *elective* course, students *choose* to take this course. I'm wondering if, within that first week, there are any stereotypes or assumptions that students have, whether you can remember students having coming in with, that are sort of common and that you need to address or need to have conversations about, and how do you go about those conversations?

Andrea: "Absolutely, that's actually one of the activities that I have the students do in the first week, they fill out several different questionnaires, and one of them is: What are stereotypes that you have? I actually have two separate questionnaires that I give out at the same time. One, I give out to the Native American students and then another to my non-Native students. And the non-Native students, I ask them like what are some stereotypes that you feel you have: "What do you absolutely know about Native Americans?"; "What questions do you have?" And then with the Native Americans themselves, I ask: "What tribe are you from?"; "What do you know about your tribe?"; "What do you wish you knew?"; "What do you know about Indigenous leaders?"; "What events would you like us to cover?"; or "What literature would you like us to cover with authors?" I want to make sure that I'm teaching things they want to know about, but I often have to start literally from scratch. Many of them don't know how many tribes there are in Arizona, let alone in the United States. They don't know names of tribes, so I just have to figure out where is the common ground to start from. A lot of non-Native students have the very stereotypical, 'Oh well, you know, they're alcoholics, they're all brown, they have long hair, they get money from the government.' So throughout the class we will challenge those stereotypes. And we'll discuss them in an open forum, and usually we interweave it with literature and stuff that we're reading. And, I don't really think that there's been a time where they've been disrespectful or argued with me. The only time that I have arguments, and this is a set-up debate, so I intend for it to be argumentative, is when we talk about the school's mascot, which is a Native American figure. And it's really interesting because some Native American students love the mascot, some hate the mascot. Same with non-Native students—some love the mascot, some hate the mascot."

. . .

As Tim makes his way through the halls, he notices an advertisement hanging on the men's bathroom door.

It reads: "Once a Native American Warrior, always a Native American Warrior . . . Want to be The Native American Warrior? Come to Native American warrior tryouts to see if you have what it takes to be a Native American Warrior Mascot at all of the Varsity football games."

He places his hand on the announcement and rips it down out of frustration, only to walk another 10 paces to see another announcement, and then another. Shaking his head, he walks into Ms. Boxy's classroom and hands the crumpled advertisement to her.

They exchange a brief look; she says, "I saw this, too."

Ms. Boxy asks for the class's attention: "Okay, I'm going to turn this into a teachable moment. What do you guys think about the mascot tryouts? Are any of you going to try out for it?" (see Figure 3.2).

"Who would want to be a mascot?" one student asks.

"Do you think that whoever they choose to be the mascot should also be educated about what being a Native American warrior is about?" she asks.

Vince, who is Pima and lives on the bordering reservation, raises his hand and says, "Miss, um, isn't the purpose of a mascot supposed to represent the school altogether? I don't think that being a mascot has anything to do with learning whatever the mascot is. I'm just saying, cuz the purpose of having a mascot is to rally up the crowd and get everybody excited and it's not, 'Oh, I'm gonna teach you guys about what the mascot is.' I mean, if a badger was the mascot, the person in the costume isn't gonna learn about badgers and teach the crowd their knowledge of badgers."

"Nisha, what do you think?" Ms. Boxy asks.

"Personally, when I went to football games, it was always someone White as the mascot and it's kinda like a disrespect toward Native Americans because... I mean, personally, I'm fine with it, but to some people it could be disrespectful to their own people, but they should be aware that they can disrespect some people," Nisha says.

"Should we not be sensitive to the 10–15% who are Native American at Desert View?" Ms. Boxy asks.

"When you go to the game, do you go there to watch football or sit next to the mascot to ask him questions about what tribes are where?" Vince asks. "No, you go to the game to watch the game. You're not there to learn the history of Native Americans."

Keene, who is Diné and Hopi has a wrinkle above his forehead as he asks, "Wait. Are you for having a Native American as our mascot or against it?"

At this, the class laughs.

"I'm just saying: It's a game. Chill out," Vince says above the laughter.

"What does our mascot look like?" Ms. Boxy asks continuing the conversation.

"He's wearing a costume," Neena says.

"Why did you say costume? Is it truly Native American traditional clothing?" Ms. Boxy asks.

"No, it's like polyester. Like cheap cloth," Neena says.

The class laughs again.

Keene cuts through the laughter and shares his truth: "Certain Native American cultures fought because they had to. They got the whole model of what being a Native American warrior is by the movies that depicted us back in the early 1900s. I mean, there shouldn't be a mascot at all that represents a Native because we're not really

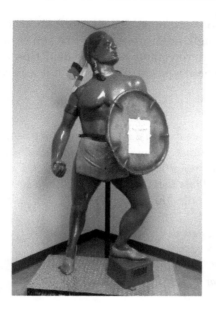

Figure 3.2 Mascot statue.

warriors. We were trying to protect something that we loved and that we weren't going to give up on." (2012)

. . .

Andrea: "But we try to understand the big picture of what mascots can represent or do represent, and the ways that impacts identity. So, it's just, it's always so eclectic. And I just love that every single class is different, but I love watching it. It evolves and evolves, but the one consistent is they're so respectful to each other, that's what I love about the class."

Timothy: "So, having been in those classes with you, I know that students started to see larger systemic injustices, particularly whose stories and knowledges are seen as facts in school and whose knowledges are relegated to the margins of curricula. And now that they're learning about Native American history and reading Native American literature, they're seeing these larger systems at play. I'm wondering: What sort of conversations do you remember having with them to share this larger narrative?"

Andrea: "I have to be real careful how I teach it. But, my big thing is, in any class I teach, I ask them to question everything. Question the authority; question me. I tell them, 'I want you guys to be thinkers when you come out of this class. I don't want you to accept the status quo. I don't want you to follow the crowd; I want you to ask the hard questions. I want you to be inquirers of knowledge. And look for things that you don't know about, understanding that the revelation might not be something that you want to hear, or read or understand. Where are you going to go with that? How are you going to use the knowledge to benefit yourself, your family and society in general?'"

. . .

Ms. Boxy provides students with a 26-page historical timeline of Native American histories in the United States. She asks them to individually read through this time-line and circle the events that they feel should be included in their history courses. They are then arranged into small groups and their task over the next week is to col-lectively construct visual timeline posters that they'll then post in the common spaces of their school.

The titles of their posters are:

- *Truths My Teacher Didn't Tell Me*
- *The Untold Story*
- *The Unknown Truths*
- *The Hidden Truth*
- *Walk in the Moccasins of a Native*
- *Truth Be Told*
- *Today's Sorrow From Past Hearts*

As students hang their posters in the hallways, they quietly move from poster to poster, writing down what they notice from each poster. Afterward, Ms. Boxy then has them write individual reflections on what they learned from this lesson.

Erin (Latina) says, "This activity showed me how much I DO NOT know about Native American history . . . It also showed me that our history classes do not really tell us the whole story, just parts of it. So in my opinion, I do not think we are being educated how we should. Native Americans played a huge part in U.S. history.

Ivan (Pima) says, "The history of Native Americans . . . is simply ignored in our history classes . . . [This activity] . . . showed us that the truth in the end is different from what we have been taught. It's nice to have one class where more students realize this too." (2012)

. . .

Andrea: "Their poster titles have always been so creative. And just their visual representation of how they want to present it. Again, it allows them that creativity to tell their story and even to tell somebody else the story, and to validate a part of history that most of us don't know. You know, and so they, they really put a lot of effort into that one."

Timothy: "So you talked a lot about wanting them to become thinkers. From what I saw, this class was a lot about reflection, providing a lot of space to think through their personal stories, what they've been taught, the schooling processes that they've come through. I'm wondering: In the years that you've taught it, have there been any students who have wanted to take that additional step of not just reflecting but enacting some sort of change."

Andrea: "I know that one year, there was the big issue about using the reclaimed waste water as snow up on their sacred mountain in Flagstaff. Literally, my entire class was gone that day because they went to protest, and I was just so proud of them. You know like I didn't mark any of them absent that day. And then when they came back, I asked them to tell me about it and teach each other what was happening. So in that instance, I know that they want to take their learning outside of the classroom. In a lot of their final reflections they are so appreciative that, at least in one class, their education centers their concerns. They appreciate that these lessons are getting out there. They say they are teaching other students outside this classroom and even their parents about what it is we're learning in here. I'm hopeful that, through this class, they have an opportunity to ignite their passion and that, maybe something that they've learned in this class might serve as a catalyst to be more civic minded and leaders in their communities."

Timothy: "When that does happen, when current events and situations occur in their communities make their way into classroom discussions, what do you do with the curriculum? Do you include materials? Do you allow students to talk about what it is that they are passionate about within that moment? How does that..."

Andrea: "Oh, absolutely! As a teacher, you've got to grab the teachable moments. And so I always ask the students what they know, and a lot of the students talk about: 'Well, my elders told me this or this about what is happening.' I say, 'Well, why don't we research this tonight? And then come back tomorrow and see what we find. Talk to your elders, talk to your families. I'll usually start the next day's class by saying: 'Let's talk about the discussion we had yesterday.' That connects the students with their family, with their culture, with their heritage.[17] So any teachable moment that I can grab, I will. And I always tell them: 'You all teach me more than I teach you.' And when they do this research and share the stories from their families, a lot of the non-Native students, they're just so shocked and say: 'We had no idea.' So it's good for all of them to get the knowledge out in whatever understanding they have of it and then we can tweak it as needed just to make sure that we are getting correct information. And I always tell students: 'If you are going to be researching it, make sure you research it from at least three sources so that you are getting—not even necessarily accurate information, but so that you can get the perspectives and decide for yourself where's the truth in all of this information that's being disseminated.

Lesson plans were usually like, kind of once I have it in place, I try and go with it. But I love it when the kids kind of pull me off track as long as it's meaningful and as long as it's engaging."

· · ·

As Ms. Boxy continues introducing the course to students, she hands them a list of the topics and subjects they will discuss in class and says, "This is a tentative schedule. Again, you guys are going to drive the class. If this (syllabus) isn't work-ing for you say, 'Ms. Boxy, let's do this or this.' We will totally go in the direction of your choosing. So I want this class to move in the direction that is meaningful to you every day. (2011)

· · ·

Timothy: "I so appreciated that you invited community members into the classroom to share their stories. I remember, particularly, when Elijah (a student in the first Native American literature class taught in 2010 and who wrote that the class felt "organic") wanted me to ask you if he could come in and share about the community conversation project he was want-ing to co-construct with students and with me. I remember your answer to that request. It was instantaneous: "Absolutely!" you said with a huge smile."

Andrea: "Yes! Those are the important teachable moments that you just have to grab. I so appreciated him coming in to share how this class im-pacted him and how he was wanting to continue to use that knowledge in new spaces."

· · ·

Elijah: *"I remember when Tim and I first talked about this group in a coffee shop and Tim told me that he would talk to Ms. Boxy to see if I could come in and talk to the class about what this group might become. Ms. Boxy accepted our invitation and soon thereafter I was standing in front of the Native American literature class, a class I had been in 2 years earlier, looking at new faces, and I was introducing them to our community group idea. I said (and I only know this because Tim recorded me talking),*

This class is pretty unique, right guys? In this class you talk about things that you don't talk about in any other classes and that's something that I'm sure some of you have probably thought about before being Indigenous people. So it's really something that you don't find in other places at all. But I . . . and Tim want to continue the talk. We want to continue talking about these things so that you can grow as a person and it helps to learn about how things have worked and the things that have happened to people.

I then had Tim share a handout I created that discussed what we were envisioning for this group. Although I did not read the handout to the class, I hoped that they would read it on their own, or at least the mission statement and be interested in attending.

Mission Statement

> *This is a critical thought group. The purpose and understanding of those involved is to better understand the history of colonialism and its effects upon Indigenous peoples. That understanding is developed by: self-reflection and critical analysis of current events."*

. . .

Timothy: "I'm remembering that those teachable moments generated such rich discussions in class. I remember students talking even after class about the adjustments you made and how much they appreciated your listening to them and changing things around to center their ideas, questions, and things happening in their immediate lives. The other thing that you did that generated such rich thinking was, instead of quizzes and tests, you had them write reflection essays that asked them to consider their thoughts in relation to the topics and subjects for a specific unit. How did you go about creating the questions for those reflection essays?"

Andrea: "What I do is I keep all of my reflection questions from every single semester. And sometimes I'll cut and paste the same questions, and sometimes I'll handwrite something that's come to me from what students have discussed. So, I mean, the reflections are all sorts of crazy. They're huge because I ask a lot of questions. But then I say: 'Within these ten questions chose five.' So that they feel like they can be proficient and can answer things they have a strong opinion on. So even though I feel like my reflections are huge, I still want them to feel manageable to the students. I just tell them: 'Take one question at a time and make sure that you have some kind of a resource to cite, to prove your point. I try and get it as close to what they would be asked in a college setting, whether or not they're planning on going to college. But I just want them to think deeply—and not to be so focused on the nitpicky questions like: 'What day did this happen?'—rather, the questions become: 'What happened? Look at it from both perspectives. Can you understand why it happened? How do you feel about it? What do you agree or disagree with?' So, they're much more open-ended questions. I want students to consider: 'How can we look at the big picture?'"

Timothy: "Why did you decide to use reflections instead of tests?"

Andrea: "I love the reflections because the kids know that there's no right or wrong; it's opinion, but they still have to support their opinion with tangible evidence. So whatever we do, like within a lesson, I always try to have my reflection questions be higher-level thinking questions that allows them to make connections. It asks them to consider questions like: What did this unit force you to think about? What made you angry? What do you agree or disagree with? But I tell them from day one: The minute you walk into my class, you hold onto every scrap of paper that I have given because then you use them for the reflections. And so, like especially with the very beginning when we do the timeline activity, I hand out a lot of writing information helping them understand that, if you think about it, history is biased. It's always been told from the European American point of view. And, again, a lot of my White kids, they get angry at it and say: 'Well, this is what I think.' But they are in a safe place and can write their truth: 'Oh this just made me mad and I don't agree with it.' But then sometimes even as they're writing, you can see within the sentence that shows their truth is being changed. They might say something like: 'Oh, well maybe, I just countered myself. Maybe I'm starting to realize a new truth.' So I definitely want them to have a safe place to write their answers and to know that whatever they write, as long as they can support it, I'm fine with it. They can't just write without justification, without supporting their ideas with information."

Timothy: "When I read their reflections and listened to the transcripts and the recordings, they say things to each other in small- and whole-group discussions. They were actively listening to other people. I know that because when they wrote their individual written reflections, parts and pieces of other students' thoughts would enter into their own writing."[18]

Andrea: "Absolutely. And what I loved about that was that they credited each other for helping them understand a certain way. Like they would write: 'Danny said such and such.' They would make sure to give others credit for helping them with their own thinking."

Timothy: "Like, they were citing each other."

Andrea: "Yes! And they still do that in their reflections; they still do that. I just love that. And that again makes me know that they are listening carefully and they're taking it in and then they're validating each other's stories. Sometimes, I push them to connect what others say with what the literature is saying as well. But just the fact that they cite each other, I love that."

Timothy: "I know it's getting pretty late and we could probably go on talking forever, so I'll ask just a couple more questions, okay?"

Andrea: "Okay. We *could* go on forever! I so enjoy our conversations. Your questions are so thorough and make me consider things more deeply."

Timothy: "That means a lot to me, thank you for saying so. Being welcomed into your class and learning with you and the students was just a really special moment in my life. Knowing that you and the other students we worked with are still willing to continue the conversation really makes me understand the importance of relationships and how research can be a meaningful reciprocation. It's also a testament to how meaningful the class was to them that they're excited to continue talking about it. I'm hopeful that whatever comes of this conversation, it will make its way back to you and back to the students you taught over the years."

Andrea: "Me too! I'm excited to learn what they had to say."

Timothy: "Okay, final question, so this might bring up some answers that you've already stated, but in your mind what does this course do? And is there anything more that this course should be doing?"

Andrea: "Well, ultimately what this course does is teach students to look at everything from a different perspective. My goal is to have the students' minds blown at what they have not been taught. And I want the class to hopefully erase some stereotypes of Native Americans, to erase some of the ignorant conceptions of Native Americans and their history.[19] And some people are going to come out of it and not change their minds at all, but at least they know why they think or feel the way that they do. The beauty of the class is to truly show the different tribes, the different cultures, and hopefully just the day-to-day ins and outs of what it means to be Native American. I often think: Where do we go from here? How can this class be so impactful that the students want to become activists especially for a Native American cause?[20] That's always my goal."

The red light from the audio recorder dims as Timothy leans forward and taps the stop-record button.

. . .

IMPLICATIONS FOR INDIGENOUS CURRICULUM AND PEDAGOGY

For many Indigenous students, classrooms are a battleground. Students are fighting for their presence in contemporary society, for their histories and stories to be valued, for their knowledges to be validated. For some, this battle they are forced to fight has led to being pushed out of school, poor attendance, low self-esteem, and failing "western academic" norms. The classroom restoried in this chapter (Native American literature) is not the norm in U.S. schools; it is the exception. Parents, like those at Desert View High School, should not have to advocate for their children to be seen, for their lives to valued and validated in schooling spaces. Children should not be faced with curricula ultimatums—regurgitate this "fact" or fail. Communities should not have their influence blockaded by school walls.

In a decolonized and critical Indigenous schooling space, the lives, stories, histories, and experiences of the students and the surrounding communities *are* the curriculum and the interactions in the home and community are reflected in the pedagogies used in the classroom. Asset-based pedagogies such as culturally sustaining and revitalizing pedagogy and critical Indigenous pedagogy, view student, family, tribal, and community knowledges as valid and worthy of being centered, sustained, and revitalized in classroom spaces. And while the lesson plans shared in this chapter—autobiographical art project, historical timeline posters, mock debates, reflection essay tests, etc.—are just a brief glimpse into the ways students' lives can be centered in classroom spaces, these are just an attempt to link to larger systems of resurgence like those shared in the other chapters of this book. Critical asset-based pedagogies push the boundaries of teaching "cultural sensitivity" or "cultural awareness." Being sensitive to, or being aware of, creates a distance from teacher and student, rather than a continued learning and growing process for all involved in the education process. We argue that educators need to be reflexive—processing their actions in relation to systemic issues and adjusting based on students' interests, desires, contributions, and needs. We argue that classrooms must move beyond respecting or making relevant "other" cultures; instead, they should work to interrogate and decenter "required" western-based content, while providing space to recenter students' cultural, tribal, and community knowledges. Tiffany Lee and Patricia Quijada Cerecer frame this argument well stating that educators must not only validate home-based knowledge, but take that crucial step to create opportunities for students to "actively participate in constructing what counts as knowledge in their classrooms and schools."[21] We believe in this cause, and we know that this work requires that we ask ourselves tough questions with complicated answers:

- What lessons and activities build solidarity and trust? What assignments provide space for students to support their thinking?
- What activities welcome students' lives, stories, and identities into the classroom space?
- How might art unleash depth to our stories?
- What classroom community norms and rules should be established in order to create spaces where students can share their truths and be in dialogue with others' truths that may not match their own?
- How do we help students develop their critical consciousness?
- When social justice movements, protests, demonstrations are occurring in the community or in the nation, what are the ways we can bring those into the classroom discussions? What are the ways we can support students in their activism? How can we support students in their own actions to resist and reject?
- How can we create spaces for students to teach each other and be impacted by the truths of another?

It is our hope that our retrospective dialogue restored in this chapter provide some answers to these and other ongoing questions in Indigenous education. What stayed with us throughout the writing of this work was the importance of creating and sustaining meaningful and dialogic relationship between ourselves and with the students we had the honor of working and learning with. In addition, we hope that what lingers with you are the ways curriculum and pedagogy can be developed in ways that aid students in their ongoing navigation to understanding and, at times, disrupting their stories and their lives as a form of resistance to repressive settler colonial systems enacted through schools.

Finally, we conclude by coming back to the purposes of this course as stated by Blasingame and Ortiz. This course was originally created to (a) repair damage done from the erasure of Indigenous stories and knowledges from dominant school curricula, (b) create a truer picture of our shared history, and (c) recognize, call attention to, and resist/reject settler colonial systems as forwarded in schooling spaces.

In our own work, together and separate, we continue to work toward these purposes for a socially just and equitable educational system. Our work continues.

NOTES

1. As co-authors of this piece, we (Timothy and Andrea) made the conscious decision to write to a particular audience—the former, current, and future students of this Native American literature course. We realize that by writing in a way that is more accessible for them, we may be marginalizing academic readers who expect in-text citations and sources for quick reference. We felt that such in-text citations detracted from the flow of our conversation and story; however, we know full well that the words, thoughts, and knowledges of others have made a direct impact on our understanding and wish to still acknowledge/cite this impact. As such, we moved such citations to these endnotes. That said, we humbly invite guests reading this piece into our shared conversation—educators, administrators, community leaders, scholar activists—as we consider the lessons learned, the impacts felt, the missed moments, and the hope for what classes like this could be in different spaces. We frame our chapter upon San Pedro and Kinloch's conceptualizing of storying and projects in humanization. From:

    San Pedro, T., & Kinloch, V. (2016). Toward projects in humanization: Research on co-creating and sustaining dialogic relationships. *American Educational Research Journal [Centennial Issue], 54*(1), 373–394.

2. Wilson, S. (2008). *Research is ceremony: Indigenous research methods.* Fernwood Publishing.

3. San Pedro, T. (2015). Silence as shields: Agency and resistances among Native American students in the urban Southwest. *Research in the Teaching of English, 50*(2), 132–153.

San Pedro, T. (2015). Silence as Weapons: Transformative praxis among Native American students in the urban southwest. *Equity & Excellence in Education, 48*(4), 511–528.

4. Wolfe, P. (2006). Settler colonialism and the elimination of the native. *Journal of Genocide Research, 8*(4), 387–409.

5. Garcia, J., & Shirley, V. (2013). Performing decolonization: Lessons learned from Indigenous youth, teachers and leaders' engagement with critical Indigenous pedagogy. *Journal of Curriculum Theorizing, 28*(2), 76–91.
   Lee, T. (2006). "I came here to learn how to be a leader": An intersection of critical pedagogy and Indigenous education. *InterActions: UCLA Journal of Education and Information Studies, 2*(1). http://escholarship.org/uc/item/92m798m0

6. McCarty, T., & Lee, T. (2014). Critical culturally sustaining/revitalizing pedagogy and Indigenous education sovereignty. *Harvard Educational Review, 84*(1), 101–124.
   Paris, D. (2012). Culturally sustaining pedagogy a needed change in stance, terminology, and practice. *Educational Researcher, 41*(3), 93–97.
   Paris, D., & Alim, H. S. (2014). What are we seeking to sustain through culturally sustaining pedagogy? A loving critique forward. *Harvard Educational Review, 84*(1), 85–100.

7. McCarty & Lee, 2014; Paris, 2012; Paris & Alim, 2014

8. McCarty & Lee, 2014; Paris, 2012; Paris & Alim, 2014

9. Archibald, J. (2008). *Indigenous storywork: Educating the heart, mind, body, and spirit.* UBC Press.

10. Desert View High School is a pseudonym.

11. San Pedro, T., Carlos, E., & Mburu, J. (2016). Critical listening and storying fostering respect for difference and action within and beyond a Native American literature classroom. *Urban Education.* https://doi.org/10.1177/0042085915623346

12. San Pedro, T. J. (2015). Silence as shields: Agency and resistances among Native American students in the urban Southwest. *Research in the Teaching of English, 50*(2), 132.

13. All caps were in the original writing.

14. Grande, S., San Pedro, T., & Windchief, H. (2015). 21st century Indigenous identity location: Remembrance, reclamation, and regeneration. In D. Koslow & L. Salett (Eds.), *Multicultural perspectives on race, ethnicity, and identity* (pp. 105–122). NASW Press.

15. "...awareness of one's self is the beginning of learning" (p. 13). From

   Deloria, V., Jr., & Wildcat, D. R. (2001). *Power and place: Indian education in America.* Fulcrum Publishing.

16. Arizona's House Bill 2281 states that school districts are not allowed to include any (non- White) "ethnic" studies program of instruction that "promotes the overthrow of the United States government. Promote resentment toward a race of class of people; Are designed primarily for pupils of a particular ethnic group; Advocate ethnic solidarity instead of the treatment of pupils as individuals. In addition to this, the bill "shall not be construed to restrict

or prohibit: courses or classes for Native American pupils that are required to comply with federal law." There are a number of federal laws that this bill might be addressing: The Indian Education Act of 1972, Title VII of No Child Left Behind, Native American Languages Act, the Indian Education and Self-Determination Act of 1975 or the Johnson-O'Malley Act of 1934.

17. "[Tribal] communities are keenly aware…that children's learning to "do" school should not be an assimilative process; rather, it should happen by engaging culture. Indeed, this education continues to be framed and lived within in a framework where larger assimilative forces and local, Indigenous forces are engaging in a "battle for power" (p. 31–32). From

> Brayboy, B. M. J., & Castagno, A. E. (2009). Self-determination through self-education: Culturally responsive schooling for Indigenous students in the USA. *Teaching Education, 20*(1), 31–53.

18. San Pedro, T. (2015). Silence as weapons: Transformative praxis among Native American students in the urban Southwest. *Equity & Excellence in Education, 48*(4), 511–528. https://doi.org/10.1080/10665684.2015.1083915

19. "Who holds the power to make curricular decisions regarding what should be taught and which voices should be silenced has to be heeded since to teach U.S. history and not include the experiences and perspectives of all ethnic groups (underrepresented groups as well as White ethnics) leaves us with an incomplete, distorted history (Banks, 2012; Banks & Chavez, 2010)" (p. 200). From

> Carjuzaa, J., Baldwin, A. E., & Munson, M. (2015). Making the dream real: Montana's Indian education for all initiative thrives in a national climate of anti-ethnic studies. *Multicultural Perspectives, 17*(4), 198–206.

20. "When Indigenous schools consider themselves as sacred landscapes where educators promote and privilege Indigenous knowledge in their classrooms and guide Indigenous students in the critical process of promoting, protecting, and preserving Indigenous languages, cultures, land, and people, it is anticipated that the next generation of Indigenous youth will become empowered to positively transform their communities. Moreover, teachers of Indigenous students should then purposefully and carefully create a space to engage students in self-reflexive and dialogic practices that inform how the students will respond to challenges Indigenous communities face. The purpose for doing so is to encourage youth to take responsibility for contributing to the future environmental, political, social, and cultural needs of their community" (Garcia & Shirley, 2013, p. 89).

21. Lee, T. S., & Quijada Cerecer, P. D. (2010). (Re) claiming Native youth knowledge: Engaging in socio-culturally responsive teaching and relationships. *Multicultural Perspectives, 12*(4), 199–205.

CHAPTER 4

THE HAWAIIAN CULTURE-BASED EDUCATION MOVEMENT

Advancing Native Hawaiian Students in Public P–12 Schools Through an Indigenous Framework

Walter Kahumoku III

OPENING *MO'OLELO*—VIEWING LIFE AND EDUCATION THROUGH A DIFFERENT LENS

One bright, hot day near the end of the school year, a principal asked me to walk a couple of blocks from his office to the seashore. As we exited the school's parking lot, I noticed two boys playfully jostling one another as they walked ahead of us. We quietly followed the youngsters down the street and when we reached the coast, the principal slowed our pace to distance ourselves from the boys. The boys skillfully criss crossed through a maze of bumpers on a busy thoroughfare and ran up a low, rolling knoll to dip into one of several tents that sat at its crest. After a few moments, we crossed the

Indigenizing Education, pages 53–73
Copyright © 2022 by Information Age Publishing
www.infoagepub.com
All rights of reproduction in any form reserved.

highway, climbed the slight hill and watched as the two, now out of their tent and bare chested, sprinted for the *kai* (ocean) where a few other children were already reveling in the surf. The principal shared,

> Brothers...both at my school...and see the girl and older boy...4th and 5th graders. All of them live in those tents we just passed. We might get them for a month or even a quarter before we are notified that they have enrolled at another school down the coast. And...all of them are Hawaiian.

Hawai'i is the home land of the Kanaka Hawai'i or Native Hawaiians and like so many other Indigenous communities, they "face continual challenges to their epistemological, axiological, and ontological essences" (Kahumoku, 2004, p. 160) that are compounded by public educational systems that act to destabilize, distort, and at times destroy their cultural and linguistic integrity (Kawai'ae'a et. al, 2018). As the 2014 Native Youth Report remarks:

> The hallmarks of colonial experiments in Indian education were religious indoctrination, cultural intolerance and the wholesale removal of native children from their languages, religions, cultures, families, and communities. The overlapping goals of this "education" and "civilization" operated as euphemisms and justifications for taking culturally and physically injurious actions against Native children and their peoples...and is why...today's Native youth continue to confront formidable barriers to success. (pp. 7, 12)

Over the last couple of decades, however, a number of Kanaka educators have pressed forward on work that improves the edification of Native Hawaiians through Hawaiian Culture Based Education (HCBE). Not only are we—Kanaka educators—seeking to improve academic abilities and knowledge in our children but we also see formal education as a means of restoring, revitalizing, and normalizing the importance of being Kanaka.

This chapter employs *mo'olelo* (stories) interwoven with definitions, research, and theory to illuminate the importance of HCBE to the well-being and future sovereignty of Kanaka Hawai'i. The intent is to chronicle this movement by providing a new definition, elucidating several of its characteristics, and highlighting the impacts of HCBE through mo'olelo. At its close, specific suggestions about extending research and advocacy for approaches grounded in Indigenous methods to educating Native children are offered.

MO'OLELO: A FIRST YEAR TEACHER'S REALIZATION

In 2007, I worked with a group of teachers who were trying to understand how to develop and implement place-based curriculum—one of the forms of HCBE. A first year elementary teacher from Connecticut shared that when the school year started, most of her students seemed excited to learn. But after a geography unit on how mountains are created, she noticed a sharp decline in student engagement. She began with a prescribed lesson from her textbook—a short reading on the "tallest" mountain in the world—Mt. Everest. After some time, one of her youngsters asked why she had not recognized Mauna Kea as the tallest mountain in the world. Admittedly, she dismissed the question as a typical student mistake; after all, the textbook was always correct. Later, she realized that the mistake was hers (and that of the textbook) and congratulated the child for speaking up but continued to use Everest and the Himalayas as examples of how plate tectonics generated mountains. She closed her story with an acknowledgment that the damage was done. Most of her students, especially those of Hawaiian ancestry, had become inattentive, inactive, and at times, insolent.

While there are countless ways to make meaning of this first year teacher's experience, one perspective is that Native learners will engage in learning processes that value what students know and are able to do. As Kanaka scholar and teacher Ka'imi Ka'iwi Kahumoku (Ka'iwi & Kahumoku, 2006) reminds us, teaching and learning should start at home and then branch out to what is unfamiliar and new. For the inexperienced educator, this is a scary proposition—how to adapt curriculum, instruction, assessment, and the learning environment to honor Indigenous children.

WHAT IS CULTURE AND WHY IS IT FUNDAMENTAL TO TEACHING AND LEARNING IN HAWAI'I?

The state of Hawai'i has perennially faced significant teacher shortages. Hawai'i's Department of Education (HIDOE) note in its 2016–2017 employment report (Hawai'i Department of Education, 2017) that between the 2013–2014 and 2016–2017 school years, the department hired an average of 1,198 new teachers annually. The HIDOE also describes that an average of 400 of these newly hired came from in-state teacher education programs, 64.5% had no previous teaching experience, and the majority of first-year educators land in schools serving large concentrations of Kanaka Hawai'i. Hawai'i P–20 Partnerships for Education (2019) convey that in addition to a high rate of hires from places outside of the islands, over 1,000 teachers resign annually and 38% of those exiting indicate that they were leaving the islands. Clearly, the islands, and in particular, Native Hawaiian community schools face a critical teacher shortage and retention issue.

Although the HIDOE and its partners have worked to remediate the high teacher turnover issue by employing induction and mentoring for all its new teachers, it has not adopted a system-wide approach that advances students' intellect and ethnic identity. According to Santamaria and

Santamaria (2012), systemic strengths-based models that capture "the reality of being members of historically underrepresented and often disenfranchised" (p. xii) have the power to "enact context-specific change in response to power, domination, access, and achievement imbalances, resulting in improved academic achievement for learners at every academic level of institutional schooling in the U.S." (p. 7). Such changes like adopting HCBE strategies are integral to supporting the growth of Native children. The data reflects that 25.13% of the total public system K–12 student population is of Hawaiian ancestry while only 9.9% of classroom teachers are Native Hawaiian (OHA, 2017). Kanaka HCBE educators have a long road ahead of them in supporting teachers—especially new hires—who work in schools serving large numbers of Kanaka children, to utilize Native knowledge, language, and other cultural teaching practices to ensure that many more of their students thrive in school and beyond.

But what is meant by the term *culture* and why is it necessary in terms of educating the Indigenous child? Grossberg (1993) refers to culture as "caught between community (social formations), totality (a whole way of life) and aesthetics (representational practice)" (p. 90) and adds that a group's culture is place and context driven. Bruner (1996) suggests that "culture shapes the mind ... it provides us with the tool kit by which we construct not only our worlds but our very conceptions of ourselves and our powers" (p. x). If we are to be concerned with how our students learn and are taught, then examining various ways in which teachers approach teaching and learning through culture-based education (CBE) is critical.

HAWAIIAN CULTURE-BASED EDUCATION

Over several decades, authors (Clark et al., 1996; Demmert & Towner, 2003; Gay, 2002; Gilbert et al., 2008; Ladson-Billings, 1995; Omizo & Omizo, 1989; Paris, 2012; Schonleber, 2006; Tharp et al., 2007; Yap et al., 2004; Yazzie, 1999) have articulated the importance of cultural methods to educating children. At the heart of these cultural strategies is an acknowledgement that incorporating a person's cultural, linguistic, and historical heritage in the process of learning is vital to that student's ability to navigate years of schooling. The confluence of these approaches highlights the need for strengths-based educational processes where a Native youngster's identity is not only valued but also becomes an integral part of teaching and learning. So what is CBE?

Recently, there has been an increase in Indigenous scholarship and initiatives working to advance CBE within mainstream education. Noted in Table 4.1, we can see five instances in which CBE is defined. Applying CBE within Native education focuses on utilizing elements of cultural

TABLE 4.1   Culture-Based Education Defined Across Native Education

	Culture-Based Education	Culture-Based Education	Culture-Based Education (Interventions)	Culture-Based Teaching	Culture-Based Education
Author(s)	Kanaʻiaupunui & Kawaiʻaeʻa (2008)	Northwest Territory's New Teacher Induction Program (2011)	Yap et al. (2004)	Gilbert et al. (2008)	Canada's Assembly of First Nations Education, Jurisdiction, and Governance's Cultural Competency Report (2012)
Definition	…refers to teaching and learning that are grounded in a cultural worldview, from whose lens are taught the skills, knowledge, content, and values that students need in our modern, global society.	…goal of culture-based education is to support all students through affirmation of their culture.…It helps [students] to be aware of their heritage and to value the accomplishments of their family, their community, and their ancestors. It builds a sense of pride and self-esteem…	…incorporates native languages and/or important elements of native culture. Culturally based interventions are deemed to be planned activities and materials designed to improve education and introduced within the education systems.	…a form of pedagogy that recognizes and integrates students' cultural traditions, values, and history and the incorporation of teaching strategies harmonious with these so as not only to preserve students' cultural knowledge but also foster their successful academic achievement.	The design of a culturally based education program demands that the program be developed locally with communities or First Nations playing an active role in developing culturally based curricula and in delivering instruction…

identity—language, sense of place, values and worldviews, practices and traditions, ways of knowing and operating, and history—to connect, and at times reconnect, Native learners to their history, heritage, and homeland. It intentionally integrates Western academics with Native content, knowledge, and skills to help students realize that education is vital to their ability as adults to contribute to themselves, their families, and their larger community. CBE moves the abstraction of education found in theorems, equations, rote memorization, and other standard U.S. educational practices into the realm of applied learning for the good of the self, family, and community.

Recently in the islands, Hawaiian CBE (HCBE) has transformed schooling to include Kanaka worldviews and values. Hawaiʻi's Board of Education ratified a set of outcomes called Nā Hopena Aʻo or HĀ (Hawaii State Department of Education 2016) to guide the way the state thinks about education. Aspects of well-being—belonging, responsibility, excellence, aloha, total well-being, and Hawaiʻi—have become outcomes to strive for by everyone employed in Hawaiʻi's public school system. Figure 4.1., Components of HCBE in the classroom, captures the core elements of HCBE, in which I expand upon the characteristics and framework for teaching in the following sections.

In such light, I propose a definition of HCBE that creates a larger context around the integration of culture, indigeneity, and education, specifically in relation to Native Hawaiians. I propose HCBE to be

> an educational approach that integrates culture—language, ways of knowing, relating, operating, and believing, places, history, home and community knowledge, and values—into teaching and learning, building bridges between the past, present, and future in the Native/Hawaiian context and beyond to improve the well-being of Native learners, their families, and communities.

The merits of this new definition are three-fold. Like other definitions, this delineation embraces relevant, sustaining, congruent, and responsive teaching approaches. Meaningful schooling is realized when teachers teach through culture to create crosswalks between home and community with modern content, skills, and dispositions expected in classrooms (Kawaiʻaeʻa, 2012). Moreover, this definition identifies the importance of empowering Indigenous children to improve their well-being as well as that of their families, and community. HCBE then becomes an educational framework that advances Native students' intellectual and academic abilities as well as their Indigenous identities. I now turn to expanding upon the characteristics of HCBE.

Characteristics of Hawaiian Culture-Based Education

A question was posed at a recent teacher training session about the validity of HCBE. "Why should I," announced one of my participants, "think

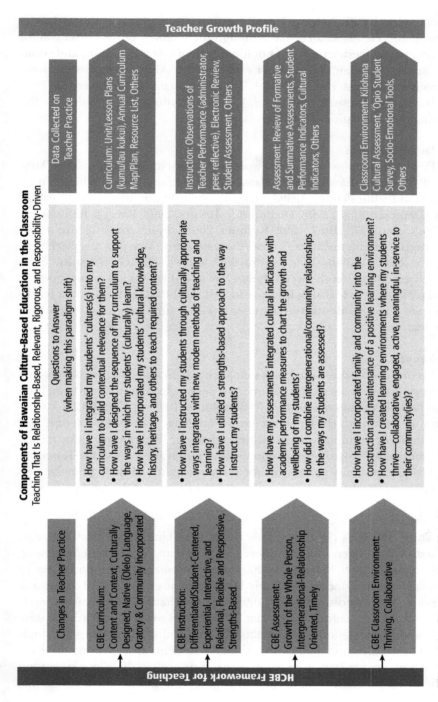

Figure 4.1 Components of Hawaiian culture based education in the classroom.

about using HCBE with my kids if they don't even think of themselves as Hawaiian?" He elaborated that although the majority of his students were of Hawaiian ancestry, most did not identify themselves as Kanaka and could not speak Hawaiian. "They don't even practice Aloha (compassion, love, devotion, kindness, charity, grace). They beat on each other every day."

In response to such statements, I suggested educators consider the following characteristics of HCBE.

Relationship-Based

First and foremost, this framework is dependent on relationships. Meyer (2003) notes that for Native Hawaiians, strong relationships between individuals fortifies connectivity, sense of responsibility, and trust. Researchers (Demmert et al., 2006; Demmert & Towner, 2003; Kaiwi & Kahumoku, 2006; Ogbu, 1978, 1987, 1992; Reyhner, 2003) report that effective teaching occurs when educators "know" their students. Tharp et al. (2007) recognize that Hawaiians value relationships and when teachers reinforce the affective connections between themselves and their students, engagement and receptivity to learning increase as well. As the adage goes, when teachers care about students, those students will in turn care about what they are learning.

Relevant

Second, beyond creating and employing a "humanizing pedagogy that respects and uses the reality, history, and perspectives of students as an integral part of educational practice" (Bartolome, 1994, p. 173), HCBE curriculum begins with a student's strengths—language, values, knowledge, and interests. For example, when a history unit about 18th century industrialization begins with significant economic and political events in the Kingdom of Hawai'i, students quickly realize the importance of their homeland to the context of what is occurring throughout the rest of the world.

Rigorous

Third, HCBE is rigorous. While Indigenous language, knowledge, and practices have been long-considered as "less-than," "old," and "meaningless" (Adams, 1988; Kahumoku, 2004), recent research and reports (Alaska Department of Education & Early Development et al., 2012; Castagno & Brayboy, 2008; Ladson-Billings, 1995) suggest that HCBE promotes levels of academic and cultural rigor that far surpasses western educational standards and expectations. As Gay (2002) states, culturally responsive education requires "having high expectations for students and ensuring these expectations are realized, are what make a difference" (p. 3). Rigor is elevated as learners perform at high levels of cognitive, linguistic, socio-emotional, physical, spiritual, and psychological achievement and excellence (Native Hawaiian Education Council, 2011; Yamauchi et al., 2008).

Responsibility

Finally, and possibly most important, HCBE advances a stronger sense of responsibility in Native Hawaiians. Ladson-Billings (1995) in her work on culturally relevant pedagogy advises

> that "good teaching" requires three propositions: (a) Students must experience academic success, (b) students must develop and/or maintain cultural competence, and (c) students must develop a critical consciousness through which they challenge the status quo of the current social order. (p. 160)

Through HCBE, schools become places to revamp existing norms, practices, policies, and beliefs into applied learning situations that endeavor to improve learners' academic abilities while solving critical issues impacting their families and communities.

These four R's represent characteristics of HCBE that began appearing in courses conducted in learning environments throughout Hawai'i's schools and communities. As a strong foundation for teaching and learning, these principles have strengthened relationships between *kumu* (teacher) and *haumāna* (students), the curricular content and context that are relevant and rigorous, and a stronger sense of responsibility are producing remarkable results in student performance indicators, especially in the areas of reading comprehension and math (Kana'iaupuni et al., 2017). As we advance our understanding of the impacts on students by the use of HCBE, we hope to expand its use throughout prekindergarten to higher education.

TEACHING THROUGH A HAWAIIAN CULTURE-BASED EDUCATIONAL APPROACH

There are four shifts in teaching practice when teaching through HCBE: curriculum, instruction, assessment, and classroom community building. What has been commonly shared among secondary and higher education is the belief that content and rigor are the primary purposes for teaching. Although curricular content is still fundamental to the growth of students, we have realized that our students, whether Hawaiian or not, will not readily embrace American history or chemistry if the educator does not first begin developing trusting and respectful relationships among the students. Community building among teachers and students sets the stage for active participation and student engagement with one another and the academic content. Thus, for teachers to be effective, they must transform what they teach, how they deliver that content, how they determine a learner's growth over time, and build a strong classroom community.

Curriculum

In terms of curriculum, teachers are asked to adjust the content and context of what is being taught by starting with the strengths of students. Even when Indigenous youth do not know their heritage language and history, many island educators who start with traditional knowledge to encourage students to understand algebraic functions see increased student interest and engagement (Kana'iaupuni et al., 2010). When an earth science lesson is taught through traditional planting processes, Hawaiian students experience a growing sense of pride in who they are as well as success on standardized tests. I am reminded of a middle school teacher from Utah, who teaches Native Hawaiian youth, commenting, "After working on a stream restoration project, my students are quick to say how *akamai* (brilliant) their ancestors were."

As teachers develop their curricular units and lessons, they answer three fundamental questions:

- How have I integrated my students' culture(s) into my curriculum to build contextual relevance for them?
- How have I designed the sequence of my curriculum to support the ways in which my students (culturally) learn?
- How have I incorporated my students' cultural knowledge, history, heritage, and others to teach required content?

HCBE curriculum utilizes Native/Indigenous/traditional/family/place/ community-based content (e.g., "kuleana" which is having responsibility for oneself and the broader community through stewardship and having a keen awareness of the relationship between past–present–future) as a strong starting point for teaching Kanaka Hawai'i students. These questions provide the classroom instructor ways to shift the content and context of what they are teaching to be much more relevant and meaningful for their learners.

Instruction

In addition to the curriculum, HCBE encourages educators to transform how they deliver their content. Indigenous youth tend to enjoy visual, hands-on, and direct experiences while applying real-world activities. They also tend to see the overall picture before the details and are creative, holistic, reflective, collaborative, imaginative, concrete learners while simultaneously processing learning experiences by observing before performing and connecting with the land (Swisher & Dehyle, 1989; Tharp & Yamauchi, 1995). Moreover, D'Amato (1988) warns that Indigenous collective value systems clash with the Western ideologies. Hawaiian children work well in collective processes and their academic performance improves when they care about others as well as themselves (Tharp et al., 2007). HCBE teachers also employ wait time and other instructional strategies to accommodate for culturally appropriate learning modalities (Yamauchi, 1998). Teachers who utilize strengths-based, grounded instructional strategies are able to affirmatively answer two fundamental questions:

- How have I instructed my students through culturally appropriate ways integrated with new, modern methods of teaching and learning?
- How have I utilized a strengths-based approach to the way I instruct my students?

HCBE encourages the use of culturally appropriate measures to chart the growth of the whole being.

Assessment

Beyond what is being taught and how students are instructed, assessments and evaluations must blend academic performance measures with indicators that describe the success of the whole, culturally competent person. We are now looking at ways to do more than simply translating English-based assessment tools into the Hawaiian, or another Indigenous, language. We are now developing assessments that are written not only in Hawaiian but contexted through a Hawaiian lens. In addition, measurements of growth must have a level of sensitivity to linguistic and cultural differences and be constantly calibrated for disconnects between the learner and what is being assessed (Diller & Moule, 2005). Through HCBE, assessing and determining progress:

(a) capitalizes on student' cultural backgrounds rather than attempting to override or negate them; (b) is good for all students; (c) is integrated and interdisciplinary; (d) is authentic and child centered, connected to children's real lives; (e) develops critical thinking skills; (f) incorporates cooperative learning and whole language strategies; (g) is supported by staff development and preservice preparation; and (h) is part of a coordinated, building-wide strategy. (Klug & Whitfield, 2002, p. 151)

In addition, HCBE assessment can be successful when teachers are able to positively answer four fundamental questions:

- How have my students integrated cultural indicators with academic performance measures to chart the growth of the whole person?
- How did I combine intergenerational/community relationships in the ways my students are assessed?
- How have I included authentic and performance-based assessments and measures to chart the growth of my students?
- How have I created a viable assessment system that accounts for multiple measures of growth—intellectual, physical, spiritual, emotional, and others—that integrate cultural ways of knowing and believing with contemporary educational practice?

Classroom Community Building

The final area of transformation when using HCBE in the classroom is the ability of teachers to create and sustain positive empowering learning environments where Native students thrive. It is a safe, supportive setting that nurtures students' physical, mental, intellectual, socio-emotional, and spiritual health (Woodhouse & Knapp, 2000) and promotes active participation of parents, families, and the larger community. A students' self-efficacy is enhanced through strengthened relationships and a sense of responsibility for their family and community as well as other teachers, students, and themselves.

HCBE learning environments also are responsive to the learning needs of Indigenous students. As Barnhardt (2005) recognizes, these environments align with the collective processes found in Native communities. Indigenous students work cooperatively to: complete tasks, operate as individuals and team members (e.g., pairs, small groups, large groups), and promote positive behavior amongst all (e.g., ha'aha'a [humility], koa [courage], lōkahi [balance], mālama [caring]). Tharp et al. (2007) suggests such culturally compatible work environments create arenas where students' use of social reinforcement to check behavior and teachers apply a balance of high expectations with a real sense of aloha—care for each and every student.

If teachers are to successfully maintain HCBE-positive learning environments, two fundamental questions must be addressed:

- How have I incorporated family and community into the construction and maintenance of a positive learning environment?

- How have I created learning environments where my students thrive—collaborative, engaged, active, meaningful, in-service to their community(ies)?

The development of HCBE and the growing efforts to implement this Indigenous educational model across learning contexts for Kanaka youth, families, and our communities has been far-reaching and offered lessons learned to ensure its success. I wish to return to the power of moʻolelo through the following examples of where and how HCBE has been shared and used. The following two moʻolelo present promising results from the application of HCBE.

HAWAIIAN CULTURE BASED EDUCATION MOʻOLELO

Success Moʻolelo #1: HCBE Professional Development for Teachers

In 2010, the Kamehameha Schools working in partnership with this state's Department of Education embarked on improving the well-being of Native Hawaiian students through HCBE training for teachers. The program, Teacher Institutes (TI), provided professional development credits to teachers when they took a course from an expert HCBE instructor.

In a program evaluation report produced by the Pacific Policy Resource Center (2014), during the 2013–2014 school year, 36 teachers embarked on a year-long course to develop and implement HCBE approaches to the teaching of English language arts (ELA) in one of the most rural parts of Hawaiʻi. Twenty-one participants completed the course and of those, approximately 17 participants reported that they experienced a variety of meaningful learning experiences that led to improvements in their classroom practices. TI participants recounted concrete learning experiences and continual instructor support to redesign, implement, monitor, and refine culturally relevant ELA (Wonders) curriculum developed by McGraw-Hill. Participants were taught to use the Moenahā (Indigenous teaching and learning) framework to guide their redesigned curriculum through Hawaiian-congruent instructional strategies; to collect data about the growth of students through culturally appropriate formative and summative assessments; to create environments rich in language, culture, traditional knowledge and practices; and to involve parent and community experts.

The data captured through analysis of teacher reflections paired with student behavioral and academic indicators provided the following impactful results. Teachers in many instances replaced prescribed (Wonders

generated) curriculum with place-oriented resources and topics. Participants reported increased student engagement and, in some cases, improved
reading comprehension and writing skills amongst learners. As one teacher
indicated, in her unit on heroes (Wonders 4th Grade), the heroes selected
by the prescribed curriculum did not reflect the backgrounds nor interests
of her students. In addition, she realized that for several of her English
language learners (ELL) from the Marshall Islands who struggled to comprehend English, as well as being in a foreign country and public school
system, she needed to replace the prepared readings and topics with those
that these students could understand and were relevant to them. When
she added a well-known South Pacific navigator, Mau Piailug, to the list of
choices, four male Marshallese students seemed to become very animated
and engaged. They became the experts and in terms of the project, proudly
presented their findings about their hero to their peers.

Furthermore, TI participants praised the course for broadening their
understanding of learning styles and contextualizing the need for differen-
tiation. The Moenahā framework presented a critical way to construct daily
lessons that attended to four different types of learners—relationship-ori-
ented, thinking-oriented, task-oriented, and creativity-oriented. When implemented, the teachers saw improvements in students' ability to work individually, in groups, and in large class discussions. They identified that fewer
students were confused and unable to complete tasks while more learners
understood what they were asked to accomplish and state why—especially
in relation to the ELA standards being covered. This type of teaching increased confidence and engagement among their learners. These results
correlate with a study conducted by Kanaʻiaupuni et al. (2010) that linked
the use of HCBE strategies and increased math and reading comprehension among Kanaka learners.

TI participants also reported the integration of families and community
members in their children's educational experiences (see Figure 4.2). One

Changed Ways of Working With Parents and Community

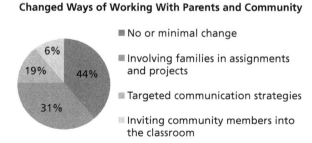

Figure 4.2   HCBE impact on family and communities.

participant asked students to interview family members as a part of a family history project that concluded a social studies/ELA unit. Other teachers utilized an Indigenous, positive communication protocol to increase family awareness of the great strides their children were making in their classes. A few teachers invited family and community members into their classrooms as a part of an applied learning strategy. An Indigenous expert in Native fishing traditions was brought into a class to link math concepts to help students see the practical application of what they were learning.

Many highlighted increased motivation to improve their pedagogy because, as one teacher explained, as she shared newfound ideas and strategies with other workshop participants, they "became excited and saw me as the expert. That made me feel so good because no one prior to this class said to me that what I had to offer was worth anything" (Kamehameha Schools' Teacher Institutes Event Report, 2014, p. 3). Just as the program encouraged teachers to develop safe, positive learning environments for their students, so too did the program instructors develop and maintain a safe, enriching environment in which collaboration, critical thinking, intergenerational and multi-subject learning could exist.

The impact on learners was profound. As stated earlier, TI participants reported increased student engagement as evidenced by expressed excitement to share with others, increased attentiveness, improved focus (being "on task"), increased inquisitiveness, and more frequent risk taking (e.g., speaking in front of the class). Figure 4.3 highlights this improvement.

During focus group interviews, participants also reported fewer behavioral issues, increased attendance, and increased perseverance when tasks and assignments were especially difficult. When applying HCBE strategies, teachers noted surges in students' ability to be independent critical thinkers. This program exemplifies how teachers can, through HCBE transformational learning experiences, implement culturally grounded approaches that improve not only teaching practices but also sustained student growth.

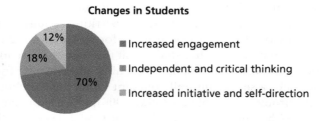

Changes in Students

- Increased engagement
- Independent and critical thinking
- Increased initiative and self-direction

12%
18%
70%

Figure 4.3   Changes in student levels of engagement in education.

Success Mo'olelo #2: HCBE and Advanced Placement English

Throughout her career, scholar and high school educator Ka'imipono Ka'iwi has studied English and in particular Hawaiian literature with the purpose of improving the ways in which she teaches her Native Hawaiian students. As she recognizes the ways in which Native people think and operate, their epistemology and ontology are often "interpreted by Western perspectives as "backward," "sentimental," or "naïve" (Ka'iwi, 2006, p. 90). She has built a collection of Hawaiian literature written in both English and Hawaiian so that she, along with colleagues, could tap into modern and ancestral knowledge to support the revitalization of Hawaiian identity in students while advancing their ability to read and write more effectively.

In 2009, Ka'iwi petitioned the College Board organization to approve a new comparative literature advanced placement course high school students would take during the senior year. She applied the HCBE principles to the course content, approach, delivery, and assessment. Ka'iwi's AP Comparative Literature and Composition course was approved in the Spring of 2010 and she began her first class in the 2010–2011 school year.

There are two unique aspects about her students. First, all of them are of Native Hawaiian ancestry. Although the State of Hawai'i does not track the number of students who take AP courses by ethnicity, in separate conversations with high school English teachers from across the state, Ka'iwi realized that very few Kanaka students even consider taking the highly intense and rigorous course. As a corollary, the Native Youth Report (2014) indicates that American Indian and Alaska Native students are the least likely to attend a high school that offers Advanced Placement courses and less than 1% of the Native youth population take these classes. The stark reality is that very few Native students have access to and are prepared well enough to take and pass an Advanced Placement course.

The second startling feature is that less than half of them take prerequisite honors courses in preparation for her class. For most, this is the first time they experienced such an intense, rigorous, and demanding course. Moreover, although all are recommended by their previous English teachers to take the course, Ka'iwi notes that many do not come into her class prepared for the deep thinking and extensive writing required when one does literary analysis. These two aspects make for, as she says, high levels of anxiety and frustration among her students at the start of the school year.

Ka'iwi utilizes not only the Moenahā teaching and learning framework but also establishes a set of culturally relevant literary assessment tools to guide students through text analysis (Ka'iwi, 2006); which she exemplifies in her chapter (see Chapter 5). She starts her course with Hawaiian literature to instruct students on how to conduct literary analysis. She builds upon that foundation through her comparative approach, connecting traditional

Hawaiian and Pacific literature with classic AP works (e.g., *Things Fall Apart, King Lear*) normally found on the exam. "This pattern," she states, "of starting at home and then build bridges to others, has really helped my students to start with what they know best and from that strong base, read through other less familiar literature with more confidence and aptitude."

The results have been incredible. When compared to other high school juniors and seniors who take the AP English test in Hawai'i, her students pass with phenomenal rates. Over 3 years, her students perform at least 20 percentage points above the state average and when compared to the national average, at least 14% above those (Kahumoku, 2016). Through the use of HCBE, Ka'iwi and her students have replaced notions that they are "less-than" and "incapable" with clear indications that they are Kanaka learners who have successfully strengthened their own Indigenous identity and their academic prowess.

CONCLUSION

The story of that fateful day when I walked alongside a principal out to the seashore to watch two youngsters join a few others in the kai has become pivotal to why I and other Kanaka educators believe that HCBE significantly advances the growth of Native Hawaiian and other children in Hawai'i's public schools. While we acknowledge that there are other factors in a student's life that are outside of our control that we are unable to remedy, we firmly believe in the power of culturally grounded approaches like HCBE that create meaningful curricular content, student-aligned instructional strategies, applied assessment tools, and positive learning environments that together, help our Native children to thrive.

To accomplish such great feats within schools, we must address the needs of ethnic minority and Native learners when they come to our doorstep. As the 2014 Native Youth Report (2014) argues:

> Although the challenges facing native youth today may seem insurmountable, tribal nations and their communities are proving that it is possible to overcome these obstacles with focused, strategic efforts. Those who serve Native students are developing innovative programs grounded in both high academic expectations and tribal values and traditions, and beginning to reverse more than two centuries of oppressive and stifling policies. In addition, over the last six years, the Administration has created new programs [in the Education Department (ED) and Bureau of Indian Education (BIE)] to support building tribal sovereignty over education. BIE and ED entered a Memorandum of Agreement to improve two-way communications between the two agencies and address common issues affecting AI/AN students. In addition, ED increased the emphasis in its Title VII formula grants, on the

need for school districts to provide culturally-relevant education for Indian students. (p. 27)

The lessons learned from decades of work in culture-based education and moreover in the context of Hawai'i and with learners of Hawaiian ancestry are valuable. Clearly, the body of research and study on culturally grounded, Indigenous and Native education offers concrete foundations for expanding HCBE throughout Hawai'i and beyond. As we acknowledge that all that is being taught in schools throughout the world is cultural—that is, that education teaches through a cultural lens—we should no longer debate the merits of culture-based strategies. Instead, we should increase our understanding through research and further examination of how to employ successful culture-based approaches for Native and diverse learners. By honoring who they are and where they come from in the ways we structure learning experiences, such transformed education will go far in the quest to not only close achievement gaps but restore the integrity and well-being of the Indigenous soul.

The context and examples within this chapter are but a step toward such transformation. It is also not meant to be definitive nor absolute; there is still so much more to explore, test, and report. Educators and those who touch the lives of students must continue advancing HCBE as a potential means of strengthening the lives of our Native youth. To this cause, I, along with others, continue this powerful work.

REFERENCES

2014 Native Youth Report. (2014). *Executive office of the president.* https://obamawhite house.archives.gov/sites/default/files/docs/20141129nativeyouthreport_final.pdf

Adams, D. W. (1988). Fundamental considerations: The deep meaning of Native American school, 1880–1900. *Harvard Educational Review, 58*(1), 1–27.

Alaska Department of Education & Early Development, Alaska Comprehensive Center, Alaska Native Educators, and Education Northwest. (2012). *Guide to implementing the Alaska cultural standards for educators.* https://education.alaska.gov/standards/cultural

Assembly of First Nations Education, Jurisdiction, and Governance: Cultural Competency Report. (2012). http://www.afn.ca/uploads/files/education/8.1.pdf

Barnhardt, R. (2005). *Creating a place for Indigenous knowledge in education: The Alaska Native Knowledge Network.* http://www.ankn.uaf.edu/curriculum/articles/ray-barnhardt/pbe_ankn_chapter.html

Bartolome, L. (1994). Beyond the methods fetish: Toward a humanizing pedagogy. *Harvard Educational Review. 64*(2), 173–195.

Castagno, A., & Brayboy, B. M. J. (2008). Culturally responsive schooling for Indigenous youth: A review of the literature. *Review of Educational Research, 78*(4), 941–993. https://doi.org/10.3102/0034654308323036

Clark, E. R., Nystrom, N. J., & Perez, B. (1996). Language and culture: Critical components of multicultural teacher education. *The Urban Review, 23*(2), 185–197.

D'Amato, J. D. (1988). "Acting": Hawaiian children's resistance to teachers. *The Elementary School Journal, 88*(5), 529–542.

Demmert, W. G., Jr., Hilberg, S., Beaulieu, D., Rawlins, N., Tharp, R., & Yap, K. (2008). *Indigenous culture-based education continuum* [Unpublished manuscript]. Woodring College of Education, Western Washington University.

Demmert, W., & Towner, J. (2003). *A review of the research literature on the influences of culturally based education on the academic performance of Native American Students.* Northwest Regional Educational Laboratory.

Diller, J. V., & Moule, J. (2005). *Cultural competence: A primer for educators.* Wadsworth.

Gay, G. (2002). Preparing for culturally responsive teaching. *Journal of Teacher Education, 53*(2), 106–116.

Gilbert, J. E., Arbuthnot, K., Hood, S., Grant, M., West, M., McMillian, Y., Vincent Cross, E., Williams, P., & Eugene, W. (2008). Teaching Algebra using culturally relevant virtual instructors. *The International Journal of Virtual Reality, 7*(1), 21–30.

Grossberg, L. (1993). Can cultural studies find true happiness in communication? *Journal of Communication, 43*(4), 89–97.

Hawaii State Department of Education. (2016). Nā Hopena Aʻo (HĀ). http://www.hawaiipublicschools.org/TeachingAndLearning/StudentLearning/HawaiianEducation/Pages/HA.aspx

Hawaii State Department of Education, Employment Report SY 2016–2017. https://www.hawaiipublicschools.org/Reports/EmploymentReport2016-17.pdf

Hawaiʻi P–20 Partnerships for Education (December, 2019). *Education to Workforce Report.* http://hawaiidxp.org/files/Rpt_Education_to_Workforce-EDU_2019-12.pdf

Kahumoku, W. (2004). A tragic Indigenous Moʻolelo: The decline of Kanaka Maoli linguistic identity. *Kuleana ʻŌiwi Press.* http://www.ulukau.org/elib/collect/oiwi3/index/assoc/D0.dir/doc415.pdf

Kahumoku, W. (2016). *Culture based approaches to educating children training workshop.* Presentation at Mana Academy, West Valley City, Utah.

Kaiwi, M. K. (2006). Grounding Hawaiian learners—and teachers—in their Indigenous identity. *Hūlili: Multidisciplinary Research on Hawaiian Well-Being, 3*(1), 27–36.

Kaʻiwi, M. A., & Kahumoku, W., III. (2006). Makawalu: Standards, curriculum, and assessment for literature through an Indigenous perspective. *Hūlili: Multidisciplinary Research on Hawaiian Well-Being, 3*(1), 183–206.

Kamehameha Schools' Kauhale Kīpaipai. (2014, April 24th). *Teacher institutes' event report. Teacher response.*

Kanaʻiaupuni, S., Ledward, B., & Jensen, ʻU. (2010). Culture-based education and its relationship to student outcomes. *Kamehameha Schools Culture-Based Education.* https://documents.sd61.bc.ca/ANED/educationalResources/StudentSuccess/Cultural_Based_Education_and_its_Relationship_to_Student_Outcomes.pdf

Kanaʻiaupuni, S., Ledward, B., & Malone, N. (2017, April). Mohala i ka wai: Cultural advantage as a framework for Indigenous culture-based education and student outcomes. *American Educational Research Journal, 54*(1S), 311S–339S.

Kawaiʻaeʻa, K. K. C. (2012). *Kūkohu: Ka Nānaina Kaiaola o nā Kaiaaʻo ʻŌlelo HawaiʻI* (A study on the cultural ecology of Hawaiian-medium and Hawaiian immersion learning environments) [Unpublished doctoral dissertation]. Union Institute & University.

Kawaiʻaeʻa, K., Kahumoku, W. K., Hussey, S. M., Krug, G. K., Makuakāne-Drechsel, T. H., Duarte, M. P., & Watkins-Victorino, L. (2018). Keaomālamalama: Catalysts tor transformative change in Hawaiian education. In E. A. McKinley & L. T. Smith (Eds.), *Handbook of indigenous education*. Springer, Singapore. https://doi.org/10.1007/978-981-10-1839-8_35-1

Klug, G. J., Whitfield, P. T. (2002). *Widening the circle: Culturally relevant pedagogy for American Indian children*. Routledge.

Ladson-Billings, G. (1995). But that's just good teaching! The case for culturally relevant pedagogy. *Theory Into Practice, 34*(3), 159–165.

Meyer, M. (2003). *Hoʻoulu: Our time of becoming*. ʻAi Pōhaku Press.

Native Hawaiian Education Council. (2011). *Native Hawaiian education council needs assessment report.* http://nhec.org/wp-content/uploads/2014/06/NHEC-Needs-Assessment-Report-2011-09.pdf

Northwest Territory's New Teacher Induction Program. (2011). http://www.new teachersnwt.ca/culture_based_education.html

Office of Hawaiian Affairs. (2021). *Native Hawaiian data book.* https://www.ohadata book.com/fr_updates.19.html#EDU

Ogbu, J. (1978). *Minority education and caste: The American system in cross-cultural perspective*. Academic Press.

Ogbu, J. (1987). Variability in minority school performance. *Anthropology and Education Quarterly, 18*(4), 312–333.

Ogbu, J. (1992). Immigrant and involuntary minorities in comparative perspective. In M. A. Gibson & J. U. Ogbu (Eds.), *Minority status and schooling*. Garland.

Omizo, M. M., & Omizo, S. A. (1989). Art activities to improve self-esteem among Native Hawaiian children. *The Journal of Humanistic Counseling, 27*(4), 167–176.

Pacific Policy Resource Center. (2014). *Kamehameha Schools' teacher institutes program evaluation report.*

Paris, D. (2012). Culturally sustaining pedagogy a needed change in stance, terminology, and practice. *Educational Researcher, 41*(3), 93–97.

Reyhner, J. (2003). *Native language immersion*. Northern Arizona University, Arizona. https://eric.ed.gov/?id=ED482031

Santamaria, L. J., & Santamaria, A. P. (2012). *Applied critical leadership in education: Choosing change*. Routledge.

Schonleber, N. S. (2006, April 8). *Culturally relevant education and the Montessori approach: Perspectives from Hawaiian educators.* Paper presented at the Annual Meeting of the American Education Research Association, San Franciso, CA. https://eric.ed.gov/?q=ED493188&id=ED493188

Swisher, K., & Deyhle, D. (1989). The styles of learning are different, but the teaching is just the same: Suggestions for teachers of American Indian youth. *Journal of American Indian Education*, 1–14.

Tharp, R. G., Jordan, C., Speidel, G. E., Au, K. H., Klein, T. W., Caldins, R. P., Sloat, K. C. M., & Gallimore, R. (2007). Education and Native Hawaiian children: Revisiting KEEP. *Hūlili: Multidisciplinary research on Hawaiian well-being, 4(1),* 269–317.

Tharp, R. G., & Yamauchi, L. A. (1994). *Effective instructional conversation in Native American classrooms. Educational Practice Report: 10.* http://eric.ed.gov/?id =ED372896

Woodhouse, J. L., & Knapp, C. E. (2000). *Place-based curriculum and instruction: Outdoor and environmental education approaches.* http://files.eric.ed.gov/fulltext/ ED448012.pdf

Yamauchi, L. A. (1998). *Research from the National Center for Research on Education, Diversity, and Excellence (CREDE): Sociohistorical influences on the Hawaiian Immersion program.* Presentation for the College of Education colloquium series, Honolulu, HI.

Yamauchi, L. A., Lau-Smith, J., & Luning, R. J. I. (2008). Family involvement in a Hawaiian Language Immersion Program. *School Community Journal, 18(10),* 39–60.

Yap, K. O., Towner, J., Beaulieu, D., Kushman, J., Demmert, W., & Tharp, R. (2004). *Experimental research in culturally based education: an assessment of feasibility.* Northwest Regional Educational Laboratory (NWREL)

Yazzie, T. (1999). Culturally appropriate curriculum: A research-based rationale. In K. Swisher & J. Tippeconnic (Eds.), *Next steps: Research and practice to advance Indian education* (pp. 83–106). Appalachia Educational Laboratory. http:// files.eric.ed.gov/fulltext/ED427902.pdf

CHAPTER 5

TRANSFORMATIVE PRAXIS

Rooted in Home "Before" Looking Elsewhere

Monica A. Ka'imipono Kaiwi

Early in my career as a native Hawaiian "English teacher" of Native Hawaiian students, I observed firsthand my bright and motivated students, who were born and raised on one of the most isolated archipelagos in the Pacific, struggle to comprehend stories in our English anthology—a collection of stories/poems written by authors who live more than 2,500 miles away from our island home. The context (setting, landscape) and content (characters actions, values, and practices) were foreign to their personal experience and worldview. As native English speakers, my students could easily read the words, but they strained to grasp the context's specific nuances, symbolism, and interpretation required to fully "comprehend" the author's story/poem (message, theme). I knew that my Native Hawaiian students were equally as intelligent as my former students in San Diego, California who were reading the same text within their familiar contexts of "home"; yet my Hawaiian students' access to comprehension was not equivalent.

Indigenizing Education, pages 75–79
Copyright © 2022 by Information Age Publishing
www.infoagepub.com

As *Kanaka Maoli* (Native Hawaiian), we are descendants of ancestors who for thousands of years read the nuances of the sky, the land, and the ocean. A generation after missionaries converted our oral language into writing, "91–95% of the Native Hawaiian population" were able to read and write in our own language, *'Ōlelo Hawai'i* (Office of Hawaiian Affairs, 2017). Within a 100 year period of time over 70 newspapers were published in Hawai'i, generating nearly a million pages of text written in 'Ōlelo Hawai'i, currently archived at Bishop Museum (Arista, 2010). It is upon this deep legacy of literacy and the dissertation work of Dr. Manu Aluli Meyer on Native Hawaiian epistemology that I began working to build bridges between our Native Hawaiian worldview and the worldviews of literature from throughout the world. The most effective "bridge building" strategy that I utilize in my classroom is a comparative approach to teaching literature—beginning at home with the familiar and then branching out to literature from elsewhere.

By setting the foundational context of the literature as being from our Native Hawaiian culture and home, Hawai'i, a comparison of similarities and difference becomes a bridge for analysis and dialogue. By way of illustration, Aluli Meyer's dissertation identifies her second "epistemological theme" as "the notion of *'āina* or land." She further explains, "how physical place is, in essence, an extension of spirit." *Kupuna* (elders) expressed 'āina as "that which feeds," shaping an individual's "differences and values" (Aluli, 2003). A literary counterpart to 'āina is "setting," defined as an "environment or surrounding in which an event or story takes place" (LiteraryDevices Editors, 2013). While "setting" references an inanimate context within which a story is told, from a Native Hawaiian epistemological perspective, "'āina" may be an active participant/character in the shaping of a protagonist/antagonist. By offering an additional lens to the discussion of setting in a story, a bridge is built with the potential to broaden and deepen critical analysis.

In my College Board accredited Advanced Placement Literature and Composition course, I couple *Waimea Summer*, the first novel written by a Native Hawaiian, John Dominis Holt (1998), with Chinua Achebe's (1999) novel, *Things Fall Apart*. I utilize the theme of "external conflict" to link the novels since both stories highlight the devastation of colonization on Indigenous cultures and people. Although students recognize similar colonial experiences, the most powerful moments are when we tackle the differences and work to navigate through unfamiliar beliefs and practices that may challenge their sense of "right" and "wrong."

I have witnessed students becoming "stalled" when they encounter an event(s) in a story that doesn't "fit" with their worldview. To illustrate, when reading Achebe's (1999) *Things Fall Apart*, my students experience a clash of culture 14 pages in when Okonkwo's father, Unoka, "an ill-fated man" is "carried to the Evil Forest and left there to die" (p. 18). Both the concept of abandoning an elder and labeling the forest—our kupuna—as "evil" is beyond their comprehension; they can read and comprehend the words but the clash of worldviews and values "stall" them as readers. In fact, students often come to class and state, "I hate this book, and I don't want to read it any more." If Achebe's book stood in isolation, it would be difficult to move many students beyond page 14; however, with *Waimea Summer* (Holt, 1998) fresh in their minds, I can ask students to step back a moment and imagine how someone in Iowa or Africa would read *Waimea Summer* (Holt, 1998); they too would not understand some of our perspectives.

When reading *Waimea Summer* (Holt, 1998), my Native Hawaiian students are the "inside" reader, with front-seat access to comprehend context specific nuances, symbolism, and interpretations. However, when reading *Things Fall Apart* (Achebe, 1999), they are the "outside" reader, a position to which they need to bring curiosity and respect for differences. By using *Waimea Summer* (Holt, 1998) as the familiar comparative piece, the discussion of similarities and differences between the two novels builds the bridge between familiar and unfamiliar literature from places far away.

The strategy of a comparative approach to literature is not limited by grade level. For over 50 years, Shel Silverstein's (1964) *The Giving Tree* has been a staple—a "canonical" title—of elementary classrooms in the United States. The story's main characters include an iconic "apple tree" with its multiple usages (i.e., providing branches to play in; as well as apples and branches to sell; a trunk from which to carve a boat; and finally, a stump to serve as a place of rest at the end of a long life). The Silverstein tree sacrificially gives and gives to meet the needs of the young boy who grows into an old man. *The Giving Tree* advocates that a noble purpose of one's life is to give unconditionally for the benefit of another (Collins, 2014). However, on an island in the Pacific where 'ulu (breadfruit) and mangoes grow on trees and apples are shipped in Matson containers, the context of "an apple tree" is as foreign as the concept of giving without reciprocation. As with my AP students, the contrast of the story's setting and the character's values with those of our Native Hawaiian culture contends that context can/does affect comprehension.

In the case of the *The Giving Tree*, when a common theme of "a tree giving for the better of another" is used to link a Native Hawaiian children's story, *No Ke Kumu 'Ulu: The 'Ulu Tree* by Kawehi Avelino (2008) to Silverstein's *The Giving Tree*, the comparative conversation again creates a bridge between the two. The Amazon Prime (n.d.) synopsis of Avelino's text *No Ke Kumu 'Ulu: The 'Ulu Tree* (2008) reveals a comparable story of sacrifice grounded in Hawai'i as place and likens the familiar "'ulu" (breadfruit) tree to the unfamiliar "apple tree;" thus, creating a bridge between the familiar and the unfamiliar:

Kū, the great Hawaiian akua (god) of the uplands, forest, and the deep sea, comes from the faraway land of Kahiki to settle in Hawaii as an ordinary mortal. After a time, he takes a wife and raises several children, while providing for them as a mahi ʻai (a farmer, planter), and lives in peace, dignity, and plenty. Then, the rains no longer come; the streams and springs begin to dry up, and the crops wither. Without food or water, his ʻohana (family) and the people are faced with the hardship of famine. Unable to bear their suffering, Kū sacrifices himself by burrowing deep into the earth. Soon, from the spot where he descended, the sprout of a breadfruit tree appears. The first of its kind in Hawaii! Kū's generosity and his amazing plant ʻulu, or breadfruit, helps to save his ʻohana and the people from the famine. Today, the ʻulu tree continues to grow throughout Hawaii and its nourishing fruit is still treasured as a food source.

Elementary teachers who implemented this particular lesson—*No Ke Kumu ʻUlu/The Giving Tree*—shared that for the first time their students understood and identified the "theme" in *The Giving Tree*, when in the past they struggled. This exemplifies the point that critical conversation builds comprehension when the discussion of books is in comparison rather than isolation.

Experiences expressed in stories from throughout the globe may be "universal" in topic and humanity; however, the reader's "interpretation" of the "universal" experience is rooted in one's personal epistemology. As educators, when we root our learners in the familiar, the culture and place of their native ancestors who were shaped and fed by the ʻāina (land) upon which they lived for generations, we empower them to branch out beyond our home island to explore and to appreciate other worldviews.

REFERENCES

Achebe, C. (1999). *Things fall apart.* Harcourt Brace & Company.

Aluli Meyer, M. (2003). *Hoʻoulu: Our time of becoming: Hawaiian epistemology and early writings.* ʻAi Pohaku Press.

Amazon Prime. (n.d.). *No Ke Kumu ʻUlu/ The ʻUlu Tree (English and Hawaiian Edition)* [Synopsis]. Retrieved August 31, 2017 from https://www.amazon.com/ Kumu-Ulu-Tree-English-Hawaiian/dp/0873361555

Arista, N. (2010, May). Navigating Uncharted Oceans of Meaning: Kaona as Historical and Interpretive Method. *PMLA, 125*(3), 663–669.

Avelino, K. (Author), & Furchgott, E. (Illustrator). (2008). *No Ke Kumu ʻUlu/ The ʻUlu Tree* (L. Andrews, Trans.). Kamehameha Publishing.

Collins, W. (2014, April 10). 10 things Shel Silverstein's *The Giving Tree* taught us (Besides giving, that is). B&N Reads. https://www.barnesandnoble.com/ blog/10-things-shel-silversteins-the-giving-tree-taught-us-besides-giving-that-is/

Holt, J. D. (1998). *Waimea Summer.* Ku Paʻa Publishing Incorporated.

LiteraryDevices Editors. (2013). Setting. http://literarydevices.net/setting/
Office of Hawaiian Affairs (2017). *A native Hawaiian focus on Hawai'i public school system, SY2015*. Ho'ona'auao (Education) Fact Sheet, 2017(1).
Silverstein, S. (1964). *The giving tree*. Harper Collins Publishing.
Walk, Ka'ano'i. (2014). "King Liholiho led the Hawaiians' amazing rise to literacy in the 1820s" (p. 3). https://19of32x2yl33s8o4xza0gfl4-wpengine.netdna-ssl .com/wp-content/uploads/A-Native-Hawaiian-Focus-on-the-Hawaii-Public -School-System.pdf

SECTION II

REVITALIZING AND SUSTAINING INDIGENOUS LANGUAGE

CHAPTER 6

TEACHING FOR HÓZHǪ́ AND WÓLAKȞOTA

Relationships, Wellness, and Language Revitalization at the Native American Community Academy

Tiffany S. Lee

Indigenous philosophies of education view learning and the development of children holistically (Cajete, 1994; Kawagley & Barnhardt, 2004). The overall well-being of children takes into account their social, emotional, intellectual, cultural, and physical development. Diné philosophies of learning articulate this type of development as achieving hózhǫ́, which in Diné, refers to balance, harmony, beauty, happiness, and self-fulfillment (Benally, 1994). Similarly, wólakȟota is a Lakota concept for peace, tranquility, and the embodiment of what it means to be human and living by Lakota values (Lakota Language Consortium, 2016; personal communication, A. D. Flying Earth, October 19, 2016). Achieving hózhǫ́ and wólakȟota is rooted in Indigenous Peoples' relationships. Relationships are the cornerstone of Indigenous community life. They are how Indigenous People come to

Indigenizing Education, pages 83–97
Copyright © 2022 by Information Age Publishing
www.infoagepub.com
All rights of reproduction in any form reserved.

understand the nature of their community, their identity, and their role for contributing to their community (Cajete, 2015).

Teachers, community members, and administrators at the Native American Community Academy (NACA), a grade kindergarten through twelfth grade charter school in Albuquerque, New Mexico, have created a language education program that engages a pedagogy of relationships in an effort to teach for hózhǫ́ and wólakȟota. The program is rooted in building students' relationships with each other, with cultural values, and with the land and their communities. This chapter will underline NACA's transformative language education program delivered in a tribally diverse school setting and urban community. Strengthening students' relationships through their heritage languages aims to achieve a state of hózhǫ́ and wólakȟota, and in turn, provide additional resources for learning and for integrating Indigenous understandings of well-being. It is a contemporary example of self-determination in education expressed through decolonizing and culturally sustaining/revitalizing pedagogy (Lee & McCarty, 2017) and results in nation and community building for Indigenous Peoples.

THE NATIVE AMERICAN COMMUNITY ACADEMY AND WELLNESS

NACA is a public charter school serving elementary, middle, and high school students in Albuquerque, New Mexico, a city of approximately 600,000 in a state that is home to 23 sovereign Native American nations. Approximately 5,500 Native American students are served by the Albuquerque public schools. NACA opened in the fall of 2006 to approximately 60 students in sixth and seventh grades. It has served for the last 10 years close to 400 students in Grades 6 through 12. In Fall 2016, NACA added a kindergarten and 1st grade class with plans to add a grade each year until it is fully functioning as a K–12 school. With the goals of serving the local Native community and offering a unique approach to Indigenous education, a statement on their website reads "NACA is a small school that focuses on identity through culture & language, holistic wellness, community & family, and academic preparation." It would be the same citation as the next 2 quotes that follow but it is in paragraph 3 (NACA, n.d.a., para. 3).

NACA's mission is to provide a holistic education focused on "strengthening communities by developing strong leaders who are academically prepared, secure in their identity and healthy" (NACA, n.d.b, para. 1). To achieve this mission, the school community identified six core values that are integrated into all aspects of the school through the curriculum, pedagogy, assessment, policies, and school climate. Those values include: respect, responsibility, community/service, culture, perseverance, and reflection. The six core values align with an overall focus on wellness for NACA students. NACA's articulation of this focus reads, "Wellness is an important part of NACA's holistic and integrated curriculum. It is implemented with meticulous attention to provide the balance necessary for a child to truly succeed as a student—and more importantly—as a human being" (NACA, n.d.c, para. 1).

MY STORY WITH NACA

I learned about the idea to create a Native-centered charter school from its founder, Kara Bobroff. We met over lunch to discuss her idea—she had received an Echoing Green fellowship, which supported her as a social entrepreneur and educator to lay the foundation for the school. Over the course of her fellowship, she organized community meetings with families, educators, researchers, tribal leaders, and other interested folks to discuss the vision and mission for the school. NACA is in its 16th year now. I have served on NACA's governance council since its inception, and I have worked with teachers on curriculum and language education programming and planning. Most importantly, I am a parent of two boys at the school, and an auntie to many young relatives attending the school.

My boys have attended NACA since the sixth grade; one graduated in 2016 and the other in 2019. With the support of our family and communities, NACA has influenced my boys to become more strongly connected to their multiple Native heritages of Diné, Lakota, and Cochiti Pueblo. While NACA was relatively new when they started and does not have the state of the art facilities many other public schools are afforded, this had not deterred them from loving their school because of the relationships they have with their friends, teachers, and the curriculum that challenges them to think critically and consider multiple points of view, with the foundation of how everything they are learning connects to Native people and communities. They are able to learn Diné and Lakota language, and they have engaged in cultural and educational exchanges in New Zealand, Hawaii, and Washington DC, not to mention the many opportunities to participate in other summer programs because of the connections NACA has made with these programs. Most importantly, my boys' heritage and youth identities are valued and nurtured at NACA.

PEDAGOGY OF RELATIONSHIPS TO ACHIEVE HÓZHÓ
AND WÓLAKHOTA

Based on my lived experience working with NACA and my research there, I have concluded that NACA is engaging in a pedagogy of relationships through its activities to achieve a state of hózhǫ́ and wólakȟota for its students. In summary, NACA's pedagogy of relationships is enacted through its student-centered education, which then privileges and prioritizes the relationships the school creates between families, staff, teachers, and its students. NACA's pedagogy of relationships is also realized through its core values (respect, responsibility, community/service, culture, perseverance, reflection), which provide the basis of all interactions, activities, and experiences at NACA. Correspondingly, the outcomes of NACA's pedagogy of relationships results in a focus on the whole being of students and in states of hózhǫ́ and wólakȟota.

As previously noted, hózhǫ́ is a Diné term for harmony, balance, beauty, well-being, and peacefulness. Hózhǫ́ is the basis of many traditional ceremonies, the most powerful one known as Hózhǫ́ǫ́jí Iiná (Blessing Way ceremony; Benally, 1994). Diné scholar Herbert Benally has written extensively about a Diné philosophy of learning and applies it to contemporary educational contexts. In particular, Benally (1994) has articulated four branches of knowledge and skills for achieving hózhǫ́: (a) proper development of the mind—"that which gives direction to life"; (b) skills that enable survival—physical needs, sustenance, becoming self-reliant; (c) positive relationships—emotional needs—k'é—"gathering of families"—"enriching and deepening relationships of mutual support within the family and community"; and (d) understanding and relationship to one's home and physical environment—"respect and reverence for all creatures." He asserts that the purpose of learning from this Diné perspective is "to gather knowledge that will draw one closer to a state of happiness, harmony, and balance" (p. 30)—hózhǫ́.

Benally (1994) states the four branches of knowledge and skills enable one to "survive and understand their relation to all the other phenomena" (p. 25). In other words, attaining the four branches of knowledge and skills provides one with understanding and accepting their interconnections with the natural world and with their place or role in the world.

In speaking with Mr. Flying Earth (former executive director and Lakota language teacher at NACA—see his accompanying chapter), who was one of the first teachers and visionary founders at NACA, about the meaning of hózhǫ́, I asked him if there were similar concepts in the Lakota language. He taught me about the concept of wólakȟota. He explained that wólakȟota is the manifestation of what it means to be a Lakota person, as one who embodies Lakota values. He said it is the "state of how humans should interact with each other." He stated it is often translated as "peace but it also involves the harmonious and virtuous nature that someone or something holds" (personal communication, October 19, 2016). Lakota values come to the forefront and are apparent in a person who embodies wólakȟota . It is similar to Benally's interpretation of achieving hózhǫ through the four branches of knowledge, which involve the embodiment of Diné values and expectations for behavior or interaction with others. They both aim to achieve balance and harmony according to their respective values.

These Indigenous concepts are similar to Cajete's discussion of finding face, finding heart, and finding foundation (1994). Cajete uses this Aztec metaphor to describe the purpose of Indigenous education—finding face is finding one's true identity, finding heart is finding one's passion, and finding foundation is the context or community from which one expresses their identity and passion. Benally, Flying Earth, and Cajete's discussions involve a holistic understanding of what it means to become complete and to be a human being. Achieving hózhǫ and wólakȟota in communal and educational contexts is grounded in the relationships people develop with one another, with their culture, and with their place or land.

Numerous scholars have written extensively about the significance of relationships in education. They address the impact of a complex range of relationship experiences. Noddings (1988, 2013) work on caring, authentic relationships in education has been highly cited. She asserts that a caring disposition among teachers is a moral orientation to teaching and an aim of moral education. She emphasizes the importance of teachers and students spending time together to build trust. Similarly, Bartolome's work on humanizing pedagogy emphasizes relationship and trust building between teachers and students (1994). However, she asserts humanizing pedagogy and relationships require teachers' political clarity (2004) about the historic, systemic role of schools in fostering inequity in education. She discusses the problems with educational approaches that promote one overarching structure across schools, such as a one-size-fits-all approach. She argues that there is a belief among educational leaders and policy makers that underachievement can be fixed by a particular teaching method and that schools are neutral, apolitical sites that students are expected to conform to, but there is not an interrogation of the schools. She contends an interrogation of schools is necessary as they may be the source of the problem in terms of their curriculum, structure, climate, teaching methods, and their continual failure of students, while also blaming students for those failures. Understanding issues related to educational inequities empowers teachers to find political clarity and humanize students. They recognize their own biases and limitations, and in turn, are motivated to provide a caring, just, additive, and level playing field. Humanizing pedagogy moves students from passive positions to active ones because it requires teachers to develop meaningful, reciprocal relationships with students, their families, and communities.

Very recently, a national study of 605 teachers found that they believe social and emotional learning (SEL) is critical to student success in and out of school (Civic Enterprises, 2013). SEL involves self-awareness, self-management, social awareness, relationship skills, and responsible decision-making. These teachers, who were 77% women and 86% White (7% African American, 6% Hispanic, and 1% Other), came from K–12 public schools across the country and varied widely in backgrounds of students and schooling contexts. The findings showed that teachers understand, value, and endorse SEL for all students, believe SEL helps students achieve in school and life, and they identify key methods to accelerate SEL in schools. SEL is very related to the philosophy behind achieving hózhǫ́ and wólakȟota. SEL prioritizes students' identities and their relationships to others. The fact that a large population of non-Native teachers supported and endorsed SEL speaks widely to the significance of education being conducted in humanizing and holistic ways with the goal of students who embody hózhǫ́ and wólakȟota.

In a statewide study across public schools in New Mexico, Jojola et al. (2010) examined best educational practices from the perspectives of Native youth, parents, community members, and teachers. They found that participants discussed positive and reciprocal relationships as integral to the schooling process. This study asked participants about their most effective and ideal educational experiences across seven critical areas, including what it means to be an educated Native American person, language, curriculum, pedagogy, accountability, the school climate, and their vision for the future. In each area, participants described the importance of healthy, positive, respectful, and reciprocal relationships as an attribute of best practices in those respective areas. The researchers explained this overall effect in their summary report of policy findings as:

> Successful relationships by schools are achieved when opportunities for interactions between students, teachers, staff, and the tribal community are provided that develop healthy, professional, and caring relationships; classroom learning is built on the values on mutual respect and reciprocity; and teachers make an effort to learn about the community and the social conditions that affect their student's lives. (p. vi)

Like SEL, successful relationships is an attribute of achieving hózhǫ́ and wólakȟota, and this study confirmed its significance and value among Native students, families, and educators.

Research on teacher–student relationships in education has also been significant for demonstrating the contrasting, counter effects of poor, negative relationships between students and educational leaders in their schools. Martinez (2010) investigated the experiences of high school age Native youth through an analysis of power operations in curriculum, extracurricular activities, and daily interactions. One of her major findings related to how the youth's lived experiences and culturally based knowledge were often not validated or "counted" as knowledge by the school system. Youth felt disenfranchised, but not disempowered, and resisted and challenged those school-based acts that confronted their sense of identity and worth.

Similarly, Quijada-Cerecer (2013) examined the experiences of Native youth who attended a public high school adjacent to their home Native Nation's boundaries. She found that the Native youth disclosed "how staff, teachers, and students dismissed their Indigenous knowledge through (a) the way(s) in which relationships are formed and sustained and (b) school policies and rules specifically related to order and discipline" (p. 593). Relationships between the Native youth and the teachers they described in her study often reflected one of teachers' inattention, neglect, and uncaring attitudes and the racialization of the students' identities as Native youth. Quijada-Cerecer explained that this treatment by teachers was one way for teachers to maintain order and to allow students to fail as opposed to legitimizing them as learners.

These scholars have all demonstrated that the significance of relationships, whether poor and negative or supportive and caring, impact student learning and success in school. Kulago (2016) argues further that schools have a responsibility to engage with families and communities in ways that are in congruence with the community's collective practices. Family, community, and education are inseparable in this context and when viewed through the Diné concept of k'é, a Diné family and community practice for showing love, care, support, and responsibility to one another (Benally, 1994; Kulago, 2016). In this regard, relationships are a priority and reciprocal, and schools can promote student success by understanding, aligning, and actively engaging families and communities on principles grounded in k'é and a pedagogy of relationships.

MY RELATIONSHIP WITH NACA

As I noted earlier, I am a parent at NACA. But I have had multiple roles as a current governance council member, volunteer, and I also actively connect my university students in Native American studies to internship and other volunteer opportunities at NACA. I have worked with NACA's language program in several ways. In 2008, I coordinated a summer language immersion camp at the school for Diné and Lakota language learners. NACA was also included in the statewide study I referenced earlier (Jojola et al., 2010), and that I co-coordinated with a team of researchers from 2008–2010 investigating promising educational practices for Native students as defined by students, teachers, parents, and community members. I have informally maintained interactions and discussions over the years in my role as a parent and governance council member with the Diné and Lakota language teachers at NACA.

The relationships I have developed over the last 16 years with teachers, parents, and staff is not just as "researcher" but intersects my roles stated above in multiple ways. My primary purpose, along with other teachers, parents, and staff, is to support NACA and its students to build a community.

NACA teachers, parents, and staff prioritize the relationships they have with students, with one another, and with the local communities. In my research with NACA's language program, I found the program promotes relationships in three significant ways. The program promotes (a) relationships with each other (peer to peer, peer to teacher), (b) relationships to cultural values and protocols, and (c) relationships to land/place/communities. The outcomes of this relationship-based approach are students' ability to connect their heritage language to each other, to the cultural values of their families and people, and to the land and community. The result is a transformative language education program that is achieving hózhǫ́ and wólakȟota, and that aligns with the wellness philosophy of NACA. In the sections below, I elaborate on NACA's relational approach in each of the three manners.

Learning Language Through Relationships With Each Other

The Diné language teacher, Ms. Tsosie,[1] says she utilizes the students' friendships with one another to create a stronger bond with each other and to promote language learning in engaging ways (interview, November 2, 2015). She creates games or competitions to introduce new vocabulary where students have to respond to statements they make about one another. For example, one student may state a condition about a fellow student through Diné language, "David is hungry." David would respond "Yes, I am hungry" or "No, I am not hungry." Other students can also respond, "Yes, he is hungry." It becomes a game and competition in that students are tested to be the first to respond and to show their correct oral use of the language. This simple activity strengthens students' connections to each other and to the language. She continues this game outside of class in between class periods and at lunch with other conditions such as s/he is a liar, skinny, deaf, leader, and so on. The activity is significant because it embodies qualities of teasing and humor. Native people have utilized teasing and humor to teach the morals and values of the community, and to celebrate life with one another (Deloria, 1988). Ms. Tsosie's educational practice to involve teasing and humor reinforces the students' relationships with each other through traditional Native practices.

Assessment practices in the language courses are also inclusive of promoting relationships. Former Lakota language teacher and Executive Director, Mr. Flying Earth, does not assess students for content knowledge alone; he also evaluates students based on their development as caring and empathetic human beings and on the quality of relationships they have with one another. He explained his assessment practices this way, "Evaluations for me and how I measure them, I establish a relationship with the students right away...I've created a relationship that every one of the students is like my relative. They're all like my little nieces and nephews" (interview, November 4, 2009). He looks for his students to demonstrate respect, compassion, and helpful behavior with others as relatives would do, as these are also attributes associated with the way the Native language is used and how Native people treat one another. In essence, assessing students is not based solely on students' academic performance, but it includes their behavior as human beings within the context of Indigenous-based values. This holistic approach to assessing students through nurturing family-like relationships supports students' connections and bonds to one another. It serves as an important illustration of his aim to achieve hózhǫ́ and wólakȟota with his students.

The effect of promoting deep relationships among students has been their greater sense of self-confidence and pride in their Native heritage. Mr. Flying Earth shared what a parent of one student had noticed about her child. NACA recently added two sections of Zuni language courses, and the instructor has incorporated planting and gardening to teach through the language (and promoting relationships to land). The parent said her child teaches her younger sibling what she is learning in Zuni, and she felt if her child was not learning Zuni, she would not be as excited about *being* Zuni (interview, October 28, 2015). This student is embodying the principles of states of hózhǫ́ and wólakȟota with regard to her language and identity, which include kinship, love, and belonging. Ms. Tsosie referred to the significance of embracing one's heritage when learning their Native language when she said, "I think one important thing that I always go back to is their identity. Identity has a lot to do with how they address themselves, how they respect themselves and others and their community." Learning their Native language develops their relationships with their fellow peers and siblings but also, and perhaps more importantly, with themselves.

Learning Language Through Relationships With Cultural Values and Protocols

In this section, I share how NACA's language program integrates the development of students' knowledge of cultural values and protocols associated with their respective Native languages. In this sense, students develop a relationship with the language to culture beyond simply learning the mechanics of language use. For example, when discussing how a Native language summer program might begin, another Diné language teacher from the summer program, Ms. Yazzie, said,

> Start the program a little earlier, maybe starting a prayer or making the kids run, just to get them into the groove of things, and also us [teachers], as well, and just having a circle of prayer, maybe before, like on the field, and have them run and—always to the East.

The practice of rising early, saying a prayer, and running East is a Diné-centered practice common in many daily activities and ceremonies and signifies aspects of the states of hózhǫ́ and wólakȟota.

Ms. Tsosie also felt Native students should interact with elders for language learning to promote learning the language through natural, home-like contexts. She put this into practice by having her students participate in "situational Navajo" (Holm et al., 2003), which is a form of role-playing using everyday situations and contexts for speaking the language. She described one situation where she has her students role-play and thereby learn the culturally appropriate way of interacting with visitors to your home. She said they learn

> the etiquette of when someone comes to visit you, how you tell them come in, wóshdéé', and they shake your hands, and you also address them by who they are to you. If it's an aunt, uncle, grandma, grandpa, then you always ask them to have a seat and offer them a drink and something to eat.

This context helps students learn their Native language through a culturally relevant and appropriate method that contributes to cultural continuity.

Engaging students in cultural activities to reinforce the language was also difficult. Ms. Tsosie and Ms. Yazzie co-taught a summer Diné language immersion course and tried to integrate a number of culturally-based activities. For example, they incorporated sand painting but found teaching the techniques and vision for creating a sand painting required advanced knowledge of the language. However, teaching through cooking or cleaning or other everyday household activities were more familiar to students and stimulated their connections to the language. Using the language based on how it is used by their family and relatives in their home communities gives the language a more familiar context, and as Ms. Tsosie said, "That way the kids can make that connection with the language and how language is used in a home, [with] livestock, just daily life."

Another Lakota teacher, Mr. Awayake, utilized a similar cultural context for learning Lakota and reinforcing values and protocols. Cultural values and protocols were shared through the set up of a tipi during the summer language immersion camp. He said,

> We went in, put up the tipi and tried to stay in the language the whole time, and kind of the incentive of that particular activity was to look at gender differences within traditions historically, and also to learn languages not associated with classroom, necessarily... so they can hear kind of some of the subtleties, and also, just to kinda look at socially, and get a glimpse of it because we did some reflection about tipis and what they mean, you know? And what they mean within Lakota culture, who puts them up. The women put them up and carry them. They're the caretakers of the home and what it is, how many people live in there, typically. Is there other designs on there, and if so, where and how those designs get put on there, and also we had the chance to cover a little bit about stereotypes and misconceptions

While the students learn and practice Lakota language through the process of setting up a tipi, the cultural significance and value of the tipi to Lakota culture are also reinforced. This is an example of how students develop a relationship to cultural protocols through the language when they learn about gender roles, the home, and the traditions associated with the tipi. The language camp included other experiential activities for the students such as a sweathouse experience, sports activities, cooking, and a family meal, all conducted in the Native languages through an immersion approach.

Again, Mr. Flying Earth discussed some of the outcomes he has observed with students who have participated in these courses and camps, along with the reinforcement from the school's overall mission and focus on wellness. When asked about how the courses and school have impacted students, he said one Lakota student "took to anything cultural at NACA" (interview, October 28, 2015). This student learned to lead the NACA powwow round dance song, he went on a school sponsored trip to South Dakota to prepare for a Sun Dance ceremony, and participated in the Sun Dance for 2 days. His behavior at those events reflected a state of hózhǫ́ and wólakȟota through his helpfulness, caring of others, and respectful conduct. Similarly, Mr. Flying Earth shared how learning Lakota at NACA for an alumnus has invigorated her life to continue learning Lakota. She is studying linguistics and anthropology in college with the goal of studying and teaching Lakota in the future, and with these goals, contributing to cultural continuity.

Learning Language Through Relationships With the Land/Place/Community

Mr. Flying Earth felt one of the challenges of teaching Native languages at NACA is their urban context. Being situated in Albuquerque, he stated

NACA needs to be intentional in connecting the language to the history, people, places, and especially to the land. Developing students' relationship to land/place/community through the language is a form of community accountability that the school is practicing. It acknowledges the interrelationship between Native people's land, language, and culture. The Zuni teacher establishes a relationship to land for his students through his Zuni gardening and planting approach to language learning. Additionally, as mentioned earlier, students are given opportunities to participate in Lakota Sun Dance ceremonies in South Dakota, further reinforcing the connections between land, language, and ceremony for students.

On another occasion, all NACA 9th and 10th graders went on a piñon (pine nut) picking field trip on the Sandia Mountains, East of Albuquerque. Piñon picking is a common practice among Native peoples of the Southwest, and Ms. Tsosie shared how they integrated cultural protocols and Indigenous knowledge of the land during the event. They started with a prayer and practiced seasonal traditions, such as providing an offering of white corn to the trees and the earth from where they were going to take the piñons.

Ms. Tsosie shared that being outside, in the mountains, using the language, and connecting the experience to Indigenous knowledge excited and engaged the students, particularly those students she felt who were less engaged academically at school. She stated many of the students had experienced piñon picking with their families and were able to demonstrate their knowledge, their fine motor skills, and teach each other. The physical challenge, the cultural significance, the parent involvement (many parents chaperoned), and the setting in the mountains exemplified NACA's wellness philosophy in practice and promoted relationships based on hózhǫ and wólakȟota.

Challenges and Complexities

While NACA is having an impact on students' overall well-being through their holistic mission and their language courses specifically, the depth with which the students learn to understand, speak (and for some of the languages, read and write) their Native languages is imprecise. NACA is not an immersion school and is only able to offer its Native language courses for one and a half hours each day. Ms. Tsosie reported that the students tell her they need to hear the language around them all the time to encourage and sway them to use it outside of class. It is hard for them to use it outside of class when they are immersed back into English language environments (interview, November 2, 2015). This is particularly prevalent today given the heavy emphasis on English-based standardized tests in the content areas of English reading, writing, and math.

Adding to this challenge, the society that surrounds NACA students who attend this urban area school is dominated by an American, English-based environment that often marginalizes and is frequently hostile toward Native peoples in the city. This layer of interaction and at times oppressive surroundings adds to the complexity of providing an Indigenous-centered education aiming to achieve hózhǫ́ and wólakȟota. How NACA moves forward to confront these challenges of the city's hostile and oppressive conditions can help inform our efforts in enacting Indigenous education for transformative nation and community building.

The teachers have come to a realization that they are not going to exit student speakers with high levels of fluency. Instead, they aim to exit conversational speakers, yet there is not a clear definition of what this means across the languages and across the language communities. Their goal is primarily to motivate the students toward lifelong learning of the language, or in the words of Mr. Awayaki, the goal is "to spark the ancestral spirit of their language. Speaking the language gives power; I feel power when I speak it" (interview, August 14, 2014). They want students to connect to this sense of power to inspire their continued learning of the language when they leave NACA.

CONCLUSION

Creating a rich cultural learning environment entails much more than honoring Native peoples on a specific day, week, or month. NACA is a school that embodies the culturally based values, knowledge, and practices of Indigenous Peoples throughout their mission, curriculum, pedagogy, assessment, and school climate, and they are truly living culturally and creating a rich environment for learning. The relationship-based pedagogy in the language courses aligns with current scholarship by many in the field of Indigenous education and with Indigenous philosophies and practices of education in their communities.

We are beginning to observe now the impact of NACA on its alumni. Many of the students in the first graduating class of seniors in 2012 have graduated from college in 2016. Several have returned over their winter and summer breaks over the years to volunteer at NACA or to give presentations on their experiences in college. Several alumni work at NACA in various capacities, such as the middle school girls' basketball coach, as an out-of-school time coordinator, and very recently, one graduate returned to become a Native literature teacher. NACA is providing a place of employment and a place for students to give back. They are continuing with honoring and supporting their relationship to the school. It demonstrates coming full circle for a school that creates authentic relationships with students and families and engages in humanizing pedagogy centered on Indigenous values for land, culture, and family. Students' language learning is embedded in this holistic educational context that is relationship-based. Relationships are the cornerstone of community life for Indigenous Peoples and how Indigenous People come to understand the nature of their community, their identity, and their role in contributing to their community. Framing a school and language program around relationships that enhances students connections to each other, to their cultures, and to land is achieving hózhǫ́ and wólakȟota.

NOTE

1. All names of research participants cited in this chapter are pseudonyms. Some names given represent terms in the Native language that exemplify the character of the individual. For example, Mr. Awayake can simplistically be translated to Mr. Caring. However, Mr. Flying Earth is not a pseudonym. He has given permission to use his real name and his commentary on his story at NACA accompanies this chapter. NACA has also given permission to use their actual name in this publication.

REFERENCES

Bartolome, L. (1994). Beyond the methods fetish: Toward a humanizing pedagogy. *Harvard Educational Review, 64*(2), 173–195.

Bartolome, L. (2004). Critical pedagogy and teacher education: Radicalizing prospective teachers. *Teacher Education Quarterly, 31*(1), 97–122.

Benally, H. (1994). Navajo philosophy of learning and pedagogy. *Journal of Navajo Education, 12*(1), 23–31.

Cajete, G. A. (1994). *Look to the mountain: An ecology of Indigenous education.* Kivaki Press.

Cajete, G. A. (2015). *Indigenous community: Rekindling the teachings of the seventh fire.* Living Justice Press.

Civic Enterprises. (2013). *The missing piece: A national teacher survey on how social and emotional learning can empower children and transform schools.* Report for the Collaborative for Academic, Social, and Emotional Learning (CASEL).

Deloria, V. (1988). *Custer died for your sins: An Indian manifesto.* University of Oklahoma Press.

Holm, W., Silentman, I., & Wallace, L. (2003). Situational Navajo: A school-based, verb-centered way of teaching Navajo. In J. Reyner, O. V. Trujillo, R. L. Carrasco, & L. Lockard (Eds.), *Nurturing Native languages* (pp. 25–52). Northern Arizona University.

Jojola, T., Lee, T. S., Alcantara, A., Belgarde, M., Bird, C., Lopez, N., & Singer, B. (2010). *Indian education in New Mexico, 2025.* Public Education Department, Indian Education Division.

Kawagley, O., & Barnhardt, R. (2004). *Education Indigenous to place: Western science meets Native reality.* Alaska Native Knowledge Network. www.ankn.uaf.edu/EIP

Kulago, H. (2016). Activating Indigenous knowledge to create supportive educational environments by rethinking family, community, and school partnerships. *Journal of Family Diversity in Education, 2*(1), 1–20.

Lakota Language Consortium. (2016). *Lakota dictionary online.* http://www.lakota dictionary.org/

Lee, T. S., & McCarty, T. L. (2017). Upholding Indigenous education sovereignty through critical culturally sustaining/revitalizing pedagogy. In D. Paris & H. S. Alim (Eds.), *Culturally sustaining pedagogies: Teaching and learning for justice in a changing world* (pp. 61–82). Teachers College Press.

Martinez, G. (2010). *Native pride: The politics of curriculum and instruction in an urban public school.* Hampton Press.

Native American Community Academy. (n.d.b). *Who we are.* https://www.nacaschool .org/apps/pages/index.jsp?uREC_ID=1663943&type=d&pREC_ID=1813044

Native American Community Academy. (n.d.b). *Mission and vision.* https://www .nacaschool.org/apps/pages/index.jsp?uREC_ID=1663943&type=d&pREC _ID=1813049

Native American Community Academy. (n.d.c). *Wellness and support services.* https:// www.nacaschool.org/apps/pages/index.jsp?uREC_ID=1663962&type=d& pREC_ID=1813077

Noddings, N. (1988). An ethic of caring and its implications for instructional arrangements. *American Journal of Education, 96*(2), 215–230.

Noddings, N. (2013). *Caring: A relational approach to ethics and moral education.* University of California Press.

Quijada-Cerecer, P. D. (2013). The policing of native bodies and minds: Perspectives on schooling from American Indian youth. *American Journal of Education, 119*(4), 591–616.

CHAPTER 7

TRANSFORMATIVE PRAXIS

Wólakȟota—Reclaiming Language and Unlocking Identity

Anpao Duta Flying Earth

My name is Anpao Duta Flying Earth. I am Lakota, Dakota, Ojibwe, and Akimel O'odham, and I grew up on the Standing Rock Reservation. For as long as I can remember, my foundational ideology and worldview was formed from, and continues to be based on, a Lakota perspective and value system that is grounded in relationships with all things. I call myself "Lakota" and while this term is often associated with a political identity based on a cultural nuanced archetype by society, I associate myself with the philosophical attributes of the word's meaning. The word "Lakota" means peaceful or virtuous, with roots in the origin stories of our people. It is meant to describe the nature and character of all those who consider themselves Lakota. That is, the word is a descriptor based on expectations of conduct rather than a label or title related to identity. Furthermore, wólakȟota is a value that is used to explain the state or manifestation of this relationship; many people define it as "peace."

Indigenizing Education, pages 99–104
Copyright © 2022 by Information Age Publishing
www.infoagepub.com

I have often heard people talk about how important language is to a person's identity, especially as it applies to Indigenous People. I have come to believe that one fully begins to understand the importance of language when language is experienced firsthand. Growing up, neither my mom nor my grandmother spoke any of our languages (Lakota, Dakota, Ojibwe) fluently. This was due in large part to the combination of the detrimental effect of boarding schools and paternalistic federal Indian policy. As a result of these turning points in Indigenous history, my family's retention and teaching of languages was forever changed. Despite these negative impacts, Lakota language was always present in my home. My grandmother and mother recognized that an important practice in bringing back our languages is to name children in our languages. Because names often become the first manner in which a person's identity is formed, my grandmother emphasized to her children (my mother and uncle) that they give their children names in our languages. Each of my siblings and first cousins were all given names in Lakota or Ojibwe. Additionally, Lakota and Ojibwe vocabulary and phrases were used regularly in my upbringing. I do not think I knew my grandmother's name until I was about 5 or 6. I only knew her as *Uŋčí* (grandmother in Lakota). I was raised to understand, in principle and practice, that language is important to who we are as Lakota.

I began to understand the power of my Indigenous language when I started to use, experience, and understand its true utility. It is deeper than a topical or superficial attempt to gain cultural capital. At the root of its meaning, language learning unlocks a deeply meaningful understanding of who you are, *wólakȟota*. This, added with history, philosophy, oral stories, and so forth, begins to create an understanding, embodiment, and truth of who we authentically are meant to be. This is not taught in most schools and in fact, was intentionally and systematically removed from our Indigenous youths' school experience through the violently assimilative boarding school era, preceded by violence and entitlement validated by western expansion via Manifest Destiny and followed by Americanized educational institutions within reservations and in urban areas that by law our children are expected to attend. There was, and I would argue continues to be, a direct attempt to disrupt this sacred connection to oneself through language as an intentional effort to disrupt intrinsic cultural excellence and power.

My family's story of language continues with the healing of our language disconnect through ceremony and song and reclaiming its everyday use. I started learning my language more deeply through understanding the nuances and meanings of traditional Lakota songs. During one of the singing sessions, one of my uncles said something that changed the way I thought about language. He said, "Don't sing anything unless you know what it means." It was probably more of a scolding than a piece of advice but it has stuck with me. Within it contains a key piece of how I think of the utility of language. Language holds a story of who we are as people, a value and knowledge system that is understood better the more you understand the nuances of how to use the language. Expression of emotions and intentions are easier in our languages. Jokes are funnier. There is power in our languages when it otherwise might feel like empowerment is found at a premium. Our languages allow us to connect to ourselves in a manner that has been previously repressed due to trauma and colonization. Language is medicine.

There is a spiritual and metaphysical understanding of language that is unlocked when an individual sings and/or prays in their traditional tongue during ceremonies. This experience provides a deeper level of communication with self, community, and ancestry. Something spiritual and sacred is activated when given the opportunity to experience this type of expression, wólakȟota. I began to delve deeper into experiencing language in ways that extended beyond the basic learning of vocabulary, numbers, colors, animals, and so forth. I began to experience and understand that generations upon generations of my ancestors used language to express the same emotions we express as we sing and pray for the healing and restoration of our peoples and lands. There exists an entirely different connection to the ancestors when this occurs, that is, the combination of emotion, spirit, expression, and communication. In this sense, language becomes powerfully connected to everything. It embodies wólakȟota.

In Albuquerque, New Mexico, I attended an information session about a school that was seeking to open its doors that focused on identity through culture and language, holistic wellness, and academic preparation for college as a means to support leadership and youth. These pillars were intended to be delivered in a way that complemented and strengthened each other—not at the expense of each other. I was intrigued by this because through my own education I experienced in Americanized school systems on and off the reservation, I was conditioned to believe that culture cannot exist in concert with academic preparation, nor vice versa. Moreover, there was seldom a thought of holistic wellness that considers the needs of the whole child, not only restricted to their intellectual/academic well-being. I was eventually invited to become part of the founding team of this school, the Native American Community Academy (NACA), which initiated a new journey for language learning and validation of an Indigenous identity through instruction and connection to community.

It should be noted that this school would not have been possible if not for the work of our previous generations and their commitment to maintaining identity, culture, and language of diverse populations of this country's Indigenous People. Yet, I must emphasize that there existed no blueprint for how to exercise cultural and spiritual self-determination through an educational setting, particularly in an urban setting. There were no textbooks that taught the convergence of holistic wellness, academic preparation, and students' identities. Creating curriculum and instruction that did this was not easy. Advisors to NACA from various institutions, organizations, and communities stepped forward to help articulate and create the framework for how this would look at various grades and levels of development. It was through the power of the community that the initial vision for NACA was created.

During the initial years of our school, we met students who for the first time in their education felt proud to speak of their participation in their cere-monies, dances, and traditional doings among their peers. They did not have to hide or fly under the radar within the public school system. They became surrounded by peers who also felt it was important to be part of a community and family that participated in cultural practices, traditions, and calendars. They also immersed themselves among peers who were still in the process of just beginning to explore their Indigenous identity. In class, they were invited to bring in pieces of their identity to strengthen what they were learning in class through, for example, Indigenous authors and content. That is, they were not being told the story of the Pueblo Revolt, Navajo Long Walk, and other historical events through a text book, but through the direct and pur-poseful engagement of elders and family members.

One day during the first year of our school, one of the students ap-proached me with a book and asked me to help her read it. The book she handed me was a Bible written in the Dakota language, which had been her grandfather's. It was clear to me that her family had had this book for a very long time. She had probably wondered about it for a long time and for some fateful reason that day, asked me what the language meant. This opened a door for us to begin lessons of language. It opened an opportu-nity for me to teach her the bit of the language that I knew. These lessons continued regularly during the first year of our school.

Before the second year began, I was asked by the principal of the school to teach Lakota language classes. I initially felt uneasy about saying yes be-cause I did not feel that my level of proficiency was adequate to equip me to be a teacher of the language. I pondered the opportunity for a long time. I called my uncle and talked with him about this opportunity. What he told me is that "you have a responsibility to teach students what you know." This small piece of advice proved profound to me. I realized that everyone has to start somewhere in support of language learning. You do not necessarily need to be a fluent speaker in order to begin teaching it.

We started our Lakota language class with roughly 25–30 students. I quickly discovered that teaching Lakota language in New Mexico was going to be different than teaching the language in South Dakota. Many of the students who had family in South Dakota had never been there. Thus, their exposure to Lakota language was limited. This was a challenge for me be-cause I had to seek a way to unlock the power of language for students who had not experienced it firsthand in their own lives. I also quickly realized that for students to learn their language, who did not otherwise have access to it, was a life changing experience. Part of this process required that every student became my niece and nephew, while on a larger scale, everyone in the school also became each other's kin. Our school became a community of relatives, rather than a system of teachers and students. For me, I took seriously the traditional role of an uncle whose responsibility is rooted in traditional education, discipline, and accountability to Indigenous values. For students to experience this type of identity development with teachers creates a special connection among themselves and their peers.

Two of the nieces who gravitated to this language learning most intensively were Maggie Seawright and Lenny Morgan. Both of whom are Lakota yet had limited contact with their Lakota land base. The language provided a roadmap to a journey through parts of their identity. I was able to take both of them and their classmates to South Dakota where they took part in healing and coming of age ceremonies that unlocked intimate parts of their identity. From Grade 7 to Grade 12, they were able to engage this part of their Lakota identity through language learning during some of their most formative years of their personal development. I believe that the power of language that I described earlier began to be experienced by these two nieces and their peers. They organically became the generation for whom education was very different than what I had experienced, that is an education that is rooted in Indigenous paradigms. It was encouraged that they insert their identity into their learning. They found pride in their Indigenous identity, within the constructs of a school. I slowly began to realize that these young Lakota women were beginning to experience the same spiritual and metaphysical understandings of language that I initially had through singing. Yet the difference was, they were doing so as part of their educational journey. We all, as students and teachers, have come to recognize that this journey was and remains a long and ongoing process.

In 2016, I was able to take both of these nieces back to my home reservation of Standing Rock and the Oceti Sakowin/Sacred Stone Camps where an immense Indigenous, nonviolent, grassroots resurgence occurred in a movement to protect the land and water. At the center of the movement, is an almost 1,200 mile long oil pipeline that has since been built just north of Standing Rock's current reservation boundary and crosses the Missouri River. The youth of Standing Rock were a catalyst for this movement determined to protect the largest river in North America against extractive industries.

I initially intended to travel home to support my people by myself. When my nieces heard of my plans, they asked to join me in support of their community in the collective mobilization around protecting our waterways and lands for future generations. They understood the magnitude of the gathering and what it meant for our people and the generations to come. They knew that what was happening at Standing Rock is tied to who they are. I feel strongly this speaks lengths about who they are and their commitment to their identity and people; a commitment that largely derives from their initial and ongoing years of language learning and identity development at our school. The movement at Standing Rock is this generations' critical movement much like Wounded Knee or Selma during the civil rights era and what has happened at Standing Rock will impact the work ahead for generations to come. Today, Indigenous youth and their communities continue this fight in defense of our land and water, having been empowered by the movement at Standing Rock.

In the months following the Standing Rock stand for our water, one of our NACA alumni captured this commitment to identity, language, and our people embodied by our students during a graduation address when she said, "We are the dreams of ancestors and the nightmare of colonialism." The next iteration of Indigenous education, I believe, must hold youth at the center of this concept of wólakȟota and challenge the things that are not in alignment with who we believe that we should be. I believe that this is our responsibility to continue the evolution of education for our people by picking up the work of our ancestors and past relatives. We must enact and move forward a vision for the next wave of education for and by our community and work tirelessly to create that education.

CHAPTER 8

CHIKASHSHANOMPAAT BÍLLI'YA

The Chickasaw Language Is Forever

Kari A. B. Chew (Chikashsha)

Drawing on research with Chickasaw citizens committed to Chikashshanompa' (Chickasaw language) reclamation work, this chapter focuses on how Chikashshanompa' learners and teachers engage in nation-building as they work to ensure the continuance of Chikashshanompa' for future generations. Complementing Michelle Cooke's chapter about teaching university Chickasaw language courses, I draw upon findings of 5 years of research during 2010–2015 with Chickasaws committed to learning, teaching, and actively using Chikashshanompa'. Together, we dedicate our chapters to the life's work of Jerry Imotichey (1938–2016)—Michelle's co-instructor and a language teacher to both of us. Jerry passed on in 2016, having inspired many with his love for his first language and passion for teaching others.

As a Chickasaw citizen and language learner, my research is inherently personal. I begin this chapter by introducing my own journey toward reclaiming my Indigenous heritage language. I then explore the significance of language reclamation and current language programming to

Indigenizing Education, pages 105–120
Copyright © 2022 by Information Age Publishing
www.infoagepub.com

nation-building. Next, I discuss my use of a culturally-grounded research methodology to conduct interviews with Chickasaws exceptionally committed to language reclamation. These interviews offered key insight into themes central to the vitality and efficacy of Chikashshanompa' reclamation, including a (a) raised critical Chickasaw consciousness, (b) conception of Chikashshanompa' as cultural practice, and (c) (re)valuing of language learners. Ultimately, I argue that the stories of Chikashshanompa' learners and teachers demonstrate the importance of sustaining cultural and linguistic practices to social change, empowerment, and nation-building.

A PERSONAL COMMITMENT TO LANGUAGE

Chokma, saholhchifoat Kari. Chikashsha saya. I was 20 years old when I first learned to use my language, Chikashshanompa', to introduce myself as a Chickasaw person. By that point in my life, I had said these same words many times in English—"Hello, my name is Kari. I am Chickasaw"—but they always felt empty, void of connection to my people and places from which I came. Speaking Chikashshanompa' grounded me in a deep sense of continuity—a connection both to my Ancestors and to generations to come. It was an experience "more than memory or remembering" that left my life forever changed (Ortiz, 1992, p. 9). I awoke to the centrality of Chikashshanompa' to the continuance of Chickasaw cultural identity, and could no longer ignore my felt sense of responsibility to learn and care for the language.

Raised in southern California, hundreds of miles from the Chickasaw Nation, I did not hear my heritage language as a child. In fact, no one in my family had spoken Chikashshanompa' for generations. The story of language loss in my family began in 1837, with my Ancestors' forced removal from their southeastern homelands to Indian Territory (present-day Oklahoma). My great-great-great-grandparents were among those displaced. Having lost so much, they sent their children to English-language boarding schools with the hope of securing a better future for them. It was a choice not "of freedom but a practice of control—a way to create an acceptable place for themselves in a different world" (Cobb, 2000, p. 37). Subsequent generations in my family learned to speak English as a first and only language. I am the first to begin learning, and thus reclaiming, Chikashshanompa'.

My own family's experience of intergenerational language loss is not unique among Chickasaws, and consequences of large-scale language shift are evident across the Chickasaw Nation. Out of over 70,000 enrolled citizens, fewer than fifty—all born in the mid-1950s or earlier—speak Chikashshanompa' as a first language. Based on this statistic alone, most schemas designed to measure the health of languages classify Chikashshanompa' as severely endangered (see Krauss, 2007). While there is little doubt that colonization and enduring and relentless pressures of assimilation have profoundly threatened the continuance of Chikashshanompa', these numbers fail to capture Chickasaw people's renewed and growing desire to know the language. Between 2011 and 2015, for example, the number of participants in language programming (including classes, camps, clubs, and/or outreach visits) increased from 900 to 1,800 (Anoatubby, 2014, 2015). What is more, a small number of exceptionally committed Chickasaw language learners have emerged as highly proficient language users and leaders of current multigenerational language reclamation endeavors.

CHIKASHSHANOMPA' RECLAMATION AS NATION BUILDING

Indigenous languages "have been forcibly subordinated in contexts of colonization" (McCarty & Nicholas, 2014, p. 106). As such, language reclamation entails the social process by which Indigenous Peoples (re)claim "the appropriate cultural context and sense of value that the language would likely have always had if not for colonization" (Leonard, 2011, p. 141). In this way, language reclamation becomes an essential means by which community members engage in nation building—"the conscious and focused application of [an Indigenous] people's collective resources, energies, and knowledge to the task of liberating and developing the psychic and physical space that is identified as [their] own" (Brayboy et al., 2012, p. 12).

While nation-building occurs in many forms, reclamation of cultural identity and language must be at the center (Brayboy et al., 2012). The understanding of language reclamation and, therefore, nation-building, as a social process emphasizes the agency of people in "asserting the prerogative to learn and transmit the language...in a way that reflects the community's needs and values" (Leonard, 2011, pp. 154–155). In other words, language reclamation is not about *fixing* Indigenous languages—which are and have always been vital—but instead about "people 'doing language' together in meaningful ways" (Fettes, 1997, para. 8). In this way, Chickasaw people are working not simply to stabilize or renew our language, but to assert our humanity by strengthening our cultural identity and resisting hegemonic legacies of colonization. When we, as Indigenous Peoples, know who we are and express who we are in our languages, we embody both resiliency and resistance.

Within the Chickasaw Nation, language reclamation has been deeply connected to nation-building at both the tribal government level and in the lives of individual citizens. In the last decade, Chickasaw citizens have recognized the severity of language loss and expressed unprecedented desire to know their heritage language. In response, the Chickasaw Nation established the Chickasaw Language Revitalization Program in 2007. The small staff, comprised of language learners and Elder fluent speakers, has focused its efforts on providing language programming accessible to all Chickasaw citizens and grounded in a vision for the emergence of new generations of Chikashshanompa' speakers.

Critical to language continuance is the rebuilding and strengthening of intergenerational relationships. Out of less than 50 Elder first language speakers, about 30[1] have committed to sharing the language in some way with younger generations. Members of this (great-) grandparental generation who are actively involved in language reclamation efforts share a desire to ensure the continuance of Chikashshanompa' and Chickasaw identity by teaching those dedicated to learning the language (Lewis, 2011).[2] For Chickasaw learners who do not have speakers in their family, these Elder speakers often take on the role of another set of grandparents, enabling the restoration of intergenerational language transmission within Chickasaw families and the community—the domains where Chikashshanompa' is rooted and can be cultivated (Chew, 2016). In the following section, I provide a brief overview of the language programming that existed at the time of my study, which I completed in 2015.

Language Learning Programming

During the time when I was doing research, the Chickasaw Language Revitalization Program offered programming for youth—including a children's language club, high school language class, family and culture camps, as well as the BakBak Youth Stickball Program—however, most language programming focused on adult learners. Adapted from the model implemented in Indigenous communities in California (see Hinton et al., 2002), the Chickasaw Master–Apprentice program was an effective model for adult language learning. From 2007 to 2015, the program supported one-on-one teams, comprised of a language learner and an Elder fluent speaker, for up to 3 years. Pairs completed 10 hours of oral language immersion per week. While the program produced several highly competent language learners, it required an investment of resources, in terms of time and speakers, that was not sustainable. As a result, the one-on-one master-apprentice model was phased out and, in 2015, replaced by a group language immersion model.[3] While fewer learners are served by the group model, those who do participate spend more time learning the language and have increased financial support for their efforts.

In addition to language immersion programs, learners living locally could take credit-bearing coursework in the language. In 2009, East Central

University (ECU), in partnership with the Chickasaw Nation, began offering a series of four Chikashshanompa' courses focused on examining the linguistic structures of the language. Typically taught by a team comprised of an Elder speaker and experienced language learner, the ECU course utilized Munro and Willmond's (2008) Chikashshanompa' grammar as a central text, covering units sequentially over the four courses. Because the text focused on examining the linguistic structures of the language, the course was not designed to produce fluent speaker-users of the language. Instead the goal was to impart student language learners with a strong understanding of and ability to talk about Chikashshanompa' grammar, a skill that would equip them as more effective language learners and teachers, especially when they pursued learning opportunities outside of class. Still, while the students who enrolled in the course were often Chickasaw or Native American, only a small number had prior experience learning the language through the Master–Apprentice Program, language courses at the high school level, or other community language programming. Often those students who were committed to learning the language participated in community language programming concurrently with their enrollment in the courses. Retention of students through the four-course series was consistently a challenge, and enrollment tended to drop for the higher-level courses. Still, dedicated language learners, including those who were non-degree seeking, consistently enrolled in and completed the four-course series.

With over two-thirds of enrolled Chickasaws residing outside of the Chickasaw Nation jurisdictional area (Morris, 2016), the Chickasaw Language Revitalization Program has long been concerned with how to make Chikashshanompa' accessible to all citizens regardless of where they live. For years, the only resources available to citizens-at-large were texts, including Chickasaw dictionaries (Humes & Humes, 1987; Munro & Willmond, 1994), an introductory language workbook created by fluent speakers (Thompson et al., 1994), and a grammar of the language (Munro & Willmond, 2008). In 2009, the Chickasaw Nation released a free Anompa: Chickasaw Language Basics app which includes audio recordings of common words and phrases. In 2016, the first of four levels of Rosetta Stone Chickasaw was released.[4]

While current language reclamation efforts are dynamic, they are happening on a relatively small scale within the Chickasaw Nation. In 2015, only about 3% of enrolled tribal members engaged in language revitalization programming, either through classes, camps, clubs, and/or outreach visits (Anoatubby, 2015). Among these 3%, interest in and attitudes about Chikashshanompa' varied, with some Chickasaws desiring only to know greetings and common phrases and others still restructuring their entire lives around language reclamation. The learners and teachers whose stories inform this chapter fall into this exceptionally committed latter group who are the driving force behind current language reclamation work within the Chickasaw Nation.

ASKING IN A CHICKASAW WAY

Interested in Chickasaw people's motivations to learn and teach Chikashshanompa', I began researching Chickasaw language reclamation efforts in 2010. I identified poignant themes across generations, including: (a) Elders' strong desire to ensure Chickasaw continuance through teaching the language to others, (b) parents' sense of responsibility to pass the language to their children, and (c) youth and young adults' yearning to speak Chikashshanompa' as they developed consciousness of their Chickasaw identity (Lewis, 2011). This research pointed not only to the potential for the restoration of intergenerational language transmission, but the critical role of language learners in ensuring the continuance of Chikashshanompa'. Seeking to learn more, I conducted additional fieldwork in 2014 and 2015.

As I looked toward exploring the nuanced and diverse experiences of exceptionally committed language learners, asking my questions in a Chickasaw way was a priority. Because I am a Chickasaw person and language learner, my research about Chikashshanompa' reclamation was inherently personal and required me to work from a protocol which embraced—rather than erased—my cultural identity and personal relationships with other Chickasaws involved in language work. To this end, I utilized a culturally-grounded methodology which has arisen out of Chickasaw-authored scholarship and is "rooted in place, built on relationships, and sustained over a period of time" (Guajardo et al., 2008, p. 8).

Upholding the call for ethical and transformative Indigenous research (Smith, 1999), Chickasaw scholar and language activist Lokosh (Joshua D. Hinson, 2007) outlines a protocol for conducting research about, with, and for the Chickasaw community. Based on a Chikashshanompa' verb meaning "to ask," the Chikashsha asilhlha' protocol includes six ethical guidelines:

1. Respect the house (chokka'), clan (iksa'), and tribe (okloshi').
2. Be visible to the community.
3. Listen and observe before questioning.
4. Reciprocate gifts.
5. Be careful with knowledge that is given.
6. Be humble.

Using the cultural metaphors of house (chokka'), clan (iksa'), and tribe (okloshi'), Chikashsha asilhlha' emphasizes respect for the immediate family, extended family, and tribal nation. Grounded in respect for these relationships, I did my best to work with research participants in a way that was humble, careful, and also transparent (see Chew & Hinson, 2021).

Interviewing was a important means to collect data. As Hopi scholar Sheilah E. Nicholas (2008) writes, "Language shift is an unprecedented phenomenon, a lived experience of an oral society, therefore, accessible primarily through the oral narratives of the people themselves" (p. 64). Altogether, I interviewed 21 participants representing Elder, middle, and youth generations. Eight had participated in my previous study, which enabled me to consider individuals' engagement in language reclamation over a period of about 5 years. I also interviewed new participants who the Chickasaw Language Revitalization Program and community members identified as being exceptionally committed and talented language learners. Interviews were comprised of three parts: (a) a focused life history, (b) details of experience, and (c) reflection on the meaning (Seidman, 2006). This model provided a structure for participants to tell their stories about what it means for a Chickasaw person to reclaim Chikashshanompa'. In the following sections, I discuss the profound insights Chickasaw people shared through interviews into the phenomenon of language reclamation and what enables Chikashshanompa' continuance.

ENABLING LANGUAGE CONTINUANCE AND NATION BUILDING

Often—and problematically—language is treated as a *thing* that can be made "more homogenous and predictable by establishing standards, printing dictionaries, and writing textbooks and curricula" (Fettes, 1997, para. 3). This view of language, however, is detrimental to the goals of language reclamation because it separates languages from their speakers. Instead, a theory of language reclamation "must begin with the speakers, with people 'doing language' together in meaningful ways, and work out from there" (para. 8). The following sections discuss three themes common to the stories of language learners and teachers who are doing language together in such a way that enables language continuance and promotes nation building. These themes include the raising of a critical Chickasaw consciousness, engagement with Chikashshanompa' as cultural practice, and a (re)valuing of language learners.

A Critical Chickasaw Consciousness

A critical Indigenous consciousness entails the "awareness of the historical and broad oppressive conditions that have influenced current realities of

Indigenous People[s'] lives" (Lee, 2009, p. 318). As a result of colonization and forced assimilation, Chickasaws experienced abuse and discrimination for speaking Chikashshanompa' and asserting their cultural identities. As such, a core component of Chickasaw language reclamation includes raising consciousness of the historical and ongoing suppression of Chickasaw people and our language and (re)awakening to a cultural identity in which Chikashshanompa' is central.

Often this raised Indigenous consciousness is developed at the transition to adulthood (Lee, 2009). Clovis, a young adult language learner whose family instilled in him a strong sense of pride in his Chickasaw and Choctaw heritages, exemplified this experience. While he "grew up knowing who [he] was" and with exposure to his heritage languages, he did not actively seek out Chikashshanompa' until he went to college. Though the language was not part of his academic studies, learning about other Indigenous communities as part of his Native American studies degree inspired him to seek out Chikashshanompa'. He explained:

> I have a little more knowledge of things that happened in the past that I was unaware of before because . . . it's not taught in schools. It's either taught at home or . . . you teach yourself or you learn from others that you find out have knowledge in whatever you're looking for, whether it be history, whether it be language, whether it be dances, whether it be ceremonies, whatever it is.

As Clovis points out, a critical Chickasaw consciousness is not taught through a formal Western education. It develops within family and through participation in the community over time—and when the individual becomes ready to (re)turn to this knowledge.

Importantly, the raising of critical consciousness is part of the lifelong journey toward becoming fully Chickasaw (Nicholas, 2008), and is experienced across all generations. An example of the ways in which Elders, too, have experienced the raising of critical Chickasaw consciousness came rather candidly during an interview. Explaining the importance of the language in his life, Jerry, an Elder fluent speaker and language teacher, stated: "[The language is] in my heart." He continued, "I guess it's kind of like the old saying: 'Once an Indian, always an Indian.'" Immediately after saying these words, he stopped and began to laugh. Jerry recognized the absurdity of describing his sense of identity in words employed by the colonizer to emphasize the perceived savagery and homogeneity of Indigenous Peoples. Reclaiming the saying, Jerry then exclaimed: "No! Once a Chickasaw, always a Chickasaw. Language is it."

For many, the process of (re)awakening to one's cultural identity was spurred by a feeling of loss and separation from that identity. Lonna, an adult language learner residing outside of tribal jurisdictional boundaries recalled asking as a child, "What did it mean to be Chickasaw?" The daughter of a boarding school survivor who did not openly share her Chickasaw language or heritage, she always felt that something was missing. Lonna remembered, "It was always like everybody else had their culture and they understood what they represented." It was not until adulthood, after her mother's passing, that Lonna began to actively pursue the language as a means to reconnect with the Chickasaw community in Oklahoma. Building on this sentiment, Lokosh, a learner who grew up outside of the Nation and later returned, explained:

> You're removed from it [the culture] and you say to yourself, "Well, I go back and play [stick]ball.[5] That's cool. I can sing. That's cool. I'm a tribal artist." But what's *the* thing that is Chickasaw through and through? That's the language.

The sentiments of these learners affirm that "language is not only a means to communicate thoughts and reminiscing of the past, it also positions one as part of the community that has a tradition and a past" and, importantly, a future (Wan et al., 2015, p. 118).

Colonization has centered on the erasure of Chickasaw cultural identity through the separation of Chickasaw people from land, family, and consequently language. This means that an essential component of nation building is the act of "counteracting generations of miseducation" about what it is to be Chickasaw (Akoto, 1992, p. iv). For learners and fluent speakers alike, a raised consciousness of what it means to be Chickasaw in the face of language shift prompted a strong sense of agency in asserting Chickasaw cultural identity and encouraging language reclamation (Lee, 2014). As Jerry pointed out, this requires the rejection of Western constructions of Chickasaw people as "Indian" and toward Chickasaw conceptualizations of what it is to be human. The words of language learners and Elders reflect that a deep and full understanding of Chickasaw cultural identity requires the language.

Chikashshanompa' as Cultural Practice

Importantly, language is just one of many ways to engage in one's culture. Studying the impact of language shift on Hopi young people, Nicholas (2009) found that even without a strong foundation in their heritage language, youth developed a strong sense of cultural identity by "living Hopi" through active participation in religion, customs, and traditions. Further, language was not limited to "talk," but encompassed oral tradition as a "'total communicative framework' manifest in song words, prayer, teachings, ritual performances, religious ceremonies, and cultural institutions" (Nicholas, 2009, p. 333). Many Indigenous Peoples understand this oral tradition as the means through which they are instructed "how to be a people in heart, thought, behavior, and conduct as they pursue life's fulfillment" (Nicholas, 2014, p. 64). The understanding of Chikashshanompa' as cultural practice is critical because it shifts emphasis from the language itself to how Chickasaw people are deepening a sense of cultural identity through the language.

Significantly, youth and young adult students who were learning the language had much insight into the importance of Chikashshanompa' as cultural practice. One student, Ezra, who studied the language in high school explained that he often used the language outside of class. He recalled a distinct memory of serving food to Elders at a community event:

> I remember [one Elder] coming up and saying, "Yakkookay [thank you]." I remember the sense of pride and love, you know. I know what he said and I'm able to answer him back, and we were able to speak. Now, it lasted about thirty seconds and a lot of them Elders got words that are way over me, but to be able to have that few seconds is what counted.

What Ezra did in these moments extended far beyond the exchanging of niceties in the language. He upheld a cultural value showing respect to an Elder by greeting him and serving him a meal. Although one does not need to be proficient in the language in order to serve Elders, the significance that Ezra attaches to this memory of language use reflects that Chikashshanompa' is what Nicholas (2009) calls the "missing piece" to deep and full understanding of the totality of a Chickasaw way of being. By using the language in this cultural context, he engaged in a process of acquiring essential Chickasaw values and concepts. Several years later, Ezra reflected again on this memory—thinking not only of the hope he himself experienced as a language learner but also of the hope this Elder must have experienced when a young person answered him in the language. In Ezra's view, this memory encapsulates what it means to reclaim one's language, to use it with purpose, and to ensure its continuance across generations.

Lonna, like Ezra, also offered insight into what it means to enact Chickasaw values which are understood in the context of the language and cultural practice. Describing the challenge of learning language without being around fluent speakers, she stated:

> It's like making dumplings. An experienced dumpling maker knows how to make them because it's the way she's always done it. If you read the recipe, though, there would be no way you could figure it out unless you had somebody there to teach you.

In Lonna's view, language learning is a social activity that, much like the preparation of traditional dumplings, is difficult to do in isolation. Without an experienced teacher who has knowledge of the language and how it should be used, an essential component of the language learning process will inevitably be lacking. This metaphor of dumpling making can also be understood another way. A Chickasaw person can learn to make dumplings relying on English—"the recipe"—without knowledge of the language. As Lonna indicates, however, something would be missing: "There would be no way you could figure [the culture] out unless you had [the language] there to teach you."

The stories of youth and adult language learners alike provide important insight into the significance of language as cultural practice to nation building. Reclaiming Chikashshanompa' is a lifelong pursuit in which one gradually and continually develops sophistication in increasingly esoteric domains. This process of accessing and acquiring deep cultural knowledge through in-depth language study can be likened to an iceberg (Barnhardt, 2008), in which the visible tip of the iceberg above sea level represents surface culture. Submerged and unseen is the body of the iceberg representing deep cultural knowledge, which will only be accessed by some language learners who choose and are invited by the community to dive beneath the surface of the ocean that is the language. Nation building begins with individuals' reclamation of deep and full understanding of Chikashshanompa' as cultural practice and grows outward.

(Re)Valuing of Language Learners

The devaluing of Indigenous heritage language learners is a legacy of colonization. Expectations of failure loom over Indigenous language learners, who have been characterized within scholarly literature and, in some cases, their own communities as "dysfluent" or inherently unable to acquire their heritage languages (Meek, 2011). Such deficit views of Indigenous youth contribute to a damaging notion that these language learners are inherently unable to speak their languages or that they have intentionally "abandoned" their heritage languages in favor of a dominant language (McCarty et al., 2014; Meek, 2011; Wyman et al., 2014). Both research and experience demonstrate that is not the case. The (re)valuing of language learners counters internal colonization allowing for the (re)building of relationships which enable and reinvigorate language reclamation work.

Bradley, a Chickasaw student enrolled in the ECU college course shared a powerful perspective on the way in which the ability to learn Chikashshanompa' is a special gift. He explained, "You can always have people who can bead, can always have people who can play stickball, but you can't always have people who remember the language." The language is a living entity and once it goes to sleep and is no longer spoken, it is difficult to reawaken. Bradley recognized that part of his responsibility as a young person was to learn and remember the language throughout his life. In his view, skills like beading and playing stickball can be taught more easily than the language. As a result, he did not feel the same urgency to learn how to bead as he did to learn the language because he could learn how to bead anytime. The language, on the other hand, may not always be accessible to him. Bradley's statement further indicates that the ability to learn and remember the language is a gift and life calling that not every Chickasaw person has.

Importantly, Bradley recognized a unique gift in himself as a language learner. The Chikashshanompa' classes he was taking at school strengthened his sense of identity and helped him to find his place in his family and community. He explained that members of his family had unique talents—such as beadwork or crafting stickball sticks—which contributed to Chickasaw cultural continuance, but no one spoke the language. Over time, Bradley's family began to esteem him a keeper of knowledge of the language, turning to him to teach them and answer questions. Not only that, the community began to notice as well. Because of his demonstrated commitment to learning Chickasaw in his high school courses, the student was selected as an aide for the classes during his senior year. Together, an internal and external recognition of language learner's talents and gifts motivates and sustains their engagement in language reclamation.

Nearly all the language learners I interviewed as part of this research described being inspired both by Elder speakers and, importantly, by one another. For Clovis, a primary source of motivation to continue to learn and use the language was working with others and seeing one another's progress. Clovis explained of learning with others, "I think we kind of push each other [to learn and use the language more] without really knowing." By valuing each other's accomplishments as language learners, these language learners formed strong bonds to one another. Significantly, these bonds around the language have enabled language learners to envision themselves continuing the legacy of current Elder language keepers. These language learners especially enjoyed seeing Chikashshanompa' Elder speakers, who were longtime friends, visit with each other and speak the language. Clovis explained, "It's just amazing to sit there and listen to them . . . They start talking over each other and cutting words off. Listening to them do that is something to look forward to." Not only did Clovis feel inspired by these Elders to continue learning the language, but he was able to see himself and his coworkers in them. He reflected, "It'd be pretty neat if me [and my coworkers] could sit around and talk Chickasaw being not Elders, but semi-young still. It'd be pretty neat to sit around and talk with each other."

Clovis's vision of himself as a "semi-young" competent speaker-user of Chikashshanompa' is significant because it speaks strongly to Tara Yosso's (2005) notion of aspirational capital, or "the ability to maintain hopes and dreams for the future, even in the face of real and perceived barriers" (pp. 77–78). Such ability, especially among younger generations, is critical both to cultural continuance and to nation building. As Yosso further explains, "These aspirations are developed within social and familial contexts, often through linguistic storytelling and advice... that offer specific navigational goals to challenge (resist) oppressive conditions" (p. 77). For language learners, aspirations of carrying the language forward have developed within a community context which values their talents as language learners and contributors to language reclamation work. Importantly, this valuing occurs as those involved with language reclamation build relationships within, between, and/or across generations.

CONCLUSIONS

When I began my research with Chickasaws involved with language reclamation work in 2010, I learned that many were motivated by a sense of urgency of language decline—a *fear* that the language could be lost forever. Four years later, when I returned to conduct both new and follow-up interviews, this fear was overshadowed by a force much more powerful: hope. As one language learner powerfully asserted, "I'm not afraid of [Chikashshanompa'] going to sleep anymore... I'm not afraid of that." Chickasaw people are choosing to prioritize Chikashshanompa', restructuring and dedicating their lives to ensuring the continuance of the language. As a result, for the first time in recent history, fluent speakers and language learners alike are able to envision a future where Chikashshanompa' is spoken (Chew, 2019).

During one especially memorable interview, Elder speaker Jerry reflected on how his perception of language learners and the importance of language reclamation had evolved over time. For years, he had been skeptical of younger generations' interest in the language. In fact, when the Master–Apprentice Program began in 2007, he declined to participate, saying that he did not believe teaching the language was good or appropriate work. Jerry explained:

> When this language thing began to be told about in the Indian communities [and] when [younger generations] began to hear [the language], they began to want to learn. I told them (which is wrong), "If I teach you, who are you going to speak to? There's nobody else... that speaks it... [and] I'm not going to live forever."

Jerry had internalized the belief that the language was destined to perish with his generation—what he perceived to be the last generation of fluent speakers.

What is significant about Jerry's statement is his admission that the belief he had once firmly held was wrong. After being asked repeatedly to be a master language teacher and taking time to think about it, he finally agreed. To his surprise, he came to embrace teaching Chikashshanompa' as rewarding and worthwhile. Not only did he agree to participate in the Master–Apprentice Program, he co-taught the ECU language courses and assisted with language immersion programming. The younger people he worked with were eager to learn, and what is more were becoming proficient users of the language. Seeing their dedication and progress inspired Jerry to ask again: "If I weren't here anymore, who's going to carry [the language] on?" This time he answered—with absolute conviction—of the committed language learners he had taught, "They'll be the ones to carry it on." Jerry's statement speaks powerfully to the central role of language to cultural continuance and to nation building.

ACKNOWLEDGMENT

A Wenner-Gren Hunt Postdoctoral Fellowship supported the writing of this book chapter.

NOTES

1. There are a number of reasons why some speakers choose not to teach Chikashshanompa'. Many speakers have experienced immense trauma associated with speaking their Indigenous language.
2. Published under the author's maiden name.
3. At the time of my study, the Chikasha Academy group immersion approach had not yet begun. Most adult research participants had completed the Master–Apprentice Program. (For more information about this approach, see Hinson, 2019; Morgan, 2017.)
4. This language software was not yet released at the time I conducted my research.
5. Stickball is a traditional game central to Chickasaw culture and spirituality.

REFERENCES

Akoto, K. A. (1992). *Nationbuilding: Theory and practice in Afrikan centered education.* Pan Afrikan World Institute.

Alberson, Y., Thompson, C., Imotichey, J., & Howard, G. (1994). *Introduction to Chickasaw.* Various Indian Peoples Publishing.

Anoatubby, B. (2014). *The Chickasaw Nation progress report* [Progress report]. The Chickasaw Nation.

Anoatubby, B. (2015). *The Chickasaw Nation progress report* [Progress report]. The Chickasaw Nation.

Barnhardt, R. (2008). Creating a place for Indigenous knowledge in education: The Alaska Native knowledge network. In D. A. Gruenewald & G. A. Smith (Eds.), *Place-based education in the global age: Local diversity* (pp. 113–134). Routledge.

Brayboy, B. M. J., Fann, A. J., Castagno, A. E., & Solyom, J. A. (2012). *Postsecondary education for American Indian and Alaska Natives: Higher education for nation building and self-determination* [ASHE Higher Education Report]. John Wiley & Sons.

Chew, K. A. B. (2016). *Chikashshanompa' ilanompohóli bíyyi'ka'chi* [We will always speak the Chickasaw language]*: Considering the vitality and efficacy of Chickasaw language reclamation* [Unpublished doctoral dissertation. University of Arizona.

Chew, K. A. B. (2019). Weaving words: Conceptualizing language reclamation through culturally-significant metaphor. *Canadian Journal of Native Education, 41*(1), 168–185.

Chew, K. A. B., & Hinson, J. D. (Lokosh). (2021). Chikashshaat asilhlhat holissochi [Chickasaws are asking and writing]: Enacting Indigenous protocols in academic research and writing. *Native American Indigenous Studies, 8*(2), 1–28. https://doi.org/10.5749/natiindistudj.8.2.0001

Cobb, A. J. (2000). *Listening to our grandmothers' stories: The Bloomfield Academy for Chickasaw females, 1852–1949.* University of Nebraska Press.

Fettes, M. (1997). Stabilizing what? An ecological approach to language renewal. In J. Reyhner (Ed.), *Teaching Indigenous languages* (pp. 301–318). Northern Arizona University.

Guajardo, M., Guajardo, F., & Casaperalta, E. D. C. (2008). Transformative education: Chronicling a pedagogy for social change. *Anthropology & Education Quarterly, 39*(1), 3–22.

Hinson, J. D. (2007). *To'li' Chikashsha inaafokha: Chickasaw stickball regalia* (Unpublished master's thesis). University of New Mexico.

Hinson, J. D. (Lokosh). (2019). *Nanna ittonchololi' ilaliichi* [We are cultivating new growth]: *Twenty years in Chikashshanompa' revitalization* [Doctoral dissertation, University of Oklahoma]. SHAREOK. https://hdl.handle.net/11244/323267

Hinton, L., Vera, M., & Steele, N. (2002). *How to keep your language alive: A commonsense approach to one-on-one language learning.* Heyday.

Humes, J., & Humes, V. M. J. (1987). *A Chickasaw dictionary.* University of Oklahoma.

Krauss, M. (2007). Classification and terminology for degrees of language endangerment. In M. Brenzinger (Ed.), *Language diversity endangered* (pp. 1–8). Mouton De Gruyter Press.

Lee, T. S. (2009). Language, identity, and power: Navajo and Pueblo young adults' perspectives and experiences with competing language ideologies. *Journal of Language, Identity, and Education, 8*(5), 307–320.

Lee, T. S. (2014). Critical language awareness among Native youth in New Mexico. In L. T. Wyman, T. L. McCarty, & S. E. Nicholas (Eds.), *Indigenous youth and multilingualism: Language identity, ideology, and practice in dynamic cultural worlds* (pp. 130–147). Routledge.

Leonard, W. Y. (2011). Challenging "extinction" through modern Miami language practices. *American Indian Culture and Research Journal, 35*(2), 135–160.

Lewis, K. A. (2011). *Pomanompa' kilanompolika chokma (It is good that we speak our language): Motivations to revitalize Chikashshanompa' (Chickasaw language) across generations.* (Unpublished master's thesis). University of California, Los Angeles.

McCarty, T. L., & Nicholas, S. E. (2014). Reclaiming Indigenous languages: A reconsideration of the roles and responsibilities of schools. *Review of educational research, vol. 38: Language diversity and language policy and politics in education* (pp. 106–136). American Educational Research Association.

McCarty, T. L., Romero-Little, M. E., Warhol, L., & Zepeda, O. (2014). Genealogies of language loss and recovery: Native youth language practices and cultural continuance. In L. T. Wyman, T. L. McCarty, & S. E. Nicholas (Eds.), *Indigenous youth and multilingualism: Language identity, ideology, and practice in dynamic cultural worlds* (pp. 26–47). Routledge.

Meek, B. A. (2011). Failing American Indian languages. *American Indian Culture and Research Journal, 35*(2), 43–60.

Morgan, J. (2017). *The learner varieties of the Chikasha Academy: Chickasaw adult language acquisition, change, and revitalization* [Doctoral dissertation, University of Oklahoma]. SHAREOK. https://hdl.handle.net/11244/50825

Morris, T. L. (2016). An example of excellence: Chickasaw language revitalization through technology. In L. E. Dyson, S. Grant, & M. Hendriks (Eds.), *Indigenous People and mobile technologies* (pp. 293–304). Routledge.

Munro, P., & Willmond, C. (1994). *Chikashshanompaat holisso toba'chi* [Chickasaw: An analytical dictionary]. University of Oklahoma.

Munro, P., & Willmond, C. (2008). *Chikashshanompa' kilanompoli'* [Let's speak Chickasaw]. University of Oklahoma Press.

Nicholas, S. E. (2008). *Becoming "fully" Hopi: The role of the Hopi language in the contemporary lives of Hopi youth—A case study of Hopi language shift and vitality* [Unpublished Doctoral dissertation]. University of Arizona.

Nicholas, S. E. (2009). "I live Hopi, I just don't speak it"—The critical intersection of language, culture, and identity in the lives of contemporary Hopi youth. *Journal of Language, Identity, and Education, 8*(5), 321–334.

Nicholas, S. E. (2014). "How are you Hopi if you can't speak it?": An ethnographic study of language as cultural practice among contemporary Hopi youth. In T. L. McCarty (Ed.), *Ethnography and language policy* (pp. 53–75). Routledge.

Ortiz, S. J. (1992). *Woven stone.* University of Arizona Press.

Seidman, I. (2006). *Interviewing as qualitative research: A guide for researchers in education and the social sciences* (3rd ed.). Teacher's College Press.

Smith, L. T. (1999). *Decolonizing methodologies: Research and Indigenous Peoples* (1st ed.). Zed Books.

Wan, R., Renganathan, S., & Phillip, B. (2015). What is the point of us talking? Ethnic language and ethnic identity in Northern Borneo, Malaysia. *Humanities and Social Sciences Review, 4*(1), 109–120.

Wyman, L. T., McCarty, T. L., & Nicholas, S. E. (2014). Beyond endangerment: Indigenous youth and multilingualism. In L. T. Wyman, T. L. McCarty, & S. E. Nicholas (Eds.), *Indigenous youth and multilingualism: Language identity, ideology, and practice in dynamic cultural worlds* (pp. 1–25). Routledge.

Yosso, T. J. (2005). Whose culture has capital? A critical race theory discussion of community cultural wealth. *Race Ethnicity and Education, 8*(1), 69–91.

CHAPTER 9

TRANSFORMATIVE PRAXIS

Keeping the Fire Burning: The Impact of Community Indigenous Language Teachers in the Classroom

Michelle Scaggs Cooke

I am a second-language learner. Growing up, I did not hear Chikashsha-nompa' spoken. I was not even sure who the last fluent speaker in my family was until I reconnected with my Chickasaw grandmother in 2007. She lived in Denver, Colorado, and had not been involved in raising my father, so my exposure to Chickasaw culture was nonexistent. In fact, I did not even receive my CDIB (Certificate of Degree of Indian Blood) card until I was 30 years old. My grandmother told me her brother had spoken the language, but he had passed away several years before. As a result, I heard Chikashsha-nompa' spoken for the first time when my family and I moved to Ada, Oklahoma, in 2007, and I began working for the Chickasaw Nation. It sparked a fire in me to learn my language, to reconnect on a deeper level with my ancestors, and to honor their memories. I signed up for one of the first Chickasaw courses offered at East Central University (ECU) in Ada, and purchased *Chikashshanompa' Kilanompoli'* (Let's Speak Chickasaw; Munro &

Indigenizing Education, pages 121–126
Copyright © 2022 by Information Age Publishing
www.infoagepub.com
All rights of reproduction in any form reserved.

Willmond, 2008), the grammar textbook required for the course. Learning even the basics of my heritage language took a great deal of dedication, but the reward of the course was taking the language outside the classroom and using it in other settings like at home with my family and with fellow coworkers. I encouraged my 10 year-old son and 6 year-old twins to join the programs offered by the Chickasaw Nation language department, and we attended an annual family immersion camp. Through those activities, I learned along with them. Learning Chikashshanompa' became a personal journey—and an emotional one at that—because as I learned my language, I also learned my culture. I wanted to understand enough Chikashshanompa' to hold a basic conversation and to understand what fluent speakers were saying to one another, so I could better connect with my elders.

I began working for the Chickasaw language revitalization program in 2012 as scholar-in-residence where I researched and wrote about Chickasaw history. In the fall of 2013, the language program asked me to teach Chickasaw I and II, the first two courses in the four course series that I had recently completed at ECU. While I did not feel quite qualified in my Chikashshanompa' fluency, I did feel comfortable in front of a classroom, and was excited to have the opportunity to share what I had learned in these courses with students. I had earned a master's degree in English, completed coursework toward a doctorate in rhetoric, and had previously taught university-level English composition courses. While I knew teaching an oral Indigenous language would be a very different experience, I was fueled by my passion for the language my ancestors spoke, and began preparing my syllabus.

Initially, I planned my courses around the *Let's Speak Chickasaw* (Munro & Willmond, 2008) textbook, striving to use teaching methods similar to those my instructors implemented in the language courses I took in high school and college. The textbook consisted of 20 units, each with vocabulary, lessons and exercises for the learner. My goal was to cover the first 10 units in Chickasaw I and the next 10 in Chickasaw II. Because there are no quizzes or tests in the book, I planned to create exams throughout the semester to track the students' progress. I quickly realized that learning Chikashshanompa' was a different experience than what my students were used to in their other classes. Most language classes are formatted with a book that is broken down into topics like "food" or "travel" and include a vocabulary list relevant to that topic. While the text included a CD with recordings of a fluent speaker saying words in Chikashshanompa' to provide the learner with pronunciation examples, it was not enough support for the students. Thankfully, the textbook was not the only language-learning resource. Chikashsha (Chickasaw) community elder and fluent speaker Mr. Jerry Imotichey was willing to coteach every class with me.

You had to love Jerry. He was always so unassuming and laid back. I felt like I could never say anything wrong in his eyes, as long as I attempted to say it in Chikashshanompa'. Although I had never experienced it first hand, I had heard from others that this had not always been the case. It seems at one point he had refused to teach the language to new learners, stating his language was bound to die with his generation. Somewhere along the line though, he had a change of heart, and I am eternally grateful. Nothing can be more defeating and embarrassing to a new learner than a fluent speaker criticizing their attempts to speak their language. Even one negative experience can cause a new learner to turn away from their attempt to learn the language and culture. Language learners should always be encouraged, and Jerry knew that.

At the beginning of the first class, I introduced myself in Chikashshanompa', "Chokma, saholhchifoat Michelle," and Jerry did the same. After our introductions, I had each student introduce themselves in Chikashshanompa'. While learning greetings and introductions in the first week of a second language class is common practice, the lesson takes on different meaning for heritage language learners. Being able to say who you are in your own language empowers a person by connecting them on a deeper level to their ancestors. It burns the fire brighter inside of you to know that you are keeping your language alive and inspires you to learn more. After each student told us their name, I asked them what they wished to accomplish from the class that semester. While students shared goals ranging from learning vocabulary to participating in dialogue, one student stood out. He wanted to learn enough Chikashshanompa' to understand what his grandmother was saying when she prayed at their Sunday meal.

This student's response changed the perspectives of the students, who were in their 20s to 40s, and had little experience with Chikashshanompa' prior to enrolling in the course. Although many of them had grown up hearing the language, they, like me, were from families that did not speak Chikashshanompa' to them. One student in the class had grandparents who spoke Chikashshanompa', but only to one another—never to their children or grandchildren. They still carried over the ideals from their childhood of needing to speak English in order to be successful in what they termed the White man's world. I would soon discover this was pretty standard in our Chikashsha community. Most students did not grow up around fluent speakers—and if they were fortunate enough to have a relative that spoke Chikashshanompa'—they often found them reluctant to teach the other members of the household citing their fear of rejection from the non-Native community.

When the student shared his desire to know his grandmother's prayer, I could see the rest of the class realign their goals with his. Suddenly, many were inspired to learn more than vocabulary words. They realized they could learn to communicate, and they could make a difference in this battle against language shift. Maybe they did not all have a fluent grandmother at their Sunday meals, maybe they were not even Chickasaw, but nonetheless they understood his need for that connection. It was an emotional moment for me. I realized what was being lost each week at that table and at other tables in our Chikashsha community. Jerry's role, as a fluent speaker, became central to confronting this dilemma.

Initially, I was not sure what Jerry's role would be as my co-instructor. No one had really defined it for me, but I had seen what his role was when I was a Chikashshanompa' student at ECU. He had a great friendship and partnership with the instructor. He was there to correctly pronounce the vocabulary words and make any needed corrections to the students' pronunciations—and we always needed them. At first, I followed this model closely. I would spend time breaking down the exercises in the book to the students through our mutual understanding of English grammar. This meant working through the chapter exercises section by section, and when questions arose, stopping and explaining the Chikashshanompa' grammar exercise as I would an English grammar exercise. The major drawback to the textbook was that it did not provide an answer key for the exercises, so if I was unsure of an answer, I turned to Jerry for clarification. I had thought I would rely on Jerry for oral listening skills and pronunciation exercises for the students, but Jerry's role in my classroom ended up being something much different. As the semesters unfolded, the students' and my relationship with Jerry developed and changed our language-learning experience. His role transformed from one of a teacher to one of a surrogate grandfather who taught us his language through love and laughter. Jerry became the heart of the class.

As an elder, Jerry rarely corrected a student. If we asked him how to say something in Chikashshanompa', he would almost inevitably reply, "How would *you* say it?" In this way, Jerry allowed us to attempt a translation free from fear of criticism. As we became more comfortable with one another, we began to ask Jerry more about himself, more about being Chikashsha, and more about Chikashshanompa'. He shared stories about his childhood. When he told us stories in Chikashshanompa', we tried to translate them, much to his amusement. At the end of the semester, I had the students each attempt to translate a children's book to Jerry in Chikashshanompa' (again, with much laughter).

While Jerry was the heart of class—breathing life into the language—I took on a more formal role. I developed the curriculum, administered the examinations, graded the assignments, and supported the students in their learning wherever I could. Some students took longer than others to pick up the words, the structure, and the grammar of the language. As an instructor, it was my responsibility to understand this and to acknowledge that each student learns in different ways. I incorporated spatial (visual), aural (auditory), linguistic (verbal), and tactile (physical) ways of learning into the classroom. For example, to reach my spatial learners I would write the words, exercises, and examples on the whiteboard. The aural and tactile learners would learn best when I had the students sing simple songs like "Head, Shoulders, Knees, and Toes" in Chikashshanompa'. Jerry would read the vocabulary aloud and the student would repeat after him which would help the linguistic learners. I would also integrate social and individual learning opportunities by allowing the students to play games as a group in Chikashshanompa' or work independently on textbook exercises.

With each new semester, I supplemented the textbook with new ideas of my own and integrated some fun additional resources for the students. Jerry was always supportive. One of the most popular games we played in class was UNO. While it allowed me to incorporate Chikashshanompa' color and numbers, it also created an opportunity for the students to talk to each other and communicate beyond their vocabulary lessons. Of the materials I developed, crossword puzzles and word searches were among Jerry's favorites. In fact, that was the last conversation I had with him before he passed in 2016. He called me to see if I could make him some new "puzzles" in Chikashshanompa', which I was both honored and delighted to create for him.

Through my journey with Jerry, I discovered that there are many different ways to reach second-language learners that can leave a lasting impact on them, and community Indigenous educators are one of them. By enrolling in a college course, these students agreed to visit a traditional college classroom 3 hours a week, take quizzes and exams, and have their knowledge graded and assessed by colonial standards, just to keep their language alive. But it was worth it to these students—they were doing anything they could to keep that fire burning. Accomplishing this goal speaks to the role of our students as nation-builders. By earning college degrees that included a foundational understanding of their Indigenous language, the students were equipped to contribute to our community and other Native communities. While I acknowledge that textbooks are an important part of learning a language in the university setting, they are not the only part. As Indigenous educators, it became Jerry's and my role to impart a unique perspective on the language classroom by sharing our cultural backgrounds and personal uses of the language. Part of learning language is being passionate about learning that language, and then keeping that passion burning, and I cannot think of a better person to help instill that passion than an Indigenous educator—someone who was born with the fire of their ancestors burning deep inside them. Language acquisition does not come overnight, or over a semester. It is a long, hard journey, but a journey where you have the opportunity to build your Indigenous nation, to further the education of other Indigenous students, and to meet people who have a lasting impact on your life.

REFERENCE

Munro, P., & Willmond, C. (2008). *Chikashshanompa' Kilanompoli'* [Let's speak Chickasaw]. University of Oklahoma Press.

CHAPTER 10

EDUCATIONAL LEADERS CENTERING YUUYARAQ AND ASSERTING RHETORICAL SOVEREIGNTY TO SUPPORT YOUTH DEVELOPMENT, LINGUISTIC SURVIVANCE, AND CLIMATE CHANGE ADAPTATION

Ataugg'aq Grant Kashatok
Leisy Wyman

Inuit educational leaders in the Far North play important roles in school-level reforms that honor local desires to center schooling around Indigenous values, knowledge systems, relationships, and languages, increasing youth well-being and community involvement in bilingual education (Tulloch et al., 2016). Centering Indigenous storywork and language learning in schools

Indigenizing Education, pages 127–151
Copyright © 2022 by Information Age Publishing
www.infoagepub.com
All rights of reproduction in any form reserved.

also supports the kinds of knowledge sharing, relationship building, and intergenerational communication that positions Native nations to address deep challenges from a place of wellness. In this chapter, we highlight how Ataugg'aq Grant Kashatok (co-author 1), a veteran Yup'ik principal, used specific genres of Yup'ik teachings and stories (John, 2010) in the Yup'ik language to foster Yup'ik young people's development, sustain Yup'ik language learning, and make space for collective thinking in Newtok, Alaska at a time when the tribe was facing imminent dislocation as some of the first climate change refugees in the United States. Contextualizing Grant's work in relation to Leisy Wyman (co-author two) and others' research with Yup'ik elders, educators, parents, and youth, elsewhere, we discuss principals as influential educational policy makers (Menken & Garcia, 2010) who can infuse Indigenous teachings and languages in schools. We also highlight ways that Yup'ik language planning supports youth development, relates to climate change adaptation, and fosters the kinds of relationships that contribute to Native nation-building in the Far North and elsewhere.

For 13 years, Grant was one of the only Yup'ik, and Yup'ik language speaking, principals in the Lower Kuskokwim School District (LKSD), a school district serving 22 Yup'ik villages and the regional hub town Bethel, off the road system in Southwestern Alaska. Newtok, where Grant was principal of the K–12 school, is one of a small number of village communities where children enter school speaking Yup'ik as their first language, in a Yup'ik region navigating Indigenous language maintenance, endangerment, and renewal (Wyman et al., 2010). Newtok is also the first of 31 Alaskan villages that need to be relocated due to melting permafrost, decreased arctic sea ice, increasing storms, erosion, and flooding related to global warming (Cochran et al., 2014). At the time of this writing, Newtok leaders had negotiated with government representatives for almost 2 decades to plan and find resources to move the community to a new site, navigating what Indigenous scholars critiqued as a "governmental and institutional no man's land" of bureaucracy (Wildcat, 2014, p. 511), as riverbank erosion approached villagers' houses, and sinking land, deteriorating infrastructure, related public health issues, and intensifying storm surges created increasingly dangerous conditions.

Many media pieces focused on the intense stresses Newtok community members experienced as they prepared to move in subgroups to Mertarlik, a new village site over nine miles upriver, over multiple years, starting in 2019. As principal, Grant served as an educational advocate in discussions between local leaders and over 20 government agencies involved in the village move. He also worked to promote student bilingualism, while navigating many layers of federal, state, and district policies, and challenges of running a school in rural Alaska (Richardson, 2011). Grant's comments on climate change were highlighted in media focused on Newtok villagers' fears, as they faced climate change dislocation. Scholars have analyzed the Newtok case, as well, to raise critical awareness of the dramatic rates, impacts, and environmental injustices of arctic climate change. Indigenous scholars and activists have highlighted Newtok to underscore the importance of relationships in climate change adaptation (Wildcat, 2014; Whyte, 2019), the possibilities of Indigenous and non-Indigenous collaboration and knowledge exchange (Barnhardt & Kawagley, 2005; Cochran et al., 2014), and the roles of institutions as key resources for environmental justice, tribal climate change adaptation, and collective continuance (Whyte, 2014). Collaborative research projects with Yup'ik community members have documented the ecological observations and climate change perspectives of Yup'ik elders from Newtok and neighboring villages (Fienup-Riordan, 2010, 2014). Little media or scholarly work to date, however, has focused on the transformative work of Yup'ik educators who supported youth in the school, or the ways that Yup'ik language use played an integral role in knowledge sharing, intergenerational communication, the development and maintenance of meaningful relationships, and climate change adaptation during this important era in Newtok history.

In this chapter, we highlight Grant's work in Newtok to discuss how principals serve as important policy makers in schools, as many Inuit communities across the Far North grapple with the complexities of Indigenous language sustainability, climate change adaptation, and assert Inuit sovereignty. Synthesizing research on Indigenous knowledge systems, language planning, and environmental justice, we also discuss the potential for schools to serve as key resources for Indigenous intergenerational learning, language maintenance and renewal, climate change adaptation, and self-determination.

To orient our reflections of Grant and others' work with Yup'ik traditional knowledge and language in schooling, we begin by briefly sharing how we worked together as educators in the 1990's, and how our pathways and discussions developed since then. We briefly overview research on connections among traditional genres of teachings, stories, subsistence, and the Yup'ik language within *Yuuyaraq*—the way of the human being. We then present Grant's firsthand account of how he shared Yuuyaraq in morning sessions to help youth access Yup'ik knowledge, understand their relationships to humans, animals, and the environment, and support collective thinking in school. Relating Grant's efforts in Newtok to Leisy and other's language planning research in LKSD, we also share how multiple Yup'ik actors have drawn upon "narrative practices and their associated ideologies as acts of resistance and persistence" (Kroskrity, 2012, p. 13) in the face of language endangerment, and highlight complexities and possibilities facing educators who share traditional Yup'ik oral teachings as a form of survivance—creative resistance and survival (Vizenor, 2008). In addition, we discuss how Yup'ilk community members assert rhetorical sovereignty—"the inherent right of peoples to determine their own communicative needs and desires" and "decide for themselves the goals, modes, styles, and languages of public discourse" (Lyons, 2000, p. 449)—as they renew positive relationships to Yup'ik knowledge, language, and the environment in schools, contributing to Native nation-building.

POSITIONING OURSELVES

For almost 3 decades, as colleagues and friends, we have had long-running conversations related to education in the Yup'ik region, discussing topics ranging from Yup'ik oral tradition, language planning and policy, family and community life, and activism, to race and gender in village schools. We met in Grant's home village of Qipneq in the early 1990s, when Grant was working as an elementary teacher's aide and high school basketball coach, and Leisy was a high school language arts teacher in the K–12 school. We first got to know one another when Grant led his high school team through an exciting basketball season and historic district championship, and Leisy chaperoned the team on many overnight trips.

In the following years, we talked often about events in the community and school. Leisy started working on a project with students and Yup'ik educators inviting elders and other community members to school to share teachings, stories, and personal experiences. At a Tribal leader's request, Mary Jane Mann, Elena Dock, Alice Fredson, and Leisy expanded the work to address Yup'ik language planning in the community. During the project, Grant shared his longrunning interest in Yup'ik knowledge and oral teachings with Leisy in many conversations, offering periodic recommendations for the work. Together, we also brainstormed ways that the work could transform curriculum and pedagogy, and the relationship between the school and the community. Grant's mother, Qussauyaq Katie Kashatok, also generously talked to students as an elder in the project (Fredson et al., 1998).

As we wrote this chapter, we both vividly recalled when Grant came to Leisy's classroom to discuss a book called *Yuuyaraq: The Way of the Human Being* (Napoleon, 1991), that was being used in Alaska Native policy making circles at the time. In *Yuuyaraq*, Harold Napoleon discussed how an epidemic referred to as yuut tuqurpallratni, "when a great many people died," devastated Yup'ik communities in the early 1900s, and how the epidemic and concurrent missionization led to intergenerational disruption, historical trauma, and contemporary issues in Yup'ik communities. Napoleon called on community members to use storytelling to break silences around histories of colonization, rebuild community, and assert self-determination with government agencies. Grant encouraged Leisy and youth to engage in the vision of self-determination discussed by Napoleon and other leaders in

Yuuyaraq (1991). At the same time, he advocated for recognizing the many ways that Yup'ik elders and families had continued to pass on central teachings and cultural practices, sharing joy and sustaining a rich Yup'ik way of life, in spite of the painful history and related forms of trauma portrayed. This early dialogue shaped many of our ongoing conversations about survivance—creative resistance and survival under hostile and challenging circumstances (Vizenor, 1994, 2008)—in years following.

Later, we co-authored a chapter reflecting on racial tensions we had observed among teachers, youth, and community members, and related power dynamics and forms of racism in the school where we had worked together, suggesting strategies that White teachers could use to develop respectful relationships with Yup'ik community members (Wyman & Kashatok, 2008). I (Grant) earned my teaching certificate and worked as a high school teacher. I then decided to become a principal because I wanted to show our kids that it doesn't take an outsider to make a difference. When outsiders come in, they often have a missionary attitude, that they're here to "save us." We can save ourselves. I (Leisy) went to graduate school to learn more about youth bilingualism/biliteracy and Indigenous languages. I was honored to work with community members to publish elders' teachings and stories in Yup'ik (Fredson et al., 1998), conduct engaged research on Yup'ik youth language development and linguistic survivance (Wyman, 2012), and collaborate on district language planning research (Wyman et al., 2010). As a White researcher, I continue to develop projects with Indigenous educational and Tribal leaders, seeking to apply decolonizing research frameworks, and cultivate relationships of respect, reciprocity, responsibility, and accountability (Brayboy et al., 2011) in work alongside Indigenous community members.

Over the decades, on our different pathways, we stayed in touch, sharing personal experiences starting families and raising children to young adulthood, and experiences from our work. From our different positionalities, we also continued to discuss Yuuyaraq, elders' traditional teachings and stories, youth development, school-based language planning, connections to land, and Native nation-building along the way. Below, we synthesize related research, before Grant connects these themes to his work with Yuuyaraq as a principal.

YUUYARAQ, YOUTH DEVELOPMENT, AND THE YUP'IK LANGUAGE

Yuuyaraq, the way of the human being and Yup'ik knowledge system. contains environmental knowledge and ways of teaching and learning that have enabled Yup'ik people to sustain their livelihoods in a unique subarctic environment for millenia (Barnhardt & Kawagley, 2005). Many Yupiit

(Yup'ik people) underscore the centrality of Yup'ik-speaking elders' oral traditions, pedagogical uses of traditional storywork (Archibald, 2008), and the Yup'ik language within Yuuyaraq.

As Yup'ik scholar Arevgaq Theresa John (2010) writes,

> Yuuyaraq is defined as...an absolute unified social web. This web is represented in our social infrastructures of kinship, health/physical and mental, form of prayer/rituals, spiritual enlightenment, leadership, and teasing. There is a relationship in storytelling genres in dance and oral stories that represent people's historical and contemporary accounts, describing their social, cultural, and subsistence lifestyle. (p. 3)

Yup'ik traditional knowledge involves a vast narrative repertoire, including detailed rules for living that children and others can master through a lifetime of listening (Fienup-Riordan, 2014, p. 96). Yup'ik elders emphasize how traditional teachings based in compassion and love can change human behavior, and the world from a Yup'ik epistemological standpoint that emphasizes the power of mind and teachings to push individuals to a good life (Fienup-Riordan, 2005). "The ancient Yup'ik traditional knowledge system was shared orally through qanruyutet (advice), qulirat (personal accounts and stories), and qanemcit (oral narratives)" in Yup'ik (John, 2010, p. 28). Qanruyutet also includes multiple genres that serve as "traditional educational frameworks" including, but not limited to, inerquutet (warnings about improper ways of living) and alerquutet (instructions and advice about proper ways of living; John, 2010, p. 52; Fienup-Riordan, 2005, 2010). The maintenance and resurgence of Yup'ik dancing, once banned by Moravian missionaries, serves as a related form of multimodal storytelling (John, 2010) and Yup'ik survivance.

Elders' teachings and stories in Yup'ik are often described as key means through which youth have traditionally acquired Yup'ik knowledge on views of subsistence, relationships, and knowledge of the environment within Yuuyaraq (Barnhardt & Kawagley, 2005; Fienup-Riordan, 2010; Wyman, 2012). The Yukon-Kuskokwim Delta, the Yup'ik homeland, is marked by abundance; many villagers participate in year-round subsistence practices. Residents of coastal villages (like Newtok) fish; hunt birds, seals, and walrus; and gather eggs, berries, and other tundra plants as important food sources. Adults share land pedagogies and curricula (Simpson, 2014), encouraging youth to observe, learn, and pitch in (cf. Paradise & Rogoff, 2009) alongside relatives practicing subsistence starting as young children. As youth take up increasing responsibilities over time, they develop interdependence with family and community members, sharing food, resources, and practices in a framework that supports relationships to one another and the environment. Community structures and expressive practices related to subsistence shape sociocultural processes that provide youth with "skills and knowledge important both for survival, and [. . .] the formation of meaning, identity, and cultural connection as a lived process" (Rasmus et al., 2014, p. 729). Sharing resources and strategies also "constitute resilience processes organized at the community and cultural level" that "build strengths and protection in young people and foster healthy and adaptive development" in Yup'ik youth (Rasmus et al., 2014, p. 729). As youth grow up participating in subsistence, they gain increasing awareness of Yup'ik perspectives of human development that underscore the importance of respectful, reciprocal relationships with elders, family, and community members, animals, the land, ella—the sentient universe, as well as the importance of working hard, being a good person and living a piniq (good, strong) life in a unique landscape. Many villagers also view subsistence as the more dependable part of mixed rural economies, and critique how media frames their lifeways as impoverished, offering counterstories of the richness of their subsistence way of life (Wyman, 2012; for related discussion see Ivanoff, 2016).

Discussions of Indigenous language survivance focus on "Indigenous languages as elements embedded in communities, histories, and spaces, rather than extracted from them" (Davis, 2017, p. 54). Yup'ik language expresses and reinforces Yuuyaraq in many ways. An elaborate demonstrative system, for instance, orients Yup'ik speakers and listeners to direction, shape and visibility, movement, accessibility, locations of objects in relation to slopes, rivers, sloughs, and bodies of water, and specific, related motion verbs (Charles, 2011; Woodbury, 1998; Wyman, 2012). Yup'ik terms relate ecological knowledge of plants, animals, land conditions, the atmosphere, and potential environmental risks like rotten ice (Reo et al., 2019). Yup'ik place names highlight notable environmental features, and historical experiences in particular places, while the enclitic-gguq (someone else says/said) can be used to quickly note when speakers are sharing teachings from previous generations (Fienup-Riordan, 2005; Woodbury, 1998). The Yup'ik language, and Yup'ik teachings and stories, also provide insight into ways that Yupiit (Yup'ik people) have maintained relationships and adapted to annual seasonal events and ecological changes historically (Climate and Traditional Knowledges Working Group, 2014).

Many young people's peer-directed practices further reinforce connections among Yuuyaraq, Yup'ik identities, and the Yup'ik language, as youth egmirte (pass on) ecological knowledge. In one study, for instance, I (Leisy) witnessed how youth used the Yup'ik language with one another in their everyday talk about subsistence. Stronger Yup'ik speakers used mostly Yup'ik and culturally specific hand gestures to share stories and things they were learning on the land. Even youth who referred to themselves as "losing their language" showed linguistic survivance—the use of Indigenous languages, communicative practices, and/or translanguaging to connect to community and express collective identities under challenging circumstances

(Wyman, 2012)—and sustained ties between Yup'ik language, subsistence, unique cultural identities, and ecological knowledge by using Yup'ik terms, discourse markers, names, and hand gestures, and subsistence-related prayers, in otherwise English subsistence stories and talk.

Regional youth leaders, such as Byron Nicholai of Tooksook Bay, demonstrate linguistic survivance as they share Yup'ik dancing and newer cultural forms like Yup'ik rap through social media, advocating for Yup'ik youth wellness and Yup'ik language and culture. Many Yup'ik youth also express interest in learning Yup'ik to communicate with elders and grandparents, participate in community life, and maintain Yup'ik for future generations (Charles, 2011; Wyman, 2012). Yup'ik youth and adults also seek, find, and share linguistic knowledge and stories of language learning on social media sites (Gilmore & Wyman, 2013) and in university classes (Charles, 2011).

Yup'iit have shown survivance by adapting and developing processes contributing to community growth under historical circumstances threatening their annihilation (Brayboy, 2005) ranging from epidemics and missionization, to oppressive language policies and boarding schools designed to destroy Yup'ik language, intergenerational relationships, ways of living, and village communities. In the 1960s, a landmark civil rights case ended the Alaskan boarding school era. Soon thereafter, village communities gained local high schools and Yup'ik bilingual elementary education programs (Gilmore & Wyman, 2013). Since the 1970s, the Lower Kuskokwim School District (LKSD) has sustained one of the longest-running attempts in the United States to offer school-based Indigenous language instruction. Yup'ik school district administrators and village language teachers have acted as educational language planners and policy makers, promoting Yup'ik language learning and Yup'ik/English bilingualism/biliteracy in community meetings, professional institutes, materials and assessments, elementary programs, and a secondary curriculum based in elders' teachings (McCarty et al., 2015; Siekmann et al., 2013; Wyman et al., 2010).

Through considerable language planning efforts, Yup'ik educators have made important spaces for Indigenous knowledge and language in schools. At the same time, ongoing educational injustices and instabilities related to the predominance of short-term, White principals and teachers (Lipka et al., 1998; Wyman & Kashatok, 2008), damaging assumptions about the possibilities and purposes of bilingualism (Wyman, 2012), state-imposed high stakes testing (Wyman et al., 2010), and the simultaneous adoption of Western curricula have continued to silence teachings that are central to Yup'iit people— such as predicting weather based on local observations—in educational institutions (Siekmann et al., 2013), and contribute to language shift. New media, and changes like increasing migration have placed additional pressures on the intergenerational sharing of oral traditions and efforts to maintain the Yup'ik language, even as Yupiit are using media to foster new spaces for intergenerational communication (Wyman, 2012). Many adults and youth have expressed concern that elders' talk and Yup'ik language learning opportunities have diminished over time, and are looking for ways to contribute to sustaining and revitalizing education (see McCarty & Lee, 2014).

Sustaining the Yup'ik knowledge and value system through the Yup'ik language is essential to Yup'ik leaders, as they draw on Yuuyaraq to self-govern, affirm their identities, foster important relationships, and guide community planning in a wide range of village and regional institutions, and use bilingualism/biliteracy to negotiate regulations and resources with outside agencies (Gilmore & Wyman, 2013). In ongoing negotiations over sovereignty and self-determination, Yup'ik people also maintain boundaries by choosing not to document or translate certain teachings and stories, to prevent outsiders from misappropriating Yup'ik knowledge or practices. In this chapter, we respect these boundaries.

Within this overall context, principals play important roles shaping possibilities for Indigenous education, linguistic survivance, opportunities for intergenerational communication and collective thinking, and Native nation-building in local schools. In the next section, Grant describes how he renewed the everyday sharing of Yuuyaraq, incorporating teachings and stories and sustaining Yup'ik language learning in morning meetings with students and others in Newtok.

RENEWING QANRUYUUTET AND CREATING SPACE FOR INTERGENERATIONAL LEARNING

Growing up in Kipnuk, Alaska, in the 1960s, our family didn't have amenities like books and television, so my mother told a lot of stories. These stories were important to teaching one how to listen and listen closely. We were instructed through the telling of inerquutet (warnings about improper ways of living), alerquutet (instructions and advice about proper ways of living), and qanruyuutet (advice) stories. Each morning, my parents would wake us up for school and give us some inerquutet or alerquutet for the day. They did this everyday as I was growing up. One premise or reason adults talk to kids is so that they know how to listen on a basic level. But also, when kids are talked to by parents, they know the parameters of acceptable behavior.

When I first got to Newtok, we didn't have any of the instructions being shared about Yuuyaraq. An aha moment for me came when I had a talk with my mom, and asked, "How come they don't talk to kids like they used to talk to them?" She was 80; after asking the question, I realized it's *my* turn to talk to the kids. She gave me all the speeches, now I have to do it. Youth need instruction daily, conditioning them to be able to listen to adults. Because some parents, especially our young parents, aren't providing this kind of instruction at home, when I became a principal here in Newtok, I decided we would provide Yuuyaraq guidance to these students, as my parents provided for me as I was growing up. I talked with Panigkaq Agatha John-Shields who was principal at Ayaprun Elitnaurvik, the Yup'ik immersion school located in Bethel, and the only other Yup'ik principal in LKSD at the time. Agatha shared how, at Ayaprun Elitnaurvik, they were structuring their morning meetings around inerquutet and alerquutet. I thought about how it connects with how we were raised, and we decided to do the same thing.

For years when I was principal in Newtok, we talked about inerquutet and alerquutet at school at the start of every school day in morning meetings with students. When I led the meetings, I used a poster by Loddie Jones, a respected veteran educator in LKSD who was one of the founders of the Ayaprun Elitnaurvik immersion school. Loddie's mother, a Yup'ik elder, was asked "What kind of children do you want?" The poster lists her response of Yup'ik values and I had it by the gym door. The poster covers Yup'ik themes related to survival, sharing food, respecting your elders, and others in Yup'ik. I chose weekly themes from the poster to make sure we covered the values and referenced the poster in the morning sessions.

When I talked, some elders would be there, and I tried to invite the whole community. We had some regulars that showed up, and they would talk to the kids about the weekly theme, as well. For example, one week was about survival. I shared a related teaching, and then somebody else would stand up and say, "This is what I know." Although we chose specific themes, the values and lessons were all related. Parents came to appreciate the way we regularly shared these teachings with youth; some even came to the school to hear the morning teachings.

TRADITIONAL STORIES, MISTUUQ LEARNING, AND CONNECTING THE DOTS

Traditionally, elders weren't expected to "spell out or theorize" meanings of stories; youth were expected to listen intently without interruption, assuming they would understand what they needed to learn from stories later, as "understanding and knowing occur over one's lifetime" (Mater, 1995, p. 33; see also Archibald, 2008; Meek, 2019). As each school year started in Newtok, I would stand up in front of veteran and new teachers to tell the string story about Tuvraq. Making and changing a figure similar to a cat's cradle to visually represent the story, I would start by explaining there are nukalpiaqs who provide food for their families and then there are Tuvraqs who provide for the whole village. I would make the Tuvraq figure. As the story continues, Tuvraq drops his qetrutni (belt) and takes off his alimatek (mittens), so he can do the work necessary to feed the whole village. What people don't realize is that the reason he is a great hunter is because he approaches his catch hiding himself behind a tree. The last figure in the string story is of the horizon with the tree and Tuvraq, with his catch in his hand. Where I grew up, you can see for many miles; the word for being able to see objects and people from afar is "mistuuq." I then share with teachers that mistuuq can also relate to experiences. What we do in our classrooms are going to be learning experiences which forever change our students.

In my morning sessions with students, I shared traditional stories, which require a different approach to learning and require another level of understanding, than listening to the direct teachings. One sometimes has to wait a long time to understand why a story was told to the audience. One of the stories I use with students is of tutgaraurluq (grandson). He becomes of age to go hunting on his own, so his grandmother made him a bow and arrow set. She instructs him to go out to the tundra and hunt, and specifically tells him, "Bring back what you catch!" Tutgaraurluq goes out and immediately catches a mouse. As he holds it up by the tail, he wonders how he and his grandmother are to share this for dinner. He decides it is too small and cooks and eats the mouse by himself. He then goes a little further and catches a muskrat and he eats that one, too. And on and on it goes—he catches a beaver, then a seal, then a bearded seal, a walrus then a whale! He decides to go back to the grandmother after catching a whale.

When Tutgaraurluq goes to his grandma's house, he realizes he has become a giant. The grandmother sees him and asks, "Is that you, Tutgaraurluq?" When he answers in the affirmative, his grandmother instructs him to jump through the window. The windows of past sod houses were in the center of a dome-like structure where the door always faced the sun. Even though he doesn't want to crush his grandmother, Tutgaraurluq climbs onto the house and jumps through the window. She is standing below the window holding out her needle with the eye showing. Tutgaraq falls through the eye of the needle and comes back to his normal size. All his catch falls out of him and the grandmother says, "What a great hunter you are!"

For years I listened to that story, never thinking about the many lessons embedded in it. My own mom never explained why she was telling the story. Traditionally, one is expected to reflect on the story over the course of many years to be able to take up the lessons embedded in it. The more I tell the story to youth, I realize I need to make sure I explain why the story is told. This is a quliraq (fantasy story) as opposed to a qanemciq (story based on facts). When the boy begins to not follow his grandmother's directions by not bringing his catch home, he becomes a monster. By following his grandmother's words to jump through the window and the eye of the needle, he becomes human again.

It is also a story about how boys grow up to be men. As children, when we first become aware of things, we only think about ourselves and do not worry too much about the family or the whole village. When we grow up, we have to come to terms with learning how to be a community member. There are many practices that Yup'ik community members use to stress related teachings. For example, we give our first catch from hunting to everyone in the community. All across the Yukon Kuskokwim Delta, when a boy or a girl catches their first catch, be it a seal or a moose, they share it with the whole town, with preference going to elders first, then the rest of the village. When asked why people do this, most people just say, "Because we've always done it that way!" The real reason is to teach the young boy about his place in the Yup'ik world. He has to learn to think of others, rather than just himself. This teaches the young hunter that you are part of a bigger picture. It's not all about you, it's about the community. When you think about the practice of giving away food, it is a survival practice that our ancestors developed in a harsh environment that allows people to help each other, especially elders, children without parents, and widows. We need practices that encourage people to help one another, and sharing food is a very Yup'ik practice that continues today.

As part of the *Alaska Step Progress Report*, my staff and I surveyed youth about the morning meetings. On the survey, one thing kids said they liked was how I told stories about a long time ago, since I explained, "This is why people do this, sharing food" or "This is how it's connected to the Yup'ik values."

Another story I use in talking to our students is about the blackfish as he swims up the river, singing a song:

> Avani avani avakakaarani yauvani taluyaruaqumta taluyapuut civluki aqsaagka nangugtagka tartugka nangugtagka ai—aluqi aluqi acimnek camaken tagyugci acimnek camken tagyugici aarraarrangemta naum nulian pilqiataq calqiataaq augalasiyugyaaqngamaa qiyauq qiyauq qauq panigavluarci yurayuvagtuuq panigavluarci yurayuvagtuuq.

> Over yonder, over yonder, somewhere over there, way over there, if we pretend to set up fish traps, our fish traps we would set them, stretch our stomachs, stretch our kidneys, come up underneath me, come up underneath me, where is your wife, that does things, wants to be someone, your daughter is a good dancer, your daughter is a good dancer.

When the blackfish comes upon a blackfish trap, the blackfish observes that some of the fish are dead and the trap is not a new one. Some of the wood on the trap is broken. In the first visit to a human community, it is trashy. The second time the blackfish visits, he sees a trap that is clean, so the blackfish chooses to be caught by the owner of that trap. The blackfish story underscores Yupik spiritual beliefs that animals offer themselves when they deem hunters worthy; hunters recognize the animals' offerings by taking and treating subsistence foods and by-products respectfully. Household members help ensure that animals return to offer themselves by treating others well, helping elders without pay, sharing subsistence foods with those in need, working hard, and treating their households with care (Lipka et al., 1998). The blackfish story also has environmental lessons embedded in it. The blackfish wants to be caught by people who keep their environment clean.

When I told stories, I explained to youth,

> When I was growing up, this is how it was told to me. And as Yup'ik thinkers, we are supposed to make the connection somehow, when we are ready for it. But since you guys (youth) are learning in this kass'aq (White) world, I am connecting the dots for you. We Yup'iit think way down the road, and all learning is mistuuq.

I have students think about how we are acting, and how all learning is mistuluni (coming clear from a distance). Another main lesson is that animals watch us, so if we want to catch a lot, we have to take care of our environment. When I explained the reasons for the stories and instructions, youth said they could see why their parents were telling them things.

STORYWORK AND LINGUISTIC SURVIVANCE IN SCHOOL

The "nature of survivance is unmistakable" in efforts to pass on "native stories . . . traditions and customs" Vizenor, 2008, p. 1; Kroskrity, 2012; Wyman, 2012), such as Grant and community members' efforts to socialize youth through use of elders' qanruyutet and stories. Schools can also "forge a space for the holistic development and well-being of Indigenous children by attending to their academic achievement through Indigenous languages, knowledge systems, and values" (Lee, 2016, p. 1) in contexts of language endangerment. In Newtok, I (Grant) always held our morning sessions in Yupik because the kids we taught are first language Yupik speakers. One of the things we were trying to do is support all kids so they know Yup'ik, and one reason we shared instructions in Yup'ik is to have a connection to language maintenance. It's essential to give these instructions in Yup'ik. We have to be able to hear the language for it to make sense. In our school, where everybody spoke Yup'ik and understood each other in English, if we tried to share lessons in English, we would lose a lot of meaning.

Newtok is one of a handful of Yup'ik villages where children come to school speaking predominantly Yup'ik; many youth in other villages enter school speaking mostly or only English (Wyman et al., 2010). Sharing traditional Indigenous stories in English, however, typically results in "weak translations" that lose meaning, humor, and artistic expression (Archibald, 2008). While many cultural aspects transfer across languages, it can also be difficult to translate words in Indigenous languages that invoke ways of life, and key perspectives on how to be in caring, kin-like relationships with others (Lee, 2016; Lyons, 2010). "The continuity of intricate, complex, delicately tuned, deeply interwoven systems," like Yup'ik demonstratives can be disrupted in language shift (Woodbury, 1998, p. 256), causing intergenerational miscommunication (Wyman, 2012). Talented Yup'ik educators like Walkie Charles of the University of Alaska-Fairbanks are renewing these systems through Yup'ik language instruction. This kind of language reclamation takes careful work drawing on insider understandings of Indigenous lifeways, young peoples' situations, and Indigenous homelands (Charles, 2011).

Bringing Indigenous teachings and stories in Indigenous languages into schools involves other kinds of "radical translation," as well, since the storytelling purpose, teller/audience relationships, and authoritative structures shaping the storytelling event differ from a more traditional storytelling setting. "Ideologies of language, ways of evaluating storytelling"—and, often, accompanying assumptions about learning—"differ and must be negotiated as stories are recontextualized in new spaces (Nevins & Nevins, 2012, p. 143). Adults may encounter complexities using teachings in Yup'ik to foster intergenerational relationships and understanding, given different epistemologies in Indigenous knowledge systems and Westernized school systems, the presence of non-Indigenous teachers, and/or intergenerational and sociolinguistic changes in Yup'ik communities. While youth themselves may understand Yup'ik teachings as "coming from a place of care, respect, responsibility, and kinship" and respond positively, non-Yup'ik educators may misunderstand Indigenous teachings as "scolding in nature" (Lee, 2016). One White principal, for instance, told me (Leisy) that youth where he worked were "beaten down." The youth he referenced, in contrast, proudly told me that youth and adults in their village were inerquq—disciplined, and how they appreciated the strong, positive influence of elders' talk on their community. They also described how some of their most confident and respected peer leaders were takaryuk—respectful and attentive towards adults and elders (Wyman, 2012). As Theresa Arevgaq John (2010) explains:

> To inerquq a person is to give him or her advice about an action that needs to be changed. The core focus is on people who need guidance and direction in life. For example, when a youth or an adult breaks the qanruyutet or traditional values and principles, a local expert will approach that individual and set him or her aside in private to address the behavior that needs to be changed. The rule is not to embarrass the person but to kindly point out his or her weaknesses in life. (p. 54)

In the village above, multiple youths expressed appreciation for this care and concern and described elders' regular teachings as a source of community strength. One young mother told me (Leisy) how grateful she was that elders talked with youth, noting, "People here respect their elders, and elders talk to their young, their kids or their grandchildren, and not just leave them alone." Young hunters also described reciprocal relationships in interviews, talking about helping elders with chores without pay, and how elders shared their "good gifts" and "power of mind" to help them with hunting success and a piniq (good/strong) life (Wyman, 2012).

As people wrestled with language shift to English, however, some parents noted how young children were misinterpreting inerquutet and alerquutet. One father commented in an interview,

> I try to pass them (the inerquutet) on, but when we talk to them, they think we are angry at them, from the tone of voice and the facial expression. They misunderstand that, and they'll say, "Daddy-m nunuraanga (scolded me)," when we tell 'em not to do this or that. My grandma said a person will only give advice if they love that person. [...] Even if we inerquq our children, they think nunuryukluteng (we are scolding them).

In another study, Yup'ik educators noted how "Yup'ik has strong empathy built into it," but how, in language shift, "If you pay attention to it, you'll see that students' behavior changes. You know, they lose sense of their awareness... their sense of how to present themselves" (Wyman et al., 2010, p. 29). I (Grant) have seen how, even when children speak Yup'ik, kids may think they are being nunuq'd (scolded) when they are talked to, if they don't hear instructions regularly at home.

Oral traditions and stories can serve as "vehicles of cultural and linguistic reproduction" in communities working to maintain languages and cultural values in language shift/endangerment, even as youth may need assistance making sense of community and language-specific ways of sharing and denoting collective wisdom (Kroskrity, 2012, pp. 13, 16). In communities working through dynamics of language shift, endangerment, and renewal, adults may need to adjust communicative practices to help youth understand Yup'ik teachings and stories in ancestral languages. In one Yup'ik village where students had wide-ranging Yup'ik skills, a White principal hired an elder consultant to support youth, after a school shooting elsewhere in the region. Yup'ik educators pointed out to me (Leisy) how the elder was particularly good at adjusting his Yup'ik language use for students' various ages and language abilities, using simplified Yup'ik to help youth with lower Yup'ik levels, as he regularly talked to students about the past, historical changes, and shared inerquutet and alerquutet. Students, teachers, and staff strongly praised how the elder's efforts supported youth well-being and improved the school climate (Wyman, 2012). It is also notable that Grant got the idea to share inerquutet and alerquutet in school from a Yup'ik principal who used qanruyutet with students in a well-regarded immersion school for children entering school as non-Yup'ik speakers.

These examples show how educators may need to pay close attention to young peoples' comprehension as they share storywork in Indigenous languages with Indigenous language learners. Nevertheless, they underscore how storywork can produce powerful results in schools for youth with varying Indigenous language competencies, including beginning language learners.

PRINCIPALS, EDUCATORS, AND LINGUISTIC SURVIVANCE

Principals are important on-the-ground policy makers in Yup'ik-serving schools, given their influence over the ideologies, interactional norms, policies, programs, hiring processes, teaching assignments, and accountability systems that provide, or undercut, resources for Indigenous language learners. In the early 2000s, multiple LKSD village principals were undermining historic Yup'ik language programs as they interpreted high stakes assessments in relation to damaging language ideologies, guided community meetings, and distributed program resources (Wyman et al., 2010). Another village study showed how a White principal's historic push to cut back bilingual education, and years of subsequent principal turnover, maintained linguistic hierarchies and damaging assumptions about bilingualism in school, complicating school-based language planning efforts, and contributing to family language shift (Wyman, 2012). After these studies, LKSD worked to educate principals about bilingual education, and the importance of Yup'ik. Research in Nunavut, Canada has shown how Inuit principals can positively influence Indigenous language programs, assessments, ideologies, and interactions; broaden opportunities for learning and sharing Indigenous teachings; support efforts to coordinate culturally responsive curriculum across classrooms; offer key professional development opportunities for Indigenous and non-Indigenous school personnel; and engage elders and parents in schooling (Tulloch et al., 2016). In 13 years, however, Grant was one of only three Yup'ik principals in 27 schools in the district. Individual White principals in LKSD have supported Yup'ik as a social and/or academic resource in schools. It is rare, though, for principals to understand what is happening in Yup'ik language programs, let alone to have the cultural sensitivity, experience, and knowledge needed to connect entire schools to Yuuyaraq, and deep collective thinking about survival, adaptation, and the future through storywork and the Yup'ik language. In 2017, Grant commented,

> Whenever I leave my job eventually, I'll probably be replaced by a kass'aq (White) principal. When he or she comes in and tries to talk about specific understandings of Yup'ik values, will he or she know as much as I do? No, I think it would be very hard for him or her. We have stories I grew up with, verbal and other kinds of stories, like string stories. Specific elders also told

stories that I pass on. If you didn't grow up with those things, and tried to share them in English, the message wouldn't be quite the same. To really help youth understand... It's a unique place in the world where we are, and there are a lot of things the kids are learning from me that they are familiar with. The weak link is when you only hear English and don't know Yup'ik terms to really get the message.

However, from my perspective (Grant), I wouldn't want to glamorize my experience trying to support the sharing of Yup'ik teachings, or to say, "In order for language survivance and so forth, it won't work unless there is a Yup'ik principal." It certainly makes it strong, but that would be taking away from teachers across LKSD. While we have discussed Grant's work to highlight the influence of principals in school-based Indigenous education, Yup'ik teachers' efforts were also essential for teaching and learning throughout Grant's time in Newtok. Educators extended the learning taking place in Grant's morning sessions that emphasized youth listening to adults, for instance, by supporting young people's Yup'ik speaking and literacy development in their classes. Grant and Newtok teachers' collective work also underscored how schools can promote Indigenous language and culture within a rigorous curriculum that prepares youth to be tribal citizens who enter higher education and enact self-determination and sovereignty (McCarty & Lee, 2015). During the years I (Grant) was principal, before recently retiring, the high school graduation rate went up dramatically, as did numbers of high school youth attending competitive math and science programs and college attendance. Every year, LKSD youth filled out a school climate and connectedness survey; looking at data across LKSD, our figures were a lot higher than some other schools.

From the start of LKSD's bilingual programs, Yup'ik teachers have been key language planners, pushing back on Westernized schooling to make space for Yuuyaraq and Yup'ik language learning. They have learned from one another's efforts in classrooms, village schools, and summer institutes. Even in cases where they have lacked or only seen partial support from principals, many have come up with innovative ways to engage youth and/or community members in language planning and renewal (Siekmann et al., 2013; Wyman et al., 2010). They have also shown how Indigenous educators can attend to the "multilingualistic 'vitalities' emerging from the mouth—and hands—of children"; "think about implications for language pedagogy and curriculum, evaluation and assessment" (Meek, 2019, p. 108); and take action to support Indigenous knowledge and language in schools.

Another Newtok example shows how visiting Indigenous artists, as well, can serve as influential educators, using school spaces to support intergenerational storywork, multilingualistic vitalities, and rhetorical sovereignty through cultural performance. Newtok community members endured almost two decades of increasing erosion, storm surges, deteriorating infrastructure, and related public health issues, while a Newtok planning group worked through complex and challenging negotiations with 25 government agencies, tribal groups, and nongovernment agencies (Cochran et al., 2014). As the community's situation grew increasingly dangerous, reporters from multiple media outlets also descended on the village of 400, to get global warming crisis stories from youth and adults in English.

Given how many media folk came to Newtok, I (Grant) saw how people didn't want to be interviewed, and how the media spotlight brought additional stress to community members. But one play called *Before the Land Eroded We Were Here* was different. A team of Alaska Native and Indigenous writers and artists came to Newtok to learn what it was like for community members to have to move to the new village site of Mertarlik, and get a sense of community members' lives during this time. The artists asked students to translate and deliver an invitation to community members to come share their experiences. Youth initially got no responses from community members. The playwrights asked students how they translated the invitation, "What are you saying? How come we have zero community members coming to participate?" The invitation was in Yup'ik, but youth were using the word for "interview." Community members said, "No, we are not going to be interviewed." When the playwrights and students shifted to ask community members, "Tell us some stories," people started coming to school, sharing historical stories, and personal observations and experiences in Yup'ik. Martha Kassaiuli, a youth who was in the first group of community members to lose their homes and relocate, had written poems about what it was like to live next to the eroding river, seeing waves crashing into the shore, getting really close to her house, reflecting on her fears, hopes, and the power of the land. The playwrights integrated community members' stories and Martha's poetry into the script. In the play, Newtok youth acted out the perspectives of community members and animals like taryaqvuk (king salmon), read Martha's poems, and danced traditional Yup'ik dances, singing stanzas in Yup'ik and English. The students performed the play in Newtok and Anchorage to packed audiences, receiving strong and emotional positive responses. The young performers ended the play by declaring in unison, "We were here, we are here, we will be here" (Estus, 2020).

By connecting to Indigenous knowledge, language, and modes of inquiry to cultural performance, artists created the conditions for community members to determine their communicative needs and desires; shape the modes and languages of public discourse (Lyons, 2010); and affirm holistic and enduring relationships to humans, animals, and land. In our final section, we revisit Grant's morning sessions, to consider ways that centering Yup'ik storywork, language, and critical Indigenous pedagogy in schools can support the kinds of deep relationships, frameworks, and institutional changes that are key for strategic climate change adaptation.

YUUYARAQ, CRITICAL INDIGENOUS PEDAGOGY, AND CLIMATE CHANGE ADAPTATION

Indigenous leadership, knowledge systems, and languages in schooling are especially important, as Indigenous Peoples "become aware of, understand, prepare for, and adapt to climate impacts" (CTKW, 2014; Wildcat, 2014; Whyte, 2019). Recent scholarship stresses the need to base climate change science and solutions on Indigenous and Western knowledge systems (Barnhardt & Kawagley, 2005), and how Indigenous knowledge systems can provide an important ethical framework that can complement Western earth science and guide climate change adaptation (Cochran et al., 2014). As communities identify and solve local issues critical for self-reliance, (Cochran et al., 2014), the "practical and philosophical traditions" in Indigenous storywork also illuminate the "fabric of relational qualities" that create kin-like relationships centered in "high levels of trust, strong standards of consent, and genuine expectations of reciprocity" (Whyte, 2019, p. 5). Such kin-like relationships are key for fostering "mutual responsibility in coordinated action," as communities seek just, culturally informed solutions for addressing urgent demands and losses of climate change adaptation (Whyte, 2019, p. 5).

From a Yup'ik perspective, "environmental change is directly related not just to human action—overfishing, burning fossil fuels—but also to human *interaction*" (Fienup-Riordan, 2010, p. 69). A common saying in the Yup'ik region is, "The weather/nature follows its people." If the people become complacent in their teachings, and related actions, then the weather is going to become bad. Through our (Grant's) morning meetings, we tried to make that connection with the students, to have them pass this on to their kids, when they become parents. Newtok is greatly affected by climate change, and it's quite prominent in our kids' minds that the land is sinking. There's no more permafrost. We are seeing new species of insects, birds, and some fish. The kids and people are witnessing that and other changes occurring.

During my time as principal, Mary George, an elder, commonly got on the radio, reminding people in Newtok that we need to take care of the land because the land takes care of us. The worse we get at not listening to alerquutet and inerquutet, the more the environment will follow its people. In school, we mostly talked about global warming in reference to what we heard growing up. When we were growing up, elders would say that there will come a time when winter will not seem like winter anymore. And it's been true in recent years. In 2016, for example, we still had open water about five miles down the river from us in December, when traditionally the river would freeze up in October. We had 4 to 5 months of crossable ice on the river, instead of 6 months. Only 4 months! One spring it was so warm we had our river ice break up by April 30, instead of close to June. Our discussions about climate change from a Yup'ik lens in morning meetings helped the students get a perspective on all of that.

Reviewing the impacts of climate change on multiple Indigenous Peoples in the United States and Indigenous perspectives and visions of climate change adaptation, Wildcat (2013) underscores how

> the first peoples of this land understood something scientists and policy makers need to understand, now more than ever, if humankind is to sustainably address the incredible negative climate change impacts facing not only tribes but all of humankind on this Mother Earth—sustainability requires the recognition and restoration of reciprocal relationships between people and places. (p. 514)

To solve intense environmental problems of global warming, Yup'ik "elders maintain that we need to do more than change our actions, e.g., efforts to reduce by-catches and carbon emissions. We need to correct our fellow humans" (Fienup-Riordan, 2010, p. 69).

As an educational leader serving a community impacted by environmental injustice and facing increasing environmental threats, Grant used Yupik teachings to foster a space where Yup'ik youth could access deep Yup'ik beliefs about the connections among humans, animals, the land, and ella—the universe. In Grant's daily practice of sharing inerquutet and alerquutet and quliraat in Yup'ik, he moved far beyond commonplace, narrow definitions of parental or community school involvement to one of critical engagement by creating a dialogic space in school where Yup'ik educators and community members could share lived experiences, and discuss Yup'ik values, teachings, cultural continuity, survivance, and renewal in the face of imminent dislocation. By placing current events within a Yup'ik worldview, Grant framed challenges and offered guiding principles for students moving forward, raising young people's awareness of Yup'ik epistemologies and beliefs about the importance of human–human, human–animal, and human–land relationships, and the ways in which "one's actions elicit reactions in a responsive world" (Fienup-Riordan, 2014, p. 96).

Simultaneously, Grant created opportunities for Newtok Indigenous and non-Indigenous educators to engage notions of critical Indigenous pedagogy. "Critical Indigenous pedagogy provides a lens for teachers to examine the history as well as the current social, ecological, health, and political issues facing Indigenous communities with students" engaging "issues of survivance (Vizenor, 1994) which draws upon Indigenous sources for guidance" (Garcia & Shirley, 2012, p. 89). Importantly, by inviting elders and other adults to share observations and Yup'ik views of survival, weather changes and extreme weather events in their Indigenous language, Grant made space for community members to make sense of the present and discuss climate change adaptation from "collective histories of having to be well-organized to adapt to environmental change," and the disruptions of "colonialism, capitalism, and industrialization" (Whyte, 2017, p. 154).

CONCLUSION

"Indigenous languages are linked to the epistemologies that guide the identity formations of Indigenous Peoples and are the means to deeply understanding and becoming a people" (this volume, p. xxix). "Indigenous language revitalization movement(s) happening around the world" are also "an attempt by Native peoples to assert rhetorical sovereignty" (Lyons, 2010, p. 139) as they "seek paths to agency and power and community renewal" (Lyons, 2000, p. 449). There are multiple ways that Indigenous leaders, educators, and allies can address the challenges of our times, honoring Indigenous teachings, stories, languages, expression, and dialogue, making intergenerational space for community members to share their experiences, in their own voices, on their own terms. Above, we have shown how Grant and other educators in the Yup'ik region have actively worked to support Yuuyaraq—the Yup'ik way of life, fostering positive youth development and sustaining the Yup'ik language, while helping youth understand challenges facing their communities and access Indigenous educational frameworks and relationships needed for climate change adaptation.

As we shared, leaders may need to negotiate layers of complexities as they seek to use Indigenous knowledges to support youth in communities facing historical disruptions in knowledge sharing, language shift/endangerment, and/or dramatic climate change. Using oral narratives in institutions like schools also relies on the efforts and judgment of experienced linguistic and cultural brokers like Grant who can draw upon life experiences, relationships, deep familiarity with Indigenous knowledge systems and epistemologies, and knowledge of contemporary institutions to frame stories in meaningful ways with youth. As Indigenous genres, epistemologies and approaches to youth development come up against dominant societal ways of talking with youth, Indigenous educators and parents may need to address changing interactional norms to renew the emotional framing of teachings like inerquutet, so youth interpret these as genres of care, concern, and love. They also need to take into account young people's previous experiences with Indigenous storywork, community-based developmental processes, and language learning.

Many examples in the Yup'ik region raise deep questions about ways that Yup'ik educational leadership, teacher preparation, and school-based instruction might be organized to support survivance and rhetorical sovereignty in language planning, governance, and Indigenous climate change adaptation. Relationships of trust, accountability, and reciprocity are crucial for fostering just, urgent, collective action in the face of pressing challenges like language endangerment and global climate change. These kinds of relationships also take time and concerted effort to develop in institutions like public schools that have been tools of colonialism, and resistant to Indigenous transformation (Whyte, 2019). Nevertheless, Indigenous Peoples are showing how centering schooling on Indigenous relationships and languages can foster Indigenous youth wellness, academic success, and language revitalization (Lee, 2016; McCarty & Lee, 2015). Our examples further demonstrate how Indigenous principals, elders, and educators can meet youth "where they are at" in a deeply self–reflective praxis that underscores Indigenous knowledge, language, family, and community, youth well-being, learning, expression, and connections to the environment.

The Yup'ik leaders and educators above are modeling survivance and fostering positive youth development. They are also developing sacred landscapes in schools and community institutions that "promote and privilege Indigenous knowledge" and "guide Indigenous students in the critical process of promoting, protecting and preserving Indigenous languages, cultures, land and people" (Garcia & Shirley, 2012, p. 89) in the face of deep sociolinguistic and ecological challenges. Finding new ways to draw upon Yup'ik knowledge, teachings, stories, epistemologies, language, and histories of survivance and adaptation, they are asserting sovereignty and laying the groundwork for Native nation-building in the present and into the future.

ACKNOWLEDGMENTS

We are thankful to Yup'ik ancestors, elders, educators, parents, and youth who have shared their wisdom, and Qussauyaq Katie Kashatok for sharing her teachings and stories with Grant and others. We are also grateful to Jeremy Garcia, Valerie Shirley, and Hollie Kulago for their invitation to participate in this volume, and critical insights, encouragement, and patience. To Perry Gilmore, shared mentor and friend, we express our deepest thanks, as well.

IN MEMORY OF GRANT

Grant unexpectedly passed away shortly before publication of this chapter. Revisiting these pages brings great heaviness, along with boundless gratitude for Grant's friendship and generosity, and our dialogues over the decades. In addition to his love of Yuuyaraq and comments on climate change, Grant was known for his brilliant, active mind and his commitment to Indigenous education. It is easy to imagine how Grant would have eagerly engaged and appreciated the rich array of ideas, offerings, insights, and guiding directions from Indigenous contributors in this book, which he was proud to be part of. I am grateful to the editors for providing the impetus and space for Grant to share some of the perspectives, stories, and practices that he viewed as being central to his efforts, in a life dedicated to youth, families, communities, human and more-than-human relations, and education in the Yup'ik homelands. Grant's positive influence on generations of Yup'ik youth lives on, even as a great many deeply miss Grant's stories, insights, generous actions, wry comments, teasing, jokes, and laughter. I take heart in the ways that Yup'ik and other Indigenous educational leaders, knowledge keepers, practitioners, communities, families, and youth are moving forward.

REFERENCES

Archibald, J. (2008). *Indigenous storywork: Educating the heart, mind, body, and spirit.* UBC Press.

Barnhardt, R., & Kawagley, O. (2005). Indigenous knowledge systems and Alaska Native ways of knowing. *Anthropology and Education Quarterly, 36*(1), 8–23.

Brayboy, B. (2005). Toward a Tribal critical race theory in education. *The Urban Review, 37*(5), 425–446.

Brayboy, B. M. J., Gough, H. R., Leonard, B., Roehl, R. F. H., & Solyom, J. A. (2012). Reclaiming scholarship: Critical Indigenous research methodologies. In S. D. Lapan, M. T. Quartaroli, & F. J. Riener (Eds.), *Qualitative research: An introduction to methods and designs* (pp. 425–450). Jossey-Bass.

Charles, W. (2011). *Dynamic assessment in a Yugtun second language intermediate adult classroom* (Unpublished doctoral dissertation). University of Alaska-Fairbanks.

Climate and Traditional Knowledges Workgroup. (2014). *Guidelines for considering traditional knowledge in climate change initiatives.* http://climatetkw.wordpress.com/

Cochran, P., Huntingon, O., Pungowiyi, C., Tom, S., Chapin, F. S., Huntingon, H., Maynard, N., & Trainor, S. (2014). Indigenous frameworks for observing and responding to climate change in Alaska. In J. Maldonado, R. Pandya, & B. Colombi (Eds.), *Climate change and Indigenous Peoples in the United States* (pp. 49–60). Springer.

Davis, J. (2017). Resisting rhetorics of language endangerment through Indigenous language survivance. In W. Leonard & H. Korne (Eds.), *Language documentation and description, vol 14* (pp. 37–58). El Publishing.

Estus, J. (2020). Climate change as art: 'My culture in beautiful...I am glad I am Yup'ik'. *Indian Country Today.* https://indiancountrytoday.com/news/climate-change-as-art-my-culture-is-beautiful-im-glad-i-am-yupik

Fienup-Riordan, A. (2005). *Wise words of the Yup'ik people: We talk to you because we love you.* University of Nebraska Press.

Fienup-Riordan, A. (2010). Yup'ik perspectives on climate change: "The world is following its people." *Etudes Inuits/Inuit Studies, 34*(1), 55–70.

Fienup-Riordan, A. (2014). Linking local and global: Yup'ik elders working together with one mind. *Polar Geography, 37*(1), 92–109.

Fredson, A., Mann, M. J., Dock E., & Wyman, L. (Eds.). (1998). *Kipnermiut tiganrita igmirtitlrit: Qipnermiut tegganrita egmirtellrit [The legacy of the Kipnuk elders]*. Alaska Native Language Center.

Garcia, J., & Shirley, V. (2012). Performing decolonization: Lessons learned from Indigenous youth, teachers and leaders' engagement with critical Indigenous pedagogy. *Journal of Curriculum Theorizing, 28*(2), 76–91.

Gilmore, P., & Wyman, L. (2013). An ethnographic long look: Language and literacy over time in Alaska Native communities. In K. Hall, T. Cremin, B. Comber, & L. Moll (Eds.), *International handbook of research on children's literacy, learning and culture* (pp. 121–138). Wiley-Blackwell Publishers.

Ivanoff, L. (2016, November 6). Why can't media portray the rural Alaska I know? *Anchorage Daily News*. https://www.adn.com/alaska-life/we-alaskans/2016/11/05/why-cant-media-portray-the-rural-alaska-i-know/

John, T. (2010). *Yuraryararput kangiit-llu: Our ways of dance and their meanings* (Unpublished doctoral dissertation). University of Alaska, Fairbanks.

Kashatok, G. (2017). Interviewed in "What it's like to live in a place being erased by climate change." *NBC News*. https://www.nbcnews.com/feature/flashback/video/newtok-alaska-is-relocating-due-to-climate-change-what-it-s-like-to-live-there-1083635779757

Kroskrity, P. (2012). *Telling stories in the face of danger: Language renewal in Native American communities*. University of Oklahoma Press.

Lee, T. (2016). The home–school–community interface in revitalization in the USA and Canada. In S. Colonel-Molina & T. L. McCarty (Eds.), *Indigenous language revitalization in the Americas*. Routledge.

Lipka, J., Mohatt, G., & the Ciulestet Group. (1998). *Transforming the culture of schools: Yup'ik Eskimo examples*. Lawrence Erlbaum Associates.

Lyons, S. (2000). Rhetorical sovereignty: What do American Indians want from writing? *College Compass and Communication, 51*(3), 447–468.

Lyons, S. (2010). There's no translation for it: The rhetorical sovereignty of Indigenous languages. In B. Horner, M. Lou, & P. Kei (Eds.), *Cross language relations in composition* (pp. 127–141). Southern Illinois University Press.

McCarty, T. L., & Lee, T. S. (2015). The role of schools in Native American language and culture revitalization: A vision of linguistic and educational sovereignty. In W. J. Jacob, S. Y. Cheng, & M. Porter (Eds.), *Indigenous education: Language, culture, and identity* (pp. 341–360). Springer.

McCarty, T. L., Nicholas, S. E., & Wyman, L. T. (2015). 50(0) years out and counting: Native American language education and the four r's. *International Multilingual Research Journal, 9*(4), 227–252.

Meek, B. (2019). Language endangerment in childhood. *Annual Review of Anthropology, 48*, 95–115.

Menken, K., & Garcia, O. (2010). *Negotiating language policies in schools: Educators as policymakers*. Routledge.

Napoleon, H. (1991). *Yuuyaraq: The way of the human being*. Center for Cross Cultural Studies, University of Alaska Fairbanks.

Nevins, M. E., & Nevins, T. J. (2012). They don't know how to ask: Pedagogy, storytelling, and the ironies of language endangerment on the White Mountain

Apache reservation. In P. Kroskrity (Ed.), *Telling stories in the face of danger: Language renewal in Native American communities.* University of Oklahoma Press.

Paradise, R., & B. Rogoff. (2009). Side by side: Learning by observing and pitching in. *ETHOS, 37*(1), 102–138.

Rasmus, S., Allen, J., & Ford, T. (2014). "Where I have to learn the ways how to live": Youth resilience in a Yup'ik village in Alaska. *Transcultural Psychiatry, 5*(5), 713–734.

Reo, N. J., Topkok, S. M, Kanayurak, N., Stanford, J., Peterson, D., & L. Whaley. (2019). Environmental change and sustainability of Indigenous languages in Northern Alaska. *Arctic, 72*(3), 215–228.

Richardson, J. (2011). On the edge, in the center. *Phi Delta Kappan, 92*(6), 4.

Siekmann, S., Thorne, S. L., Arevgaq John, T., Andrew, B., Nicolai, M., Moses, C., Lincoln, R., Oulton, C., Samson, S., Westlanke, J., Miller, G., Winkelman, V., Nicholai, R., & Bass, S. (2013). Supporting Yup'ik medium education: Progress and challenges in a university–school collaboration. In S. May (Ed.), *LED2011: Refereed conference proceedings of the 3rd International Conference on Language, Education and Diversity* (pp. 1–25). The University of Auckland.

Simpson, L. (2014). Land as pedagogy: Nichnaabeg intelligence and rebellious transformation. *Decolonization: Indigeneitty, Education & Society, 3*(3), 1–25.

Tulloch, S., Metuq, L., Hainnu, J., Pitsiulak, S., Flaherty, E., Lee, C., & Walton, F. (2016). Inuit principals and the changing context of bilingual education in Nunavut. *Etudes Inuit Studies, 40*(1), 189–209.

Vizenor, G. (2008). Aesthetics of survivance: Literary theory and practice. In G. Vizenor (Ed.), *Survivance: Narratives of native presence* (pp. 1–23). University of Nebraska Press.

Whyte, K. (2014). Justice forward: Tribes, climate change and responsibility. In J. Maldonado, R. Pandya, & B. Colombi (Eds.), *Climate change and Indigenous Peoples in the United States* (pp. 9–22). Springer.

Whyte, K. (2017). Indigenous climate change studies: Indigenizing futures, decolonizing the Anthropocene. *English Language Notes, 55*(1–2), 153–162.

Whyte, K. (2019). Too late for Indigenous climate justice: Ecological and relational tipping points. *WIREs Climate Change* 2020e11: e603

Wildcat, D. (2014). Introduction: Climate change and indigenous Peoples of the USA. In J. Maldonado, R. Pandya, & B. Colombi (Eds.), *Climate change and Indigenous Peoples in the United States* (pp. 1–7). Springer.

Woodbury, A. (1998). Documenting rhetorical, aesthetic, and expressive loss in language shift. In L. Grenoble & L. Whaley (Eds.), *Endangered languages: Current issues and future prospects* (pp. 234–258). Cambridge University Press.

Wyman, L. (2012). *Youth culture, language endangerment and linguistic survivance.* Multilingual Matters.

Wyman, L., & Kashatok, G. (2008). Getting to know the communities of your students. In M. Pollock (Ed.), *Everyday antiracism: Getting real about race in school* (pp. 299–304). New Press.

Wyman, L., Marlow, P., Andrew, C. F., Miller, G., Nicholai, C. R., & Reardon, Y. N. (2010). Focusing on long-term language goals in challenging times: Yup'ik examples. *Journal of American Indian Education, 49*(1/2), 22–43.

CHAPTER 11

HOPILAVAYIT AW NAA'AYA'TIWQAM, THOSE WHO HAVE CHOSEN TO ATTEND TO THE HOPI LANGUAGE

Storying "The Making of an Indigenous Language Teacher"

Bernita Duwahoyeoma
Ada Curtis
Sheilah E. Nicholas

Siwivensi:

I had already decided to become an educator as early as 5 to 6 years old and played school with my playmates. I remember spanking them across the hand in imitation of my teacher in my first year of public school. I didn't know then that this was *qahopi*, not Hopi.

Indigenizing Education, pages 153–181
Copyright © 2022 by Information Age Publishing
www.infoagepub.com
All rights of reproduction in any form reserved.

Somi'mana:

At or around 7 and 8 years old, I started imitating the teachers I had in school. I enjoyed playing school with my peers. I would be the teacher but with my limited English, I used a ruler to basically be an authoritative figure. I held up the ruler to get their attention. I loved it when they listened.

Qötsahonmana:

At age 6 or 7, I was playing teacher using a transportable chalkboard/desk I would set up under a mulberry tree not far from my house. I don't recall who my students were—probably my cousins who were also my playmates.

Cajete (2015), in *Indigenous Community: Rekindling the Teachings of the Seventh Fire,* writes, "Very little has been written about how contemporary Native people have come into our *Indigenous selves* (emphasis added) through the work that we do. This is particularly true of Indigenous educators" (p. 1). Furthermore, Blair et al. (2003) point out that "limited attention has been paid to the preparation of bilingual and biliterate teachers" (p. 93). Both perspectives have particular application to Indigenous language teacher-educators. As co-authors, in this chapter, we reflect on our personal and professional trajectories and explore "how we came to where we are" in identifying as *Hopilavayit aw naa'ayatiwqam.* Those who have chosen to attend to the Hopi language. Interestingly, our opening reflections reveal that each of us had embarked on a journey into the teaching profession early in our lives (ages 5 to 7). Immediately noteworthy in our case is that while we charted separate and distinct trajectories, we would in due course, come together on a collective path toward finding our "true vocation" (Cajete, 2015, p. 1) in Indigenous/Hopi language revitalization.

Forty-eight years as a classroom teacher with 4 years as a Hopi language and culture teacher, Siwivensi has been locally situated in our home community of Hopi; for Somi'mana, 10 years of her journey would take her to a bilingual program serving Hispanic English language learners in Pennsylvania; and Qötsahonmana, whose teaching experiences began as a Peace Corps volunteer in Jamaica, West Indies followed with a 30+ teaching career in the Tucson, Arizona area. Our paths converged in Summer 2004 at the Hopi tribe's Hopilavayi Summer Institute, a historic initiative to provide Hopi language teachers professional development for school-based Hopi language and culture programs.

Qötsahonmana, as a consultant to the Hopi tribe's Hopilavayi Program forged a partnership with the University of Arizona's (UA) American Indian Studies Program (AISP) to assist in the Institute design and implementation.[1] In its inaugural year, 2004, she and Emory Sekaquaptewa, *Poliwisiwma,* offered two university credit-bearing courses titled, "Introduction to Indigenous Language Revitalization/Oral Immersion Methodology" and

"Basic Hopi Language Literacy Development," respectively.[2] This tribally sponsored initiative drew interest from teacher assistants employed in local K–6/8 schools whose positions included the responsibility of teaching Hopi language and culture classes, Head Start teachers, and certified classroom teachers with an interest in integrating the Hopi language into their classroom curriculum. At the time, Siwivensi and Somi'mana were certified classroom teachers in the same local community school. Siwivensi reflected that she was spurred to apply for the institute in order to pursue a long-held aspiration to learn to write and read Hopilavayi so that she could write children's books for Hopi children. Somi'mana had recently returned to Hopi from Pennsylvania and desired to explore a bilingual approach to teaching Hopi children. The institute participants were all proficient Hopi language speakers but did not read or write Hopi.[3] Ironically, while Hopi was Qötsahonmana's first language acquired in childhood, language shift from Hopi to English, beginning at Grade 3, in public schools she attended in the border town of Winslow, AZ left her with only a receptive ability in the Hopi language but not a speaking ability. In an interesting twist, Qötsahonmana developed Hopi literacy skills in Emory's, Poliwisiwma's, graduate course titled, "Hopi Culture in Language," which subsequently became a critical asset for the institute program. Oral Immersion, a research-based approach to language teaching was a key aspect of the program model premised in the resource these first institute attendees brought to the institute program as oral speakers of Hopi.[4] Over the course of seven summer institutes held during the month of July (2004–2010) (see also Nicholas, 2021), Siwivensi and Somi'mana applied their coursework toward a graduate degree (a second for Ada); in May 2010, both received a master's degree in language, reading, and culture from the UA's College of Education with a focus in Indigenous language revitalization.

STORYING OUR LIVED HISTORIES

In our respective storying, we explore "how we came to where we are" by privileging our individual life histories and lived realities. We resurface early memories of our Indigenous educational and linguistic foundations centering our family and community relationships. We also revisit and reconceptualize the tensions and challenges we each navigated to re*f*orge a collective path toward reclaiming our inherited roles and responsibilities as the *first* teachers of our community youth. Hornberger and Swinehart (2012) highlight the role of stories/narratives in their study of three Indigenous Andean teachers enrolled in an intercultural bilingual education masters program. They also illuminate the critical role of a "local space of professional development" (the higher education masters program) in which transformative experiences occur and unfold through the process of *professionalization* while engaging as educated professionals in "instances of language planning from the bottom-up" (p. 35). Hornberger and Swinehart posit that narrating their professional experiences enabled Indigenous educators to transcend their *"situaciones de la vida,* life situations"—personal and professional experiences of discrimination and marginalization as Indigenous people—toward gaining new perspectives about the link between their linguistic practices in relation to their indigeneity. In the case of David, who, by reflecting on his teaching experiences "returned" to recognizing himself as Indigenous so that he now asserted, "'I'm Quechua,' not 'I'm a Quechua speaker'" (p. 40). Engaging with the coursework provided the "wake-up call" to distinguish between these assertions of identity. Similarly, our narratives became expressions of *self-empowerment,* bringing to light the "teacher within" (Cajete, 2015, p. 12) each of us as well as giving us "voice" (Ruiz, 1991) in storying our narratives. Our narratives also reveal a transformative process originating and unfolding in the context of the Hopi tribe's Hopilavayi Summer Institute, a "local space of professional development" within which Hornberger and Swinehart (2012) state, "Professional formation enters into a dynamic with ... individuals' personal language policies, marking their adult lives with stronger identification with Indigenous language and culture" (p. 35). We recognize this process of illumination as a manifestation of and a critical consciousness (Smith, 1999) to align ourselves with *the way things should be.* Cajete (2015) describes this process as storying "the making of an Indigenous teacher"—reclaiming an Indigenous heritage of thinking, teaching, and learning (p. 13).

ITAAQATSIMKIWA, OUR LIFELINE; ITAATUMALMAKIWA, OUR LIFEWORK

Two foundational Hopi concepts, *itaaqatsimkiwa* (our lifeline) and *itaatumalmakiwa* (our lifework), mark and comprehend our life trajectories as "preordained" and "predetermined"—our destinies to become Hopi language educators. These concepts situate our professional trajectories in "community past, present, future" (Cajete, 2015, p. xvi). As Bernita, Siwivensi (from here on) explains, we became acutely conscious, *suyan maatsi'yungwa,* of our life purpose that further evoked a clarity about the path that was predetermined for us. She expressed this best using Hopilavayi and in the form of *navoti,* a Hopi teaching: "*Qa sööwu hevta; [pay hak] navoti'tangwu; [lavayit] aw unangtavi'tangwu.*" Barring a slow search or a trial and error process, having attained this understanding [of our calling] one attends to the call [of language work]. Thus, the concept of itaaqatsimkiwa, a "given way of life," was one we had each embarked upon very early in our lives and storied as the opening to this chapter. Reflection also revealed that we were encouraged by many along and through our teaching experiences. Cognizant of our positioning as the "essential link[s] between the aspects of community and the processes of schooling" (Trujillo et al., 2005, p. 2275), we each embraced our responsibility, *aw unangtavya*. Accepting this responsibility became the way to give back to our community and people; "giving back" then also offers a framework to illuminate "possibilities" for the development of contemporary theory(ies) of Indigenous education (this volume). More specific to Indigenous language education following Hornberger and Swinehart (2012), narratives of our professional trajectories inform Indigenous/Hopi language planning "from the bottom–up." These are "locally grounded insights into what professionalization and Indigenous language revitalization mean to . . . educators as they create, interpret, and appropriate . . . language education policy" (p. 37). In the Hopi case, language education policy refers to the Hopi Tribal Council Resolutions[5] that established and supported the Hopilavayi project/program initiatives.

Our narratives are further framed in specific Hopi thought that define our unfolding processes comprised of advice and instruction, healing and self-empowerment, and looking within or introspection to find ourselves and our true vocations. Siwivensi frames her 43 year teaching career with the Bureau of Indian Education (BIE) system on the Hopi Reservation in the Hopi concept of *tutavo,* advice, instruction, and counsel regarding Western education. The advent of Western education and schooling into the Hopi world in the late 1800s positioned a view of Western education as the means for *survival through co-existence* with the dominant society and as holding the potential for *enhancing* the lives of the Hopi people. Thus, each generation of Hopi implored its youth to go to school, listen, and learn the White man's language and how he thinks in order to become the "eyes, ears, and mouths" for the Hopi people in external matters and affairs that would directly impact them.

Somi'mana's story is a vivid reflection on a perplexing situation she experienced while teaching far away from Hopi in a Pennsylvania school. Her primary-aged students of Spanish heritage who identified as English language learners were provided with a bilingual education program as academic support. Comparatively, she recalled her own entry into primary school as a monolingual Hopi speaker—there was no such program support for her. Rather, her heritage language was silenced in traumatic ways and with lasting impact; this systemic silencing of Hopi language remains ongoing in the schools serving Hopi students through the implementation of external educational policies. Compelled to disrupt this process emanating from a reflective critical consciousness, Somi'mana embarked on a path of self-healing, *naaqalavtsinva,* and self-empowerment, *naa'öqalanta,* by recentering salient Hopi values at the core of her being.

For Qötsahonmana, the concept of *naamiq yori*, to look within, initiates introspection on significant incidences or "rude awakenings" to personal cultural and language shift and change. The shifting process began with her family's move 60 miles away from Hopi to the border town of Winslow, Arizona. Inevitably, entry into public school initiated the shift from Hopi to English monolingual development and its primacy into adulthood. Adult and parenthood gave rise to the effects of language shift and a critical consciousness about the importance of one's heritage language that subsequently converged in a common and shared reality with Hopi community youth and Hopi language teachers at the Hopilavayi Summer Institute.

We turn now to our storying.

SIWIVENSI, PRINTED PUMPKIN BLOSSOM

Itamumi tutavo, It was requested of us [to go to school].

Nu' Siwivensi yan Hopimaatsiwa. Nu' Musangnungaqsino. Nu' Pivwungwa. Ingu Qa'ökwavnöma, pu' ina Puhueyestewa.

My Hopi name is Siwivensi. I am from Musangnuvi Village. I am Tobacco Clan. My mother is *Qa'ökwavnöma* and my father is *Puhueyestewa*.

My mother was 19 years old when I was born. She fulfilled her Hopi wedding responsibilities when I was about 2 years old. An old photograph (Figure 11.1) shows her and I dressed in our wedding robes, evidence that

Figure 11.1 Two year old, Siwivensi with her mother dressed in their Hopi wedding robes. *Source:* Photo, courtesy of Siwivensi.

my mother had remained at my father's home for the duration of time it took to make our buckskin shoes and weave our cotton robes.[6]

My father and my grandfather were both composers of songs so that was the first form of language I was exposed to as a toddler. I danced and imitated the *katsinam*,[7] carrying around a red scarf that I often tied around my waist as a kilt. I was not shy and danced publicly. A favorite family story tells about a time I refused to go to the plaza with the rest of my family to watch the katsinam.[8] Returning home, my family found a cluster of people in our front yard watching me dance and then giving away the peaches that my grandfather had carried home from the peach orchard that morning. I was imitating the katsinam giving gifts to the spectators when they concluded a dance; I was imitating their behavior by giving away the peaches.

When I was 5 years old, my father relocated our family—my mother and me—to his job site in Heber, Arizona. For the first time, I was removed from my grandparents and my Hopi community. I suddenly became ill after the move and complained of severe stomach pains. The doctor at the hospital found nothing wrong with me, however, I continued to complain of pains so we made a trip back to our village. As soon as I set foot in the family home and reunited with my grandparents, my complaints disappeared. The medicine man laughed as he told my family that my imagined illness was really homesickness.

Going to School

I could speak only Hopi when I was enrolled in public school kindergarten for the first time in Heber, Arizona. My traumatic experiences began on Day 1. Communicating with others was totally frustrating. Other children would pull on my two long braids as they shouted, "Whoa horsey, whoa!" Some greeted me with "How" and a raised palm forward; the teacher never intervened. I didn't cry, but I was very unhappy and began to refuse to go to school. My mother didn't force me to go to school so not going to school provided more positive experiences—piñon picking with my mother—which wiped out these negative experiences from my memory. I also begged to return to Hopi to be with my grandparents, but that never happened. I did not finish out my kindergarten school year because of these negative experiences. Due to marital problems that erupted between my parents, they separated and my mother relocated the two of us to Phoenix, Arizona. We were taken in by my mother's older sister, and I was enrolled in another larger public school.

Surprisingly, my school experiences began to improve in first grade at Longview Elementary school through finishing Grade 5 at Osborn Elementary in Phoenix, Arizona. Teachers I had in succession from first through fifth grades were good teachers, trained and committed to children. Many of them took individual time with me and used my personal strengths in art, music, and dance to engage me. I blossomed with their support so that by the time my grandmother decided to bring me under her care, I was academically motivated and confident. My oral English proficiency had escalated, improving both my reading and writing skills. The extent of that growth was revealed when I entered sixth grade in a Hopi elementary school and surpassed my classmates in academics and leadership skills. Unfortunately, however, as a result of my academic success, I also endured a bad middle-school experience at the local Bureau of Indian Affairs (BIA) School.[9]

The sixth grade teacher was a large and loud African American woman who was very stern and demanding. The first time I experienced punishment at her hands was less than a month after I entered her class. She had given a Weekly Reader question and crossword puzzle assignment for homework. After lunch, this teacher set a chair in the middle of the room and started to call out students' names. When called, we were instructed to form a circle around her chair. She picked up a flat length of board and sat down on the chair asking the first student in line where or from whom he or she got the answers to their homework assignment. If they gave an answer that was appropriate to her, she allowed that student to return to their seat. If a "No" answer was given, or the answer was not to her liking, she smacked that student with the board behind a leg. We kept circling her chair, stopping and answering her question; several students were beginning to cry. Continuing to be in the circle that grew smaller and smaller, I learned that the few friends I had helped with their Weekly Reader homework that morning had passed the answers on to their friends. I was in that line getting smacked across my calves each time I answered, "I finished it on my own."

A Hopi Upbringing

During my early childhood, I was totally immersed by my family in the Hopi language and culture. Everyone spoke Hopi. The adults in my early life were actively involved in the cultural practices of our village. My father always returned to the reservation from his job to participate in his religious societal responsibilities. My grandparents were true examples of individuals who knew the importance of reciprocity according to Hopi and involved themselves in helping others. One NEVER forgets how one is nurtured from the time they develop in their mother's womb. Our Hopi way of life teaches respect and values all life. Children in their innocence are especially important. I was never spanked because this is not a part of Hopi parenting. It was the school system that brought confusion and pain to my life as a developing child. Yet, I was resilient enough to overcome that and move on.

While my formal education was riddled with more ups and downs than I reveal here, my Hopi education made it possible for me to grow up without serious damage to my sense of being. Rather, my cultural upbringing had developed into a firm sense of identity that would guide me through the rest of my life. Since sixth grade, my life has been filled with personal accomplishments in things that the non-Indigenous world regards highly as signs of success so that following high school, I took on the challenges of higher education, encouraged first by my grandparents, then my teachers and other influential people. As an older generation of Hopi, these individuals advised me to always remember my roots and come back to help our Hopi people—to become the "eyes, ears, and mouths" of the people through education. With a bachelor's degree in education, I entered the teaching field at the same school I had been in as a sixth grader (1961).

Unfortunately, throughout my 43 year teaching career, there was very little opportunity to influence or advance the direction of Westernized education *for* our Hopi students. In the latter years, data-driven standards and testing restricted culturally relevant instruction. As a trained Indigenous language practitioner, I have been attempting to make changes in my educational institution to meet the heritage culture and language needs of our Hopi students. Administrators recognize language and culture as important, but still marginalize them in terms of time allotments and equal importance in the daily curriculum.

Reflecting on my journey, I recognize that embracing Western education *did not* replace my Hopi education. It enabled me to acquire the skills and knowledge about child development, educational theories, and researched practices to deliver language and culture lessons to my students effectively and competently. English as my second language made me bilingual and bicultural; I make choices based on what I know of a life lived in a city and the one I live on Hopi. My realization is that our Hopi children are entitled to an education that does not force them to make either/or choices between the mainstream world and living their cultural lives. A personal belief is that my birth has a purpose. That purpose has been revealed in the long path it took to find others with similar roles waiting to be played. Those roles are of becoming Hopi language teachers and advocates for the Hopi way of life. Our collective path to our work "is to reclaim our inherited roles and responsibilities as the *first* teachers of our community youth." We are self-assured in acknowledging that our paths have been guided by the "teacher within" so that we now align ourselves with "the way things should be."

SOMI'MANA, SPIDER WEAVING ITS BEAUTIFUL WEB

"I wanted to become a teacher but not like the teachers I had in grade school."

Nu' Somi'mana yan Hopimaatsiwa. Nu' Songoopangaqsino. Nu' Nuvawungwa.
Ingu Puhuyesnöm, pu' ina Navotíma.

My Hopi name is Somi'mana. I am from Songoopavi Village. I am Snow Clan.
My mother is *Puhuyesnöm* and my father is *Navotíma.*

With this I go forward.[10] I am a middle child of 11 children (five older
and five younger siblings). While in the womb of my mother for 9 months,
I went through her life with her, living as a good Hopi woman with Hopi
values: Don't be lazy; Help everyone; Feed the hungry. My mother shares
the following story of my 9 months in her womb.

She got very ill and my father was miles away from the mesa top attending to the sheep. My oldest sister was doing the best she could to care for
her but her pain was not getting any better so she went to a neighbor to
come help with my mother's pain; this too didn't bring my mother any
comfort. Our mother was finally taken to the only hospital 18 miles away.
There, she was diagnosed with pneumonia and had to stay. She wasn't there
long when the Snake Dance activities began. She didn't want to neglect her

Figure 11.2. *Somi'mana* as Miss Hopi at age 20 years. *Source:* Photo, courtesy of
Somi'mana.

duties—carrying out her female role in village ceremonies—and asked her doctor to release her with a promise to return. She must have spoken well, for she was released. Maybe she got well from attending to her obligations and caring for the community, but she did not return for the follow-up. On August 24, 1956, I was born to my parents, Luella Lomayestewa and the late Harold Joseph, Sr. in the village of Songoopavi. All 11 of us siblings were delivered by my father; not one of us was born in a hospital. My mother was a strong Hopi woman; no [Western] prenatal care for any of us.

I entered this world to be identified as Hopi, born into the Snow Clan, *Nuvawungwa*, and with my Hopi name, Somi'mana. I received my Hopi name at 21 days old, and when my *so'o*, grandmother, and aunties on my paternal side gathered before sunrise to celebrate my being. My father is Spider Clan, *Piqöswungwa*;[11] therefore, my Hopi name means Spider Weaving Its Beautiful Web.

It saddens me now, that the door to all my healthy and rich cultural upbringing was closed when I entered kindergarten in 1962 at Second Mesa Day School. No one there cared to nurture our cultural background—where we lived, or what we did in our villages prior to entering the school setting itself or before and after each school day. I understand *now* that the U.S. policy was that we were not to speak our language nor be who we are; *I felt this and experienced it!* Rather, the teachers did an excellent job of enforcing the policy rules and regulations. I remember the brown paper towels neatly cut into little squares and the soap at the sink ready to be used for anyone who spoke in their Native tongue—to wash your tongue or mouth with the soap. Yes! I went to the sink, but I thank the Great Spirit that my Native tongue didn't get washed away.

Our parents, elders, and leaders were all for educating their children in the Western way. They wanted us to "become their eyes and tongues"—to bridge the gap between who we are as Hopi people and the White man and his world. We are native to this world and if this was the set up from the beginning, we would be one strong, contributing beings in the world. Instead, our caretakers were silent as we got on the yellow buses and were sent away to a place they had no input into. We all lost sight of the purpose of getting educated. We didn't become the eyes and tongues for our Hopi people; we got educated to live by U.S. policy.

Going to School

Once I boarded the bus, I would get a sick feeling in my stomach. It worsened when I got off the bus and entered the school building, and by all that was unfamiliar: the smell of the building, the sounds of opera music, the click-clack of the teachers' high-heeled shoes. Did anyone ask, "How are you

feeling?" Did anyone say, "Come, we are going to have fun learning together?" All the familiar and *right* stuff was not in the policy. We *survived* kindergarten through sixth grade in these unfamiliar and unwelcoming places.

Our sixth grade teacher, Mr. Caldwell, was considered to be one of the
best teachers in the school; he learned how to speak Hopi, stayed the lon-
gest and retired from teaching at the school. During my time in his class, I
never heard his Hopi tongue, but I remember that he played country music
in class which didn't mess with my stomach, and to this day when I hear that
familiar music, I say to myself, "Sixth grade, Mr. Caldwell." He had us mem-
orize addition, subtraction, and multiplication facts. At the end of our sixth
grade year, he made a prediction of what he thought our futures would be.
He said that I would become an airline stewardess, and I was fine with that.
But, he made one classmate upset with his prediction for her—that she
would become a housewife with lots of children. She remains upset today
with this memory because she has been employed while those he predicted
would do great things are the ones who became housewives.

Leaving Hopi

My family left Hopi for Flagstaff, Arizona (90 miles away) when my oldest brother found our father a job there. This was a difficult move for us;
we left a familiar place for one that was unfamiliar and with people we
didn't know. I became the oldest child in the household because my older
siblings were away at boarding schools, college, or trade schools. Even with
limited English, our parents were able to enroll us in school. I did well in
school; the memorization of basic math facts in sixth grade made me shine
in my classroom. I was admired by my teacher and peers. Although my
father was the only one working and financially supporting the household,
we managed weekend trips home to Hopi to check on our ranch and our
grandparents. My mother would sometimes stay to fulfill her women's society obligations which left the responsibility of "mothering" my younger
siblings in Flagstaff to me.

My family decided to move back to Hopi during my junior year in high
school. By this time, I was attending school, working (at a car wash and Grey-
hound post house), and providing for my own educational needs, so I wanted
to stay in Flagstaff and finish high school. I roomed with a Navajo woman
and paid my half of living expenses until I graduated high school with honors. I returned to Hopi in the summer of 1975 and participated in the social
dances: Hopi Butterfly, Zuni Butterfly, Paiute and Navajo. Summer came to
an end and there was funding for anyone who wanted to pursue a degree.

Becoming a Teacher

My younger sister used to tell me that I should become a teacher because she remembered that on our walks home from school, we'd stop several times so I could share with her what I learned in school that day. I would write in the sand to show her. I enjoyed sharing my knowledge, my lightbulb moments. With my sister putting those thoughts of becoming a teacher in my mind, I did follow her advice. I had a nice student teaching experience—teaching middle-class White students in the Flagstaff public school system; I applied everything I learned in my program to my teaching. I felt prepared to be an effective classroom teacher and took this experience and confidence back to Hopi. But, taking what I learned to Hopi was very different. In Hopi, my first year of teaching was in a community school (see Viri, 1980) where no lesson plans were required; we were to develop lesson plans from ideas from the students. But, how to get the ideas from the children was not part of my preparation. The Hopi students were fluent speakers of their Third Mesa Hopi dialect.[12] They did not allow me to speak or use my Second Mesa dialect; I had to speak like them to fit in, and I learned how important the dialect was. I wasn't using what I went to school for; I had no training, it was confusion, not a learning experience. Next, I went to a BIA (Bureau of Indian Affairs) [federally supported] school. I remember the words—"quality education"—on the school billboard that I saw every day. Teaching a third to fourth grade combined class with 35 students and not enough class space, I asked, how am I providing a quality education in these conditions? I wrote a letter to the principal with these concerns and a second teacher was hired. People were telling me to go for my MA in education. I did, but nothing about that first MA was about "waking me up" until my second MA at the U of A (University of Arizona) where I found the program to be fulfilling, meaningful, and purposeful. The second MA followed a return to Hopi from Bethlehem, Pennsylvania.

Bethlehem, Pennsylvania

The closure of Lucent Technology in Phoenix, Arizona, where my husband was employed, found us relocating far from Arizona and Hopi to Lucent's plant in Bethlehem, Pennsylvania. At the time, two of my three children were of school age and being close in age, they were enrolled in the same school, my daughter in second grade and my son in kindergarten. I became a parent volunteer in their school; this experience re-inspired my teacher background. I took courses at a community college and received my elementary certification. I started teaching as a substitute teacher in the Bethlehem Area School District which allowed me exposure to many elementary schools and working with preschoolers. I found working with preschoolers learning English as a second language as the perfect teaching setting for me, so I took additional courses to get certified in early childhood. I became a preschool teacher in a local school district. What we did as teachers of English language learner preschoolers was totally different from how I was taught as a second language learner of English in Arizona. We accepted these students for who they were and did not take anything away from them; whereas, for me, I was not allowed to speak my language, Hopi, at school. My two co-teachers who were from countries in South America, one from Colombia and the other from Chile, asked me if I spoke my Native language. I was thrilled to tell them I did. Their next question was if I read and wrote it. My answer was "No." They were puzzled. They both could read and write their Spanish language and in their countries, they learned in their native Spanish before moving to the United States. They were the only teachers in our school's bilingual program who did not need Spanish-speaking assistants to help them communicate with the families of their students; they did it themselves. One co-teacher told me that if an opportunity came up to learn to read and write my language, I should take it. Keeping her words in mind, I returned to Hopi in 2002 and took a teaching position at a local elementary school.

Our return to Hopi was largely motivated by my responsibility to fulfill my obligations to my women's society and my responsibilities as a paternal aunt for relatives in the grinding corn ceremony—the Hopi female puberty ceremony. My own children, who are of Hopi and African American heritage, were also questioning why they were racially "different" from those around them; they needed to learn about who they were and where they came from. Living in Pennsylvania allowed us to take weekend trips to visit their father's side of the family in Maryland, and summer trips to Arizona allowed them to visit my side of the family. In 2003, with my husband's retirement, we made the decision to move the family to Arizona; this allowed our children to participate in and learn about their Hopi culture, hear the language, and eventually become speakers of Hopi (my dream).

At the close of school for Summer 2004, I heard the announcement, "Any teachers who are interested in learning to speak and write Hopi, come by the office and pick up a form." This was the start of an empowering and healing experience. I learned to read and write Hopi and to teach my Native tongue by using an approach called *Total Oral Immersion*. The funding came from our Hopi Tribal language program which I thought would see to it that we are bringing our Hopilavayi back into our local schools. But no one came into our schools during the school year to acknowledge the work we were doing. Instead, the principals in the schools would tell us not to teach language but to use the time to get the students ready for testing. Most of our tribal leaders do not seem to understand that having your

Native tongue does not hinder one's education or test scores but enhances their academic abilities. I have learned that if you know who you are, where you come from—your Hopi identity and what it's done for you—then you appreciate it, share it in order to help our youth work from where they're at to be able to live in this world. It is a matter of finding yourself and then to go from there forward. I try to model for them that in this way they can get to where I'm at.

QÖTSAHONMANA, WHITE BEAR GIRL

"When you were a child, you were fully Hopi."

Nu' Qötsahonmana yan Hopimaatsiwa. Nu' Qalwungwa. Nu' Songoopangaqsino. Nu' Muuyit yu'ta pu' Ahölat na'ta. Niikyang Piqöshaynömnit Milton Nicholas amumi wungwa.

My Hopi name is White Bear Girl. I am Sunforehead Clan. I am from [the village] of Songoopavai. Muuyi is mother and Ahöla is my father. I was raised by Piqöshaynöm and Milton Nicholas.

During my childhood, children were active participants in daily village life until the age of six when they began "going to school." There were no tribal day care centers nor Head Start programs, and immediate and extended family members were all caretakers living the Hopi way of life— tending to their flocks of sheep, cornfields, orchards, and gardens.

My paternal grandmother, so'o, was a significant figure in my childhood. I recall being her silent but observant child shadow, helping her with daily chores the best I could but mindful of getting underfoot. I often slept at her house, only a few steps away from the home I shared with my parents. So'o's life was one of never-ending chores and I was witness to this. She was always the first to rise before daylight and stoke the remaining embers in the kitchen stove to get a fire going for breakfast—typically fried potatoes, *piqaviki*, flour tortillas, and coffee. Breakfast was a family affair, lots of talk and laughter before all went off to do their own chores. So'o's chores included, but were not limited to, several trips, two buckets at a time, to the water pump located some yards behind her house to fill the water barrel in the house, replenishing the wood bin for her kitchen stove including taking an axe to any one of the logs stacked up at the family wood pile, and feeding the chickens and horses. I recall helping her crack open apricots from the orchard and put them to dry on the roof, watching her create colorful wicker plaques, *yungyapu*, and after dinner, observing her as she hand-sewed quilt patches into beautiful quilts; she gifted me with one which I still have. Often, after dinner clean up, she would bring out either a jigsaw puzzle or the game of Chinese Checkers. I greatly admired and loved my So'o.

Going to school

My parents experienced boarding school. Undoubtedly, reminded of their experiences, they chose to enroll me in the local Mennonite operated Hopi Mission School located on the outskirts of my father's village, Kyqötsmovi. I recall always being reminded to do well in school or I might have to go to "boarding school." I attended Hopi Mission for first and second grade after which our family moved to the border town of Winslow. Vivid in my memories of going to school was that the sounds and colors of village and family life seemed to drift away upon crossing the highway and onto the school grounds. In reflection, it may have been that as a monolingual speaker of Hopi, the English language of the school context took over, essentially closing the door to the life and sounds of my Hopi world. I remember my teachers—Miss Dirk, a vivacious young woman who joined us in play during recess and laughed loudly and freely with us, and then there was Miss Penner who baffled me with her sternness—everything about her seemed inflexible, unbendable, unapproachable.

During this time, I also became a friend to the children of the White family who managed the village store. Cynthia and Kevin, sister and brother, were frequently at my house; I was never invited to their house which was not visible behind the six foot fence that encircled their house and yard. One day, out of the blue, Cynthia asked, "Are you poor?" My reply, "I don't know. I guess so." I had no clue to the meaning of the word *poor*. That night I asked my mother, "Are we poor?" She replied, "I don't know. I guess so."

Moving to town

Our move to the border town of Winslow, 60 miles away, disrupted the traditional enculturation process of becoming Hopi for me. Prior to this move, I completed the first rite of passage into the *katsina society*[13] and danced in one social dance, Butterfly Dance[14] (Figure 11.3) but I would not experience any other of the myriad cultural practices that brought members further into the esoteric realms of Hopi life. The focus of my schooling turned to preparing me for the mainstream world through Western education and all the experiences that both offered. I "put away" my Hopi to become a better speaker of English (and to avoid covert and overt criticism of my developing English) and to do well academically; this was a tragic sacrifice encouraged by my parents who did so "in my best interests" and

Figure 11.3 *Qötsahonmana* at age 6, as a Butterfly Girl dancer, in the Butterfly Dance. *Source:* Photo, courtesy of *Qötsahonmana.*

likely from their own boarding school experiences. However, I became an avid reader, a positive consequence. During junior high, reading allowed me to travel the world and to see the unfortunate plight of many peoples that sparked an intense desire to both travel and to help those less fortunate—this became my aspiration in life. With an interest in working with children having special needs, I embarked on a journey that would merge this career goal with my increasing desire to see the world; I became a U.S. Peace Corps volunteer.

The Peace Corps experience was a turning point in my life in many ways; however, reflection on this always brings to mind my childhood friend, Cynthia's question, "Are you poor?" and mine and my mother's responses, "I don't know, I guess so." Ironically, I never saw myself or my Hopi world as "poor." Also ironic is that while Cynthia's perspective described Hopi as what might be referred to as a "third-world country" and as potentially in need of external help from such as the U.S. Peace Corps volunteer organization, instead, *I* was the one seeking to "help" others I viewed as less fortunate than me. In the end, I benefited tremendously from this experience, foremost in that it was an opportunity to take a good look at myself—*naami yori,* from the outside inward, and then to look deeply within myself—naamiq yori in order to move forward with purpose grounded in a consciousness of my personal, social, and cultural identities. Following my return from my Peace Corps service, the ensuing years as a classroom teacher presented many incidents that led to a return to academia. In academia, my journey brought numerous individuals into my life space who greatly influenced me in "how I came to be where I am."

Critical Consciousness

The mainstream cliché, "Sticks and stones may break your bones; but words will never hurt me" has been central in my intuitive sense of "contradiction" conveyed about language. Subsequently, I resolved that the cliché *is* a contradiction to the Hopi perspective of the *power of words*. Since becoming a mother, a parent, I have been subtly advised "never to speak with words of anger" to my children. The lesson: Hurtful words expelled in anger are not only heard and remain in the receiver's memory, but are internalized with lasting effect and possible ominous consequences for children who are vulnerable in their emotional and psychological development. Today, as a scholar-educator who works with students aspiring to be teachers, this understanding of the power of words is forefront in my philosophy of teaching. I implore emerging teacher-educators to recognize their "power," their "role" in either nurturing the life trajectories of their students or murdering their spirit (Williams, 2005).

This inherent danger of anger can be conveyed in abundant ways. The many ways I have been influenced by Western ideologies that contradict Hopi values and thought have surfaced in numerous incidences. In the following "incident," the influence of Western feminism surfaced as a growing resentment in carrying out my "female" role of feeding my family as a working wife and mother, and in turn, manifested in the verbal and nonverbal complaints during mealtimes from my children about my cooking. I turned to my mother for advice. In the ensuing phone conversation and upon hearing the context, her response was immediate and contextualized through a Hopi teaching through the Hopi language; while she understood my predicament, she reminded me that I had *chosen* to become a wife and mother; thus, it was my responsibility to "feed my family"—the primary role of a wife and mother. Moreover, if I prepared the food I would serve my family with an attitude of resentment and anger, essentially, I would be feeding them my anger and resentment. Her message was profound. The positive change I initiated from this conversation and understanding has been deep and long-lasting; I have modeled this understanding for my children and have reaped the rewards and experienced the fulfillment.

Aligning myself with how "things should be" originated as a series of rude awakenings. The first was an awakening to a void in my cultural identity and subsequently to language shift in my personal life and for my children. Dr. Akira Yamamoto, a Japanese AILDI (American Indian Language

Development Institute) faculty, assured me that my language was not lost but lay deep in the recesses of my inner self, and that all I would need to do was to resurface it. Yet, as I initiated this process through literacy under the mentoring of my clan uncle, Emory Sekaquaptewa, also an AILDI faculty, my mother responded to the Hopi language I was voicing with the expression, "*Um tsayniiqe paas Hopiningwu.*" "When you were a child, you were fully Hopi." These rude awakenings combined created a paradox in my mind (at the time, premised in my misinterpretation of my mother's words).[15] On the one hand, I *was* Hopi (by birthright and heritage), but on the other hand, I *had ceased* to be Hopi (as a nonspeaker). These rude awakenings led to a critical consciousness of the "messages" being conveyed and in *re*forging the path toward what I would come to understand as my "true vocation"—attending to my heritage language on behalf of our community youth that includes my own children.

WHERE WE ARE TODAY

Presently, Siwivensi[16] has completed 4 years as the language and culture teacher at the second of two K–6 schools located on the Hopi.[17] At both schools, she provided a Hopi language and culture program to the total student population attending each school (for the academic year 2019–2020, she worked with 207 students). She also offered evening adult Hopi language classes, initially targeting parents of students and then opened to community members. Somi'mana retired from the BIE (Bureau of Indian Education) school system in Spring 2019 and returned to Hopi. Immediately on her return, she was recruited as a first grade teacher at the same elementary school as Siwivensi. Prior to her retirement, she was a kindergarten teacher at an elementary school in the White Mountain Apache community.[18] Similar to her position as teacher of preschool non-Hopi students in Pennsylvania, working with Apache students, Somi'mana continued to share the Hopi language and life philosophy with her students conveyed through Hopi songs. Qötsahonmana is faculty in the Department of Teaching, Learning, and Sociocultural Studies (TLSS) in the College of Education at the University of Arizona (UA), Tucson, Arizona. In addition to teaching academic courses in language and culture in education, teacher research, and Indigenous oral tradition, she is a faculty instructor for the AILDI housed in the UA College of Education, and consultant instructor for the Indigenous Language Institute (ILI), Santa Fe, New Mexico (http://www.indigenous-language.org/). The AILDI engages undergraduate and graduate students as well as community educators and practitioners from tribal communities "to provide critical training in support of and to strengthen efforts to revitalize and promote the use of Indigenous languages across generations" (http://aildi.arizona.edu, para. 1). ILI's mission is to provide "vital language related services to Native communities so that their individual identities, traditional wisdom and values are passed onto future generations in their original languages" (http://www.indigenous-language.org/, para. 1).

CONCLUSION AND IMPLICATIONS

Our professional trajectories while influenced by preparation in Western institutions and teacher education programs nevertheless reveal how the essence of how and what we think—internalized as our cultural and linguistic foundation—continues to align with "the spirit of Indigenous thought" (Cajete, 2015, p. xvii). As Siwivensi states, "Western education did *not* replace our Hopi education, but rather, resurfaced for us the relevance of the Hopi way in our contemporary lives." While our Western education experiences were riddled with traumatic ups and downs, our cultural and linguistic upbringing thwarted any serious damage to our cultural and social identities; our subsequent language work restored our well-being through which we gave voice to the teachings of our ancestors. Hornberger and Swinehart's study findings confirm longitudinal diachronic accounts of changes in people's linguistic repertoires which demonstrate that "marginalization experienced as adolescents was not a permanent state of affairs . . . nor does alienation become a fixed part of a young person's identity (despite persistence in memory)" (citing Woolard, 2011, p. 642). This speaks to the memories of insult and humiliation for Siwivensi of the physical abuse at the hands of her teacher for doing her homework, and for Somi'mana, images of the paper towel squares and soap "at the sink ready to be used for anyone who spoke in their Native tongue." Our narratives collectively concur that anchored in a firm sense of identity and provided with a distinct cultural and linguistic map (ways of knowing, being, and doing), we each navigated Western education and the mainstream world to achieve, according to Siwivensi, "what the non-Indigenous world regards highly as signs of success"—academic and professional success. The overarching implication is that Indigenous/Hopi language planning from the bottom–up must go beyond revitalizing the language focused on producing a new generation of speaker-users toward re-instilling an Indigenous/Hopi identity that deeply considers the relation of linguistic cultural practices to a contemporary meaning of Indigeneity (Hornberger & Swinehart, 2012).

Importantly, our narratives point to the critical role of the Hopilavayi Summer Institute as the "professionalization context" in which we engaged in renewal of Indigenous/Hopi knowledge, identity, and cultural and linguistic practices as educational professionals. The Hopilavayi (Hopi

Language) Summer Institute, by its name, and recruiting Hopi speaking individuals privileged local identities in "shifting the indexical value [and valuing] of... language" (Hornberger & Swinehart, 2012, p. 43); a stark move away from our educational experiences that viewed our heritage language as a "problem" (Ruiz, 1984) to be eradicated through educational policies and practices. Within the institute context (2004–2010), we engaged in multiple "instances of language planning from the bottom-up" (Hornberger & Swinehart, 2012, p. 37). The following is an excerpt of one "instance" of language planning, a commitment articulated by one cohort of institute attendees to align with self-identifying as Hopilavayit aw Naa'ayatiwqam, Those who have chosen to attend to the language:[19]

Our Belief: Our Hopi way of life is made complete with the Hopi language.

Our Children: Our children will extend our Hopi way of life.

Our Mission/Our Responsibility: We believe in our children and that is why without laziness we support them. So that our children will not forget the Hopi way of life and with the Hopi language, live by means of it. This is what we are thinking.

Hornberger and Swinehart (2012) describe such an instance of language planning as "co-construction and negotiation of linguistic expertise and pedagogical knowledge" (p. 48) that illuminates and calls attention to "speakers and repertoires, and on the actual resources that speakers deploy in actual contexts" (citing Moore et al., 2010, p. 1). We have amassed a body of work that has important implications not only for our own language practices (e.g., oral language use as well as Hopi literacy development) and pedagogical epistemologies (e.g., language teaching premised in local knowledge), but for the sustainability of continued future language planning at this grassroots level. Moreover, the transformative process has taken us beyond our classroom educator roles through our work with others as Hopi language teacher practitioner-mentors. We have participated in text production, local and national conferences, teacher research, and Hopi language teaching as well as language teacher preparation in our respective arenas.

The professional narratives of the Indigenous Andean educators resonate deeply for us.

Similarly, individually and collectively, we have weathered and transcended the struggles associated with our cultural roots and identities toward commitment and activism in support of Hopi language revitalization; our early pride in culture and language internalized in childhood has persisted and evolved into recognition and advocacy of the importance of "living Hopilavayi" in all spheres of our everyday lives. As Nery, an Andean Indigenous educator states, "If we don't do it, who will?" (Hornberger & Swinehart, 2012 p. 40).

The importance of the Hopilavayi Institute as a professionalizing space forefronted for us, the value of Hopi and what professionalization might mean in deconstructing schooling as previously being "a Westernizing threat" (Hornberger & Swinehart, 2012, p. 40) to one in which schooling, as Somi'mana states, "is about waking [us] up" to our potential "to model [for our children] ... our Hopi identity and what it's done for [us] ... to appreciate it ... so they [too] can get to where [we're] at"—a state of well-being and moving along the trajectory of community rebuilding.

(RE)VISIONING THE ECOLOGY OF HOPI EDUCATION— (RE)BUILDING COMMUNITY/NATION

[Màasaw] gave us specific instruction that we must honor our covenant; that we have to hold on to and protect our Hopi way; and that we must not forget who we are.
—Ben Nuvamsa, 2011

Cajete (2010) writes, "It is the history of colonization that guides Indigenous scholars [and educators] in their advocacy for 'coming back to our collective Indigenous power'—often referred to as 'empowerment'" (p. 1127). This chapter described the reflective and reflexive processes—tutavo, instruction; naaqalavtsinva/naa'öqalanta, self-healing/self-empowerment; naami yori/naamiq yori, self-reflection/introspection—we, as Hopi language educators employed to search/research our individual and collective understanding of colonization relative to Indian education through our lived realities and experiences. Instruction, self-healing/self-empowerment, and self-reflection/introspection comprise the theoretical framing of reclaiming our empowerment. The Hopilavayi (Hopi Language) Summer Institute became our site of empowerment (Cajete, 2010). As Siwivensi noted, according to mainstream perceptions, each of us had achieved academic and professional "success" in our individual life journeys; this was our shared "language of experience" gained through our participation in the Western educational system that we brought to the empowerment process in the context of the institute. The institute also became the site of a "formal relationship" forged between the Hopi tribe and the University of Arizona to address "Hopi language loss" (Hopi Tribal Council, 1994) through "institutionalizing the instruction of the Hopi language in community- and school-based programs" (Hopi Tribal Council, 1998).[20] In the following, we narrate the holistic process of theory, search/research, and praxis as emerging, intersecting and evolving in the *liminal space* created by the institute. We illuminate and articulate the ways in which a local site of professionalization offered a re-envisioning of Hopi/Indigenous community/nation rebuilding. That is, rebuilding a community's foundational capacity premised on "local educators' efforts to 're-emplace' and 'rescale' the Hopi language in the lives of Hopi children, families, and communities...in the non-traditional domains of the classroom and school" (McCarty et al., 2012, p. 52).[21] Here, we point out that most of the institute participants attended out of *personal* desire and choice—para-educators to more effectively carry out their language teaching responsibility in school-based Hopi language programs, certified teachers to create spaces for the Hopi language in their own classrooms, and community members to work with youth in their village communities. We also provide highlights of our work with community youth in planning and implementing the practicum component of the institute program, *Hopinaatuwpi*, self-rediscovery through Hopilavayi.

Over the course of seven summer institutes (2004–2010) and alongside para-educator institute participants, we worked to revision the ecology of traditional Hopi education as "conceptual well-springs for the 'new' kinds of educational thought...needed to frame the exploration of an appropriate Indigenous [Hopi] educational philosophy" (Cajete, 2010, p. 1126) through consciousness raising (Smith, 2003) and seeking *rejuvenation, renewal*, and *restoration*. Here, "renewal," "rejuvenation," and "restoration," of our community spiritual well-being are inherent in the notions of continuity—*how things should be*—expressed in the Hopi word, *powata*, to make right, put in order (Hopi Dictionary Project, 1998, p. 434) and sovereignty. This conceptual pathway returned us to the understanding that we, *Hopiit*, the Hopi people, do not merely exist—*itam qa paysoq yeese*; there is purpose to our existence articulated in ancient knowledge, navoti, prefaced and reiterated in the words, "We, at that place [and time] *received* (emphasis added) our life path; what kind of life we were to lead was made known to us" (personal communication, E. Sekaquaptewa, November 10, 2006).

At the core or the Hopi lifeway is the cultivation by hand of "the small, humble ear of corn that would grow in fields watered by rain," a commitment "to live by the reciprocity-based social institutions that were necessary to insure the well-being and survival of the community," and "to accept the responsibility to live on this land in a way that would preserve its natural bounty" (Sekaquaptewa et al., 2015, pp. 3–4). Importantly, the act of "receiving" references a binding reciprocal relationship—a covenant, an agreement, *namiyuku*—between those who would become the Hopiit and *Maasaw*, guardian steward of the fourth world. Not only does this remote encounter and covenant remain indelible in Hopi memory, but as ancient knowledge, navoti, it "contains the very essence of [Hopi] tribal sovereignty" (Brayboy et al., 2015, p. 3). The specific instruction(s) given by Maasaw "that we must honor our covenant; that we have to hold on to and protect our Hopi way; and that we must not forget who we are" (2011, website)" still resonate. Thus, Hopi sovereignty encompasses, as Onondaga

Elder Oren Lyons (2007) asserts, "the skill to hear the instructions... to be responsible... to look out for the future of our children" (p. vii). Inherently, this entails a critical consciousness about our accountability and responsibility to Maasaw and the generations to come, namely, that we must attend to "raising Hopi people who are caring, sharing and self-sufficient" (Sekaquaptewa et al., 2015, p. 5)—through preserving the ceremonies and cultural practices essential to teaching them proper human behavior and character to make them citizens among all people (James, 1974).

In our searching/researching process, we further recognized that the traditional Hopi education and "curriculum" is comprehensive, complete, and remains in place, *paas pasiwta*. As a collective of language educators, we shared this "language of experience" acquired through participating along with others in the Hopi way of life, one becomes Hopi, *Hopiqatsit ang nuutum hintsakme', Hopisinoniwtingwu;* we embodied and "lived" this traditional curriculum, *implicitly,* in our contemporary daily lives through myriad forms of "language as cultural practice" (Nicholas, 2008). Acutely aware that our Hopi pedagogy has worked effectively and efficaciously for thousands of years—we repositioned ourselves as "caretakers of the language"—*Hopilavayi aw naa'aya'tiwqam,* those who have chosen to attend to the language—a role inscribed with the inherent responsibility as linguistic and cultural transmitters for our community youth ensuring that our children will be equipped with this knowledge and prepared to assume the reciprocal responsibility to the past, present, and future/continuity. Providing this essential linguistic access describes a movement of our revisioning toward *community/nation re-building* that concurrently addressed: (a) implementation of tribal language initiatives; (b) implementation of tribal and school-based language programs; and (c) instructional pedagogical development, "processes by which a Native nation enhances its own foundational capacity for effective self-governance and self-determined community and economic development" (Jorgensen, 2007, p. xii). Thus, the language work undertaken in the liminal space of the Hopilavayi Summer Institute centered on the Hopi concept of "community" as an *identity* that carries the idea that everyone must be united in "hearts, minds and efforts... [and] persist with the determination to follow the same body of beliefs and practices" for the well-being of the community (Sekaquaptewa et al., 2007, p. 5); the institute participants assume a critical role in fostering the rejuvenation of this identity for our youth.

From 2004 to 2010, the institute offered a rigorous program of language teaching professionalization: introduction to language revitalization, oral immersion methodology for language teaching, lesson planning and materials development, action research, basic Hopi language literacy development, and a practicum experience in creating an oral immersion event for community youth—Hopinaatuwpi, self-rediscovery through Hopilavayi.

The Hopinaatuwpi would become an integral component of the institute program in bringing together the language educators and community youth in this liminal space.

We listened, heard, and privileged the desires of youth who wanted to "talk Hopi" so they could talk to their So'o, grandmother, make their mothers proud, and understand what is going on in the *kiva* as well as asserting that talking Hopi every day should be the norm, and posing the challenge of talking Hopi to them to see if they might understand. In turn, institute participants, who were also parents and grandparents, wanted community youth to have *respect* for the Hopi way of life, understood as emanating from an understanding of the core principles and values *implicit* in Hopi cultural and linguistic practices. "Teaching" Hopi language, then, required that Hopi principles and values be made *explicit* to the youth because, as Emory Sekaquaptewa stated, "Language is not separate from the practice of culture. Language is one of the ways culture is understood" (Emory Sekaquaptewa, personal communication, March 24, 2004). The 2005 *Naatuwpi*, centered on the principles and values: "When one is being Hopi, one is industrious, self-respecting, respecting of others, and being happy." Seemingly mundane everyday activities and cultural practices: sweeping the floor, shelling corn, hoeing weeds in the garden/field, planting corn, learning kinship terms for family members, and making music and dancing provided the context for "language as cultural practice" and the means for internalizing implicitly learned values of industriousness, respect, fulfillment, and well-being embedded in the accompanying language forms. Community youth ranging in age from 4 years to 26 attended; survey responses from learners and parents described the Naatuwpi experience as transformative: The youth were engaging family members with the Hopi learned, expressing that language learning was fun and a positive experience. The 2010 Naatuwpi also engaged young adult/adult learners with language learning of ritual language used at baby naming ceremonies as well as that of *tsukula-vayi*, clown language; *Tsutskut*, ritual clowns are important cultural teachers of Hopi morals and principles.

The language work undertaken within the liminal space of the Hopilavayi Summer Institute exemplifies the *possibilities of sustainability* of community/nation rebuilding while illuminating "possibilities" for the development of contemporary theory(ies) of Indigenous education "rooted in a transformational revitalization of our own expressions of education" (Cajete, 2010, p. 1132). However, the challenges to the sustainability of community/nation rebuilding—the seven year duration of the Hopilavayi Summer Institute and the 10 year lapse of movement—are the reality played out within "a geography of struggle and 'resistance' [and] 'persistence' against entrenched ideologies about the viability of Indigenous languages, their place within a history of institutional exclusion and discrimination, and current policies and discourses of high-stakes accountability ... that exert powerful tensions and obstacles for creating and sustaining educational opportunities and spaces for language teaching and learning" (McCarty et al., 2012, p. 53). Nevertheless, while securing a viable position for Hopi language and culture in the school curricula has not been realized, our transformations underlie a deeper sense of responsibility and obligation to current and succeeding generations of Hopi to understand their Hopi identity; *Itam it aw naa'ayatota*. We tasked ourselves to attend to the language.

NOTES

1. At the time, Qötsahonmana was a doctoral student in American Indian studies at the University of Arizona, Tucson. She is from Songoopavi Village on Second Mesa.

2. Emory Sekaquaptewa, Poliwisiwma, Hopi Research Anthropologist in the UA Bureau of Applied Research and Anthropology (BARA), self-taught linguist and appellate court judge for the Hopi tribe was from Kykotsmovi Village, Third Mesa.

3. The Hopi language remains primarily an oral language in use. The Hopi tribe adopted the orthography used in the Hopi Dictionary: A Hopi-English Dictionary of the Third Mesa Dialect. *Hopìikwa Lavàytutuveni*, 1998.

4. The Hopilavayi Summer Institute followed the nationally and internationally renowned model of the AILDI, housed in the College of Education at the University of Arizona (see www.aildi.com). Qötsahonmana's own experience with AILDI as a student, co-instructor, research assistant, program coordinator, and currently faculty spanned the years from 1991 to the present. In addition, she had conducted a year-long professional development project for a local K–6 school working specifically with the school's Hopi language and culture program. Subsequently, the Hopi tribe partnered with the Department of Language, Reading, and Culture (now the Department of Teaching, Learning, and Sociocultural Studies) to offer courses.

5. This history is documented in the following Hopi Tribal Council resolutions. H-129-94 approved the Hopi Language Assessment Project (HLAP) to quantify Hopi language shift and loss. The HLAP was conducted in 1997 confirming significant language shift from Hopi to predominantly English in households surveyed. Following dissemination of HLAP results, H-022-98 approved the Hopi Language Education and Preservation Plan (HLEP) establishing the Hopilavayi project under the umbrella of the Hopi Culture Preservation Office. H-010-2006 reiterated the "language survival goals" stated in the Hopi Pötskwani'at 2002 including teacher training and certification in Hopi language and culture, the establishment of formal relationships with universities as well as mandating all schools to include a Hopi language curriculum. Moreover, H-010-2006 designated trust funds from the Title IV of the Arizona-Florida Land Exchange Act of 1998, PL 100-696 "in accordance with this resolution."

6. In the Hopi culture, men are the weavers that includes weaving the wedding robes for the bride of the groom; the groom is their clan relative. Likewise, Hopi men are the moccasin makers. In Hopi tradition, the bride remains at the groom's home for the duration of time it takes to complete making the wedding robes and buckskin boots for her and her children (indicates that completing the wedding ceremony itself may occur long after the couple begin their lives as husband and wife). During her stay, the bride demonstrates her industriousness.

7. Spirit beings that have control over the rains.

8. During the summer, the katsinam come from their home at *Nuvatukwi'ovi* or *Kiisiwu* (San Francisco Peaks) to bring moisture to Hopi farmers' fields and to remind the Hopi people to adhere to the Hopi way of life through their song and dance which they perform in the village plaza.

9. "Formerly known as the Office of Indian Education Programs, the Bureau of Indian Education (BIE) was renamed and established on August 29, 2006, to reflect the parallel purpose and organizational structure BIE has in relation to other programs within the Office of the Assistant Secretary-Indian Affairs." www.bia.gov/bie

10. Somi'mana states that opening with this phrase is her way of acknowledging that "once you realize where you're at"—attaining a critical consciousness— you go forward.

11. *Piqöswungwa*, Bear Strap Clan, belongs to a phratry made up of all the clans that came across the carcass of a dead bear during their migrations: *Honngyam*, Bear Clan, *Piqösngyam*, Bear Strap Clan, *Tsorngyam*, Bluebird, and *Kohkyangngyam*, Spider Clan. These totems signify separate identities and serve as reminders of some significant thing that helped them survive as a group during their travels. They are clan relatives, therefore, they can call their children by names that represent any of their related clans. (Bernita Duwahoyeoma, email communication, July 8, 2020).

12. "Most Hopi speakers regard the language as having three dialects: First Mesa Hopi, Second Mesa Hopi, and Third Mesa Hopi. The dialectal differences are apparent in the pronunciation of syllables containing vowels with a grave accent (à, è, ì, ò, ù)" (Nicholas, 2008, p. 31).

13. "Initiation into the katsina society or *katsinvaki* 'is the first ceremony in which Hopi children participate, being the initiatory step into a society [the esoteric realm]' (Sekaquaptewa, 1985, p. 23) traditionally occurring at seven or eight years of age" (Nicholas, 2008, pp. 148–149).

14. One of a host social dances through which Hopi youth come to know their kinship roles and responsibilities, particularly between a paternal aunt and her nephew reinforced through dancing (B. Duwahoyeoma, personal communication, January 1, 2017).

15. The appropriate translation for my mother's words was, "When you were a child, you were a fluent Hopi speaker." Hopi was my first language but as an adult, I struggled to speak Hopi after "putting it aside" at age eight.

16. We use our Hopi names as one of the "conditions" we establish in our Hopi language teaching environments under which we can empower ourselves.

17. She decided to retire with the federally initiated transition from Bureau of Indian Education (BIE) schools to that of grant schools; however, the new language and culture teaching position was opened and prompted her return to teaching in this positon.
18. Her teaching post away from Hopi was necessitated by the transition of the Hopi BIE to grant school status. This move allowed Somi'mana to maintain her employment status in the BIE school system.
19. This was drafted and exists in the Hopi language version. This is a "loose" translation into English.
20. Policy implementation—tribal and school—of Hopi culture and language programs has been primarily assumed by Hopi community members employed as bilingual para-educators or teacher assistants in existing school-based programs.
21. "Applying and extending Blommaert's (2010) notion of sociolinguistic scale—the stratified vertical ordering of sociolinguistic resources across time, space, and (we add) place—we explore how macro level policies are complicit in truncating or "scaling down" Indigenous language resources... [and] then examine the interaction of macro level policies with local language practices and the displacement and fragmentation of Indigenous language resources." Our analysis of ethnographic case studies showed "how local Indigenous and non-Indigenous educator–researcher–activists are 're-scaling' Indigenous language resources by re-emplacing them in the non-traditional domains of the classroom and school (cf. Pietakäinen, 2010)" (McCarty et al., 2012, p. 52).

REFERENCES

Blair, H., Paskemin, D., & Laderoute, B. (2003). Preparing Indigenous language advocates, teachers, and researchers in Western Canada. In J. Rehyner, O. Trujillo, R. L. Carrosco, & L. Lockard (Eds.), *Nurturing native languages* (pp. 93–104). Northern Arizona University.

Blommaert, J. (2010). *The sociolinguistics of globalization*. Cambridge University Press.

Brayboy, B. M., Faircloth, S. C., Lee, T. S., Maaka, M. J., & Richardson, T. A. (2015). Sovereignty and education: An overview of the unique nature of Indian education. *Journal of American Indian Education, 54*(1), 1–9.

Cajete, G. (2015). *Indigenous community: Rekindling the teachings of the seventh fire: Toward an evolving epistemology of contemporary Indigenous education*. Living Justice Press.

Cajete, G. A. (2010). Contemporary Indigenous education: A nature-centered American Indian philosophy for a 21st century. *Futures, 42*(10), 1126–1132.

Hopi Dictionary Project. (1998). *Hopi dictionary/Hopìikwa lavàytutveni: A Hopi-English dictionary of the Third Mesa Dialect*. The University of Arizona Press.

Hopi Tribal Council. (1994). *Hopi Tribal Council Resolution: H-129-94*. Hopi Tribe, Office of the Tribal Secretary.

Hopi Tribal Council. (1998). *Hopi Tribal Council Resolution: H-022-98*. Hopi Tribe, Office of the Tribal Secretary.

Hopi Tribal Council. (2001). *Hopi Tribal Council Resolution: H-119-2001.* Hopi Tribe, Office of the Tribal Secretary.

Hopi Tribal Council. (2006). *Hopi Tribal Council Resolution: H-010-2006.* Hopi Tribe, Office of the Tribal Secretary.

Hornberger, N. H., & Swinehart, K. F. (2012). Not just *Situaciones de la Vida:* Professionalization and Indigenous language revitalization in the Andes. *International Multilingual Research Journal, 6*(1), 35–49.

James, H. C. (1974). *Pages from Hopi history.* The University of Arizona Press.

Jorgensen, M. (2007). *Rebuilding native nations: Strategies for governance and development.* The University of Arizona Press.

Lyons, O. (2007). Foreword. In M. Jorgensen (Ed.), *Rebuilding Native nations: Strategies for governance and development* (pp. vii–x). The University of Arizona Press.

McCarty, T. L., Nicholas, S. E., & Wyman, L. T. (2012). Re-emplacing place in the "global here and now"—Critical ethnographic case studies of Native American language planning and policy. *International Multilingual Research Journal, 6*(1), 50–63.

Nicholas, S. E. (2008). *Becoming "fully" Hopi: The role of the Hopi language in the contemporary lives of Hopi youth—A Hopi case study of language shift and vitality.* Unpublished doctoral dissertation. University of Arizona, Tucson.

Nicholas, S. E. (2021). A Hopi model of heritage language teacher preparation: The Hopilavayi Summer Institute. In L. Crowshoe, I. Genee, M. Peddle, & J. Smith (Eds.), *Sustaining Indigenous languages: Connecting communities, teachers, and scholars* (pp. 89–106). Northern Arizona University.

Nuvamsa, B. (2011). *Nuvamsa responds to defeated Hopi Tribe Constitution Draft 24A.* https://beyondthemesas.com/2011/01/28/nuvamsa-responds-to-defeated-hopi-tribe-constitution-draft-24a/

Ruiz, R. (1984). Orientations in language planning. *NABE Journal, 8*(2), 15–34.

Ruiz, R. (1991). The empowerment of language-minority students. In C. E. Sleeter (Ed.), *Empowerment through multicultural education* (pp. 217–227). SUNY Press.

Sekaquaptewa, E., Hill, K. C., & Washburn, D. K. (2015). *Hopi Katsina Songs.* University of Nebraska Press.

Sekaquatewa, H. (1985). *Me and mine: The life story of Helen Sekaquaptewa (as told to Louise Udall).* University of Arizona Press.

Smith, G. H. (2003). *Indigenous struggle for the transformation of education and schooling.* Alaska Federation of Natives (AFN) Convention. Anchorage, Alaska.

Smith, L. T. (1999). *Decolonizing methodologies: Research and Indigenous Peoples.* Zed Books.

Trujillo, O., Viri, D., Figueira, A., & Manuelito, K. (2005). Native educators: Interface with language and culture in schooling. In J. Cohen, K. T. McAlister, K. Rolstad, & J. MacSwan (Eds.), *Proceedings of the 4th International Symposium on Bilingualism* (pp. 2274–2284). Cascadilla Press.

Viri, D. F. (1980). *Hopi education: Integrating past, present and future.* Hotevilla-Bacavi Community School.

Williams, R. A., Jr. (2005). *Like a loaded weapon: The Rehnquist court. Indian rights, and the legal history of racism in America* (pp. 33–70). The University of Minnesota Press.

SECTION III

ENGAGING FAMILIES AND COMMUNITIES IN INDIGENOUS EDUCATION

CHAPTER 12

CENTERING INDIGENOUS PHILOSOPHIES OF COMMUNITY IN FAMILY, COMMUNITY, AND SCHOOL ENGAGEMENT

Hollie Anderson Kulago
Tsiehente Herne

TWO SHORT STORIES

This chapter begins with two short personal stories from the authors. We came into relationship with one another through an Indigenous teacher education program at a small college in upstate New York, within the original homelands of the Haudenosaunee Confederacy (also known as the Iroquois Confederacy) which spans across New York state and Ontario, Canada. Hollie is Diné and originally from the Navajo Nation in the northeastern part of Arizona. She was the director and faculty for the Indigenous teacher education program. Tsiehente is Kanien'keha:ka (Mohawk) originally from Akwasasne, NY. She is currently an in-service teacher and was a

Indigenizing Education, pages 185–211
Copyright © 2022 by Information Age Publishing
www.infoagepub.com

student in an Indigenous teacher education program. We begin with these stories because they represent significant points in our lives when we came to understand what it meant to draw upon the power of community to support an education that leads to our continuance as Indigenous people. In this chapter, we theorize ways that lifeways and certain concepts that are taught through ceremonies can guide Indigenous family and community engagement to support the overall well-being of our students.

Hollie's Story[1]

When the first baby of our new generation, my niece, was born to my oldest sister, my two other sisters, my mom, and I stood in the hospital room taking turns holding and admiring our beautiful baby girl. With so much love and excitement, we talked to her, introduced ourselves to her, welcomed her, and within that, my second oldest sister asked, "Who's going to tie her hair?" My sisters, my mom, and I laughed because the *Kinaałdá* (Diné puberty rights ceremony) was to be held a good 13 years away, but we knew the seriousness of that question and we were already planning for the ceremony. My oldest sister said, "Mom, of course." We all agreed, and continued to happily welcome our daughter, knowing that our *Tsénahabiłnii* (Sleepy Rock People) clan would continue on for another generation. This experience always comes to mind when I think about educational goals from a Diné perspective because it references the Kinaałdá and the teachings of *k'é*, which is later discussed in detail. The goals of the Kinaałdá are steered toward the continuation and existence of our people through collaborative support from the family and community.

Tsiehente's Story

When I was 15 years old, I watched my mother gather young boys, uncles, leaders, and family members from the Kanienkeha;ka Territory to witness and be a part of my younger brother's ceremony to transition from boyhood to *ronenkentá:ron* (young man). Coming from Haudenosauee homelands of Upstate New York and my mother being a Bear Clan Mother, I listened to her talk most nights about trying to provide support for her children that would be about culture, and in hopes of deterring an introduction to drugs or alcohol. When she talks about the uncles and aunties that work alongside her she states, "We live what we love, we are not in the confines of Western curriculum; that is the key difference to what makes us unique and what makes us work" (Lousie Herne, Kanien'keha:ka, personal communication, August, 2020). I remember spending 4 days at my uncle's home during the *Oheró:kon* (word they use to reference the rights of passage ceremony) fasting ritual in the woods, helping with various chores, including putting down prayers for my brother. In that moment, being with my *kahwatsí:re* (family), visiting, playing, praying, helping bring wood, cooking for helpers, or watching the fire and observing the support my brother received, I realized it was something I wanted to experience too. Why would I want something so beautiful to only be for the boys? So, I asked my cousin to come with me to ask my mom to do something similar with the girls since I was older than my brother, I figured it would be worth a shot. It was only fair that the girls be allowed to have their own Oheró:kon ceremony. I wanted my family to see how proud I would be and how strong I could be. Not knowing what that entailed or what that all meant, I knew I wanted to be given the opportunity to experience something unexplainably difficult, but yet so beautiful to endure. I wanted to see that we, as young women, could do something other than party and get into trouble, by cultivating a tradition of critical thinkers who embody aspects of survivance based on our own traditions and teachings. With these experiences, we would be able to bring many kahwatsí:res together, to hear the kahwatsí:res tell stories to their young initiates and to witness relationships mended through ceremony for the young men and women. When I participated in the Kanien'keha:ka Oheró:kon rites of passage, I found my self-worth and established a sense of identity through my experience in ceremonial fasting. Throughout my journey, my experiences in ceremony have given me the chance to tell my story through my own language, create dialogue with other youth, and teach other communities the importance of rites of passage. Since then, every year, I am asked to visit and talk to the youth about my experiences at the yearly Oheró:kon gathering. Sometimes I am just a witness, other times I am an aunty to a niece who does not have one which helps me, the young woman, and many other volunteers, become family and build relationships. This is a way we continue to help the youth throughout their journey as young boys or girls transitioning to adulthood. The knowledge and the power of knowing through our old ways of ceremony and tradition is happening because my mother created a safe space of learning and experiencing that has rippled across Haudenosaunee territories to revitalize our sense of family and community.

INTRODUCTION

In this chapter, we share our stories of educational experiences that were specifically organized to ensure the survival and existence of our Native nations. These experiences often are, or originate from, ceremonies. We refer to these experiences as educational experiences because they were consciously designed with specific goals for learning certain knowledges, values, and processes for youth as they grow into healthy contributing adults. The stories point to the ways that these experiences are collective educational experiences that cannot be successful without the relationships with, and engagement of, the families and communities. Afterall, they are educational experiences that ensure that the *lifeways* of our people will continue to exist. Tsalagi scholars Jeff Corntassel and Tiffany Hardbarger (2019) state that there is an urgency for Indigenous Peoples to regenerate *lifeways*, "which are the ways in which complex relationships and governance are nurtured and honoured within a community context, and are the driving forces behind Indigenous sustainable practices that promote community health and well-being" (p. 88). As authors of this chapter, we share our stories to describe the lifeways that guide our work as educators. The stories highlight the components of the educational experiences that have ensured the continued existence of our nations. We theorize what these components could look like in schools.

We set the context starting with a brief description of relevant historical events that have created the necessity of this chapter. That is, a brief description of United States educational strategies and goals for Indigenous Peoples are reviewed to describe how Indigenous children were purposely separated from their families and communities. The description demonstrates how necessary it is for us in the contemporary context to return to educational approaches that center and perpetuate our Indigenous philosophies which are rooted in relationality and necessitates the engagement of the family and community in educational settings. Then, an overview of frameworks that help us understand the current contexts and approaches to Indigenous education will be reviewed to position this work within components of critical and culturally sustaining Indigenous pedagogies, and family and community engagement.

After the context is set, the theoretical framework of an Indigenous philosophy of community (IPhC) is used to describe two educational experiences by the co-authors. The experiences point to ways that education for the reproduction and continuance of a people is guided by a sense of relationality (Holmes & Gonzales, 2017) and communality (Cajete, 2015). Hollie will describe her understanding and experiences with the Kinaałdá and the concept of *k'é* which will reveal the significance of her opening story and the framework used in her research study. Tsiehente will describe how the concepts taught through Oheró:kon have helped her understand what her students need in school to feel that they are supported and valued. Each of these descriptions demonstrate ways that family and community are crucial to the healthy growth of our youth. The collective agency that defines the IPhC is then re-centered as a strength of Indigenous Peoples to be used in educational spaces, specifically in relationship to school.

In the last section, we describe how the concepts inherent to the Diné and Kanien'keha:ka educational experiences described can be central to the ways that they envision and/or practice their engagement through family and community engagement. Hollie shares findings from a qualitative research study (Kulago, 2011) that investigated how Diné youth defined community. Tsiehente describes how her role is guided by her Kanien'keha:ka ways of knowing to support her students, in ways that other teachers cannot, as a teacher and aunty. The experiences shared within this chapter extend from and continue to pose important questions that guide our work. We wonder: What if the knowledges, concepts, and practices of survival taught through Oheró:kon, Kinaałdá, and other ways that we demonstrate value of our youth and their futures, were in the daily processes of schooling? What is possible for our youth and Native nations when relationships and engagement between school, families, and community are intentional about centering and perpetuating Indigenous philosophies of community to support the holistic well-being of the youth and to strengthen the communities? We invite the reader to consider ways that Indigenous philosophies and ways of knowing are centered in your work or how they can become central so that you support the holistic well-being of Indingeous youth, families, and communities.

HISTORY

Many historical events led up to the disruption of the communal way of living for Indigenous Peoples. Western schooling, which specifically for this chapter we refer to as U.S. American education, was considered the solution to the Indian problem aimed to assimilate, civilize, Christianize, Americanize, detribalize, and deculturalize Indigenous Peoples with the intentions to disconnect us from our lands (Adams, 1995; Huff, 1997; Lomawaima & McCarty, 2006; Reyhner & Eder, 2004; Spring, 2001). The attacks on the tribal ways of life which were considered "socialistic and contrary to the values of 'civilization'" (Spring, 2001, p. 28) were identified as insufficient and failed in the attempts to civilize Indigenous Peoples. "Civilized" meant embodying the virtues of private property (Grande, 2015), meaning that the ownership of land as property was civilized, and living in relationship with the land was not. It was believed that once the Native Americans[2] were detribalized (disconnected from the land), they would fully assimilate into mainstream capitalistic America (Reyhner & Eder, 2004; Spring 2001). U.S. schools also promoted and continue to promote individualism. Underlying this idea was the belief that the Indigenous Peoples should become individualized with individual wants: "He will say 'I' instead of 'We' and 'This is mine,' instead of 'This is ours'" (Oberly, as cited in Adams, 1995, p. 23).

Ultimately, within the context of settler colonialism, the goal of U.S. education was to eliminate the Native presence which meant to eradicate the culture of Indigenous People. The hearts of our cultures that were targeted, were our reverence and responsibilities of our relationships to our people and our land. Corntassel (2012) states that the "disconnection from our lands, cultures and communities has led to social suffering and destruction of families" (p. 88) which begs us to consider the ways that "colonization systematically deprives us of our experiences and confidence as Indigenous peoples" (p. 88) and directly links to the disintegration of our community health and well-being. Specific tactics were used to separate our children and their schooling experiences from their families and communities with attempts to completely sever those ties.

Hopi/Tewa scholar Jeremy Garcia (2019) states that the menacing impacts of colonialism from the establishment of the first missionary schools and throughout time through various policies, continue to impact families and communities today. He also reminds us that "schools [should] not only understand and problematize the effects of settler colonialism, but [should] recognize the strength of Indigenous epistemologies and ontologies that determine Indigenous notions of family and community" (Garcia, 2019, p. 76). With the understanding that our Indigenous notions of family and community were intentionally and systematically disrupted, we should work to identify and center our philosophies within the work we do as Indigenous teachers in order to heal those severed ties. There are various ways that we can center our philosophies and strengthen our communities within the learning experiences of Indigenous students as described by multiple scholars through the continuous development of critical Indigenous family and community engagement.

INDIGENOUS FAMILY AND COMMUNITY ENGAGEMENT

Indigenous resurgence urges us to turn away from colonialist practices and reclaim and perpetuate relationships grounded in land, culture, and community to strengthen Indigenous nationhood through everyday actions (Corntassel, 2012; Corntassel & Hardbarger, 2019; Simpson, 2017). The process requires that we center, empower, and activate Indigenous knowledges and philosophies. As teachers with critical Indigenous consciousness, we know the histories that have led to the disruptions in our ways of knowing and being. It is up to us to provide educational environments that work to heal "soul wounds" (Jacob, 2013) and "cultivate the heart" (Shirley, 2017) through everyday acts of resurgence (Corntassel & Hardbarger, 2019) for our students who might feel the wounds as well, and/or be confronted with various emotions as they process new levels of critical consciousness.

Yakama scholar Michelle Jacob (2013) identifies the concept of the "soul wound" as an "important jumping-off point to analyze the importance of developing a critical healing approach" (p. 11). Originally coined by Eduardo Duran (as cited in Jacob, 2013), the concept of the soul wound describes how colonial violence inflicted upon Indigenous ancestors resulted in the historical trauma that continues to impact Native peoples (Jacob, 2013). Jacob explains that if "the traumatic response to colonialism goes unaddressed and unresolved, then healing the soul wound will not happen" (p. 11). She uses this framework to analyze ways that Yakama activists outside of the classrooms have worked to heal the soul wounds still felt within the community through decolonizing praxis. Through descriptions of three case studies, Jacob reveals a Yakama decolonizing praxis that could lead to healing social change. To promote healing social change according to Jacob, we must (a) understand Indigenous bodies as sites of critical pedagogy through such things as dance, language speaking, and traditional food harvesting; (b) center social justice praxis to build moral communities by such things as engaging the youth and elders in caring and knowledge-sharing relationships; and (c) utilize grassroots Indigenous resistance as a mechanism to dismantle colonial logic by recognizing the soul wounds that need healing and "to do it" (Jacob, 2013). Like in Jacob's description, we know the soul wounds that need to be addressed when we think about the severed relationships, and the importance of the family and community relationships with the school and the education of our children. We can use this understanding as a "jumping-off point" as well, to rethink ways that we build relationships between schools, families, and communities rooted in our Indigenous philosophies of community.

Diné scholar Valerie Shirley (2017) warns us that when "educators teach into these risks that move students into an emotional space where the stories of oppression stir up such emotions, it is crucial for educators to consider the ways in which they can navigate youth through this emotional space" (p. 166). She proposes that within an Indigenous social justice pedagogy (ISJP), educators *cultivate the heart* by drawing upon aspects of Indigenous epistemologies to heal and empower the youth. Shirley states that in ISJP,

> Indigenous epistemologies are purposefully infused in the daily structure of the learning environment...drawing on Indigenous knowledge systems to create an environment where young people begin to privilege, promote, revitalize and center their Indigenous ways of thinking and being. (p. 167)

She goes on to explain that "cultivating the heart toward empowerment is an essential step that sets the stage for students to consider the ways in which they can contribute to the betterment of both their classroom community and their Indigenous community in general" (p. 167). Centering

Indigenous ways of knowing throughout the daily structure of the learning environment can extend outward to ways that teachers of Indigenous students engage family and community by centering Indigenous philosophies of community in their approaches. Similarly, Corntassel and Hardbarger (2019) state that the "everydayness" and perpetuation of centering Indigenous knowledges addresses the immediacy for renewing aspects of everyday Indigenous life, specifically, relationships. To "perpetuate" is to practice repeatedly with an understanding that there is an obligation to carry on and to engage everyday acts of Indigenous resurgence and nationhood (Corntassel & Hardbarger, 2019). Within this chapter, we describe how we felt empowered by our ways of knowing as we share stories of our supportive educational experiences, and how we work to cultivate similar relationships with families and communities.

Theoretical Orientations

As with classroom pedagogy, seeking to approach other areas of education for Indigenous students through critical and culturally sustaining/revitalizing processes is necessary to the well-being and empowerment of Native communities and nations. Two significant frameworks have emerged in recent literature that contribute to our understanding of the possibilities of significant Indigenous family and community engagement with schools. Both call for a critical awareness of the ways that schools have "attempted to detach us from our languages, culture knowledge systems, and original landscapes" (Garcia, 2019, p. 77) and continue to marginalize Indigenous families through racism, invisibility, exclusions, tokenism, and false decision-making (Bang et al., 2019). Garcia (2019) and Bang et al. (2019) provide guidance in how to navigate these relationships in ways that empower the families, communities, and students.

First, Garcia (2019) describes a culturally sustaining Indigenous family engagement (CSIFE) framework that calls for processes to engage family and community through school. According to Garcia, the CSIFE framework:

1. Creates spaces for critical dialogues that empower individuals, validate identities, and co-construct spaces for collective agency for Indigenous education.
2. Is a cross-generational healing process that contextualizes histories within ourselves, schools, and the contemporary moments, in recognizing colonial constructs that impact us.
3. Indigenizes and sustains family and community engagement.
4. Embraces and respects the diverse family dynamics.

5. Empowers family and community to be change agents and advocates whose actions are rooted in social justice and survivance.
6. Cultivates family and community engagement for self-education, self-determination, and sovereignty (Garcia, 2019, pp. 84–86).

Garcia's framework seeks to lead educators through a reflexive process and to sustain Indigenous knowledges that center how to be in relationship with others so that Indigenous teachers, families, communities, and students can advocate and advance educational goals through collective agency.

From an Indigenous resurgence framework, Bang et al. (2019) state that Indigenous families are central to the strength of Indigenous nations and theorize "four main facets of family engagement that contribute to Indigenous resurgence" (p. 792). The four facets are:

1. learning from and with our lands, waters, and more-than-humans is integral to Indigenous family engagement;
2. multigenerational and lifelong learning are integral to Indigenous education and therefore foundational for Indigenous family engagement;
3. relationships and collaboration with non-Indigenous educators and systems need new forms of partnership that recognize and cultivate everyday Indigenous resurgence; and
4. equitable and transformative collaboration with families leads to rigorous academics and higher achievement for Indigenous students (Bang et al., 2019, p. 792).

Bang et al. (2019) explicitly focus on "promising practices and everyday resurgence in families and beyond" by focusing on perpetuating "Indigenous families' and communities' ways of knowing and being to combat colonial enclosures" (p. 798). Furthermore, they encourage spaces where families and communities can engage in imaginative and creative ways to envision their realities, including within schools and other educational spaces.

From these two frameworks, it is evident that schools are spaces where families and communities should engage in the sustaining, perpetuating, and generating of a resurgence of Indigenous ways of knowing and being. The frameworks point to three specific components that are demonstrated in the stories shared in this chapter. First, critical awareness and dialogue is essential in understanding the various family histories and dynamics as to "empower individuals, validate identities, and co-construct spaces for collective agency" (Garcia, 2019, p. 84). When there is a sense of collective agency, Garcia (2019) claims that "Indigenous families and communities can then draw on this collective agency to advocate for equitable outcomes in educational settings" (p. 84). Bang et al. (2019) claim that for schools to collaborate with Indigenous families, they must first acknowledge the "historical legacy of settler-colonial education on Indigenous communities" (p. 797) and be mindful of the types of processes used. Furthermore, they claim that using Indigenous forms of deliberation, diplomacy, and decision-making as collective processes open up space and create new pathways for family leadership and engagement (Bang et al., 2019). In Tsiehente's story, she describes how the families and leaders in her community saw the need to revitalize the rights of passage ceremony so that the youth could transition from childhood to adulthood in a ceremony to provide them with the necessary knowledge and tools to become healthy Kanien'keha:ka community members. It was a collective effort, and still is, to set the goals and make the ceremony successful. The teachings and family support that Tsiehente received during her participation in the ceremony continue to guide her as she advocates for her students and works to empower them through Kanien'keha:ka teachings.

Secondly, both frameworks point to ways to indigenize family and community engagement once critical awareness and self-reflection has become a continuous process. Bang et al. (2019) state that there is "an unwavering reach for well-being, love, fierce grace, and strength that enflesh Indigenous ways of knowing and being in the here-and-now" (p. 799). Garcia (2019) states, "Indigenous values, knowledge, language, ceremonies, and connections to place make up our claim to indigeneity" (p. 84). These statements point to the significance of centering Indigenous philosophies and lifeways to guide the practices that schools use to engage families and community members. By centering and intentionally perpetuating Indigenous philosophies and lifeways we will also be able to intentionally refuse ongoing colonization (Bang et al., 2019). With Indigenous philosophies at the foundation of family and community engagement, we would be able to enact "the processes by which our knowledges and ways of being have come to be" and could lead to family and community engagement as critical sites of learning and resurgence (Bang et al., 2019, p. 799). An important step in this process is to promote cross-generational healing (Garcia, 2019) and multigenerational and community learning (Bang et al., 2019) so that Indigenous knowledge can be shared by elders and other knowledgeable community members. Bang et al. (2019) state that "multigenerational and community learnings are key aspects to Indigenous pedagogy and ways of knowing and being" (p. 802). Garcia (2019) claims that the source for healing across generations and building strength is found within Indigenous epistemologies. These frameworks call for a centering of Indigenous philosophies with guidance from various knowledge keepers. The Diné youth in Hollie's research study claim that they wanted and needed to build positive relationships with their elders because they have been told to respect elders, including teachers, but they felt that the older generations judged the youth too harshly. One youth described how he understood why some teachers were harsher than others, and highlighted the need for intergenerational healing:

> I think we need to earn our respect [from teachers], because it all reflects back on how our elders were raised. And during the Navajo Long Walk, [the Navajo] got abused... [The soldiers] abused children and everything and [the Navajo] didn't know how to act to other people and that's how [the Navajo] are today and, maybe we need to respect their values and what they believe.

The values to which the youth participant was referring were those of helping each other, treating each other with respect, and learning from their elders. He engaged his critical thinking about the history of the people to heal the relationships so that he could then learn from his teachers and elders.

The third component important to our discussion includes the goals of self-education, self-determination, and sovereignty of Native nations. These goals should be cultivated through Indigenous family and community engagement and partnerships. With collaborative decision-making and goal setting, schools can identify issues that are important to the families and community. Indigenous students, families, and community members should be able to see themselves "as part of the larger process for sustaining not only their cultural knowledge and values, but to engage in transformative results that impact self-determination and create opportunities that reinforce our rights to sovereignty" (Garcia, 2019, p. 86). Additionally, schooling should be connected to the students' lives which "requires explicit connections between learning opportunities and community wellness such that youth can visibly see the impact of their learning and leadership within their communities" (Bang et al., 2019, p. 802). Ultimately, the partnerships and approaches to engagement should "critically consider whom family and community engagement policies and practices are meant to benefit and whether or not these actions are fulfilling their purpose and toward what ends" (Bang et al., 2019, p. 806). In Tsiehente's story below, she describes how the school discouraged teachers to get involved in the lives of their students, specifically when the youth wanted to organize actions to support the Tyendinaga Mohawk blockade in which many of their family members participated to stand in solidarity with the Wet'suwet'en heredity chiefs as they opposed construction of a pipeline through their territory. Tsiehente was proud of her students because they were taking action to support the sovereignty of another nation, but she was also upset with the stance that the school took. As a teacher and community member, she got caught in the middle of the goals of her community and the goals of the school.

These frameworks are meant to inform policy, practice, and research. We describe our work and theorize from the perspectives of a teacher and a researcher. Indigenous teachers and researchers are essential to perpetuate Indigenous lifeways centered in Indigenous philosophies and ways of knowing.

INDIGENOUS PHILOSOPHIES OF COMMUNITY

Indigenous philosophies of community (IPhC) are the source from which teachers can draw to organize their frameworks for Indigenous family and community engagement. IPhC guides the protocol of how to engage in all situations and are built on familial responsibilities and relationships and are aimed at survival (Kulago, 2016). Holmes and Gonzalez (2017) describe *relationality* as "coming to know oneself through the contextual constellation of relationship" which instructs how education "strives towards the whole and ethical development of the person situated in the collective" (p. 219). Tewa scholar Gregory Cajete (2015) claims that "Indigenous Peoples have always been intimately aware of our 'communality' . . . our sense of communality is the basis of our identity as distinct peoples" (p. 66). Indigenous ways of knowing position us to always be in relationship. Cajete (2015) claims that to rehumanize our communities from the disempowering nature of colonization and to work towards self-healing, teaching, and learning should seek to restore communal ways to Indigenous peoples which position us in relationship with all aspects of the natural world. Centralizing the concepts of IPhC including relationality and communality, is critical in promoting the collective agency as described in the previous section because it puts individuals in relationship with others where they do not stand alone. It is critical in promoting the collective agency of the families, communities, and schools to make decisions for the well-being of the youth and to strengthen their communities. When the families, community, and schools engage with each other through IPhC, they would inherently advocate for the holistic development and support of the youth. In the educational experiences we describe in the next section, we identify concepts that are specific to our Native nation's IPhC.

Diné Educational Experience and K'é

The Diné educational experience of which I, Hollie, have identified as crucial to the continuance of the Diné is the Kinaałdá. I do not speak for all Diné or believe that this is the one way that all Diné interpret the Kinaałdá. This is my description of a complex and multifaceted ceremony that I describe for the purposes of this chapter. The Kinaałdá is a 4-day puberty ceremony for girls as they transition to womanhood. As mentioned in my opening story, for some, this is a ceremony of which the preparation starts as soon as a baby girl is born. Throughout the 4-day ceremony, the girl is taught many lessons, by many different people. The girl is the most important person in the ceremony, and the lessons revolve around the goals of keeping respectful relationships (Roessel, 1993). The family selects an older woman to "tie the girl's hair." This woman becomes the teacher, mentor, and ultimately, the person who the parents want their daughter to be like. During the 4 days, the girl is referred to as the Kinaałdá and it is believed that she is "holy" and the Diyin Dine'e (Holy People) are with her. Because of this status, she must do all she can to be the best Diné person she can be because she is basically setting the groundwork for the type of adult she will become. She must take care of her physical health by eating only natural foods and running to the East three times a day; her mental health by being thoughtful, a problem solver, decision maker, and critical thinker; her emotional health by being generous, caring, unselfish, strong, positive, helpful, and all the positive virtues valued by Diné; and her spiritual health by praying, and engaging in various ceremonial practices. She is taught how to be a good relative and embody k'é (relationships of respect). On the final night, family, friends, and community members are invited to sing and to bless her and her life with various prayers. This ceremony is the educational experience that ensures our existence as Diné because it celebrates our young women's physical ability to reproduce and teaches her what it means to be a good woman (mother/caretaker) and carry on the concept of k'é. The relationships she gains and strengthens with all of the people who contribute to her ceremony demonstrate their concern for her future (Kulago, 2011). Respectful relationships that are cooperative, generous, and appreciative are demonstrated through the support offered to her from relatives and family friends. Ruth Roessel (1981) claims that "sharing is the cornerstone of this experience" (p. 82) because no family could have enough food on its own to carry out all the responsibilities associated with the ceremony. This ceremony, educational experience, happens because of the support of the family and community in any way that they are able to contribute to the health and well-being of the Kinaałdá.

As I have described elsewhere (Kulago, 2011, 2012), the concept of k'é speaks directly to the way relationships of respect and interdependence should exist between people. K'é has been defined as kinship, clanship, peace, love, kindness, cooperation, thoughtfulness, friendliness, and respectful relations with nature and others (Lamphere, 1977; McCarty & Bia, 2002; McCloskey, 2007). The teaching of k'é was the specific reason that the Holy People of the Diné created the Kinaałdá puberty ceremony for females to ensure our existence, survival, and reproduction. The importance of the ceremony is to teach females about how to be "good" mothers/caretakers and women. "Good" mothers taught their children how to build and value relationships. They modeled for their children how to treat other people and nature through a worldview of k'é.

It is important to note that k'é is not simply one thing but means all the positive virtues previously described based on the context in which it is used. For the purposes in this chapter, I describe k'é through four qualities that we should embody to continue our positive existence as Diné—the qualities we should embody to be good people. The first quality that the community should embody is the basic knowledge and recognition of each other as family or relative. Recognizing kinship through clans demonstrates knowledge of who you are, how you should relate to people, and how other people relate to you. Also, in nature, we recognize relationships with certain natural elements as family. The second quality is that of maintaining harmonious relationships by expressing love, compassion, friendliness, kindness, and trust as one would to family members. The third quality is sharing with one another and being generous, unselfish, and thoughtful of others. The fourth quality is being able to depend on one another and being dependable oneself. In a qualitative research study, I investigated how Diné youth define community in which the youth pointed to these qualities as they explained the various ways that they felt they should be supported but were not always (Kulago, 2011).

If we consider the Kinaaldá ceremony as a formal educational experience, then we can consider k'é as the educational goal, and the means of education. Thus, the goal of this educational experience is to teach the young person how to be a useful and contributing adult to strengthen the community, through her experience with the community during her ceremony. The ceremony is successful because all involved contributors have a common goal. They all want to ensure the positive future for the girl. They want her to be a "good person" and have the proper values that will contribute to the community as a whole when she becomes an adult. None of the people who contribute expect any materialistic individual gain from the ceremony but value the spiritual and emotional benefits. In this process, the girl understands that her cooperation is of utmost importance. All the people who help are depending on her to bring blessings upon them. All members supporting the ceremony have a responsibility and role that contributes to the overall good of the community.

Kanien'keha:ka Educational Experience and Key Concepts

Throughout my teaching career, I, Tsiehente, have learned that Oheró:kon (Under the Husk) rites of passage brings me back to my community. Oheró:kon is the name that is used to describe a rites of passage ceremony held during a child's transition from boy/girl to young man or young woman which is an important transition in any young person's life because they are provided with tools and cultural teachings that they will utilize throughout their lifetime. Clan Mother Louise Herne describes what she sees during the Oheró:kon journey for young women when she states, "Watching a young woman, who had no empowerment of her own because she was living inside a narrative that was handed to her, [come] into her own...it's so amazing to watch, watching her fail, [then] stand up, [get] left out, [and become a] part of [the community] again" (Louise Herne, Kanien'keha:ka, personal communication, August, 2020). She describes how challenging it is for a participant but also how the participant finds the power within herself to create her own narrative. I have experienced this special tradition which has contributed to the confidence I get when telling my story of the 8 years that I have participated and fasted during the ceremony. It continues to give me guidance and wisdom that I could not have received anywhere else. In this journey I found purpose and identity in who I am and want to become, personally and professionally. This has led me to my passion for teaching and educating children through an Indigenized curriculum.

In this ceremony, the youth participate annually with weekly teachings or lectures from local community members. The weekly teachings are incredibly important for every youth to attend as they are sustaining a transformative tradition that models how we talk to each other, how we educate our youth and most importantly having those uncomfortable conversations in healthy ways. The ceremony is held during the spring/summer seasons and it takes 4 years to complete. Their first year of fasting, they are with their community. They must complete the next three by themselves and on their own. The ceremony is a fasting journey that brings youth and adults back to the basics of survival without food and water for a period of time. Their fasting journey teaches them how to make sacrifices for when they start their family and for themselves. It teaches them necessary skills to be self-reliant and self-aware of their environment. Fire keeping is also an important component of the ceremony. Not only do the participants keep a fire burning for warmth, but it is for prayer as they drop tobacco into the fire. The way the participants care for the fire, clean and not messy, symbolizes how they want to keep their families. One of the most important components of the ceremony is the importance of family and community. Family and community members contribute to the ceremony in multiple ways. There are lead aunties and uncles, who are knowledgeable and respected adults and are not always related by blood but help guide the participants through their journeys.

In the years that I took to complete my Oheró:kon journey of transition from a young girl to now a woman, I gained a great deal of respect and admiration for the people that made it happen and continue to make it happen every spring season. People on the outside of the ceremony don't get to see the hard work the families do by having healthy conversations with the young children and teenagers. It is a very beautiful sight to see families that were in need of healing their relationships coming together in ceremony to make sure their children do not have the same life difficulties that they did. Through my experiences, I learned the importance of having an aunty and uncle, and I aspire to carry myself the same way they did. I chose two aunties whom I really admired growing up to guide me through my Oheró:kon journey. They were crucial because they taught me how to use the necessary tools to survive while being on the land, and also the knowledge of what it means to be an Onkwehón:we (the original people) woman. To this day I work alongside them in the community and the education system.

Fifteen years ago, as a result of major concern for the youth by a few leaders and parents, the traditional ceremony was revitalized within our community through lots of research and long conversations with many elders. Throughout years of revitalizing the ceremony, the concerned community members searched for stories and knowledge keepers which has led to Oheró:kon evolving into a beautiful continuously culturally evolving ceremony that brings families and communities back together to our original teachings. The reason we call it "Under the Husk" or Oheró:kon is because our sacred corn is symbolic of prosperity and wisdom contained within. Each kernel contains its purpose in a young person's life and why they were born into the world. When we peel back the layers of husks to reveal the living core, we reveal the beautiful corn the same way we do with our youth—we pull back those layers of childhood and adolescence to reveal a young man or woman presented back into the community. Fortunately, the initiative was taken to revitalize a once lost tradition of our puberty rites ceremony to a normalized gathering of teachings and practices that are happening every year. What I know about our rites of passage is that it is forever evolving as we learn more and respond to the context, and it is one of the few spaces that value our youth, that listen to them, and acknowledge them for their presence and great intellect. I try to do this in my classroom by giving the students choice and centering the curriculum within cultural teachings and ceremonies.

The educational experiences described in this section provide theories of Indigenous education that are specifically designed for continuance of the people and their lifeways guided by Indigenous philosophies of community. The theories presented here center, value, and celebrate the youth and their futures. With the concept of giving back to the community with their own unique talents and skills to share with the community.

CONCEPTUALIZING PRACTICE: INDIGENOUS PHILOSOPHIES OF COMMUNITY

In this section, Hollie describes the concept of k'é through the findings of her qualitative research study that involved Diné youth. Tsiehente describes her own experiences as a community member and teacher and the decisions she makes for her practice as she centers Kanien'keha:ka (Mohawk) IPhC concepts. Both provide descriptions of how concepts from educational experiences provided through ceremonies can be applied within and at the foundation of school. We invite the reader to think about concepts from their communities and IPhC that can help cultivate the heart (Shirley, 2017) and heal soul wounds (Jacob, 2013) by supporting Indigenous students through their Indigenous ways of knowing.

Cultivating K'é at School

In a qualitative study (Kulago, 2011), I, Hollie, asked Diné youth participants[3] about how they define community and how community and school partnerships can be created to support the success and well-being of them and their peers. The findings of the study concluded that the youth ultimately name qualities that align with the concepts of k'é. Although the study began with "academic success" as the goal for creating effective community and school partnerships, academic success took a backseat to the overall well-being of the youth. It was concluded that once the holistic well-being of the youth was provided, academic success would follow. The participants stated that there were members of the community that were not always positively supportive of the youth and saw the school as a place where healing could happen and spread out into the community. The participants described qualities that people should have in order to strengthen the community to more effectively support the youth. This idea makes community and family engagement with school crucial to the well-being of the students and the strengthening of the community.

The Possibility of Cultivating Community in School

The foundation of a community centered in k'é is the recognition of others in the community. This recognition directly aligns with the first quality of k'é described previously as the basic knowledge of each other in the family. Through the use of the Diné clan system and the recognition of clans, a person demonstrates knowledge of who he or she is, how he or she should relate to people, and how other people should relate to him or her. Although the clans identify our relations, and not everyone has or knows their clans, the concept of k'é goes beyond kinship ties because it focuses on the way we behave based on caring relationships in general. The participants of the study described how a basic recognition of other people is important to youth. They agreed that not being judged or ignored would be a good first step to creating positive relationships with the youth. They stated that they needed to feel this type of recognition by school faculty and staff, by their peers, and by the community. They also reflected on their own perspectives of others and admitted that they did the same and consciously worked to be more open-minded and understanding. The basic recognition of other people without judgment is what the participants felt from their families. The feelings of familial relationships are the foundation of k'é.

Once there is a basic recognition of people and relationships, maintaining harmonious relationships by expressing love, compassion, friendliness, kindness, and trust as one would to family members is necessary. The maintenance of harmonious relationships as a quality of k'é, was described by the participants as the ability to trust others and to be trusted in the community. The participants claim that trust is a key factor in creating a supportive environment for the youth. The participants stated that building relationships of trust with peers and adults would help the youth make positive decisions and help them talk through issues they had or get resources they needed. By approaching the youth with relationships of love, compassion, friendliness, kindness, and trust, the youth would find quality relationships where they felt like they could be themselves and still be valued and supported.

Sharing with one another and being dependable, generous, unselfish, helpful, and thoughtful are other important qualities of k'é that promote the maintenance of positive relationships and something the youth want to feel. The youth stated that selfishness and not thinking of how one's actions affected their motivation and positivity and needed to be addressed in their community. Some of the participants stated that many people will only offer to help others if they were getting paid or getting something material out of it. They felt like some of the adults who should be helping them did not understand them or approach them as youth in need of guidance. All of the participants stated that they were raised in families where they were encouraged to be helpful, especially towards elders. Not only is this quality necessary for building relationships with the elders, but it is also necessary for building relationships with the other adults of the community.

Additionally, being able to depend on one another and being dependable oneself is an important component of k'é. As one participant stated, "Everyone needs everyone" (Kulago, 2011, p. 163) in order for the community to function positively. K'é acknowledges the dependence we have on each other and also that we are all being depended on and have a role to play. The constant acknowledgment that we need each other could promote a sense of self-worth to many youth and others in the community. The youth saw their role as taking the initiative to be more helpful towards their community members as a way to contribute to the strengthening of the community such as helping elders and learning the language. They envisioned school as the place where being positive and contributing community members could be taught, and then spread throughout the community.

The Diné youth felt that there was a mismatch in some places between what they have been taught in terms of how to act and live as Diné in community with others, and what they actually experienced in their community. They felt some of their community members were not always positive in the ways that they viewed the youth and therefore didn't necessarily feel supported. The youth theorized that the qualities of k'é should be practiced in the school in order to heal the community. Historically, Indigenous youth were intentionally separated from their families and communities by Western schooling and those severances are still affecting our communities. The participants positioned schools as the place to learn and practice those qualities. Families and community engagement are crucial to the process of healing.

Oheró:kon Concepts at School

Before I, Tsiehente, participated in the Indigenous teacher education program to become a certified art teacher, I was a high school Mohawk language teacher that served 70% Native Americans. Throughout my teaching career, I have always worked hard to support and be there for all students, regardless if they would use their language or not as I am one of the few teachers that is from the same community as my students. I prioritized skills to be successful as a good human being in addition to thriving academically. It's important that I advocate for them when it comes to school issues and for them to know they have allies and support. When I first began teaching at the public high school that served a majority of Native American students, I could see the non-Native teachers favoring the non-Native students over our own Native students. This bothered me so much because they were being stereotyped and mistreated because of the color of their skin or who their family was. It was very evident that they treated Native students differently and expected them to learn and behave like the other students in the classroom. So, much of my teaching career became teaching other teachers how to treat our Native students by modifying their lessons and being culturally sensitive and aware of their differences. More often than not, the staff had misconceptions of the students which were completely wrong and inaccurate because they were basing their ideas on their skin color and assumptions of the community they represented. I remember having a conversation with another teacher (non-Native) and she began talking very negatively about a particular student, which I found inappropriate. I knew this student and understood their family background which was difficult, so school was a safe place for them during the day. When this teacher began gossiping the way that she did, I immediately got up from my chair and started walking away, her expression changed and she asked, "Where are you going? Did I say something wrong?" I turned around and said, "I am not going to sit here and listen to you trash talk a student who I know very well and comes from the community that I come from which you look down on. It is not just him but also the community I come from which you consider is too rez." I continued on,

> How dare you? You're supposed to serve all students' needs and learn about where they come from economically, culturally, and their educational experiences. From the sounds of it, you have no idea what these students have been through when they walk through that door, so you have no right to make those awful comments.

The teacher was in complete shock and began apologizing profusely, not realizing the tone she was setting in her room and to other staff members. From that day forward, I began my work in supporting those students as much as I could in ways that the other teachers were not able or willing to.

Many teachers who did not support the students refused to acknowledge the history that our students' families have faced, how education was not an easy experience in history and present day. I began to work on having students recognize the Two-Row Wampum. The Two Row Wampum is a living treaty; a way that the Haudenosaunee and Dutch established an agreement for their people to live together in peace in which each nation was to respect the ways of the other and to discuss solutions to the issues that came before them. The Haudenosaunee made a belt to record a peace agreement between the two nations. The belt has two purple rows running alongside each other representing two boats. One boat is the canoe with the Haudenosaunee way of life, laws, and people. The other is the Dutch ship with their laws, religion, and people in it. The boats were to travel side by side down the river of life. Each nation is to respect the ways of each other and would not interfere with the other (Two Row Wampum-Guswenta, 2018). I used this treaty to remind the students of how they are always living in the Haudenosaunee row, with the European ship in the other row, and how they need to have balance in both as they navigate their own lives.

Meaning, in the Haudenosaunee canoe, they can practice language, ceremony, songs, and teachings of our people and history, while on the European ship they need Western education, and are living in a modern home, buying food from the grocery stores, and watching tv or playing video games. I took all my teachings from what I have learned in Oheró:kon and began to support my students through our Haudenosaunee ways of knowing and utilizing our local community historians to help create cultivators and critical thinkers.

Necessity of Indigenous Knowledge

Due to these experiences and as an Indigenous teacher, I knowingly and consciously bring the Haudenosaunee teachings into the classroom. I have learned how essential it is for me to sustain our Indigenous knowledge; thus I go back each year to Oheró:kon fasting week to watch our youth finish and complete their 4 days of fasting by having their aunties, uncles, family, and community support them through their process. I have witnessed the ceremony evolve from five young boys fasting in the mountain with a few supporters to seeing every seat at the longhouse filled every Sunday. The people come to talk to the youth and prepare them to be with the land. The revival of this tradition has caused a ripple effect across Haudenosaunee country and now more than ever the youth are asking for it and parents wanting it for themselves. When you have something so interconnected with a sense of community, sense of family, and a sense of belonging, the positive change you see, and the ways youth transform is because the youth know that the support comes from a place of love and nurturance. That is what I try to center my own teachings around for my students in the classroom. I work to bring the important teachings of Oheró:kon into my classroom to holistically support the youth and provide space for opportunity for expression of oneself. I want the students to know the responsibility of fire keeping and taking care of themselves, the recognition of sacrificing for their families and communities is a Haudenosaunee way of being, and the love, hope, and support of their families and community will always be there. I do this by being present and advocating for the youth in the educational spaces that I am most often in. This also occurs in my active role in the community where I interact with many of the students outside of school.

Throughout the years since my ceremony, not only do I still consider the two women my aunties but also, they are two women who know what it means to be good human beings. I consider them lifelong role models and change makers to our youth. It is important for the students to have positive role models who may not always be related but to know where they can go for guidance and direction. Similar to the fasting journey, aunties and uncles should be available to help guide students through their Western educational journey within schools.

Another important concept that I took away from my fasting journey is the importance of presence; for being there for someone even when they say they do not need it. During the ceremony, love and support is provided not only from families, but from the ceremonial helpers and community members who are willing to help guide them along the way. The ceremony teaches how important it is for families to show up and be there for their children, and to guide them in ways that can help them move forward in positive ways through important life decision-making. It also helps to mend broken relationships and promote healthy behaviors. Also, the elders and presenters nurture the youth during the ceremony by taking the time to teach and share their wisdom

We promote important cultural histories and ceremonies by giving students the opportunity to talk about their experiences (if they are in Oheró:kon) and how it has changed them and their relationships. Incorporating teachings especially from our creation story which talks about important values we carry throughout Oheró:kon, includes teachings about the fire keeping and what that represents, to why fasting for 4 days is required to learning about medicines that are grown locally. Students should know the process and speech that goes along with it. We want students to feel included and valued for their experience and have a voice in spaces that they often are not allowed to talk.

I find that as more youth participate in Oheró:kon, the youth are enacting the teachings from the ceremony, the basics of survival and the symbolism of fire keeping, and sacrificing for their families and community. They are taking better care of themselves and are looking for ways to give back at such a high level. Youth crime rates have dropped according to local police data reports. Youth are gathering, not for parties but for singing or dancing, or helping the community in productive ways. They are showing up and being present. This is because they know their supports are there when they need them. This support has helped young adults leave their community for Western educational credentials and come back with a purpose to help the community. As a teacher, I can see the effects that the participation in the ceremony have on the students in school. I build upon that in school and can reference certain ways of knowing and being because I know they understand and value the concepts. I can talk to them as an "Aunty" in school and be respected.

Aunty and Teacher. With me now being a lead aunty in Oheró:kon, and a teacher at the high school, I struggle with certain community issues that affect our kids on the daily. Because the youth are connecting to their Indigenous knowledges and lifeways, they are finding their voices and advocating for their community. Oheró:kon created a foundation for youth to find themselves with the support of family and community. This shows that not only are our youth very important to us and the next seven generations, but they will be our future leaders, knowledge keepers, and language holders. Through our ways of the Haudenosaunee, the youth are beginning to become diplomats and delegates to our ways of life in using the language and ceremonies in and around the communities. As the students and their communities take on issues that impact our lifeways, I do worry about their mental, physical, and overall health. This puts me in an interesting position because there are times when the school asks us as teachers, not to be involved in student or community issues.

Most recently, the Tyendinaga Mohawk blockade in Ontario, Canada became a focal point for the nationwide protests in solidarity with the hereditary chiefs of the Wet'suwet'en opposing the construction of the Coastal GasLink Pipeline through their territory in central British Columbia. My community, including the youth, are continuously impacted by the violence that happens because of big corporations trying to pollute the little land we have left. This led the community to stand in solidarity with the Wet'suwet'en. The students wanted to organize a walkout to support their family members who participated in the blockade. The initial talks about students doing a walkout was denied because it was during school hours and the students did not want to get suspended. The students and staff came together to find resolutions, and the students thought it was more impactful if they held an information session with staff and students about the issues they face. This took place after school in the local auditorium and a good crowd showed up in support. Three students stood up with pride and talked about important matters. As faculty and staff, we were told by the principal of the high school not to get involved in community issues. When I was told not to be involved, that put me in a place of resistance because of who I am and how I am in support of what the youth and community members were standing up for. Being a teacher and a community member should be an advantageous position but when the school does not want to be involved, it is a difficult place. The other administrators and teachers who are not Haudenosaunee who may not live in the community, can go home and not have to worry about the same issues we face, and they do not understand how to support the communities that they serve. This puts me in an uncomfortable spot because not only do I teach the students during the week about language and ceremonies at school, but I also teach them about ceremony and language during the weekend in the community. It is impossible for me not to be involved in the youths' lives because that is my passion. And that's what I struggle with as a teacher and lead aunty to all the youth, I feel like I have to walk a very fine line between my career and my duty as a community member. Regardless, if I were to lose my job over supporting the youth who are trying to educate other youth about current Indigenous issues, especially in climate change, then I have no problem with that. I became a teacher to do exactly that, support them, teach them, and acknowledge them for the amazing individuals they are.

DISCUSSION

The stories, educational experiences, concepts, and practices that were described reveal how the education of our young people are considered from the very beginning to teach for the continuance of the lifeways of our Native nations. These types of experiences are often prepared for throughout the lives of the children and were created specifically to ensure the existence of the people. The ceremonies and the concepts taught within have important implications for how our Indigenous youth should be centered, valued, and nurtured throughout their educational experiences, including in school.

The Diné youth demonstrated a critical awareness as they described how they were not always supported by the community in the ways they were taught to be Diné and continued to seek positive and trusting guidance. What the youth describe as an unsupportive community at times, points to the soul wounds caused by colonization that still impact the community today. As stated, these wounds need to be addressed or they will continue to linger and negatively affect our communities (Jacob, 2013). The youth were able to envision their school as a place where qualities of k'é could be practiced. They point to the components of the two frameworks mentioned earlier (Bang et al., 2019, Garcia, 2019) of centering Indigenous knowledges and strengthening Native nations. They theorized that if such qualities were taught, valued, and practiced in school by all involved, these qualities would move outward to the community. The youth call for their Diné lifeways to become a part of the school environment that is intentional about strengthening the community. They see this as a way to holistically support the well-being of the youth and to perpetuate a positive community where they could feel comfortable in reaching out without being judged. The collective contribution of knowledge keepers, elders, and other Diné community members could provide the knowledge to inform practice which points to the need for Indigenous family and community engagement with the school. The youth in this situation ask an important question that has been asked by many: What if practicing and perpetuating Indigenous lifeways in school could strengthen these practices in the community?

The Kanien'keha:ka parents and community members clearly centered their knowledge keepers, elders, and anyone who could offer information when they sought to revitalize Oheró:kon because the collective knowledge and memories were vital to their goal. As the Indigenous family and community engagement frameworks claim, critical awareness and collective agency can provide the capabilities for families and community members to establish and advocate for their own educational goals (Bang et al., 2019; Garcia, 2019). This led to the Kanien'keha:ka community and youth becoming change agents and advocates for their land, languages, and ways of knowing. The effectiveness of the ceremony is now evident as described by

Tsiehente when she states that youth are gathering for singing and dancing, youth crime rates are lower, and the youth are leading movements and become diplomats for their people. The community in this instance should be engaged when discussing the educational achievement of the youth in schools. The school should be reaching out to the family and community members to collaborate in ways that would encourage the school to incorporate Indigenous lifeways in the everydayness of their practice. However, as stated, Tsiehente had a difficult time being an aunty and a teacher because the school encouraged teachers not to get involved in the issues that the community faced. When the youth enacted the teachings learned through the revival of the Oheró:kon, they were empowered to speak up and take action to stand in solidarity with the Wet'suwet'en. The protection of the lands and waters were at the forefront of the community's mind and therefore affecting the students. Tsiehente knew this as a community member and continued to stand with the students as they planned their actions. Such instances seem like the opportune time to promote equitable and transformative collaboration with families and communities that could lead to rigorous academics and higher achievement for Indigenous students. This situation points to an important question: How could the issues facing the community become teaching moments and opportunities to engage students in their academics in ways that would strengthen their Native nations rather than punish the students and teachers involved?

The types of family and community engagement that center the healing of relationships between community and school for which this chapter calls, would benefit from the components described by Garcia (2019) and Bang et al. (2019). Specifically, by promoting critical awareness and dialogue to promote collective agency, centering Indigenous knowledge and multigenerational healing and learning, and working towards goals to strengthen Native nation sovereignty and self-determination, Indigenous family and community engagement would support the overall well-being of the youth. The Diné youth felt that they were not always supported in the ways they were taught to be Diné and sought positive and trusting guidance from their families and elders. The Kanien'keha:ka family and community members knew that their youth needed the Oheró:kon in order to save them from destructive behaviors, so they worked and continue to revitalize the ceremony as a collective. Both of these stories recognize wounds that still affect us as Indigenous Peoples and we look to our Indigenous knowledges to help cultivate our hearts (Shirley, 2017) as we shed layers of colonization.

NOTES

1. I have obtained permission from my family to share this story in this chapter.

2. Though we use the term "Indigenous" throughout the chapter, we also use "Native American," "Native," and other terms that specific authors used when we reference their work.
3. I did not have a personal relationship with the youth but we were from the same community and I am an alumni of the high school they attended at the time.

REFERENCES

Adams, D. W. (1995). *Education for extinction: American Indians and the boarding school experience, 1875–1928.* University Press of Kansas.

Bang, M., Montaño Nolan, C., & McDaid-Morgan, N. (2019). Indigenous family engagement: Strong families, strong nations. In E. McKinley & L. Smith (Eds.), *Handbook of Indigenous education* (pp. 789–810). Springer.

Cajete, G. A. (2015). *Indigenous community: Rekindling the teachings of the Seventh Fire.* Living Justice Press.

Corntassel, J. (2012). Re-envisioning resurgence: Indigenous pathways to decolonization and sustainable self-determination. *Decolonization: Indigeneity, Education & Society, (1)*1, 86–101.

Corntassel, J., & Hardbarger, T. (2019). Educate to perpetuate: Land-based pedagogies and community resurgence. *International Review of Education, 65,* 87–116.

Garcia, J. (2019). Critical and culturally sustaining Indigenous family and community engagement in the education. In S. B. Sheldon & T. A. Turner-Vorbeck (Eds.), *The Wiley handbook of family, school, and community relationship in education* (pp. 71–90). John Wiley & Sons, Inc.

Grande, S. (2015). *Red pedagogy: Native American social and political thought* (10th anniversary ed.). Rowman & Littlefield.

Holmes, A., & Gonzales, N. (2017). Finding sustenance: An Indigenous relational pedagogy. In D. Paris & H. S. Alim (Eds.), *Culturally sustaining pedagogies* (pp. 207–224). Teacher College Press.

Huff, D. J. (1997). *To live heroically: Institutional racism and American Indian education.* State University of New York Press.

Jacob, M. M. (2013). *Yakama rising: Indigenous cultural revitalization, activism, and healing.* University of Arizona Press.

Kulago, H. A. (2011). *Diné youth define community: Finding routes to school and community partnerships* [Unpublished doctoral dissertation]. Purdue University.

Kulago, H. A. (2012). Theorizing community and school partnerships with Diné youth. *Journal of Curriculum Theorizing, 28*(2), 60–75.

Kulago, H. A. (2016). Activating Indigenous knowledge to create supportive educational environments by rethinking family, community, and school partnerships. *Journal of Family Diversity in Education, 2*(1), 1–20.

Lamphere, L. (1977). *To run after them.* University of Arizona Press.

Lomawaima, K. T., & McCarty, T. L. (2006). *To remain an Indian: Lessons in democracy from a century of Native American education.* Teachers College Press.

McCarty, T. L., & Bia, F. (2002). *A place to be Navajo: Rough Rock and the struggle for self-determination in Indigenous schooling.* Lawrence Erlbaum Associates.

McCloskey, J. (2007). *Living through the generations: Continuity and change in Navajo women's lives*. University of Arizona Press.

Reyhner, J. A., & Eder, J. M. (2004). *American Indian education: A history*. University of Oklahoma Press.

Roessel, M. (1993). *Kinaałdá: A Navajo girl grows up*. Lerner.

Roessel, R. (1981). *Navajo women in society*. Navajo Resource Center, Rough Rock Demonstration School.

Shirley, V. J. (2017). Indigenous social justice pedagogy: Teaching into the risks and cultivating the heart. *Critical Questions in Education, 8*(2), 163–177.

Simpson, L. B. (2017). *As we have always done: Indigenous freedom through radical resistance*. University of Minnesota Press.

Spring, J. H. (2001). *Deculturalization and the struggle for equality: A brief history of the education of dominated cultures in the United States* (3rd ed.). McGraw-Hill.

Two Row Wampum-Guswenta. (2018). *Onondaga Nation*. https://www.onondaga nation.org/culture/wampum/two-row-wampum-belt-guswenta/

CHAPTER 13

ENGAGING NATIVE FAMILIES IN CO-CREATING MEANINGFUL EDUCATIONAL OPPORTUNITIES AS A COMMUNITY

Danielle R. Lansing

Storytelling has been a valued pedagogy for Native people since time immemorial. When an individual becomes a listener of stories, it is often expected that they will eventually carry the knowledge forward to sustain the next generation (Archibald, 2008). It is in this same spirit that I tell my story. As a storyteller, I understand that part of my role as a Diné woman is to carry on the tradition and pedagogy of sharing valuable life lessons.

As a child, I remember listening intently to Ma'íí Jóóldlóóshi (coyote) stories told by shimásání (grandmother) and her animated voice. Her voice changing as she switched between the sly and overly confident Ma'íí (coyote) and other animal teachers. We also heard the history of our family and the hard times they endured as they lived through harsh winters, survived

Indigenizing Education, pages 213–229
Copyright © 2022 by Information Age Publishing
www.infoagepub.com
All rights of reproduction in any form reserved.

Hwééldi (The Long Walk), and also endured the changes of western society. My mother and aunt often recalled and shared stories of my great grandfather and his teachings. Cheii (grandfather) once told them how important it was to make sure he told his children stories in the safe confines of their family home, careful so none of the wisdom could escape them or be lost. Late in the evenings, when only they could learn from these valuable teachings, Cheii shared his knowledge and the wisdom of our ancestors. Now more than ever I can understand the intentionality Cheii felt as he told his stories. He knew wisdom would be needed to navigate the future that lay ahead for his children and grandchildren. I tell this story, with the intention that these teachings reach future Native teachers in our communities knowing the complexities that lay before them.

As a child, I remember being in school and feeling like my parents were invisible and not expected to participate in my education. I could feel the distant way in which my teachers interacted with my parents almost with an air of discomfort and awkwardness. It was as if my teachers didn't expect much of us. Ironically, my parents were both hard working individuals who were consumed with the everyday complexities a Native family deals with as they try to survive in the big city. They may not have been present at Parent–Teacher Association (PTA) meetings or seen volunteering at bake sales, but they were very concerned with how my sister and I were doing in school. I knew that the way my parents participated and supported our education was different. It was probably around first or second grade when I began to realize how different my family was. First of all, my parents didn't have the same school experiences that I had. They didn't grow up with their parents and families. As a consequence of living in very rural Navajo communities with minimal educational infrastructure, both of my parents attended off reservation boarding schools at a very early age. Mom left home after second grade to attend a border town dormitory program where she attended public school. Dad left home to attend an off-reservation boarding school hundreds of miles from home. They both survived assimilationist boarding school experiences that taught them to set aside their Diné ways while at school. Another way that I knew my parents were different, was the fact that we divided our time between our life in the city and life "back home." That was the term my parents used when we would pack up on Friday nights to travel back to our reservation community. Those were the best times. We would spend the weekend enveloped in the love and support of my grandparents and extended family. Even if it was a 5-hour drive and having only spent a full day "back home" it was well worth it as we drove home feeling rejuvenated and refreshed. This is the way we were able to participate in ceremonies, special occasions, harvests, and holidays. These were the instances that helped us maintain our identities as a Diné family. We received a level of familial and communal support that provided a sturdy foundation for enduring the complexities of school, work, and life. Much of what I learned from these early years still sustains me today. So yes, my mom was never a member of the PTA, we never participated in bake sales, but she served as a conduit to a greater level of support, not just for school but for life.

In my teacher education program, I remember being trained from textbooks that explained the intricacies of how to conduct effective parent–teacher conferences, develop an exciting classroom newsletter, or involve parents in field trips as chaperones. However, as I entered tribal communities as a teacher, I felt a deeper, more intimate level of support for the children. It was different from the surface level involvement that I was taught. It was the same support that I was intimately familiar with; the support that sustained me well into the future.

As an elementary school teacher, I dedicated my career to working in tribal communities located in urban and rural settings. I was fortunate to have learned a great deal while teaching in K–3 classrooms in four unique tribal communities. The schools I taught in were located in rural settings. Some maintained dormitory facilities on campus and some were in close proximity or physically surrounded by a metropolitan city. From these diverse experiences, I have gained insight into the unique ways in which parents, community members, and tribal leaders support children through their educational journeys. Recognizing and honoring the support parents provided their children helped me develop strong relationships with parents and community members. This resulted in meaningful learning experiences for everyone involved. Consequently, being able to connect and partner with families became a priority for me as a teacher. Fortunately, I've sustained many relationships with the children and families that I have taught.

Now, as a faculty member in a tribal college and university (TCU) teacher education program, I have looked for ways to incorporate my stories as pedagogy to support our future teachers in better understanding family engagement within Native communities. Many of the mainstream texts don't do any justice to describing the ways in which American Indian and Alaskan Native (AI/AN) families support their children through their educational journeys. Instead we are often confronted with a deficit discourse regarding how AI/AN children are not faring well within educational systems across Indian country. Native parents are often portrayed as apathetic or unable to socialize their children for schooling. This is why I feel it is so important to document and begin a dialogue that honors how AI/AN parents uniquely support their children. This is imperative for preservice teachers, so they can capitalize on the strengths of tribal communities and the values that will sustain their livelihood for the future. My hope is that Native educators will contribute to tribal nation building by creating classrooms that honor partnerships with parents, families, and communities to strengthen educational systems that serve our children.

METHODOLOGY: WAYS OF KNOWING
AND UNDERSTANDING

As a researcher, I have identified closely with qualitative methodologies that provide me the freedom to tell the stories of our lived experiences (Archibald, 2008; Smith, 2012). As I continue to work as an educator in tribal communities, I have come to realize the need to identify and articulate the best practices that positively impact our families and children. Part of my motivation to do this is a result of my current position as a TCU faculty member at the Southwestern Indian Polytechnic Institute (SIPI) where I teach in the early childhood education (ECE) associates degree program. I seek to develop our stories in order to document best practices unique to the AI/AN context so that we may develop programming that best meets the needs of our future teachers. Family and community collaboration in education is an integral part of our curriculum and we seek to develop best practices that align with the tribal communities we serve in order to prepare preservice teachers for the field.

Jo-ann Archibald's (2008), *Indigenous Storywork*, has been especially motivating to me as an Indigenous researcher. Her journey to learn more about Indigenous stories and their place in education as pedagogy is empowering and insightful. I am inspired to reach back to honor our ancestors' prior teachings and share the knowledge with the next generation. As a result, storytelling is the overarching methodology and framework that guides my work and informs my praxis. I have been further motivated by the teachings of Shawn Wilson (2008), who has articulated Indigenous research as a ceremony that acknowledges the relational aspects that shape our stories and allow us to gain further insight into our world. Through this process, I have reflected greatly on my own identity and how it informs my relationships with learners.

I identify as a Native woman. I am a Diné woman who has worked hard at maintaining my identity and ties to my community. I continue to move between the spaces of life in an urban setting and responsibilities "back home." My family and I regularly return to our community to fulfill duties to our family but to also rejuvenate ourselves in the comfort and security of our ancestral home, always remembering we are connected to the land physically and spiritually. This sustains us and we remain committed to who we are as Diné. What we have come to realize, is that many AI/AN families also live this lifestyle as a consequence of economic security and opportunity. These families are my relatives and I must act accordingly. As a mother, I am enacting Diné notions of K'é (kinship ties) as I support Native teachers in rebuilding culturally responsive educational experiences for children who enter classrooms each day. These too are my children and I am vested in their well-being. As an auntie, I hope to provide guidance to the preservice teachers who will utilize these lessons as a way to confront the deficit discourse surrounding Native families in order to build meaningful relationships that are realized in powerful educational experiences in the classroom, school, and community.

I keep close to my heart the relationships that I have experienced as an opportunity to learn and develop as an Indigenous educator. Part of this relationship requires a reciprocal sharing of the knowledge I have gained. To honor these experiences, and fulfill the teachings of my family, I work to articulate processes that have been successful in empowering our communities to move forward in our quest for improved educational systems.

As an Indigenous researcher, I am often confronted with the tensions of enacting Native ways of knowing and learning while simultaneously borrowing methodological tools that support the development of research that will inform academic discourse. I seek to maintain a balance between both ways of knowing. I have selected grounded theory (Creswell, 2013) as a tool to examine the process of engaging AI/AN parents in a Photovoice project to create a local cultural curriculum. Grounded theory has been particularly useful as there is a paucity of literature and explanations of best practices related to AI/AN parents and their involvement in educational practices or what is often referred to as parental involvement or parental engagement.

Grounded theory study is a qualitative research methodology used to articulate a theory for a process or action (Creswell, 2013). The process described is a phenomenon that is experienced by participants of the study. The development of the theory explains the process or practices examined. The theory that is eventually developed is derived from examining the data collected from participants who have experienced the process (Creswell, 2013). Grounded theory is especially helpful when a researcher seeks to develop a theory rather than utilize existing theories.

Part of my motivations to utilize grounded theory is the hope that new theories be developed to further the discourse of AI/AN education, ECE in an AI/AN context, as well as illustrating strengths-based perspectives involving AI/AN parents and their support of education. The intent of examining this phenomenon is to develop a theory regarding best practices in engaging AI/AN parents in determining educational opportunities for their children. This study focuses on the processes and actions that have occurred over time in order to describe the process of engaging AI/AN parents in a Photovoice project that leads to the development of culturally responsive curriculum.

As a storyteller, grounded theory is the methodology that fits well with the process of retelling and thinking about my experiences within our community. Many enduring relationships have developed along the way. As a result of wanting this work to continue in other communities, it is important to tell our story in order to inspire others to truly connect with AI/AN families.

Through these connections we can then develop responsive educational programs. Storytellers in my family and community carried forth values and anecdotes in hopes that we as listeners and community members carried on the knowledge and ultimately integrated the valuable lessons into our lives. It is just as important for me to carefully think through the ways in which these relationships have developed as a way of describing the possibilities for tribal communities. My intent is to acknowledge the capacity of our communities when optimal conditions can be replicated by future teachers who can re-build our educational systems through parental engagement.

The following are the research questions that guided this inquiry:

What processes evolve when AI/AN parents are provided the opportunity to become actively engaged in their child's educational experiences? What are the conditions and strategies necessary to keep AI/AN parents engaged in the process of developing a culturally relevant curriculum?

Context: Wakanyeja "Sacred Little Ones" Early Childhood Initiative

The Southwestern Indian Polytechnic Institute (SIPI) opened its doors in 1971 to meet the educational and vocational needs of local tribal com-munities. Located in Albuquerque, New Mexico, SIPI has served as a valu-able resource to not only local tribes, but to AI/AN from various tribal communities across the United States. Over the years, SIPI has evolved to become a national Indian community college providing technical and transfer degree programs and certificates.

At the request of local tribes, SIPI developed an Associate of Arts degree program in ECE. SIPI began offering classes in ECE beginning in the year 2000 (Martin et al., 2003). SIPI's program has been a steady resource for local tribal early childhood centers and schools training teachers and edu-cational technicians. Many SIPI graduates have transferred to bachelor's degree programs at local universities.

In 2010, SIPI opened an early childhood learning center on campus to serve as a resource to SIPI students. The early childhood center supports the ECE associates degree program as a practicum site for ECE students. Stu-dents complete two practicum experiences at the center as part of their ECE coursework. This includes experiences in infant/toddler and preschool class-rooms. A local nonprofit organization was contracted to operate the center as a Head Start and Early Head Start center serving infants, toddlers, and preschoolers. The early childhood learning center has provided a resource for not only the SIPI campus and its students, but also the greater commu-nity. The center serves 44 children. The children at the center reflect the intertribal nature of the campus community. Children from various tribes are represented as well as non-Native children from the greater community who represent a variety of ethnicities. All of the teachers at the center are AI/AN. Several are alumni of SIPI's ECE program and represent local tribes. They serve as cooperating teachers to SIPI's practicum students. The center is accredited by the National Association of the Education of Young Children (NAEYC) and has been recognized as a Head Start Center of Excellence. The center has proven to be a valuable resource in developing early childhood teachers for tribal communities. Over the years, SIPI and the early childhood learning center have strengthened their relationship as partners in ECE.

In 2011, SIPI's ECE program was awarded the *Wakanyeja*, "Sacred Little Ones," early childhood initiative, a W. K. Kellogg foundation grant awarded by the American Indian College Fund. The Sacred Little Ones initiative enabled SIPI to partner with its early childhood center to enhance programming through the inclusion of Native language and culture into early childhood curriculum. As the principal investigator and director of the initiative from 2012–2015, I have and continue to be an active participant observer of the inquiry. Throughout the initiative, 11 urban and rural AI/AN parents were consistently involved within the initiative for up to 2 years as the core group. Up to 35 families have participated in events and activities planned by the parents throughout the initiative. Teachers at the center have also become intimately involved in supporting the initiative through participation in events, parent meetings, and by providing childcare for meetings. Center leadership provided not only a physical location but a supportive environment for collaboration.

Case Study

This case study examines the use of Photovoice as a tool for engaging families in developing a framework for the integration of Native language and culture into curriculum. While Photovoice is a community based participatory research methodology, in this study, Photovoice is examined as the core phenomenon and unit of analysis. Photovoice has been instrumental in mobilizing grassroots efforts in social justice movements worldwide and has been utilized in Native communities to support curriculum development (Romero-Little, 2010). In this particular case, Photovoice was an ongoing project for parents and a means to develop curriculum.

Data Collection and Analysis

Data collection procedures included daily reflections of parent interactions within meetings, community events, and center-based events. As the

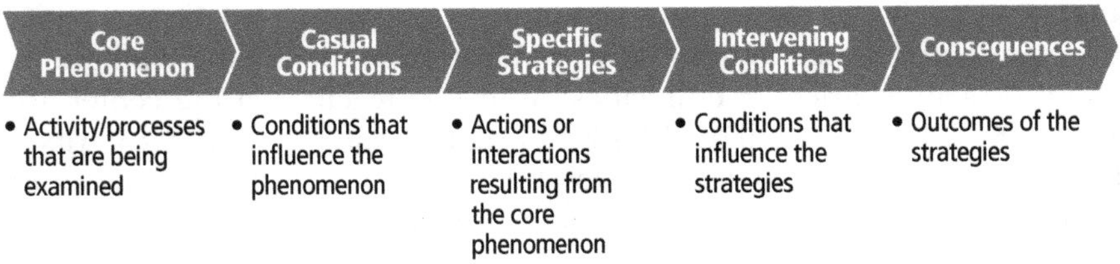

Core Phenomenon	Casual Conditions	Specific Strategies	Intervening Conditions	Consequences
• Activity/processes that are being examined	• Conditions that influence the phenomenon	• Actions or interactions resulting from the core phenomenon	• Conditions that influence the strategies	• Outcomes of the strategies

Figure 13.1 Axial coding.

researcher, I constantly moved between recording thoughts and referring back to observational notes and interactions with parents. Parents also participated in focus groups which also served as a data source. As a researcher, an integral part of the process included enacting reflective techniques with regard to the facilitation of the project and direct participation in the actual curriculum framework that was realized. This has included numerous interactions that I have had with teachers, parents, families, children, students, and community members. Memoing (Miles et al., 2014) throughout the project after parent meetings, special events, and conversations with families has been most helpful in organizing and analyzing key interactions. Other data sources have included focus group transcripts, surveys, and the actual Photovoice data. A great deal of insight has been garnered through the ongoing relationships that have been established with the program and families.

I have chosen to utilize axial coding as the means to analyze data collected. This included a structured approach where the grounded theory methodology approach included a central phenomenon, causal conditions, and strategies while intervening conditions are identified and consequences of the phenomenon are derived as a result of the process that is examined through the study (Creswell, 2013). This process then aids in articulating an emerging theory. Figure 13.1 illustrates the coding paradigm used to analyze data. Each phase is described below in relation to the Sacred Little Ones initiative.

WAKANYEJA "SACRED LITTLE ONES" EARLY CHILDHOOD INITIATIVE

Core Phenomenon

The core phenomenon is defined as the central category regarding the phenomenon (Creswell, 2013). The Sacred Little Ones initiative was a comprehensive 4 year endeavor that included various program goals and activities. This included improving our TCU teacher education program, partnering with two local early childhood centers, fostering successful transitions to the K–3 environment, empowering parents as change agents, and integrating Native language and culture into early childhood curriculum. For this study, the focus was on the processes involved in engaging AI/AN parents in developing a cultural curriculum. This included participation in the Photovoice methodology and the eventual development of a curricular framework.

Part of our Sacred Little Ones initiative goals included fostering the integration of Native language and culture into ECE curriculum and programming. As a team, we as teachers, community members, and partners thought carefully about how to move forward with defining and integrating Native language and culture. Our early childhood center serves various tribes as well as non-Native families. We approached our goals in consideration of our community. It was imperative that our team include the participation and input of our families. This was so that we could develop educational experiences that are relevant to our intertribal community. This family partnership was a unique opportunity to define our educational needs together.

The Photovoice methodology has been a helpful tool for our initiative. Our team selected the Photovoice methodology as the means to empower our parents to become active agents of change within our community. The Photovoice methodology is a qualitative participatory research methodology that engages the participants in answering a guiding question to shed light on community strengths and concerns while encouraging community action. In the case of our initiative, parents answered the following guiding question: "What knowledge is needed to become a healthy Native American?" This guiding question provided an opportunity for parents to think of all of the ways in which we could support the children in becoming well-balanced individuals. The team hosted several informational sessions to recruit interested parents. All parents were invited to participate. We did not limit this to a discussion of academic or cognitive development, but instead focused on what our children would need as a foundation for life. Data collected would provide insight needed to develop our early childhood program further. With that in mind, families began to develop their photographic responses to the guiding question. Families gathered photographs that included images from their home life, life in their tribal communities, special events, and even existing photographs from the past. Families worked for several weeks or up to 2 months to develop a collection of 10 photographs that addressed the guiding question. Throughout the process, we supported families by answering their questions, reiterating the goal of our inquiry, and by providing them a supportive network for developing their collections.

Following the development of photograph collections, the group met regularly to embark upon analysis of the data collected. These group meetings consisted of parents, two teachers from the center, and the center specialist. As the facilitator, I attended all of the sessions along with members of my project team. We gathered twice a month for a period of 14 months sharing, discussing, and reflecting on the photographs and participant reflections. Each family shared their reflections while the group was able to ask questions and discuss each photograph. The group developed thematic areas by consensus. By the time each family had shared their collections, 48 photographs had been analyzed and 10 themes had been developed. These themes then laid the foundation for three thematic units that were then developed with the help of the preschool teachers and center leadership. These thematic units continue to enhance the existing curriculum and are implemented throughout the summer. The areas of focus include community gardening, health and wellness, and Native arts. These thematic units include community-based culminating events that invite families to participate. The thematic units have been very well received by parents and have increased family and community engagement at the center.

An enduring outcome of the project was the resulting high-level ongoing commitment of parents. The core group of parents continues to be highly engaged within the center. The parents eventually decided to combine their efforts with the existing parent committee. Each month the group meets to develop educational opportunities that align with classroom curriculum while using their thematic areas as a reference. The themes now serve as a curriculum framework for the program. Parents at the center have formed a close-knit group that regularly collaborates to bring culturally relevant activities to the center. They are a strong, confident, and cohesive group of parents who consistently participate in their child's education while working to make their educational experiences culturally relevant. As a result, each parent meeting provides the opportunity for parents to contribute to the curriculum and enhance programming. This collegial group has a collaborative relationship with center leadership and teachers. New families, who enroll in the program, easily see that collaboration is the culture of the program. For example, parents have elected to create an annual "Native Harvest Feast" event in lieu of the Thanksgiving holiday. Parents plan this event as a collective group. Families sign up to bring Native foods to a communal feast where recipes are shared and families feast together. Through this event, new families see that the support for AI/AN culture and identity is central to programming and immediately participate in collaborative efforts as they feel validated and observe that sharing their culture is welcomed and the norm. Table 13.1 illustrates the results of the Photovoice inquiry.

Part of the success of the Sacred Little Ones initiative has carried over to SIPI's ECE program where preservice teachers and paraprofessionals are preparing to become early childhood educators. The center operates as a lab school where students can observe the collaboration with parents firsthand. Students learn from a valuable example that helps shape their

TABLE 13.1 SIPI Photovoice Inquiry

Photovoice Inquiry	Photovoice Themes	Thematic Units and Educational Activities
• 11 parents • 48 photographs analyzed • 1 facilitator • Preschool teachers and center administrator	• Tradition • Culture • Traditional Attire • Community • Home • Family • Role Models • Health • History • Natural Resources	• Community Garden Unit • Indigenous Health and Wellness Unit • Indian Market Unit • Special Events—Native artist presentations, pottery workshops, storytellers, Native fashion shows, fun runs, community garden project

emerging ideas of how to partner with families in programming. Students are able to observe the manner in which AI/AN identity and culture have become central to educational opportunities at the center. These practical experiences are pivotal in shaping the mindset of future teachers. It is an example of how to truly collaborate with AI/AN families. By documenting our process and best practices, this initiative can be sustained through SIPI's early childhood program curriculum for training teachers. Mainstream textbooks offer broad sweeping generalizations regarding Native American families who often get little mention. For a TCU serving tribal communities, it is important to document our best practices so that we may provide relevant curriculum to our future teachers.

Causal Conditions

Causal conditions are the conditions that influence the phenomenon (Creswell, 2013). For many of the AI/AN parents, the opportunity to participate in developing culturally relevant curriculum was an important one. So important that they were willing to commit much of their time to this long-term project. It was a chance to include culturally relevant knowledge into the educational experiences of their children.

Although many participants had relocated to the urban setting either temporarily or permanently, they still maintained ties to their tribal communities. Some families made daily commutes to take their children to our early childhood center while they completed their post secondary degree programs on our campus, or worked in the city. At the end of each day, they would make the drive home to their respective communities. Some had daily commutes up to 90 miles round trip. For many families, their decisions to relocate from their communities were out of necessity as rural settings impact their access to employment and educational opportunities. On weekends, many families return to their communities to participate within tribal and family activities and to fulfill their roles and obligations as tribal members. These experiences were pivotal to their livelihoods. Families saw the value of sustaining these relationships within their lives and worked hard to that end. There was much to be learned and gained by maintaining these ties. This is illustrated in the following reflections of Stella, a Diné and Apache parent in the program. Here she describes how important it is for her daughter to be connected to her ancestral home, even if she currently resides in the urban setting.

> My family on my husband's side and my side has livestock that they look after. Even though I live in the city, and live a city life where I do not look after livestock, my parents and my in-laws are taking a role in caring for their animals. For us to introduce where she comes from and what types of land she is a part of, will encourage her that life is beautiful and for her not to be afraid of where she comes from. I believe that is the most encouraging part of being a parent, is for her to understand that there is not only one way of life but many. This is just one part of who she is as a Navajo and Jicarilla Apache girl.

Parents understood that these Native ways of knowing would support their children far into the future. They would support children in eventually developing into productive tribal members who would eventually contribute to the future of their Native nations. This understanding provided motivation to include these important teachings within their child's educational experiences.

As parents moved between the spaces of life in a tribal community and life in the city, they practiced AI/AN notions of kinship and relationality. This included consideration for one another as relatives as well as members of a community. For example, one father continued to lead the planting event for the community garden several years after both of his children had moved on to elementary school. As a gesture of gratitude, teachers and parents would present him a gift basket after each planting event. He and other parents often realized that their work would contribute to the immediate community of parents and learners but also towards children and families who would become part of the center in the future. This motivated them to serve as role models not only for their own children, but for the community as well.

Strategies

Strategies are defined as the actions or interactions that result from the central phenomenon (Creswell, 2013). Parents participated in up to two Photovoice meetings per month. Each meeting lasted up to 2 hours in length. This included time to listen to each parent's presentation of photo reflections and providing feedback and supportive comments. Discussions included clarification of the meaning of the photographs, the message behind the image, and how it connected to the education and development of AI/AN children. Many of these collective discussions included discourse that was focused on parental beliefs, ideas for the program, and what aspects of Native language, beliefs, and culture were important to their child's education. Through these discussions, parents often found commonalities with one another across a variety of experiences and tribal affiliations. They became a cohesive group who supported one another in clarifying what was important to them. This is exemplified by Andie, a Diné mother in the program who describes what occurred during Photovoice meetings.

> I think a lot of communication and a lot of knowledge is actually shared by each presenter...you know, things that we go through on a daily basis, or as a community. Knowledge is given to us to move forward, to be strong Native Americans...and to have that knowledge as a basis to help us with our grandkids and our kids.

Intervening Conditions

Intervening conditions are the narrow and broad conditions that influence the strategies (Creswell, 2013). As Native parents, there are many conditions that influence the strategies that were employed throughout the collective process of developing a curricular framework. This project privileged the AI/AN experience through the guiding questions allowing them to fully discuss their shared experience as AI/AN parents who want the best for their children. Although they represented a variety of tribal affiliations, they all essentially had the same goals of supporting their children in becoming well balanced individuals. This included a collective belief that Native ways of knowing were key to the development of their children. Through this process many shared values emerged such as the importance of relationships and kinship ties, honoring the community through participation, and respect for each others' beliefs. Parents also understood the diversity inherent in an intertribal setting and celebrated their differences while learning more about one another.

It must be acknowledged that many of the AI/AN parents had not yet experienced a culturally relevant curriculum themselves. Many of their parents and grandparents had experienced assimilationist curricula. Many of which would be rectified by the development of this new curriculum as parents experienced a renewed emphasis on Native language and culture.

Consequences

The consequences are the outcomes of the strategies employed throughout the process (Creswell, 2013). Throughout this 14 month process, parents participated in deep and meaningful discussions that focused on their strengths derived from their collective experiences as AI/AN people. As a result, they developed a high level of commitment and engagement in their child's education. Many teachers observed the impact of this high level of engagement in the development of their children. Parents not only placed a greater commitment on their child's education, but also on the role of Native language and culture in their lives. Many families developed personal goals to participate more, take on leadership roles within the parent committee, and make the decision to learn more about their AI/AN heritage.

As a consequence of the process, parents developed a supportive network for their families that assisted them in navigating education and life in general. An integral part of this network included the center leadership and teachers. This provided a strong foundation for parent and teacher partnerships. As a result, parents and teachers have continued to collaborate to make culturally relevant educational experiences a reality.

DISCUSSION

From the onset of the Photovoice project, parents were allowed to take the lead. Parents were able to see their opinions, beliefs, values, hopes, and aspirations heard. A collegial atmosphere developed in which parents were able to collaborate with teachers and center leadership. They were able to see their opinions valued and realized through changes in the curriculum. Knowing their aspirations were heard and realized through curricular improvements was especially empowering for parents as they developed a reciprocal relationship with teachers. This experience was eloquently illustrated by Stella, a participant in the Photovoice project, as she described a curriculum project that resulted from parent input.

> We were given an advocacy voice towards the type of curriculum we want our children to be exposed to. Our parents have come together and created projects that our children are able to see in their classrooms and school grounds. For example, our planting project has been a huge influence on our children ... they get to see parents on certain days of the week pulling weeds and maintaining the garden for the children. (Photovoice Reflections, 2014)

Community values such as participation and a shared sense of responsibility were activated while parents developed a process for having their voices heard and their needs realized. As the relationships evolved, the

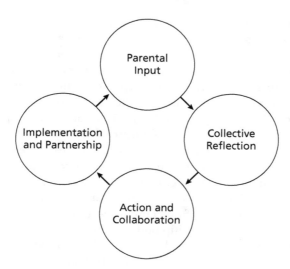

Figure 13.2   Co-creating cycle with parents.

group began to settle into a unique process. This process included time to hear parental input, usually by providing uninterrupted time to fully speak about their concerns, comments, requests, or ideas. After parents provided their input to the group, other parents and teachers in the group had ample time to collectively reflect on the ideas put forth. Next, parents and teachers were able to discuss action and possible collaborations in response to parental input. Lastly, teachers would discuss implementation of the ideas put forth by parents. This co-creating process is where partnerships and collegial relationships flourished. This iterative process was highly effective for parents. Figure 13.2 illustrates the process that developed as the project progressed.

CONCLUSIONS AND IMPLICATIONS

AI/AN parents are very interested in becoming partners in their child's education. Engaging parents to become involved collaborators requires educators to provide parents opportunities to co-create. By becoming involved in collegial relationships, parents often evoke values inherent in their tribal communities such as a shared sense of responsibility for the greater community. In doing so, they develop a school community that is reflective of the AI/AN values that are necessary in sustaining their communities and cultures. These opportunities create an educational environment that reinforces who they are as Native people.

In order to rebuild educational systems that reflect Indigenous knowledge, languages, and values, educators must think carefully about how we include parents. For AI/AN people, listening and honoring the voices and stories of our community is an integral part of the process. Storytelling and listening are the ways in which we can co-create with our families to make education relevant again in order to sustain our communities into the future. For Native people storytelling is a natural part of co-creating and carrying on our legacies into the future. This co-creating cycle is a departure from the typical communication styles of western educational systems that rely on quarterly parent–teacher conferences and the occasional note home. A high level of engagement requires a renewed commitment to listening to the stories of our people. For educators, this means that making time to hear the aspirations of our families is a worthwhile endeavor and an important aspect of relationship building and curriculum development. These are the optimal conditions that activate the relationships and motivation necessary for parents to participate in Native nation-building on behalf of our communities.

For teacher education the implications are great. Teacher educators should critically examine current practices for family engagement with a critical perspective and special attention to Native families. This includes the acknowledgement that Native families have historically been excluded from their children's schooling. In order to rectify this history, teacher training should include best practices that align with Native ways of knowing such as opportunities for dialogue, storytelling, and co-creating. Implications for praxis include an understanding that meaningful family engagement for Native communities includes making time for high levels of engagement that include opportunities for families to share their aspirations for their children and communities. This necessitates a greater level of attention to the voices of parents and careful consideration of how their input can be included in curricular and program level changes as a means to develop educational systems that better align with Native nation-building. This is a return to what tribal communities have known all along; Native nation-building starts with the hopes and dreams parents have for their children.

REFERENCES

Archibald, J. (2008). *Indigenous storywork: Educating the heart, mind, body, and spirit.* UBC Press.

Creswell, J. W. (2013). *Qualitative inquiry & research design: choosing among five approaches.* SAGE Publications.

Martin, J., Lujan, J., Montoya, V., Goldstein, G., & Abeita, K. (2003). *Request for approval: Institutional change in educational offerings* [Unpublished report].

Southwestern Indian Polytechnic Institute, Liberal Arts and Business Education Department, Early Childhood Education Program Archives.

Miles, M. B., Huberman, A. M., Saldana, J. (2014). *Qualitative data analysis: A methods sourcebook* (3rd ed.). SAGE Publications.

Romero-Little, M. E. (2010). How should young indigenous children be prepared for learning? A vision of early childhood education for indigenous children. *Journal of American Indian Education, 49*(1&2), 1–16.

Smith, L. T. (2012). *Decolonizing methodologies* (2nd ed.). St. Martin's Press.

Wilson, S. (2008). *Research is ceremony: Indigenous research methods.* Fernwood Publishing.

CHAPTER 14

TRANSFORMATIVE PRAXIS

Cherished Hopes: Building a Relationship With Families for Success

Vibeka Mitchell

I am a Diné from Naschitti, NM and grew up on the Navajo Reservation. I lived in Naschitti up to sixth grade and then we moved to Kayenta, AZ. I completed my education there and graduated from Monument Valley High School. I went off to college for 1 year at Northern Arizona University in Flagstaff, Arizona and then moved to Albuquerque where I graduated from the University of New Mexico. After I finished school, I knew I wanted to work with young children so I decided to become a preschool teacher. I got hired in 2005 and have been employed as a preschool teacher ever since. I knew I wanted to work with young children but also knew my passion was to work with Native children. When Southwest Indian Polytechnic Institute (SIPI) opened a center on their campus, I jumped at the opportunity to work at the new center. I knew working at a center on a tribal college campus would give me the opportunity to work with Native American children. I wanted the ability to be able to say that I was helping Native children become successful in the education system.

Indigenizing Education, pages 231–235
Copyright © 2022 by Information Age Publishing
www.infoagepub.com
231

Many early childhood centers have specific criteria that each program is required to follow in order to maintain funding. Our program, like many others, has performance standards that each child and teacher are required to achieve with the families. For years, I admit that I had worked on keeping those standards met without building a real relationship with the families outside of the general standards. Much of my focus remained solely on the cognitive and social development of the child. We have curriculum and assessments that are used to help the families and children grow within the program. Like many programs, we focus on the whole child including the family. The whole child concept begins with educational assessments, meeting health requirements (immunizations, physicals, dentals, and in house screenings), referrals for any services, and setting goals for the child or the family. For years, I have worked with families to keep paperwork in line and turn it in on time. I was here to make sure goals were met and parents were bringing in necessary paperwork. Part of our requirements also included a specific number of volunteer hours our parents had to fulfill. After some time, I began to feel like parents were beginning to see this as day care and not willing to volunteer or participate in school events.

Over the years, many parents began to see our program as merely a drop-off day care. This is when I began to talk with parents about keeping a consistent routine for their young child. I emphasized the importance of children arriving early for the curriculum that is taught in the morning. As a teacher, I felt like I was failing because I couldn't get parents motivated to understand the importance of our early childhood program. In addition to these strategies, teachers formally met with families four times a year to update information and create goals during the two parent teacher conferences and two home visits. The parent–teacher conferences happen at school during school hours and this meeting gives us the opportunity to have them visit the class and to show them the curriculum and schedule of the class. Home visits take place at each family's home and give us a different perspective of the child in their home. Both meetings are used to discuss the child's progress and to set goals for the child. Goals for the child can include copying their name, recognizing numbers 1–10, playing with peers. The goals are all specific to each child and are established from assessments or observations. Once goals are established for each child, it gives teachers the opportunity to make individualized plans for lessons. Making goals with the parents gives parents the opportunity to support their children at home. This partnership between teacher and parent is essential for the child's growth. I always made goals with families because it was part of the job, then I began to realize that it takes a team effort with the parents to help the child. It also takes a strong relationship between teachers and families.

It was about this time that the *Wakanyeja* "Sacred Little Ones" initiative was brought to our center to help bring culture and traditions into the curriculum. When the initiative was awarded, I was informed that most of the collaboration was going to include my class. Honestly, I was nervous because I wasn't sure how much extra work it would be. It took me awhile to learn what the purpose of the initiative was and to feel comfortable with it. I was curious about how the integration of culture and language would occur in a class that consisted of different cultures. I decided I wanted to be involved in the initiative. The main reason is that as a teacher I saw this as an opportunity to contribute to a unique process. I wanted the experience of enhancing our classroom for our Native children. Before this initiative came to us, we were limited in resources and information on how to reach out to Native communities. Since the beginning, our initiative brought presenters, professional development trainings, and materials that assisted in fostering collaboration with SIPI which created a real community. This has made our center blossom. The collaboration has transformed our center and families.

As part of the *Wakanyeja* "Sacred Little Ones" initiative, families were invited to participate in the Photovoice project. The Photovoice project is centered on families sharing their needs, wants, beliefs, and ideas that are important for their family. During the meetings, families were asked a framing question: "What knowledge is needed to become a healthy Native American?" The families took pictures that answered the framing question. Each family brought their pictures and shared their responses with the group. This included sharing the actual picture and a description of why the picture was chosen. Each parent read their narratives and discussed what was significant to their family. After all of the families presented their pictures, we all put them in groups of similarity and came up with themes. I can vividly remember each picture that was shared.

One Pueblo family's picture, for example, depicted traditional farming. A toddler was helping maintain the field. The image showed a child learning about planting and maintaining a garden. The family felt this was important for children to learn how to maintain natural food harvesting, the importance of healthy foods, and to carry on traditions. In another photo that we discussed, a child stood in her Diné clothing and had her hair wrapped up in a traditional bun. This mother explained that she wanted to present this picture because she wanted others to see the importance of dressing in traditional Diné attire. She was proud to see her daughter wear the clothes confidently and to know who she is as a Diné girl. Being involved in this process was a good way to hear the family needs and wants for their children. I began to hear the passion each family expressed for their culture and what is important for their children. This process opened a door for families and I to connect on a deeper level. Parents were sharing their most cherished hopes for their children. As I listened to each family, we became a team to help each other support the children of our community.

There were times when I would get discouraged and wonder why some families viewed our early learning centers as a day care center or drop-off center. However, that began to change as we connected with parents through our Photovoice project. For example, Angela (Diné) had her family enrolled in the center. Angela was minimally involved in center events. However, her daughter Kiesha was very smart and was very eager to learn. I did everything we could to challenge this child to her full potential before she left for kindergarten. Like many other children, Kiesha began to become interested in the meetings after school and wanted to stay with her peers whose families were participating in this project. On the circle time calendar, I would mark the days when our Photovoice meetings were scheduled. One day Kiesha saw that a meeting was being held that day after school. When her mom came to pick her up, she ran to her mom to tell her. She took her mom's hand to show her the calendar and asked if they could stay. She was so adamant because other kids told her that dinner is provided and they get to play in small groups. So that day, mom decided to stay for the meeting since her child was so interested in staying late. This one instance was a huge turning point for this family. The family then became involved in Photovoice. Angela provided photos representing her love and respect for elders, traditional games, father and daughter learning how to make bread, and running. I began to see how close she is with her extended family and how important it is for her children to know their relatives. She wanted her children to see them as role models and positive influences. The greatest accomplishment was seeing Angela begin to create goals and a stronger relationship with the teachers. This strong teacher/parent relationship helped the family grow tremendously. The family began to make progress and to want more for their family. In the end, the child went on to kindergarten very well prepared and so proud of her heritage. She knew who she was as a Native child and knew her potential in her learning. The influence of her teachers and family working together provided a strong foundation for her learning.

Eventually, Photovoice was able to help our teachers develop a summer curriculum that focused on Native themes parents had developed. This project gave the families a chance to have a "voice" in their child's education. Having this opportunity to create supportive relationships with our families has brought greater family engagement and collaboration. We took Photovoice themes and developed three thematic units. The parents were able to see their hopes and dreams developed into the curriculum. The three thematic units that were developed continue to help support our Native identity and remind us of our ties to our communities back home. Throughout the process it gave the parents a sense of pride that I hadn't seen before. I saw families step up in their involvement in the center. We had an increase in volunteers, parent meeting representation, and as a result a strong community developed at the center.

Working with families at the Head Start center is very rewarding for me as a teacher. I have seen many families grow and many children leave for kindergarten with a solid foundation of learning. Now, I know that developing strong relationships with families begins with listening. Our partnership has given many families and teachers the opportunity to have a "voice" in the educational goals and curriculum. As a result, our families know who they are as Native people and have the courage to stand up for what their families want. This was a learning experience for me and I realized how to use my "voice" to make a change. Being a part of this process reminded me of my upbringing and brought me closer to this center. I now know why I was blessed to be a teacher at this center.

CHAPTER 15

INDIGENIZING PLACE-BASED EDUCATION IN EARLY LEARNING

Co-Creating Curriculum With Indigenous Communities at a Tribal College

Nahrin Aziz

Northwest Indian College (NWIC) is headquartered on the Lummi reservation, along the Salish Sea shoreline. It is one of 37 tribal colleges and universities (TCU) within what is now named the United States of America. According to the American Indian Higher Education Consortium (2018), "Each of these [TCU] institutions was created and chartered by its own tribal government for a specific purpose: to provide higher education opportunities to American Indians through programs that are locally and culturally based, holistic, and supportive" (p. 1). This philosophy, coupled with NWIC's mission that promotes Indigenous self-determination and knowledge, guided our work.

Indigenizing Education, pages 237–257
Copyright © 2022 by Information Age Publishing
www.infoagepub.com

Over the past decade, NWIC has participated in numerous early childhood education (ECE) initiatives sponsored by the American Indian College Fund. These initiatives "[place] powerful resources in the hands of tribal college early childhood teacher education programs (and faculty), tribal college and university (TCU) early learning centers (and partners), teachers, families, and children" (American Indian College Fund, 2018, p. 2). The initiatives build on tribal communities' strengths and supplement existing robust Associate of Applied Science-Transfer in early childhood education (AAS-T ECE) degree programs. Although the focus varies slightly from one initiative to another, all of the initiatives address the following five domains to improve Native children's knowledge acquisition and application, enhance teacher preparation programming, connect Pre-K to K–3 schooling, embed Native language and culture into curriculum and instruction, and empower families as self and community advocates.

In 2016, NWIC received the Restorative Teachings Early Childhood Education Initiative grant. The 2-year initiative concentrates on coupling Indigenous knowledge and traditional ways of learning with current best practices from the early learning field. It strengthens systems of care and learning for Native children "by aiming to design culturally-responsive and adapted ECE systems, build stronger family engagement programs, and support Native family economic security directly through partnerships and access to higher education" (American Indian College Fund, 2016, p. 1).

Initially, the research team proposed to examine issues of food sovereignty and anticipated developing a children's garden featuring traditional Coast Salish plants to help contextualize food sovereignty in an early learning setting. However, the further into the initiative, the clearer it became that prior to cultivating a garden, we needed to put into place a solid curriculum, one that would help to inform us about the plants essential to the area—Indigenous to this land—and used in children's everyday lives. This revelation ultimately resulted in reforming NWIC's Early Learning Center (ELC) curriculum; therefore, informing the work (i.e., creating place-based education that embraces a tribal community's values and practices) presented in this research study.

This chapter contextualizes a study that explored the ways in which ECE faculty members at a TCU co-developed a Coast Salish place-based curriculum and pedagogy. Specifically, the purpose of this chapter is about a research study that (a) examines and understands the process of developing a Coast Salish place-based curriculum focused on family and community; and (b) assesses the impact of the Coast Salish place-based curriculum on children, families, and teachers by analyzing observational and interview data from teachers, families, and community members. The subsequent sections that follow discuss the process of developing a Coast Salish place-based curriculum with ECEs, families, and community members as well as the impact of that curriculum on child outcomes. To uncover the most successful way of creating, implementing, assessing, and sustaining a new curriculum, the research team embarked on an inquiry guided by the following questions:

1. What is the process through which an ECE degree program at an institution of higher education co-develops and implements a Coast Salish place-based curriculum at an early learning program?
2. In what ways do stakeholders find place-based education and this form of pedagogy valuable in serving the needs of children, families, teachers, and the community?

NWIC's Foundational Beliefs

NWIC's AAS-T ECE degree program adopted a set of five beliefs, based on Indigenous epistemology and corroborated by research (Aziz-Parsons, 2017; Bang, 2014; Copple & Bredekamp, 2009). These foundational beliefs continue to guide and influence our philosophy of early learning:

- Native children are extraordinarily intelligent and capable of higher-level learning.
- Teachers must foster classroom environments that respect and represent family and community values.
- There must be a focus on developmentally appropriate practices and culturally responsive teaching.
- Place-based education must be infused throughout early learning programs and curricula.
- Engaging in collective community-based work is imperative in order to effect systemic change.

While these beliefs are interconnected and interdependent, I highlight the importance of collective community-based work and place-based education to contextualize the curriculum development process and to serve as the foundation of our Restorative Teachings Early Childhood Education Initiative and this study.

COLLECTIVE COMMUNITY-BASED WORK

Lees et al. (2016) stress the importance of developing authentic collaborations with communities through building relationships between educators and tribal nations that are sustainable and mutually beneficial. They identified four different phases of partnership development and implementation:

(a) building relationships, (b) expanding responsibilities, (c) implementing shared activities, and (d) reflecting on experiences. Members of our research team engaged in these phases throughout the duration of the project and in a cyclical manner in order to implement culturally responsive teaching strategies in Indigenous education.

Developing significant and sustainable projects in tribal communities requires cultivating relationships grounded in reverence and reciprocity. In their review of relationships between First Nations and institutions of higher education, Kirkness and Barnhardt (1991) emphasized

> the need for a higher educational system that respects [Indigenous students] for who they are, that is relevant to their view of the world, that offers reciprocity in their relationships with others, and that helps them exercise responsibility over their own lives. (p. 1)

This is applicable to working with Indigenous students, as well as tribal leaders, elders, and community members.

In an effort to remain fluid and authentically grounded in a Coast Salish place-based education, as well as to ensure accuracy of the curriculum, we sought members of the local community who were familiar with the place and the educational programming to provide feedback on our process and progress. In her review of our ECE initiatives, NWIC's Board of Trustees chairperson and Lummi Nation Education Board secretary, commented, "In years past, Native children were being fit into an existing and unfamiliar educational system. But finally, now, we are creating systems that work for Native children and families" (K. Kinley, personal communication, 2017). In his review of our ECE initiatives, the director of the Xwlemi' Sche'lang'en (Lummi Nation Culture and Language) Department, noted:

> The work that you are doing with the Initiative is a true investment. You are taking stock of the presentation and protection of Xwlemi' Sche'lang'en "Lummi way of life." The Initiative aligns well with the Lummi Nation because the philosophy of Indian communities includes sense of place and it is language-based. The Initiative also embodies traditional education, because it includes children, extended family systems, language, cultural knowledge, landscape, and oral tradition. (A. S. Johnnie, personal communication, 2017)

PLACE-BASED EDUCATION

Place-based education recognizes and validates a community's unique features and strengths, thus taking a specific, asset-oriented approach to teaching and learning. It takes into consideration both land, which is concrete, and space, which is abstract (Styres, 2019). Coast Salish place-based education therefore links to not only land, water, flora, and fauna, but also organizational systems, values, and practices with which Native children are already familiar, thus making content and curriculum more purposeful, meaningful, and contextual. Brayboy and Maughan (2009) are clear on this point, when they note, "All knowledge cannot be universal in its application because of the importance of place, space, and context" (p. 10).

Because a place-based curriculum is more specific and rooted in children's lived experiences, many scholars posit place-based education prevails over standardization of curriculum. Woodhouse and Knapp (2000) describe place-based education using the following five fundamental characteristics: It emerges from the particular attributes of a place, it is inherently multidisciplinary, it is inherently experiential, it is reflective of an educational philosophy that is broader than "learn to earn," and it connects place with self and community.

These scholars highlight the essential element of relational reciprocity and postulate that educators who use place-based education as the foundation of their pedagogy believe "that education should prepare people to live and work to sustain the cultural and ecological integrity of the places they inhabit" (Woodhouse & Knapp, 2000, p. 2).

As indicated by the emphasis on standardized curriculum in public schools, place-based education is not yet widely accepted by mainstream educators. Gruenewald (2003) argues that current educational practices, which standardize curriculum and all students' experiences despite their diverse geographical and cultural backgrounds, are designed for future generations to compete in a global economy. He suggests that testing and educational standards dictate the discourse in education and challenge any notion of teaching to foster empathy or designing curriculum to explore local places. Gruenewald further laments, "In place of actual experience with the phenomenal world, educators are handed, and largely accept, the mandates of a standardized, 'placeless' curriculum and settle for the abstractions and simulations of classroom learning" (p. 8).

Concurrently, placeless curricula can be harmful for students. For example, in 2001, I taught second grade in the southeastern part of the United States, during which a standardized achievement test was administered to children ages seven and eight. One portion of the test instructed children to write a personal narrative about snow. Many of these children had never experienced snow because they had not left their city, much less their state, and thus had not traveled to different regions of the country with colder climates. This standardized achievement test neglected to consider who was doing the writing. The essay question was neither connected to the children's place nor their experiences. Consequently, these children were forced to experience failure at a young age, by being asked to write a personal narrative on a topic about which they knew nothing from firsthand experience. The implication of this situation and similar, is that standard-ized test designers and curriculum developers must consider children's lived experiences and build on their existing knowledge. Educators can and should certainly continue to assess children's analytical skills. Focusing on a concept with which they are familiar will yield richer writing samples, enabling educators to assess children's skills, knowledge, and aptitude in a more authentic way.

Presenting an approach that results in meaningful teaching and learn-ing experiences, Greenwood (2011) defines place-based education as that which utilizes students' communities and their environment as the con-text for learning experiences and curriculum development. Supporters of place-based education believe community embedded learning is a neces-sary component and that this pedagogical approach helps ensure learners take responsibility for the health of social, cultural, and ecological places they inhabit (Gruenewald, 2003). Place-based education therefore con-nects to children's experiences and is grounded in relational reciprocity, a value evident among Indigenous communities around the world.

Building on the intersectionality of place, self, and community, Sobel (2005) offers an overview of place-based education as "the process of using the local community and environment... to teach concepts... across the curriculum" (p. 6). He elaborates,

> Emphasizing hands-on, real-world experiences, this approach to education increases academic achievement, helps students develop stronger ties to their community, enhances students' appreciation for the natural world, and cre-ates a heightened commitment to serving as active, contributing citizens. Community vitality and environmental quality are improved through the ac-tive engagement of local citizens, community organizations, and environmen-tal resources in the life of the school. (p. 6)

Linking content and curriculum to family, community, and place is a seminal and frequently cited practice that improves children's motivation to learn, thereby increasing academic performance (e.g., Foerster & Little Soldier, 1977; Takano et al., 2009). Learning that is connected to commu-nity reflects and builds upon the values, practices, and experiences of the children. It also closely relates to the learners' lived experiences, thus be-coming more meaningful to them. For example, when students have access to curriculum building on their environment, values, and practices, they may have a deeper understanding of the content and are more engaged in the learning. The intersectionality of classroom, community, and place gives rise to academic success and enables young children to thrive and flourish in their early learning programs. Learners are more engaged and motivated, and exhibit prosocial behaviors when the curriculum connects to their lived experiences. In the following section, I contextualize the methodology to begin examining what this could look like in practice, especially in a tribal community that strives to create connected and relevant early learning experiences for its youngest children.

METHODOLOGY: SHARED RESPONSIBILITY AND LEADERSHIP

It is important to note that the researcher and author of this chapter is the principal investigator and project director of the Restorative Teachings Early Childhood Education Initiative, as well as NWIC's ECE program lead/ faculty member. As the project director, I facilitated the coordinating team meetings, ensuring team commitment to NWIC's mission and grant goals and documenting progress toward project outcomes. To do this, we enacted a framework based upon the American Indian College Fund's ECE Initiatives, which aimed to transform Native early childhood education from *within* Native communities (Yazzie-Mintz et al., 2015). This differs from other frameworks in which teams may work *for* a particular community. Thus, my role comprised of meeting with, seeking guidance, and receiving consultation from tribal leaders and elders as well as NWIC administrators, including but not limited to representatives of the Lummi Nation Culture and Language Department, Lummi Cultural Resources Preservation Commission, Lummi Nation Education Board, and NWIC Coast Salish Institute. During the consultation sessions, tribal leaders, elders, and community members vetted the processes, productivity, and partnerships that our project used and in which our project resulted.

Further supporting this notion, NWIC's Coast Salish Institute director recommended a community ECE visioning process through which Lummi community members defined and described current early learning opportunities as well as those desired within the Lummi Nation. Therefore, upon receiving its first ECE initiative grant, NWIC's AAS-T ECE degree program hosted an event during which attendees engaged in a visioning process developed by the late Willie Jones, Sr.[1] Participants reflected on the conditions of the past—the traditional past and the past of oppression brought by colonization—the present, and the future for their tribal nation's youngest citizens (children prenatal to age eight). The multigenerational gathering included elders, leaders, parents/families, children, and community members who shared hopes and dreams for their children, their families, and their tribal community. This visioning illuminated five ECE values that the Lummi community underscores for the education of its youngest citizens: intergenerational participation; developmentally appropriate practices; respect for Coast Salish ways of life; traditional teachings; and reclamation, restoration, and revitalization of Native language. These five values served as the foundation of our Coast Salish place-based education curriculum. By building on previous ECE initiatives and working with community members to infuse their values and practices into our work, NWIC's President asserted, "The goals and strategies of all of our early childhood education projects start with the community-based visioning processes, so our ECE initiatives therefore have become an extension of that Vision."

Emerging from the collective dialogues, we designated a coordinating team to serve as an advisory council for the initiative. The coordinating team assessed the project at monthly meetings designed to review goals, create structures and systems, celebrate successes, reflect on challenges, explore possible solutions, and identify next steps. The coordinating team consisted of project director, ELC director, curriculum developer, and curriculum coach.

The ELC director helped to align the project with other aspects of the early learning program, such as licensing regulations and participation in Early Achievers, Washington State's quality rating and improvement system. The curriculum developer helped to center our conversations on place-based education in regard to the Lummi Nation and served as a liaison between the coordinating team and Lummi Culture and Language Department, for which she worked. The curriculum coach supported teachers as they bridged theory with practice when implementing the new curriculum. While each individual led a particular portion of the project, the coordinating team worked collaboratively and creatively. We created a space that was safe for individuals with different worldviews, in which we honored multiple perspectives, supported one another, encouraged each other to take risks, and collectively solved problems in innovative ways.

Collection of Data: Developing Coast Salish Place-Based Curriculum

As part of initial and ongoing communication, we entered into a cyclical process between developing the curriculum and enacting the curriculum. To gather data for the curriculum development process during our two-year initiative, we used the following modalities: (a) family listening sessions, (b) community engagement events, (c) consultation sessions, and (d) teacher focus groups and interviews.

Family Listening Sessions

As an initial grant activity, we facilitated a family listening session. Our goal was to provide families with an opportunity to connect and share their individual and collective perceptions of what a place-based curriculum could and should entail. We hosted such an event to meet with parents and family members of young children enrolled at NWIC's ELC, and asked them, "What are the characteristics of a thriving, healthy young child?" This process enabled us to co-create a framework for the new curriculum—a Coast Salish place-based curriculum. Data gathered included conversation, observation, and artifacts. We provided various opportunities for families to convey their ideas, and as a result, families responded by voicing, writing, and drawing their concepts of student achievement and Lummi place-based education.

Community Engagement Events

We hosted a Coast Salish place-based event intended to convene community members and converse about the curriculum as it was being developed and to determine our effectiveness in serving the community's needs. For example, we hosted a multigenerational community engagement event during which parents and family members participated in traditional activities such as story sharing and cedar weaving. Prior to the event, members of the coordinating team developed a series of questions about the place-based curriculum and activities. During the event, we elicited responses from attendees via questions written on large sheets of chart paper posted throughout the room and informal interviews with individuals and groups conducted by a team member. We asked attendees to explain how the curriculum activities supported parents in raising thriving, healthy, young children and the extent to which the curriculum activities integrated Native language. As children and adults engaged in the teachings, we observed their interactions and collected their feedback both formally, via written responses to a series of questions, and informally, via individual and group conversations.

Consultation Sessions

A significant aspect of our Coast Salish place-based curriculum development was the consultation we received from leaders, elders, administrators, parents/families, teachers, and community members. To maintain authenticity and validity, representatives from Lummi Nation Education Board, Lummi Nation Cultural Resources Preservation Commission, and NWIC Coast Salish Institute reviewed content and materials to assure they were Coast Salish place-based and aligned with Lummi community values and practices; thus, protecting the integrity and accuracy of the curriculum. Consultation occurred initially to lay the foundation for the work and as well continued frequently throughout the duration of the initiative. Communication among stakeholders involved with the initiative was grounded in respect, relevance, reciprocity, and responsibility (Kirkness & Barnhardt, 1991). Relationships formed in this manner demonstrate appropriate ways of working with tribal communities, helping to ensure project success and sustainability and underscoring key indicators of community-driven development.

Teacher Focus Groups and Interviews: Assessing the Curriculum

To assess our efforts, and to promote shared leadership and responsibility, we conducted teacher focus groups and interviews with the ECEs who were implementing the curriculum at NWIC's ELC. Both the focus groups and interviews provided teachers with opportunities to share their reflections (e.g., areas of strength and for improvement) about the curriculum. These educators were responsible for using the new curriculum to facilitate purposeful teaching and learning activities with young children; therefore, soliciting their insights and evaluations were crucial to the significance, success, and sustainability of our project. We facilitated four focus groups with 12 teachers and administrators, during which we met with the entire ELC staff collectively. We gathered teachers together in focus groups because we wanted to interact with them as a collective, to share their experiences of teaching the curriculum, to hear one another's opinions and perspectives about the Coast Salish place-based education curriculum, and to consider each other's ideas and experiences around curriculum implementation. We also facilitated six interviews, during which we met with each lead teacher individually (two infant teachers, two toddler teachers, and two preschool teachers). The purpose of the teacher interviews was to gain a deeper understanding of their perspectives and experiences about implementing a Coast Salish place-based curriculum with the young children in their care.

FINDINGS: COAST SALISH PLACE-BASED CURRICULUM AND PEDAGOGY FOR EARLY LEARNING

Throughout this process, attendees at our family listening session expressed great interest and enthusiasm toward creating a new curriculum for their children. One major theme that emerged was the importance of a place-based curriculum centered on Coast Salish plants and foods. Participants stated:

> [Learning about traditional Coast Salish plants and foods is] important because my child will learn traditional practices of certain types of foods . . . Learning who we are and where we come from as Indigenous People.

> Traditional, native plants allow kids to engage with the natural world, figure out how things are connected to each other, and how we rely on our environment, all through experiential learning. [They will develop] feelings of connectedness with all worldly creatures.

Another theme that emerged from our family listening session underscored that a Coast Salish place-based curriculum is deeply rooted in identity. Participants gave the following testimonies:

[This new curriculum will] give rise to learning about identity. Children won't feel lost. They'll feel connected to their home through traditional plants and foods.

[A Coast Salish place-based education curriculum] will help the children identify "home." They will have teachings about traditional plants and foods. Identity/Pride/Whole/Balance.

At our family listening session, it became clear that the participants were invested in the development of a new curriculum as much as the research team was. This corroborates that in order for place-based education to be successful, it must be developed *within* community, not *for* community. Families expressed Coast Salish place-based education for young children as multifaceted, including physical, intellectual, emotional, and spiritual teachings. These four areas are interconnected, function as a compelling component in the lives of the children, families, and community we serve, and thus became the foundation for our new curriculum.

Implementing the New Curriculum: Honoring the Lummi Way of Life

This study revealed the ways in which stakeholders find place-based education and this form of pedagogy valuable in serving the needs of children, families, teachers, and the community. We interviewed ECEs who implemented the new curriculum at NWIC's ELC and gathered data from families at our community engagement event.

Our questions within the teacher interviews were designed to probe the impact of a Coast Salish place-based curriculum on children, and on teacher–parent partnerships, and on them as teachers. Interview data from this study indicate that teachers highly value a place-based education curriculum. Another major theme included language; and engagement emerged as teachers indicated the strengths and benefits of implementing the new curriculum.

When asked about the meaning and significance of a Coast Salish place-based curriculum, one infant teacher explained:

We do need to teach our kids what we value as people. And our kids are not going to be able to know what we value as people, until we teach what we know. We're teaching our kids different things [with the new curriculum]—we're teaching them Lummi language.

We asked further probing questions, specifically about the ways in which their teaching pedagogy has evolved as a result of the Coast Salish place-based curriculum. The same teacher expounded:

[Before implementing the Coast Salish place-based curriculum] we were not going for a walk and looking for ferns. We were just going for a walk. [After implementing the Coast Salish place-based curriculum] we really focus on trying to find the things that are in the [place-based curriculum] books. We are not just out on a walk. We are out trying to explore what is out there [in this place].

Children are now engaging more with their environment and connecting their environment to what they are learning in the classroom. When asked about how a Coast Salish place-based curriculum influences a child's learning experience, a preschool teacher illustrated:

The first day that our salmon curriculum was out, they opened up the books and they were matching the salmon pictures in the books to the salmon puppets that we had in our classroom. It's really an organic process for them...teaching moments came when we were able to sit with the children and talk about the life cycle of the salmon and what that looks like.

Salmon are an integral part of the Lummi way of life. They are honored in ceremonial practices (First Salmon Ceremony), support subsistence, and ensure economic security. The Coast Salish place-based curriculum we have designed and implemented now gives rise to Lummi children at NWIC's ELC learning about the importance of salmon and exploring the reciprocal relationship they have with it, thus helping to strengthen the connection between home and school.

The children's early learning experiences, including acquisition and application of knowledge, at NWIC's ELC have improved. Our Coast Salish place-based curriculum has motivated teachers to adopt a constructivist approach to teaching and learning. When asked to define what a Coast Salish place-based curriculum looks like in her preschool classroom, one teacher answered,

I think really letting the kids just [be] in the dirt, get in the environment and be naturalists, learn from what is around them. And then connected to our ancestors—our history, connected to where we have come from and where we're going, and just that it's like a cycl[e]...we're all connected. I think [place-based education is] being where you're at, but also being connected with the past and the future.

When asked to describe how the new curriculum influenced parent–teacher relationships and partnerships, the same preschool teacher noted:

We have started implementing activities in the classroom where we're sending home letters to parents. We sent home a letter talking about the salmon's habitat and what we as humans contribute to their habitat that's negative, and the parents brought in things and brought in plastic containers and pop containers, and plastic bags and rings and stuff that ends up in the salmon's habitat. And that particular activity also resulted in several conversations with parents... And they actually wanted to know how we interacted with those items and their children and the curriculum. That was huge.

It is important to note that these responses were not anomalies. Rather, they reflect the themes that emerged when all of the teachers reflected on the implications of enacting a Coast Salish place-based curriculum. This initiative resulted in teachers deepening their knowledge about place-based education; becoming more intentional about their teaching and learning practices; taking initiative to better engage families in their children's education on a more regular basis; and expanding their understanding of how a strong classroom to community connection benefits children, families, and communities.

Beyond Holidays and Predetermined Curricula

Prior to NWIC's Restorative Teachings Initiative, the curriculum at our ELC mirrored the curriculum at many other early learning programs across the country. It was primarily based on western holidays and thematic units that were predetermined by teachers and used year after year. While this provided young children with developmentally appropriate learning activities, it did not fully recognize a community's interests, skills, or place. As a result of partnering with the community, however, NWIC's AAS-T ECE degree program helped to enact a Coast Salish place-based curriculum for the ELC.

For many teachers, the shift to an emergent land, water, and place-based curriculum empowered them to reflect on and learn more about family and community values and practices. Teachers examined ways in which seasonal changes prompted specific community activities and incorporated this information into their lesson plans. For instance, in October, they deviated from celebrating holidays to investigating fall harvest vegetables, such as squash and pumpkins. Teachers studied local plants and animals and introduced young children to relationships to these natural elements. For example, infant teachers began their spring study with the exploration of sage and sweetgrass; continued to engage with local birds and migrating birds (birdwatching, bird books, and bird sounds in the classroom); and ended with creating a plan to cultivate early spring plants that were Indigenous to our area, all the while, developing sensory activities related to these topics. Teachers also began altering the materials they used for instructional purposes. What was once store bought, such as brushes, was now handmade using more traditional elements, such as using clumps of dandelions or cedar and dry grass or sticks to create utensils for young children with which to paint.

There was also a significant shift in the disposition about the *purpose* of teaching. Prior to the launch of the Initiative, teachers often voiced concerns about not having "planning time" built into their daily schedule, allowing them to lesson plan while at work. We now have lead teachers who are lesson planning on their own time, either at home in the evenings and on the weekends, or at NWIC's library during their lunch breaks. This is demonstrative of their commitment to their vocation and to their professional development goals. Although teachers once considered lesson planning as merely a job duty that they *had* to do, they now consider lesson planning as a responsibility that they *want* to fulfill. During a coordinating team meeting, our curriculum coach observed that the teachers were "gaining experience in learning, in ways that [they] find beneficial, that isn't accountable to anybody else." NWIC's ELC teachers were viewing themselves differently and holding themselves to higher standards and levels of expectations to which they are accountable.

One infant lead teacher reflected that by aligning her practice to Lummi values, she was teaching "*better.*" When asked her to explicate why teaching based on Lummi values and practices is "better," she responded, "Because it's [the children's] way of life. And to teach them things that they...already know is better than basically trying to teach them something else. So it's...bringing the connection from home to the center and bridging the gap." This underscores the importance of integrating a community's values into curriculum, which creates a stronger connection between school and home for learners.

Teachers as well as their administrators became cognizant of this pedagogical shift and these changes to practice. For example, when discussing observable changes in teachers' behaviors, attitudes, and dispositions during our coordinating team meetings, the ELC director responded,

> I am very impressed with how the staff have risen to the challenge of...using this kind of perspective of teaching place-based curriculum to finally focus and really jump into their planning in a much more intentional way...Now I can have a conversation about their planning and observation and teaching, and they all have a plan, they all have ideas, they all are looking forward, and they all are also looking and reflecting on what they've done and what the impact is.

These examples demonstrate ways in which implementing a Coast Salish place-based curriculum enabled us to engage in curricular reform that positively affects children's early educational experiences. Our new curriculum highlights local, Indigenous knowledge. It also reflects the community's values and practices, thus helping to restore traditional teachings. And it has resulted in teachers becoming more intentional about and reflective on their practice. As one infant teacher, who was also a student in NWIC's AAS-T ECE degree program, shared in her coursework, "The work is never over. When you think it is, think, 'How can you make things better, more meaningful, and intentional in your work and education?'" (Ayala, 2017, p. 2). This quotation is demonstrative of NWIC ELC teachers now engaging in a continuous improvement model to enhance their practice and pedagogy.

Engaging in Multigenerational Teaching: "We Are Seeing, Hearing, and Tasting the Culture Together"

Enacting a Coast Salish place-based curriculum made an impact on families and their level of engagement with their children's education. We focused our engagement evening on traditional activities including in our curriculum, such as storytelling and cedar weaving, and saw an exponential increase in attendance and participation. For instance, our family engagement event took place on a stormy and blustery night. Although temperatures dropped below freezing and the forecast warned of an overnight snowstorm, over 50 children, families, and community members attended our event, nonetheless. Families shared a traditional salmon meal and shared about their parenting experiences, while weaving, with each other. At the end of the evening, families embraced one another and left with prodigious smiles, demonstrative of a sense of pride and accomplishment that stemmed from their finished products and cedar presents that would be gifted to loved ones.

Throughout the event, families commented on the importance of and their contentment with engaging in the traditional, multigenerational teachings (i.e., storytelling and cedar weaving). This family engagement event, and others that similarly espoused a Coast Salish place-based curriculum, was successful because the learning activities enabled families, including adults and children, to enjoy one another's company and establish new relationships. Furthermore, the traditional activities embodied Native values and practices, thus strengthening the home to school connection, enhancing participants' learning experiences, and cultivating connections among community members. One parent of a child enrolled at the ELC poignantly reflected, "Weaving—when hands are busy creating beautiful pieces, people allow themselves to share with others unfiltered thoughts, feelings, [and] beliefs." This exemplified the importance of place-based education as it integrates art, tradition, environment, values, and the practice of academic and interpersonal skills, for younger and older learners alike.

Family and community members at our engagement event also evaluated the curriculum by reflecting on how the content and activities supported parents' needs. They answered:

We are exposing our children to a cultural experience.

We are bringing families together, weaving our parenting skills into strong, beautiful work.

We are supporting families by our traditional ways, values, teachings, and food!

In response to the guiding questions, attendees also considered the ways in which the curriculum activities supported families in raising thriving, healthy, young Lummi children. They responded:

Cultural things for parents and children are food for the soul and will last a lifetime. We are seeing, hearing, and tasting the culture together. *Xwlemi' Sche'lang'en* (Lummi way of life) is good.

Finally, attendees reflected on the extent to which the curriculum activities integrated Native language. They shared:

Native language was well integrated! Almost all introductions this evening were spoken in the language. And we want more opportunities to speak and hear our language.

As the above quotations exemplify, weaving values, practices, and language into content and curriculum for children and families is significant to the local community. The classroom to community connection strengthens children's early learning experiences, thus improving child outcomes (as demonstrated by their increased level of engagement), as well as results in increased family engagement with the school, with each other, and with the community. Demmert and Towner (2003) posit:

From a tribal and Native American professional perspective, the creation of lifelong learning environments and meaningful educational experiences for both the youth and adults of a tribal community requires a language and cultural context that supports the traditions, knowledge, and language(s) of the community as the starting place for new ideas and knowledge. There is a firm belief within many Native tribal communities and professional Native educators that this cultural context is absolutely essential if one is to succeed academically and to build meaningful lives as adults. (p. 1)

This notion illustrates the important role that language and culture play in terms of supporting academic success. Enacting a Coast Salish place-based curriculum has made significant changes to and an indelible impact on our ELC: early childhood educators are more intentional about and reflective on their practice; family engagement events are grounded in a community's values and practices; and educational programming and activities are more meaningful, relevant, and successful for Native children and their families.

EDUCATIONAL IMPLICATIONS AND SIGNIFICANCE: "HOPE FOR THE FUTURE"

The Coast Salish place-based curriculum developed as part of this study focuses on a people's values, practices, and language. When we asked teachers to reflect on the curriculum development initiative and share their interpretation of place-based education, one teacher described, "It has meant bringing culture into the classroom and really giving the children the history and the background of their people. And...in one word, *hope*. It means hope—hope for the future." In both homogeneous and heterogeneous communities, place-based curricula could intentionally focus on the learners and their lived experiences, beyond the standard ways of teaching, resulting in deeper connections to family, community, and environment.

Place-based education generates learning experiences that are more meaningful and relevant to young children's lives. Prior to reforming our curriculum, teachers taught generic thematic units that were disconnected from the children. For example, teachers were framing their curriculum around western holidays that were not celebrated by every child and his/her respective family. Today, teachers are crafting lesson plans that stem from the children's lived experiences and their family's/community's funds of knowledge (Moll et al., 1992), thus associating early learning content and curriculum to information with which children are familiar and in which children are interested. Moreover, our Coast Salish place-based curriculum ensures that when children move from one age group/classroom to the next, they are supported in not only their growth and development, but also their transition, because of the strong alignment that now exists among our ELC's infant, toddler, and preschool classrooms, which is a direct result of the new curriculum.

In order to enact a Coast Salish place-based curriculum, individuals should not attempt to do the work in isolation, but rather, in collaboration *within* community. Programs can strategically partner with parents/families, elders, leaders, and community members to establish a curriculum that reflects local knowledge, values, and practices. Children's learning depends on the context brought forth by their family and community, including "environment, interactions, [and] activities. The home is the center of children's development, and families are their first and most enduring teachers" (Child Care Basics, 2013, p. 58). Place-based education embraces this transformative approach to education and effects systemic change by emboldening families and communities to actively participate in a decision-making process that results in the creation and implementation of an efficacious curriculum.

In the case of the *Restorative Teachings Early Childhood Education Initiative* at NWIC, it was not merely a grant's principal investigator, or a degree program's faculty member, or an early learning program's director who spearheaded this project. Instead, there were various and numerous participants including faculty from NWIC's AAS-T ECE degree program, teachers and administrators from the ELC, and members of the Restorative Teachings ECE Initiative Coordinating Team. Local knowledge holders such as elders from the Lummi Nation, and leaders from NWIC's Coast Salish Institute, Lummi Nation Education Board, Lummi Nation Cultural Resources Preservation Commission, and Lummi Nation Culture and Language Department were vital to the process. All participants collaborated, consulted, and conferred on a regular and ongoing basis to cooperatively and collegially champion the work. Such partnerships are paramount to the success of a place-based curriculum, because the significance of a place-based curriculum is not solely the final curriculum product, but also, the process of gathering people together to co-create, apply, assess, and refine the work.

Institutions of higher education can also enact place-based curriculum. For instance, taking the process that we have created, examined, and presented in this study, NWIC's AAS-T ECE degree program will soon embark on science and mathematics curriculum development. We will participate in the same process of involving elders, leaders, and community members to guide curriculum development, instruction, and assessment designed for post-secondary students in our teacher preparation program. By building on the students' knowledge, we project that we will successfully foster a growth mindset in student teachers as they actively engage in science and mathematics learning that is deeply connected to their place, values, and practices.

Understanding the positive impact of a place-based curriculum can revolutionize the ways in which we assess not only young children's growth and development, but also the growth and development of all learners. A curriculum grounded in place is one that respects, reflects, and is infused with a learner's lived experiences. It recognizes the strength of families and the wealth of communities and can help increase learner outcomes and enhance academic achievements. It is emblematic of self-directed learning, empowers communities to serve as agents of change in schools, and aligns with the philosophies of self-determination. Equally important, it honors and validates who students are and from where students come, thus enabling them to feel entitled in and have ownership of their own education. Using familiar concepts to which learners are accustomed and can connect, educators will more accurately and thoroughly measure skills, aptitude, and knowledge. This will help to ensure that content and assessment tools are neither laden with cultural bias nor favor a small group of students who may understand certain references. Instead, a Coast Salish place-based curriculum co-created with community members builds upon learners' existing knowledge and rich backgrounds, thus resulting in meaningful and relevant experiences that best support teaching and learning.

When asked to consider what teaching at the ELC would resemble, had we not embarked on this journey of enacting a place-based curriculum, one preschool teacher made the following poignant, prolific, and profound statement:

> We would have not moved forward as far as we have...I believe our center as a whole would be a lot worse off than we are right now. And I feel like the "visioning" [with] our elders, which started way back, before we had the five principles of restorative teachings...It wasn't just [the] visioning of teachers or parents, but the elders were there, and envisioning what this could look like in an early childhood setting, and actually seeing that come forward is huge...It's the work of our elders coming through our work [as teachers] and reaching our kids—reaching the Lummi kids, reaching their family, and reaching back to their ancestors, because it's the elders bringing it forward.

This is the quintessential definition of Coast Salish place-based education. It connects learners to their environment and to their relatives from generations forward and back, rooting them in traditional teachings, values, and practices, giving rise to educational equity, and resulting in high academic standards and achievement that nurture students' identities.

NOTE

1. Willie Jones Sr. was one of the founders of NWIC and respected elder and leader of the Lummi Nation. Though Mr. Jones passed away in 2016, NWIC continues to use his visioning process as a way to ensure mission fulfillment.

FUNDING SOURCE

This Tribal College & University (TCU) Early Childhood Education (ECE) Project was supported by grants awarded to Northwest Indian College by the American Indian College Fund (College Fund). The following TCU ECE Initiatives were generously awarded to the College Fund by the W. K. Kellogg Foundation: Wakanyeja "Sacred Little Ones" ECE Initiative (Grant# P3015070); Ké' ECE Initiative (Grant# P3026203); and Restorative Teachings ECE Initiative (Grant # P3033148).

REFERENCES

American Indian College Fund. (2016). *"Restorative Teachings" early childhood education initiative*. https://collegefund.org/research-and-programs/early-childhood -education/restorative-teachings-early-childhood-education-initiative/

American Indian College Fund. (2018). *Tribal college and university early childhood education initiatives: Strengthening systems of care and learning with Native communities from birth to career*. https://collegefund.org/wp-content/uploads/2019/12/ Early-Childhood-Education-Initiatives_B.pdf

American Indian Higher Education Consortium. (2018). *Tribal colleges and universities*. http://www.aihec.org/who-we-serve/TCUmap.cfm

Ayala, C. (2017). *Early childhood education career study: Professional goal statement* [Reflection paper]. Northwest Indian College, ECED 101.

Aziz-Parsons, N. (2017). Connecting educational communities to engage in collective inquiry: Creating professional learning communities as sites of action research. *Tribal College and University Research Journal, 1*(2), 30–58.

Bang, M. (2014, August 14). *Seeing and engaging in Indigenous knowledge systems in early science education*. Keynote presentation at the biannual Washington State Department of Early Learning Tribal Early Care and Education Conference.

Brayboy, B., & Maughan, E. (2009, Spring). Indigenous knowledges and the story of the bean. *Harvard Educational Review, 79*(1), 1–21.

Child Care Basics (3rd ed.). (2013). Olympia, WA: Washington State Department of Children, Youth, and Families.

Copple, C., & Bredekamp, S. (Eds.). (2009). *Developmentally appropriate practice in early childhood programs serving children from birth through age 8* (3rd ed.). National Association for the Education of Young Children.

Demmert, W. G., Jr., & Towner, J. C. (2003). *A review of the research literature on the influences of culturally based education on the academic performance of Native American students*. Northwest Regional Educational Laboratory.

Foerster, L. M., & Little Soldier, D. (1977). Trends in early education for Native American pupils. *Educational Leadership, 34*(5), 373–378.

Greenwood, D. (2011). Why place matters: Environment, culture, and education. In S. Tozer, B. P. Gallegos, A. Henry, M. Greiner, & P. Groves-Price (Eds.), *Handbook of research in social foundations of education* (pp. 632–640). Routledge.

Gruenewald, D. (2003). The best of both worlds: A critical pedagogy of place. *Educational Researcher, 32*(4), 3–12.

Kirkness, V. J., & Barnhardt, R. (1991). First Nations and higher education: The four Rs—respect, relevance, reciprocity, responsibility. *Journal of American Indian Education, 30*(3), 1–15.

Lees, A., Heineke, A., Ryan, A. M., & Roy, G. (2016). Partnering to prepare teachers for urban Indigenous communities. *Multicultural Education, 23*(2), 13–21.

Moll, L., Amanti, C., Neff, D., & Gonzalez, N. (1992, Spring). Funds of knowledge for teaching: Using a qualitative approach to connect homes and classrooms. *Theory Into Practice, 31*(2), 132–141.

Sobel, D. (2005). *Place-based education: Connecting classroom and community*. Orion Society.

Styres, S. (2019). Literacies of land: Decolonizing narratives, storying, and literature. In L. Smith, E. Tuck, & K. Yang (Eds.), *Indigenous and decolonizing studies in education: Mapping the long view* (pp. 24–37). Routledge.

Takano, T., Higgins, P., & McLaughlin, P. (2009). Connecting with place: Implications of integrating cultural values into the school curriculum in Alaska. *Environmental Education Research, 15*(3), 343–370.

Woodhouse, J. L., & Knapp, C. E. (2000). *Place-based curriculum and instruction: Outdoor and environmental education approaches* (ED 448012). ERIC Clearinghouse on Rural Education and Small Schools.

Yazzie-Mintz, T. (Chair), Lansing, D., Pyatskowit, C., Chelberg, K., Macy, S., & Aziz-Parsons, N. (2015, November 18). *The tribal and Indigenous early childhood network: Making critical connections nationwide.* Presented at the Tribal and Indigenous Early Childhood Network Forum, National Association for the Education of Young Children Annual Conference.

CHAPTER 16

TRANSFORMATIVE PRAXIS

Indigenizing Education in Early Learning: Connecting Curriculum to Community

Oomagelees (Cynthia Wilson)

*Now' Si'am, Oomagelees se ne sna Che Xwlemi-sen ne xwnitemqen sna Cynthia,
Skano ey' etse etie schay etse ngene ne stl'i kwen e skwal e kwekwinol skwal suit sen
Ohileq kwen ena' tachel ne Si'am etie schay hey'i etse ngenene alhe xwlemi.*

Hello my friends. I am from Lummi. My Lummi name is Oomagelees and my English name is Cynthia. Over the past several years, Northwest Indian College partnered with the Lummi Nation to offer the Restorative Teachings Early Childhood Education Initiative which fostered experiential education guided by Coast Salish ways of life. This has been really good work for the children. From my heart, I would like to share a few words about my experiences in indigenizing early childhood education.

I have been living on the Lummi reservation most of my life. When I was in third grade, my family was relocated from the reservation as part of the Wheeler Act, but we always came back home. My father was a fisherman and my mother was a teacher; both were very good at their professions. While growing up in our family, I had learned it was better to be of service to the

Indigenizing Education, pages 259–263
Copyright © 2022 by Information Age Publishing
www.infoagepub.com
259

community. My mother and father, for example, were good at giving back to the community. They were good mentors to many of the community members living on the reservation and had many visitors as we were growing up. The doors were never locked, and all were welcome to have coffee and share good news. My siblings and I had taken our roles as we grew older (some eventually left on their journeys to be with the ancestors)—I personally had a deep interest in education.

This was based on the fact that my educational opportunities were not the best and I felt our children deserved a good education. When I was younger, I wanted to be in the field of education to give back to my community. In my early years, I worked with students from Kindergarten through 12th grade. I loved working with those age groups; however, it became clear that I knew very little about the teaching and learning methods for our earliest learners, children ages birth to eight. Therefore, upon earning my master's degree in education in curriculum development and technology, I decided to enroll in the Early Childhood Education (ECE) Certificate program at Northwest Indian College (NWIC). My goal was to acquaint myself with teaching methods for the early learners. I found that I did not know much about the early learners even though I am a grandmother and a great grandmother. Being a teacher of early childhood education students, I knew the method of teaching in a western academic context was different and important to know. Despite these differences, I also recognize the Lummi values of family in that when the children go into the early learning center, it should feel similar to visiting auntie's house or grandma's house. When our children walk through the doors of the learning center, they should experience the kind, loving, nurturing, and sincere care reflected in their homes. As a Lummi citizen, I value an educational experience that balances the goals and expectations of education in both Lummi and western contexts.

In recent years, I have been working with the Lummi Nation Culture and Language Program to write curriculum for our program and the schools. I was inspired to get involved with the Restorative Teachings ECE Initiative while working on my early childhood education certificate at NWIC. It had been a continuation of a project from previous years, so I was familiar with the initiative and liked the work that NWIC and the community were doing for the youth. This initiative worked to develop Coast Salish place-based materials and supported teachers in tribal and public schools.

When invited to be a coordinating team member on the project to represent the Lummi Sche'lang'en department, I could not pass it up. I enjoy writing curriculum from our cultural and linguistic lens and believe it is important for teachers to have a guide or a road map when they are working with our children. As educators and as concerned members for our leaders of tomorrow, it is essential that we look at what is important for our children once they leave their homes and begin the path of their educational journeys. Thus, when developing our curriculum for our early learners, it is of utmost significance that we engage our families and community.

The project director of the Restorative Teachings ECE Initiative, Nahrin Aziz, was also the lead faculty member for my ECE certificate classes. I enjoyed her courses and learned a great deal from her at the NWIC. She was a great instructor and mentor as I was earning my ECE certificate. We collaboratively developed the vision for the early learning center and worked together to make sure the program was successful. Working with our co-ordinating team and the teachers of the early learning center, it became apparent that we needed a plan that would be positive and meaningful in working with our Lummi school-aged children. With the project director's guidance and support, the Coast Salish place-based curriculum was possible to create. For the project, we met biweekly and adjusted the curriculum to ensure the teachers had all the materials and supplies to teach the lessons. We also worked to align efforts in developing a Coast Salish place-based curriculum with ECE policies.

Building this curriculum with the team was a critical form of education for the students, families, and communities. We want our children to be successful youth and future leaders who contribute to the Lummi Nation. It is up to us as a community to rally and help our children continue to be resilient and stand in the forefront as the leaders we want them to be. Through sustaining our Lummi culture and language, we can assist them in that endeavor. When looking at our children we know that they are unique and come from sovereign nations and we have to respect and support that. We want to help to preserve, protect, and promote what is important to the Lummi people. Language and culture are of utmost importance, and as an educational entity, we can embrace and assist with the goals to promote Lummi language and culture within our daily lessons in the classroom.

Once the process of co-constructing the Coast Salish place-based curriculum began, it seemed to naturally fall into place. We wanted to expose the children to what they already knew and had been living most of their lives, which was the knowledge associated with the environment. When we learn about the environment, we learn about the people of the land; whether it is through the water, mountains, or the plants and animals. For the Lummi people, we have held sacred the relationships with the land since time immemorial. We believe the environment takes care of the people, and thus the people must take care of the environment. Everything has a living spirit and we have to nurture all things we come into contact with to show appreciation and continue the path as Lummi people. In the Coast Salish place-based curriculum, the lesson plans enabled us to learn about the plants, animals, and the places in which we live—our surroundings—which are very significant to who we are. In order to do this, we had to examine our way of doing things and to follow a different path—a path that was identifiable to the children. A path that we needed to be on which was one that our children follow and one which the environment follows. This Lummi framework guided us in creating daily lesson plans and materials. For example, we know that our children will arrive in September eager to learn after the summer months have passed. For this very reason we needed our timeline to be seamless within our units and lesson plans for the school year. We asked ourselves, "What is important in September for the people that we serve? What is important in October, November, and so on?" Every month there was something important that we highlighted in our lessons.

This project has reinforced my values of involving families and the community in teaching the students. I appreciated the evenings we hosted for the local teachers. The families brought so much positive energy when sharing their special talents and gifts to reinforce a Lummi perspective. Everyone walked away with a gift and a newfound talent that could live on in their household. When we were at the events, such as cedar weaving or Coast Salish storytelling, you could see the special spark in the children's eyes when they worked with their family on a cultural project. From my observations, I have witnessed that bringing children and families together like this is highly memorable and special.

Incorporating the Lummi language and culture sets the tone and involves the community to ensure that we are on the right track. When we use our language in most of what we do throughout the day, it reassures and validates us as a people. So, in all of the lessons that we developed for the children, we used the language of our people and drew on the environment to guide our curriculum and instruction. When working on the Coast Salish place-based curriculum for the ECE program, we realized that it was engaging, not only for the children, but for the entire family and Lummi community.

Our people had suffered enough through colonization and it is time to sustain our Indigenous Lummi knowledge, language, and values when teaching our children. Indigenous communities deserve to be honored for who they are and what they stand for. We acknowledge that we have ways of doing things and ways of knowing that nurture who we are as a people. Thus, we continue to work hard at reinforcing our sovereignty through indigenizing ECE in ways that inspire our future leaders. Our hopes and dreams are that through our education system, our children are embraced; and through the efforts of the teachers and the community, we can take steps towards getting ready for their success. The Lummi creation story talks about the survivors of the great flood. The elders put the children in the canoe and set them off to carry on the lifeways of our people. Today, we want to do the same thing with our children. As future leaders, they can save our ways of life. This project took a lot of work in planning and coordinating invitations to Lummi families, community members, knowledge holders, and leaders. It was all important because it helped our Lummi children stand tall in all of *their* accomplishments.

CHAPTER 17

COMMUNITY-CENTERED DIGITAL STORYWORK TO REVITALIZE INDIGENOUS KNOWLEDGES

Christine Rogers Stanton

As mirrors of broader society, today's public schools often emphasize individualistic meritocracy, standardization of curricula and instruction, and accountability to state and federal governments. However, when we look beyond formal, public education, we see a different view of teaching and learning—one that embraces community knowledges and diverse ways of knowing (Battiste, 2002; Pewewardy, 2002). Within Indigenous communities, specifically, there is a tradition of collective learning, relevant and localized content, and accountability to the community (Cleary & Peacock, 1998; Wilson, 2008; Windchief et al., 2015).

The purpose of this chapter is to describe the development of and potential for community-centered digital storywork (CCDS) to enhance formal and informal learning through community engagement with six Rs (respect, relevance, reciprocity, responsibility, relationality, and representation).

Indigenizing Education, pages 265–274
Copyright © 2022 by Information Age Publishing
www.infoagepub.com
All rights of reproduction in any form reserved.

CCDS provides a strengths-based model to prepare learners, educators, and leaders to share community knowledges in ways that support Native nation-building. The model was developed in partnership with educators, leaders, and learners from multiple tribal nations.

Indigenizing education, as an act of self-determination and educational sovereignty, requires Indigenous leadership (McCarty & Lee, 2014). Given my positionality as a White scholar and teacher educator, in this chapter, I hope to represent the story of the evolution of the CCDS model with integrity while recognizing my limitations as a settler, community outsider, and academic. I am regularly humbled by invitations to learn with and from Indigenous partners, and it is an honor to provide the theoretical and scholarly context for the practical chapter co-authored by the Piikani team members who provided essential leadership during early implementation of the CCDS model. I also recognize the necessary role of White educators, scholars, and students within the process of advancing educational justice (Kovach, 2013), so I hope this chapter also proves informative for White allies, educators, and scholars.

COMMUNITY ENGAGEMENT AND FORMAL EDUCATION

Since time immemorial, Indigenous Peoples have engaged in powerful teaching and learning that is place-conscious, culturally grounded, and community or Native nation-centered. After the invasion by White settlers, these aspects of Indigenous education became targets for disruption. For example, the U.S. government forcibly removed children from their families and communities and placed them in boarding schools where they were punished for speaking their Indigenous languages and practicing their traditions. As a result of various assimilative educational models, the ties between learning environments and communities—and education and cultural transmission—have been severed in many contexts (Sabzalian, 2019).

As Grande (2015) emphasizes, accountability to Indigenous communities has long been neglected due to this "historical relationship between schooling and American Indians" (p. 16). Even today, formal educational institutions are often kept separate from communities, particularly in terms of views of content and accountability, due in large part to inaccurate views that Indigenous and community knowledges are inferior to formal academic—or "Whitestream" (Grande, 2003, p. 6)—education. Settler-colonial perspectives continue to be privileged, while the experiences and ways of knowing of peoples of color continue to be marginalized (Buras, 2008; Hickman & Porfilio, 2012; Nieto, 2004). To compound the marginalization of indigeneity, educators often enact Whitestream methods, such as teacher-centered lecture and presentation, which rely upon deficit-oriented teachers' guides and emphasize individualism and meritocracy (Brenner & Hiebert, 2010; Lavere, 2008; Levstik, 2008; Whitney et al., 2012). These values potentially conflict with the active, collective resistance to oppression and genocide—what Vizenor (2008) terms "survivance" (p. 1)—vital to many Indigenous communities and Native nations.

Similarly, today's formal educational institutions are most often held accountable to accrediting bodies and government entities, rather than to communities and Native nations. Given the diversity between Indigenous nations, reviving educational sovereignty requires educators and scholars to engage in "community-based accountability" (McCarty & Lee, 2014, p. 103). While there remains a dearth of attention to teaching practice and how it aligns with community and specific Native nation expectations, the tide is turning in terms of both research and education, as more scholars and educators are looking to Indigenous theories as they evaluate teaching within communities serving Indigenous Peoples.

CRITICAL INDIGENOUS THEORIES IN EDUCATION

McCarty and Lee (2014) advocate for educational practice that engages with the community to revitalize the many Indigenous knowledges and ways of knowing that have been "disrupted and displaced by colonization" (p. 103). To confront the gap between community and educational institutions, scholars encourage increased attention to "funds of knowledge" specific to Native nations, communities, families, and contexts (González et al., 2005). Such work acknowledges localized strengths and culturally grounded assets, thereby validating historically minoritized knowledges, increasing relevance for learners, and committing to community-based accountability. Specifically, Indigenous scholars emphasize the importance of elevating attention to community-led "desire-centered" decision-making in terms of education and educational research (Tuck, 2009). This move re-centers community and family within the process of teaching and learning, and it also diverts attention from "damage-centered" or deficit views of Indigenous communities and Indigenous education.

One of the most powerful ways to advance desire-centered funds of knowledge within Indigenous communities is to attend to the importance of story. Through validation of Indigenous counter-narratives both in terms of content and methodology/pedagogy, education can critique and confront the "legacies of colonization" (McCarty & Lee, 2014, p. 103). As Indigenous scholar Brayboy (2005) notes, "Stories are not separate from theory; they make up theory and are, therefore, real and legitimate sources of data and ways of being" (p. 430). Broadly, stories offer hope in that they carry the theories and epistemologies vital to sustain and revitalize Indigenous knowledges and Native nations.

The processes of sharing stories, and the theories that they communicate, are unique to each Indigenous community. Archibald (2008) emphasizes that such *storywork* relies upon the interactive and synergistic relationships between storyteller and story hearer. Similarly, Wilson (2008) explains that Indigenous research is a process of sharing stories and developing relationships with the hearer/reader. Within teaching and learning contexts, Indigenous scholars have applied similar storytelling/hearing theory. Kirkness and Barnhardt (2001) note that to Indigenize higher education, educators and scholars must integrate Four Rs—respect, responsibility, reciprocity, and relevance—throughout educational contexts. These Four Rs reinforce the relationship between sovereignty and education, thereby enhancing views of Native nation-building/revitalization. In a variation of the "Four Rs," Brayboy et al. (2012) note that relationships, in addition to respect, reciprocity, and responsibility, are vital for culturally responsive research, and McCarty and Lee (2014) explain that these Rs also apply to K–12 teaching and learning contexts, given their support of community-based accountability.

The revitalization of Indigenous counter-narratives demands sustained collaboration and rigorous learning. In particular, Archibald's (2008) *Indigenous Storywork* seeks to "maintain the spirit of the oral tradition" (Archibald, 2008, p. 30) through the integration of cultural and community funds of knowledge with academic skills and content. Therefore, effective storywork demands close collaboration with and participation by knowledge carriers within the community. Furthermore, it requires *work* by teachers, community members, and learners. Indigenous storywork is, therefore, not simply about telling traditional stories. It is about thinking collectively and critically to engage in the purposeful shaping and sharing of knowledges.

COMMUNITY-CENTERED DIGITAL STORYWORK

When blended with community-based participatory research practices (Northway, 2010; Stanton, 2014), storywork offers the opportunity to privilege and promote Indigenous languages, values, and knowledge systems within education and research. Additionally, use of digital audiovisual media to do storywork shows potential to align with Indigenous ways of knowing more effectively and appropriately than written documentation (Iseke-Barnes & Danard, 2007). Archibald (2019) notes the potential for audiovisual storywork—in particular, filmmaking—"to advance the critical role of land, story, and cultural protocols to the place-based political identities of Indigenous visual storytellers" (p. 19). Christian (2019) describes ways filmmaking transmits cultural knowledges through "purposefully selected sounds and visuals that speak to the genetic memories we [Indigenous Peoples] carry in our blood" (p. 49). Furthermore, Christian (2019) explains that audiovisual storywork elevates and revitalizes "a culturally specific place-based identity on particular lands" (p. 53). In terms of connecting to and centering specific Indigenous communities and Native nations, filmmaking can be a powerful tool for implementation of Indigenous storywork principles.

The initial vision for a community-centered digital storywork (CCDS) model emerged out of this recognition that audiovisual technology can support rigorous community-centered storywork research and education. Broadly, CCDS works to deconstruct Eurocentric, settler-colonial views of teaching and learning by focusing on community desires, expertise, and accountability through audiovisual storytelling. Instead of marginalizing or excluding Indigenous epistemologies, CCDS recognizes Indigenous knowledges and ways of knowing as integral to the development, shaping, and sharing of stories/histories. Additionally, CCDS engages students and community members as interactive participants in synergistic knowledge production, rather than expecting them to be passive recipients of knowledge that appears disconnected from their communities and contexts.

CCDS elements are customized to focus on community-specific needs surrounding planning, research/production (e.g., interviewing, filming, and selecting archival b-roll materials), and analysis/post-production (e.g., editing and disseminating). Initial activities focus on cultural protocol, planning, and equipment orientation, while later workshops provide time and space needed to refine interviewing, filming, and editing skills. Each series of workshops, which can span between 5 and 12 months, concludes with a community showcase, where student films are shared with community members. To apply Indigenous storywork to digital audiovisual media and intercultural contexts, CCDS participants and leaders adapt principles offered by leading Indigenous scholars, including respect, relevance, reciprocity, responsibility, and relationality, to their unique contexts. Early in the model's development, the CCDS team learned that a sixth R—representation—is also vital for effective digital storywork. Given that holism is integral to effective Indigenous storywork (Archibald, 2008), the various "Rs" intersect and overlap. For example, *respect* cannot be achieved without enacting *relevant* content, processes, and protocols.

Respect

The tenet of *respect* is foundational for community-centered research and education (Archibald, 2008; Kirkness & Barnhardt, 2001; Kovach, 2009;

Wilson, 2008). Within CCDS, *respect* underlies both the content (i.e., knowledges) and the processes of transmitting knowledges (i.e., ways of knowing) specific to an Indigenous community and/or Native nation. While there are many commonalities across and between communities, each Native nation—and each community—has its own unique experiences and methods for sharing information. For example, within CCDS work, cultural expectations may allow a community knowledge carrier to share a particular story only with a person who identifies as the same gender as the storyteller or only at a specific time of the year.

Relevance

Given the uniqueness of sovereign Native nations, collaboration with community leaders is important for defining relevant goals for education (McCarty & Lee, 2014). The CCDS process begins by engaging community members in identification of knowledges *and* ways of knowing that hold *relevance* within the specific context. In particular, care must be taken to apply Native nation-specific storytelling protocol, instead of assuming that a filmed version of a person telling a story is automatically relevant. For example, if it is culturally appropriate to divert your gaze when listening to a traditional story shared by an elder, CCDS participants may choose to pair the elder's narration with locally relevant photographs or landscape imagery to honor this contextually-specific storytelling practice.

Reciprocity

Archibald (2008) emphasizes the need to engage in storywork in a "good" way that genuinely benefits the community and Native nations (Archibald, 2008, p. 12). In addition to elevating attention to counter-narratives typically excluded within Whitestream media and curricula, CCDS showcases the work—both the products and the processes—in the community. Members of the CCDS team also share the process and products through conventional formats, such as publications and conference presentations, in order to encourage expanded validation of storywork in academic arenas.

Responsibility

Within storywork, a sense of *responsibility* to community and cultural groups is as important as an obligation to self and immediate family (Archibald, 2008). As a result, culturally revitalizing educators have a unique responsibility "to pass on" cultural knowledges and ways of knowing (Mc-Carty & Lee, 2014, p. 110). Throughout CCDS processes, participants demonstrate awareness of responsibility to the interviewees, their team members, and their broader community. For example, they often check with community knowledge carriers about editing decisions (e.g., "Are leaders within the Piikani Nation ok with this part of the story being in the film? Why or why not? What is our responsibility in terms of sharing this information within and beyond the Nation?").

Relationality

Strong relationships, including the relationships between ideas and those between peoples, are considered central to Indigenous research and learning (Cleary & Peacock, 1998; Kovach, 2009; McCarty & Lee, 2014; Wilson, 2008). Through interactions with stories and storytellers, students and scholars learn about their "historical, cultural, and current context in relation to the story being told" (Archibald, 2008, p. 32). Storywork offers many opportunities to learn about the importance of *relationality* within education and research. CCDS participants frequently note the need to collaborate with community members outside of the immediate project, which demonstrates the importance and complexity of relationships within the community and throughout Native nations. For example, participants may decide to verify editing decisions with cultural leaders to ensure stories remain intact.

Representation

Although *representation* is not included as one of the "Rs" within most Indigenous research literature, it was identified during an early CCDS workshop as integral to the storywork process. Ensuring the accuracy of representations requires active participation from community knowledge carriers, researchers, and learners. Furthermore, culturally sustaining and revitalizing representations require this participation to extend throughout the storywork process, including planning, interviewing, transcription, data analysis, development of written or digital formats, and the (re)distribution of counter-narrative knowledges. In addition, participation must center upon culturally congruent ways of knowing. For example, Archibald (2008) notes that dissecting and categorizing stories, which is standard practice within qualitative research and mainstream narrative study, potentially conflicts with Indigenous values and beliefs about holism of story.

CONCLUSION

The first CCDS initiative engaged Blackfeet Community College students in learning about and applying cultural protocol, documentary filmmaking techniques and skills, and community knowledges (see Chapter 18). Since that inaugural effort, CCDS projects have expanded to include middle and high school youth, elders, and educators from four different Native nations in both formal and informal educational contexts. Community members have demonstrated interest in production of new films documenting boarding school survivorship, language revitalization and education, and traditional practices as a means to promote wellness. For example, at a community basketball tournament, Apsáalooke youth shared trailers they had created as part of an after-school club to highlight differences between traditional tobacco use and abuse of the substance.

The CCDS model, like other forms of audiovisual expression, continues to evolve and improve. CCDS projects are simultaneously empowering and emotionally exhausting, and they have faced many challenges, including participant retention, sustainability of leadership and funding, and development of on-site technical support. For communities embarking on similar work, the technology can also prove cumbersome and intimidating. However, today's smartphones, tablets, and laptops have high quality cameras, and many are sold with easy-to-use editing software. Online tutorials can provide additional technical guidance and resources, and many of today's youth are skilled teachers in terms of technical knowledge.

As Windchief et al. (2015) explain, educators must recognize "the contributions of the knowledge keepers in our home communities as well as those who extend their lives into the wider society such that they bring home something good" (p. 280). Therefore, to indigenize education and revitalize understandings unique to Native nations, participants need to honor community funds of knowledge while advancing the desire-centered interests of the Nation. Overall, CCDS and similar audiovisual storywork models can engage learners, Indigenous knowledge carriers, and community members to advance Nation-specific views of respect, relevance, reciprocity, responsibility, relationality, and representation.

REFERENCES

Archibald, J. (2008). *Indigenous storywork: Educating the heart, mind, body, and spirit*. UBC Press.

Archibald, J. Q. Q. X. (2019). Indigenous storywork in Canada. In J. Q. Q. X. Archibald, J. B. J. Lee-Morgan, & J. De Santolo (Eds.), *Decolonizing research: Indigenous storywork as methodology* (pp. 17–21). Zed Books.

Battiste, M. (2002). *Indigenous knowledge and pedagogy in First Nations education: A literature review with recommendations.* National Working Group on Education and the Minister of Indian Affairs.

Brayboy, B. (2005). Toward a tribal critical race theory in education. *The Urban Review, 37*(5), 425–446.

Brayboy, B. M. J., Gough, H. R., Leonard, B., Roehl, R. F., II, & Solyom, J. A. (2012). Reclaiming scholarship: Critical Indigenous research methodologies. In S. D. Lapan, M. T. Quartaroli, & F. J. Riemer (Eds.), *Qualitative research: An introduction to methods and designs* (pp. 423–450). Jossey-Bass.

Brenner, D., & Hiebert, E. H. (2010). If I follow the teachers' editions, isn't that enough? Analyzing reading volume in six core reading programs. *The Elementary School Journal, 110*(3), 347–363.

Buras, K. L. (2008). *Rightist multiculturalism: Core lessons on neoconservative school reform.* Routledge.

Christian, D. (2019). Indigenous visual storywork for Indigenous film aesthetics. In J. Q. Q. X. Archibald, J. B. J. Lee-Morgan, & J. De Santolo (Eds.), *Decolonizing research: Indigenous storywork as methodology* (pp. 40–55). Zed Books.

Cleary, L. M., & Peacock, T. D. (1998). *Collected wisdom: American Indian education.* Allyn & Bacon.

Grande, S. (2003). Whitestream feminism and the colonialist project: A review of contemporary feminist pedagogy and praxis. *Educational Theory, 53*(1), 329–346.

Grande, S. (2015). *Red pedagogy: Native American social and political thought* (10th anniversary ed.). Rowman and Littlefield.

González, N., Moll, L. C., & Amanti, C. (2005). *Funds of knowledge: Theorizing practice in households, communities, and classrooms.* L. Erlbaum Associates.

Hickman, H., & Porfilio, B. J. (2012). Introduction. In H. Hickman & B. J. Porfilio (Eds.), *The new politics of the textbook: Problematizing the portrayal of marginalized groups in textbooks* (pp. xvii–xxvii). Sense.

Iseke-Barnes, J., & Danard, D. (2007). Reclaiming Indigenous representations and knowledges. *Diaspora, Indigenous, and minority education: Studies of migration, integration, equity, and cultural survival, 1*(1), 5–19.

Kirkness, V. J., & Barnhardt, R. (2001). First Nations and higher education: The four R's—Respect, relevance, reciprocity, responsibility. In R. Hayoe & J. Pan (Eds.), *Knowledge across cultures: A contribution to dialogue among civilizations.* The University of Hong Kong. http://www.ankn.uaf.edu/IEW/winhec/FourRs2ndEd.html

Kovach, M. (2009). *Indigenous methodologies: Characteristics, conversations, and contexts.* University of Toronto Press.

Kovach, M. (2013). Treaties, truths, and transgressive pedagogies: Re-imagining indigenous presence in the classroom. *Socialist Studies, 9*(1), 109–127.

Lavere, D. B. (2008). The quality of pedagogical exercises in U.S. history textbooks. *The Social Studies, 99*(1), 3–7.

Levstik, L. S. (2008). What happens in social studies classrooms?: Research on K–12 social studies practice. In L. S. Levstik & C. A. Tyson (Eds.), *Handbook of research in social studies education* (pp. 50–62). Routledge.

McCarty, T., & Lee, T. (2014). Critical culturally sustaining/revitalizing pedagogy and indigenous education sovereignty. *Harvard Educational Review, 84*(1), 101–124.

Nieto, S. (2004). *Affirming diversity: The sociopolitical context of multicultural education* (4th ed.). Pearson.

Northway, R. (2010). Participatory research: Part 1: Key features and underlying philosophy. *International Journal of Therapy and Rehabilitation, 17*(4), 174–179.

Pewewardy, C. (2002). Learning styles of American Indian/Alaska Native students: A review of literature and implications for practice. *Journal of American Indian Education, 41*(3), 22–56.

Sabzalian, L. (2019). *Indigenous children's survivance in public schools.* Routledge.

Stanton, C. R. (2014). Crossing methodological borders: Decolonizing community-based participatory research. *Qualitative Inquiry, 20*(5), 573–585.

Tuck, E. (2009). Suspending damage: A letter to communities. *Harvard Educational Review 79*(3), 409–427.

Vizenor, G. (2008). Aesthetics of survivance: Literary theory and practice. In G. Vizenor (Ed.), *Survivance: Narratives of native presence* (pp. 1–24). University of Nebraska Press.

Whitney, L., Golez, F., Nagel, G., & Nieto, C. (2012). Listening to voices of practicing teachers to examine the effectiveness of a teacher education program. *Action in Teacher Education, 23*(4), 69–76. https://doi.org/10.1080/0162662 0.2002.10463090

Wilson, S. (2008). *Research is ceremony: Indigenous research methods.* Fernwood Publishing.

Windchief, S., Garcia, J., & San Pedro, T. (2015). *Red pedagogy:* Reflections from the field. In S. Grande (Ed.), *Red pedagogy: Native American social and political thought* (10th anniversary ed.; pp. 277–282). Rowman & Littlefield.

CHAPTER 18

TRANSFORMATIVE PRAXIS

Piikani Digital StoryWork: Community-Centered Digital Stories in Practice

Brad Hall
Cinda Burd-Ironmaker
Eric Cox

Blackfeet Community College (BCC) is located on the Blackfeet Indian Reservation of North Central Montana. As one of 36 tribally controlled higher education institutions in the United States, BCC is committed to engaging in community-based research both as a way to provide insight into community issues and to provide experiential learning opportunities for students. Collaboration with partner universities has provided the opportunity to implement community-centered digital storywork (CCDS; Archibald, 2008) as a means to revitalize community-based knowledge and values central to the everyday lives of the Piikani people.

In 2014, BCC began collaborating with partners in the Department of Education and the School of Film and Photography at Montana State University (MSU) to explore development of a Piikani-specific CCDS model. We received grant funding to support the purchase of equipment

Indigenizing Education, pages 275–283
Copyright © 2022 by Information Age Publishing
www.infoagepub.com
All rights of reproduction in any form reserved.

(e.g., cameras, lighting kits, computers for editing, etc.), travel costs (for workshop participants, cultural mentors, and technical consultants), stipends for leaders, and group meals. The BCC–MSU partnership engaged participants (students, faculty, and community members) in five audiovisual filmmaking workshops, which integrated development of technical skills with learning about cultural protocol.

During the first cycle of the CCDS project at BCC, which we called Piikani Digital Histories, the Six R framework (Kirkness & Barnhardt, 2001) guided the creation of a documentary entitled *Full Circle* (https://www.youtube.com/watch?v=hBRwRflVIC8). The short film reveals the issues surrounding the urgency of saving our endangered Piikani language and culture and combines interviews with community members of all ages with archival photographs. Although MSU film students provided technical assistance, the BCC Piikani filmmakers made all of the major decisions about the production of the films: They collected, organized, and edited footage, then integrated voiceover narration and music. While the process itself sounds fairly straightforward, it proved complex—yet powerful—because of the expectation for both technical growth and adherence to cultural protocol. This chapter, which is coauthored by one of the CCDS project leaders (Brad) and two BCC Piikani filmmakers (Cinda and Eric), explores lessons we learned from the implementation of CCDS at BCC and seeks to inform future research and learning in and beyond the tribal college setting. We are all Piikani, with diverse backgrounds and interests, however, our time at BCC would provide common ground to engage in research through our formed relational bond and our own contributions to this project.

RESPECT: LEARNING THROUGH COMMITMENT, HUMILITY, AND CONNECTION

As Piikani researchers, our preexisting connectedness to community members provided us with a foundation to engage participants. *Respect* is traditionally the underlying component in the intergenerational transmission of knowledge, calling upon learners (and, in our case, researchers) to value the importance of family and other relations in revitalizing tribal perspectives and devising community-based tactics that support Native nation-building. Through our implementation of CCDS, we learned that respect must be sustained and action-oriented. The Piikani community views respect as a cornerstone for interactions and relationships.

Piikani filmmakers engaged with CCDS learned that community members participating in projects required leverage to determine conditions for participation, including preferred locations, flexibility with family/work life, and an adherence to traditional Piikani protocols as reinforced through each interaction (Bastien, 2004). For the CCDS project, this "R" became fundamental, because our research called upon us to listen to and engage with participants (e.g., interviewees) through a series of interactions, rather than single encounters, and to promote long-term commitment to our research. As Piikani filmmakers, it was important that the process not only highlight the knowledge acquired through CCDS, but also that it validate our efforts to begin community conversations surrounding issues, their problems, and potential solutions.

Through the use of respect, the *Full Circle* project framed our discussions around our culture as an asset, not a liability. We learned that community-based knowledge can teach and provide context to encourage desired changes. Respect is closely tied to humility, as it requires researchers to recognize their limitations and possibilities throughout the processes they follow. Creating *Full Circle* was humbling, as it called upon us to seek out multiple viewpoints from throughout the community instead of relying on our own knowledge. We also found we needed to recognize the times when individual opinions overlapped with what was viewed as collective knowledge. As a result, we sought out our community's "authenticity of voice" by identifying individuals who have the knowledge and experience to frame CCDS discussions around topics related to them. Many of the interviewees were recommended by community members we initially approached as potential participants, thereby enacting a process that vouched for the eventual participants being recognized within the community as having knowledge relevant to student topics. These individuals were identified principally by their community credibility as "knowledge carriers" in particular areas of Piikani filmmakers' interest.

RELEVANCE: LEARNING FROM FUNDS OF KNOWLEDGE, MULTIPLE VOICES, AND COLLECTIVE INTERESTS

CCDS seeks to inform educational approaches by strengthening and recognizing links to community funds of knowledge (González et al., 2005), while also providing Piikani filmmakers with technical training to enhance skills and promote individual strengths. *Relevance* calls upon us to provide space for the community (through both informal interactions and formal interviews) to advance CCDS goals. Our CCDS process enabled the community to build a platform for collective action. For example, knowledge transmitted through *Full Circle* has not only ignited interest in heightened language revitalization and activism among the Piikani, but has helped to guide the promotion of community-based advocacy through CCDS more broadly.

Fundamentally unique, the Piikani community required a specific approach to developing and implementing a CCDS process that effectively procures community-based knowledge and delivers it in ways that ensure relevance. We understood that our approach to research needed to be flexible, interdisciplinary, and integrative of multiple voices. For example, while we initially planned to create multiple films about different topics, we decided to combine ideas together to promote a common purpose, as identified by multiple members of the community to be a top priority for the Piikani Nation.

We also recognized that our audience is diverse and that information we share is not limited to the boundaries of our reservation. Unlike many film projects, it was essential that our film's outcome was not predetermined by us (i.e., Piikani filmmakers) alone. Instead, the inclusion of individuals who held knowledge shaped *Full Circle* as a collective story. We learned that despite the varied knowledge and experience of our Piikani filmmakers, limitations (e.g., lack of cultural knowledge or technical skills) did not define participation in CCDS; rather, the individuals' skill sets and specialized knowledge defined their roles and contributions to the project.

RESPONSIBILITY: LEARNING THROUGH EMOTION, ACCOUNTABILITY, AND INTEGRITY

With a strong sense of *responsibility*, CCDS accepts the challenge of relating the creation of audiovisual stories to broader awareness of ethical obligations, community accountability, and cultural stewardship. CCDS seeks to develop compelling, community-based messages to cultivate wide appeal on and off our reservation and to encourage the audience to relate to participant experiences, even without sharing or having any Piikani community-based knowledge background. Through this process, CCDS becomes a way to meet the knowledge transmission needs of the community, and the project also tapped into the possibilities of engaging "allies" and other non-community members in discussions surrounding the Piikani experiences. The intended purpose of this CCDS project, whether engaging localized or broad audiences, was to evoke an emotional response as a means to enhance action through interest, enthusiasm, and general concern to sustain the Piikani community goal of language revitalization.

Accountability is a principal component of responsibility and occurs continuously and concurrently throughout the CCDS process. The creation of *Full Circle* required tribal institutional review and adherence to general research procedures, including obtaining participant consent. However, CCDS demands additional levels of accountability, given the collectivity of the story and the expectations of cultural protocol. Trust between the Piikani filmmakers and participant/interviewee/educator became the binding factor in collecting community-based knowledge through CCDS.

Regardless of each participant's own opinion, we learned that there is "truth" in all messages, and acceptance of this reality allowed for reasonable discourse as well as an unprecedented opportunity to teach the possibilities of community activism and advocacy. In particular, the process required us to find participants' common ground to maintain collective continuity of community-based knowledge.

It is our responsibility to allow our stories to break down barriers to understanding, but even more critical is the recognition that a researcher's own biased tendencies may permeate a CCDS project to create barriers to the application of community-based knowledge. Since our identity inevitably impacts our work, we learned it is important to comprehend how our positionalities shape decisions about using participant information. The researcher and the participant both share an innate responsibility to share Piikani knowledges and ways of knowing with integrity. From the beginning of this CCDS project, our goal was to avoid reinforcement of common stereotypes and misconceptions, as they only scratch the surface of issues and distract from developing a deeper, more relevant understanding of the colonial legacy and contemporary challenges affecting our Piikani community.

RECIPROCITY: LEARNING THROUGH INTERCONNECTIVITY, COMPLEXITY, AND SYNERGY

Knowledge is meant to be shared to enlighten individual consciousness and help individuals and communities realize their human potential. Thus, *reciprocity* is a critical component of how knowledge is taught, learned, and applied, both within individual and collective contexts. When relaying community-based knowledges, we learned that collecting, editing, and sharing mutually sustaining interactions with participants allows each story to be distinct yet connected. This seemed to form a tapestry of diverse experiences that allowed differences in opinion to be part of an open dialogue calling upon community members to form their own conclusions. Every contribution, by every participant, is to be valued and honored by researchers, whose ability to learn perpetually is linked to how they gather experiences and then verify and accept knowledge they are receiving. In particular, digital storywork proves to be a powerful method for accountability and transparency, and with such responsibility may come risks. Through production of *Full Circle*, we learned that participants take a risk to benefit their community, as they gift their unique knowledges to Piikani filmmakers and, as a result, put their own reputation within the community on the line. Adding credibility to the CCDS process, interview participants needed to be renowned within the community for the specific knowledge-set they possess and are conveying to the project.

One common misconception is that all Indigenous Peoples are the same, and non-Indigenous Peoples often believe this even more often about specific tribal communities. In reality, there are many variations within even the smallest tribes—such groups are hardly homogeneous. Differences of opinions existed among participants throughout creation of *Full Circle*, which is what is to be expected when members of nonhomogeneous groups are asked to convey collective knowledge. Reciprocity calls upon the researcher to enact cultural protocol (such as, but not limited to, gifting) and find relevant ways to navigate differences within cultures. When applying CCDS, we found that it was important to recognize the root causes of barriers and accept personal limitations to avoid giving the impression of subscribing to one individual's particular narrative while dismissing others (e.g., political differences or cultural disagreements). As the saying goes, "don't judge what I have to say, until you have walked in my moccasins." Reciprocity compels researchers to form coalitions with participants to enable their voices to be heard, while keeping an optimistic view that even though experiences are sometimes at odds, they still provide an important view of what CCDS is trying to convey. Therefore, in order to promote reciprocity, we believe it is important to integrate all contributions by participants into CCDS projects whenever possible, as differences of opinions are tied to community history and reality and can be used to teach the complexities of collecting community-based knowledge. Through the CCDS process, researchers are consistently refining and sharing ideas about how to approach issues and project the interconnectedness of various viewpoints in a responsive manner.

The community must be the primary beneficiary of information gathered; therefore, the action, movement, and evolution of a particular issue shared through a project like *Full Circle* potentially becomes a catalyst for other CCDS research, theory, pedagogy, and practice. For example, after we screened *Full Circle* in the community, we were asked to produce another film, facilitate CCDS workshops with other BCC faculty and students, and provide guidance for the local alternative high school's digital storytelling work. We learned that, when reciprocity is valued, CCDS can create a synergistic space for open and honest dialogue among participants, so that every participant (including the researcher) can feel empowered and assured that their role benefits them, the Piikani filmmakers, and the community as a whole.

REPRESENTATION: LEARNING ABOUT COLLECTIVE
REALITY, SELF-PERCEPTION, AND HISTORICAL CONTEXT

What makes CCDS simultaneously powerful and difficult is that while audiences hold preconceived stereotypes and misunderstandings, CCDS has the potential to confront and resist those misconceptions. CCDS, therefore, challenges Piikani filmmakers to ensure that participants are allowed to decide how their community is *represented*. This becomes more complex with the context of garnering collective knowledge, as communities and individuals are within themselves unique and distinct from one another and, therefore, hold different beliefs about how knowledges should be represented. Through our work, we learned that researchers should not make irrelevant comparisons among community participants, as this leads them to subscribe to generalizations that can misinform the project's progress and cripple the CCDS process. Any effort to collect and convey community-based knowledge through CCDS can be derailed the moment trust is broken between a participant and Piikani filmmakers.

Accurate *representation* provides an opportunity to (re)claim knowledges that have been lost or changed within a community. To overcome the community's challenges and promote healing, sharing knowledges with families and neighbors allows a re-examination of how each person contributes to their nation personally, professionally, and spiritually (Bastien, 2004). The process of CCDS inquiry, when combined with personal knowledges and awareness of individual limitations, enables Piikani filmmakers to navigate spaces in ways that revitalize community-based ways of knowing. Outcomes are important in *representation,* because they are connected to how the community members see themselves and how they would like others to view them and their community as a whole.

Stories have the potential to stimulate community interest in topics that affect their daily lives, but many can be painful, controversial, or possibly damaging to community integrity. We learned that many issues we encountered through the CCDS process required us to be sensible in our selection of a project topic and to find ways to collaborate and connect ideas, rather than compartmentalizing our projects. As a result, we realized that *representation* of topics requires appreciation for overlapping topics and recognition of the ways the past continues to inform the present. *Representation* evokes a sense of how historical community-based knowledges should be applied to remain relevant so that cultural components can be operationalized to meet modern challenges.

RELATIONALITY: LEARNING FROM MENTORS, EXPERTS, AND PARTNERS

CCDS projects recognize that *relationality* is a combination of formal and informal experiences, and these experiences form the basis of Piikani filmmakers and participant interactions during the project. Throughout the process used to produce *Full Circle,* ideas were organically connected through the use of general questions to evoke responses from credentialed or recognized community "knowledge carriers." Participants who were selected to contribute to the project were recognizable within the community as "knowing" or having experience in the area of interest. Due to the complexity of issues being studied, simply living in the community was not enough for participants to effectively contribute to the CCDS project—they needed to possess specialized knowledge to avoid uninformed opinions on matters needing clarity and urgency. Unfortunately, filmmaking processes tend to ignore the bi-directionality of relationships.

In addition to recognizing the position of participants, the Piikani filmmakers in CCDS projects must also confront their own positions, especially in their efforts to explain the project and expectations of the participants. The Piikani filmmakers recognized that despite our intentional efforts to engage participants, there was no guarantee that knowledge carriers would contribute to the project. As the project progressed, several of our participants became leaders who assisted the project through informal mentoring, articulated the process to others, and helped to attract others to the project. This culturally grounded approach to recruitment puts participants at ease when working with Piikani filmmakers. *Relationality* compelled the researchers to be flexible to meet the needs of participants, who at times informally guided the CCDS process. Piikani filmmakers were not in a position to "control" the inquiry; rather, we relinquished this to meet cultural and personal needs of participants. Engagement in the project required partnership with participants throughout the CCDS process, beyond simply interviewing them. Whenever possible, participants were asked to clarify and/or provide feedback on their contributions. This exchange and collaboration made relationships stronger and built trust, allowing the project to continue.

CONCLUSION

CCDS has the potential to help students find purpose in their learning. Providing students at BCC with opportunities to engage in CCDS grounded them in their learning process through research and film production, promoted their personal contributions to the community, and furthered their understanding of traditional ways of knowledge application across educational contexts. Furthermore, as a pedagogical method, tribal colleges and schools who struggle to engage learners can create critical culturally sustaining/revitalizing pedagogies (McCarty & Lee, 2014) and curriculum by utilizing CCDS. Students can strengthen technical skills as well as learn about the community interests and concerns that contribute to their educational journeys. This project has gained interest from local school districts, alternative schools, and other organizations within the Blackfoot

Confederacy. For instance, the Crow and Little Shell Indian communities in Montana have also applied CCDS as a method for school and community-based projects.

Tribal colleges like BCC remain a critical link between Western education and the perseverance of Indigenous cultural ways of knowing. All organizations serving Indigenous communities should embrace, develop, and implement ways that initiate a critical and creative response to reinforce Native nation-building. Community-centered education efforts grounded in reciprocity, responsibility, representation, and relationality support the practical application of Indigenous ways of knowing (Wilson, 2008). CCDS is a framework by which Indigenous families and communities can collectively contribute to the promotion and preservation of Indigenous knowledge and languages.

REFERENCES

Archibald, J. (2008). *Indigenous storywork: Educating the heart, mind, body, and spirit.* UBC Press.

Bastien, B. (2004). *Blackfoot ways of knowing: The worldview of the Siksikaitsitapi.* University of Calgary Press.

González, N., Moll, L. C., & Amanti, C. (2005). *Funds of knowledge: Theorizing practice in households, communities, and classrooms.* Lawrence Erlbaum Associates.

Kirkness, V. J., & Barnhardt, R. (2001). First Nations and higher education: The four R's—Respect, relevance, reciprocity, responsibility. In R. Hayoe & J. Pan (Eds.), *Knowledge across cultures: A contribution to dialogue among civilizations.* The University of Hong Kong. http://www.ankn.uaf.edu/IEW/winhec/FourRs2ndEd.html

McCarty, T., & Lee, T. (2014). Critical culturally sustaining/revitalizing pedagogy and Indigenous education sovereignty. *Harvard Educational Review, 84*(1), 101–124.

Wilson, S. (2008). *Research is ceremony: Indigenous research methods.* Fernwood Publishing.

SECTION IV

CLOSING SECTION: INDIGENIZING TEACHING AND TEACHER EDUCATION

CONCLUSION

A Call to Action: Indigenous Teaching and Teacher Education

Keiki Kawai'ae'a
Jeremy Garcia
renée holt
Ac'aralek Lolly Carpluk
Valerie Shirley

The vitality in sustaining Indigenous youth, families, communities, and Native nations is reflected across the respective educators, families, and tribal communities who have contributed to this book. The collaborative projects are grounded in decolonization, critical Indigenous pedagogies, language revitalization, and critical engagement with families and communities; and have revealed the strength in braiding research, theory, and praxis to guide Indigenous education efforts. Vital to this process is recognizing rich cultural and linguistic knowledge systems that historically serve as foundational ideals of learning and teaching across Indigenous communities. Further, the collaborative projects lead us to an energetic call to action for Native and non-Native educators and communities to implement a transformative approach that is justice-centered and contributes to Native nation-building. Our colleagues—those who have come before—have walked and cleared the pathway for what is possible and what is yet to come. This notion of what

Indigenizing Education, pages 287–299
Copyright © 2022 by Information Age Publishing
www.infoagepub.com
All rights of reproduction in any form reserved.

is yet to come is powerfully contextualized in Anpao Duta Flying Earth's chapter, "Wólakȟota: Reclaiming Language and Unlocking Identity" (see Chapter 7), by centering Indigenous youth:

> NACA [Native American Community Academy] alumni captured this commitment to identity, language, and our people embodied by our students during a graduation address when she said, "We are the dreams of ancestors and the nightmare of colonialism." The next iteration of Indigenous education, I believe, must hold youth at the center of this concept of *Wólakȟota* [peace] and challenge the things that are not in alignment with who we believe that we should be. I believe that this is our responsibility to continue the evolution of education for our people by picking up the work of our ancestors and past relatives. (this volume, p. 104)

We, too, believe the answers are inclusive of Indigenous youth who continue to remind us of their resiliency, commitment, and agency to sustain our Indigenous lifeways and peoples. We also echo Anpao Duta Flying Earth's point that we must "continue the evolution of education for our people by picking up the work of our ancestors and past relatives."

In this final chapter, we invite Indigenous scholar-educators and allies to join our collective call to action—a call that seeks to develop, innovate, and build stronger pathways for Indigenous educators and teacher education programs. Through the Native Professional Educators' Network (NPEN), the goal is to root teaching and teacher education efforts within Indigenous epistemologies and languages—restorative acts that hold Indigenous well-being and vibrancy at the center of educational endeavors. This chapter introduces the vision of NPEN, linking its purpose with historical movements that will inform the next 50 to 100 years of educational transformation for Indigenous communities, families, and children.

FROM THE NATIVE VOICES WITHIN US

Native communities across the 50 states in the United States continue to reach deep within themselves for the answers to counteract the negative impact of Western acculturation and assimilation through a growing surge of hope across the land and waters of Native communities. It is understood that Indigenous knowledge, language, worldview, and ways of being are critical to Native people and can be easily lost if not passed across and through the generations. What we have painfully learned is how critically important Native languages, epistemologies, practices, and values are to the well-being of Native peoples and that fostering strong cultural roots in the transmission of understanding who we are and where we come from equip us with a greater sense of pride and confidence to face the future. It is important to remember that Native elders, families, and communities have provided the best of their insights and intentions leaving behind the stones from which strong Native educational foundations can be rebuilt. In this regard, William Demmert Jr. and John Towner (2002) explain:

> Traditional systems of Native American education used to transfer skills and knowledge from one generation to the next developed over thousands of years. In these systems, students were not allowed to fail. The family, clan, tribe, and responsible mentors worked with the youth until the information or task was clearly learned. The lessons were an integrated part of daily life and ceremonies, not a separate or isolated activity. (p. 1)

Over the last 20 years, and as made evident across the chapters in this book, there has been a growing surge of discussion around how to sustain and address the transfer of knowledge, values, and languages. For instance, as referenced by contributing author, Walter Kahumoku III (see Chapter 4), *culture-based education* (CBE), a term coined to express a culturally responsive model for addressing the education of Native peoples is one model that has gained attention. Shawn Malia Kanaʻiaupuni and Keiki Kawaiʻaeʻa (2008), expand this work by defining CBE as:

> The grounding of instruction and student learning in the values, norms, knowledge, beliefs, practices, experiences, places, and language that are the foundation of a culture ... Culture-based education may include teaching the traditions and practices of a particular culture, but it is not restricted to these skills and knowledge. More importantly, culture-based education refers to teaching and learning that are grounded in a cultural worldview, from whose lens are taught the skills, knowledge, content, and values that students need in our modern, global society. (p. 71)

There are a number of reasons for encouraging instruction in Native languages and cultures that include the survival and transmission of Native languages, identity, cultural knowledge, mores, and practices that lead to improved educational opportunity and increased student achievement (Kawaiʻaeʻa, 2008; Kimura, 2010; Little & McCarty, 2006; McCarty & Snell, 2011).

Recent movements in Indigenous education also include the call for *critical Indigenous teachers* (Garcia, 2020) whose curriculum and pedagogy are driven by a decolonial praxis and infuses Indigenous social justice pedagogies (Shirley, 2017) to generate a critical consciousness in youth who then become protectors and advocates for their Native nations. These unique educational models that address academic, cultural, and political goals reflect and respond to community aspirations that are vital in elevating the vibrancy of Native peoples. In order to accomplish these goals, Mary Hermes and Keiki Kawaiʻaeʻa (2014) add that education "programs [must strive to] seek an indigenization of the education system as a strength-based place from which dynamic Indigenous language and culture rich environments can further foster the cultural identity and positive sense of well-being, self-image, and homeland connection" (p. 308). Therefore, theoretical and educational models such as CBE, critical Indigenous pedagogy, and Indigenous social justice pedagogy are essential for Native schools, educators, families, and tribal nations to draw upon as they thrive toward indigenizing their education systems.

Given the growing relationships between research, theory, and praxis that continues to inform Indigenous education, we recognize the necessity to engage in ongoing dialogues that bring Indigenous theories and praxis to life. Essential to this process is acknowledging the power Indigenous teachers have in enacting, sustaining, and informing critical and culturally based Indigenous pedagogies. Thus, the call to action includes the questions of: How are we preparing Indigenous teachers to be change agents who enact critical and culturally based Indigenous pedagogies? How are they being prepared to be Indigenous teachers as Native nation builders whose curriculum and pedagogy are driven by revitalizing language, sustaining relations with families and communities, advocating for the protection of land and people, and upholding notions of self-determination and sovereignty? Finally, how are we sustaining critical and culturally based Indigenous pedagogies within current educators and educational leaders in schools, communities, and diverse learning contexts?

INDIGENOUS TEACHER EDUCATION

There are multiple types of school models and philosophies of education and indeed, no "one size fits all" approach would be appropriate in the preparation of teachers. When reflecting on the purpose, function, and role of education, there are many viewpoints and responses to the questions posed above. One might also argue that education should be responsive to family, community, and individual aspirations and that education must serve the "we," not just the "me." Native education, however, must position itself in the "we" and the need for holistic learning that attends to the development of the whole person—mind, body, and spirit. Therein lies the problem which must be addressed in the preparation and development of an educator workforce for classroom teachers, administrators, and educational support/specialist staff. What kind of preparation, development, and skill set would teachers in these kinds of schools need?

As a consortium of Indigenous educators, we believe that in order to teach in schools serving a high concentration of American Indian, Alaska

Native, and Native Hawaiian learners, teacher preparation programs must be (RE)envisioned to reflect the unique demands of Indigenous communities. This calls for teacher education programs to engage a mindshift change and think of new pathways that utilizes course instruction, observation, and practicum opportunities for modeling effective teaching strategies and providing extensive experiences in generating curriculum tailored to Indigenous contexts—where the Native language, culture, values, and goals of the Native nations are embedded throughout the learning experience.

A National Initiative: Native Teacher Education Pathways

Early initiatives across various platforms like the National Indian Education Association (NIEA), the Indian Nations at Risk Task Force of 1991, and the White House Conference on Indian Education in 1992 led to actions to address the cultural and educational needs of American Indians and Alaska Natives. In 1998, President Clinton signed an executive order (13096) that created funding opportunities to support this need. Critical to this moment was the establishment of the Indian Professional Development Program that provided funding to increase the number of Native teachers serving Native students (Archibald & Garcia, in press; Beaulieu et al., 2005). Since the inception of this federal program, many Indigenous teachers have earned their degrees to become teachers.

Few studies have been conducted to examine Indigenous teacher education. In 2001, a 3-year national research study, the Native Educators Research Project, examined 28 teacher education programs across the United States and conducted case studies in the induction year on issues of language, culture, and student achievement in their classrooms and school sites. Among the many findings, the research project revealed two critical goals for re-envisioning Native teacher education programs: (a) a focus on building resilience and relationships and (b) enriching content, pedagogy, and practice. David Beaulieu and Anna Figueira (2006) explain the importance of building resilience and relationships between Native teachers of Native students by suggesting

they must be resilient—strong in their sense of self and steadfast in their sense of mission . . . It is in the development of resilience and building relationships in a community of practice that Native teacher training efforts have sought to re-envision teacher training that shows great promise. (p. 119)

The urgency to continue developing a strong sense of self and mission is essential in re-envisioning Indigenous teacher education. There is much work yet to be done to (RE)shift the focus from Western systems to Indigenous systems of teacher preparation and development. With the growth in Indigenous theories and practices in education (as evident in the chapters in this book), it is essential to engage new research that will inform the process of Indigenous teacher education.

Over the last 3 years, the Grow Your Own (GYO) teacher education initiative has accelerated a national momentum towards addressing critical teacher shortages and the wide racial, ethnic, and linguistic disparities found in the teacher workforce (Valenzuela, 2017). These programs focus on recruiting and preparing local community members through teacher education pathways and partnerships to enter the teaching profession and teach in their communities. The underlying principles of GYO align with the creation of a national Native Teacher Education Pathway for local programs that prepare Native teachers and others to work in Native communities as well as language and cultural educational settings such as Native language immersion and schools with predominantly Native student enrollment. The creation of a Native Teacher Education Pathway as a national initiative will greatly support local programs to prepare and further advance teacher know-how through programs that tightly integrate and build upon Native philosophies of education, infuse approaches to language revitalization, and engage in critical Indigenous theories across foundations and methods courses and seminars. It is critical that these kinds of distinct teacher preparation programs are available, accessible, and supported. These unique programs would amplify those best practices that honor Native ways of learning and teaching as a strengths-based strategy designed to meet and advance rigorous academic standards and the unique cultural, linguistic, and social-emotional goals for Native education that nurtures positive cultural well-being and leads to Native nation-building. A Native Teacher Education Pathway would significantly reduce the teacher shortages and retention rates that have thwarted the ability of schools from meeting the unique needs of Native American, Alaska Natives, and Native Hawaiian students for decades. The increase of Indigenous teachers who are capable of meeting the linguistic and cultural needs of Indigenous students would assist greatly in addressing a longstanding educational inequity our children, families, and communities have endured. While Native nations are diverse and unique, there are essential programmatic elements that guide a common and distinctive Native American Teacher Education Pathway. These elements include:

1. Native Languages—to teach about and through a Native language and its cultural lens.

2. Native Understandings of Place—to understand and value place as a context for learning and to build connection to and with the place, people, language, and culture.
3. Native Culture and Knowledge—to develop a cultural mindset that transmits the knowledge, practices, mores, spiritual, and leadership understandings of the culture.
4. Native Worldview and Values—to maintain and transmit an Indigenous perspective and the worldview reflective of the Indigenous language, culture, and history.
5. Relationship with Native Families and Communities—to value and understand the family and community and to connect, collaborate, and advocate for its students.

While these essential elements offer a unique approach to developing a common Native Teacher Education Pathway, we underscore the need to continue building relations across Native educators, schools, and communities to assist in co-constructing these proposed elements. We have seen an influx of great work emerging across universities and tribal colleges and universities (TCU) as they strive to institutionalize Indigenous teacher education programs; and the momentum extends to new opportunities toward building solidarity and collective efforts among Native professionals and educators at a national and global level. The efforts to establish a national initiative across universities and TCUs would strengthen Indigenous communities and increase the well-being of Native children and their families through the process. Building a national coalition to engage Native Teacher Education Pathways is being contextualized through a recent initiative entitled, Native Professional Educators' Network which centers Indigenous teaching and teacher education.

NATIVE PROFESSIONAL EDUCATORS' NETWORK: A CALL TO ACTION

In 2015, Indigenous educators convened at the National Indian Education Association annual convention with the intent to develop a Native Professional Educators' Network (NPEN). Approximately, 50 educators across diverse educational contexts and communities engaged in a generative dialogue, seeking to describe concretely the strengths of a Native teacher. This first gathering confirmed the need for a national and strategic effort to envision, innovate, and design increased opportunities to strengthen Native education for and by Native communities. A series of discussions and collaborative visioning led to the official inaugural gathering of Indigenous educators at the 2018 NIEA annual convention held in Hartford, Connecticut. In 2018, a subcommittee was officially appointed and included the inaugural NPEN members: Keiki Kawaiʻaeʻa (University of Hawaii—Hilo), Jeremy Garcia (University of Arizona), Acʻaralek Lolly Carpluk (University of Alaska—Fairbanks), renée holt (Washington State University), Valerie Shirley (University of Arizona), and Tarajean Yazzie-Mintz (First Light Education Project). In 2019, Jason Dropik (Head of the Indian Community School, Milwaukee, Wisconsin) as a newly elected NIEA board member joined NPEN.

At the subsequent 2018 and 2019 preconvention workshop series, the NPEN committee planned and created space for educators to engage in critical dialogues regarding the state of Indigenous education across their respective contexts and to generate attention in reconceptualizing pathways for Indigenous teacher education programs. During the sessions, attendees continued to express the need for increased and targeted support specific to Indigenous teacher educators whose work is at the crux of integrating Indigenous language, culture, and education. Through these generative sessions, a vision, mission, and guiding principles were developed for NPEN.

The Native Professional Educators' Network seeks to bring educators and community members together to generate a national voice for strengthening Native place-based, culture-based, and language-based teacher education programs (Kawaiʻaeʻa et al., 2019). With Indigenous knowledge and values as a grounding framework, NPEN is a community of Native and non-Native educators who work to create changes in education systems. NPEN engages and rematriates Indigenous education through culturally based education and critical Indigenous pedagogical frameworks that calls for educators to include land-based, culture-based, and decolonization in their programs and schools. NPEN's goals are to: (a) create opportunities for educators to build networks specific to Indigenous teaching and learning principles and (b) to develop a national movement that supports the development of Indigenous teacher preparation programs. The following are NPEN strands that are guiding this effort.

Guiding Strands of Native Professional Educators' Network

In building a momentum for NPEN, four areas of focus create the spaces for continued critical conversations towards advancing Native teacher education and professional development through a national collective platform: Native community vibrancy through education; Indigenous knowledge, pedagogy, and praxis in education; Indigenous teacher education programs; and accreditation systems for Indigenous teacher education programs.

Native Community Vibrancy Through Education

Education rooted in Indigenous social and cultural systems lead toward transformative change in Indigenous communities. Indigenous and locally implemented educational efforts serve as places to enhance Native community vibrancy across the continuum of educational practices and systems (i.e., early childhood through postsecondary education and beyond—birth to elderhood—as well as family and community engagement initiatives). NPEN recognizes the possibilities of such efforts and facilitates dialogues around envisioning Native community vibrancy through education.

Indigenous Knowledge, Pedagogy, and Praxis in Education

An essential focus of NPEN is grounded in Indigenous knowledge, language, and values through curriculum, pedagogy, and praxis. Within this strand, notions of Native community vibrancy come to life as we sustain and revitalize our (re)connection to our epistemologies—our knowledge systems, kinship, ceremonies, and genealogy. This focus centers our relationships to place (i.e., land, waters), clan systems, and Indigenous philosophies. NPEN strives to engage in critical dialogues that capture the ways in which educators indigenize curriculum and pedagogy in education. With foundations of transformative education and decolonial praxis growing among Indigenous communities, the need for a national initiative that calls upon teaching and teacher education programs to shift significantly has become paramount. By drawing upon transformative models and theories such as culturally based education and critical Indigenous pedagogies, NPEN offers opportunities for collective solidarity in revitalizing and sustaining Indigenous worldviews and values that guides an educational pathway leading to Native nation-building.

Indigenous Teacher Education Programs

Indigenous teacher education programs prepare Native teacher candidates for teaching within the unique sociocultural and political contexts of Indigenous communities. NPEN seeks to create a broader space for ongoing discussions and strategic actions that actively support the preparation of holistic, critical, and culturally grounded educators. Through NPEN, Indigenous educators have an opportunity as a collective voice to (RE)envision, strengthen, and advocate for the kinds of Indigenous teacher education programs that honor and actualize our Indigenous voices, languages, cultures, and ways of knowing while building solidarity across diverse socio-cultural contexts.

Accreditation Systems for Indigenous Teacher Education Programs

The accreditation of teacher education programs is important for building capacity of Indigenous teachers. Across universities and TCUs, Indigenous teacher education programs are integrating Indigenous principles and practices to prepare teacher candidates; therefore, there is a growing need for accreditation options that acknowledge and affirm Indigenous philosophies, ways of knowing, language, culture, and place in Indigenous teacher education programs. NPEN supports accreditation systems that imbue Indigenous processes of accreditation and contribute to community vibrancy, well-being, language, and culture perpetuation, and self-determination.

NPEN's goals are intended to lead to transformative outcomes that are informed by Indigenous educators, leaders, youth, families, and communities. The members of NPEN strive to build upon the experiences, challenges, and successes of educational efforts to inform educational policies (within Native nations and at the state and national levels) and the landscape of teaching and teacher education programs across institutions and programs. We encourage all Indigenous and non-Indigenous scholar-educators and allies to join NPEN's call to action by engaging in dialogues and innovative approaches that mobilize a national movement to create a Native Teacher Education Pathway that informs the preparation of the next generation of Indigenous teachers.

We invite you to join us as we expand on this work during the annual convenings of the National Indian Education Association (NIEA). We are grateful to the NIEA as they have supported the inception of this effort. Through this coalition, we can generate new possibilities for research, theory, and praxis that informs Indigenous teaching and teacher education.

CONCLUSION

The scholarly contributions shared in this final chapter and across the chapters of this book reflect a deep level of love, care, and passion for all generations of Indigenous Peoples. Together, we are a collective whose values and commitments to sustaining Indigenous lifeways are guided by the principles of respect, responsibility, reverence, and reciprocity (Archibald, 2008). Evident across the chapters are models and collaborations that reflect the ways that indigenizing processes of research, theory, and praxis are in motion across Indigenous communities. Importantly we value the transformative approaches in how Indigenous research, theory, and praxis converge to co-construct meaningful critical and culturally sustaining curriculum and pedagogy with families and communities. It is the work with teachers, youth, families, and community members that ensures our goals, knowledges, and values in sustaining pathways that honor Indigenous sovereignty, self-determination, and Native nation-building. For example, in *Indigenizing Education in Early Learning: Connecting Curriculum to Community* (see Chapter 16), Oomagelees (Cynthia Wilson) drew on her Lummi creation story to guide efforts in carrying on the lifeways of her people. She reflects:

> The Lummi creation story talks about the survivors of the great flood. The elders put the children in the canoe and set them off to carry on the lifeways of our people. Today, we want to do the same thing with our children. As future leaders, the children can save our ways of life. (this volume, p. 262)

Through these exemplars, we document and analyze pathways for sustaining and revitalizing a distinct form of education that is decolonizing and grounded in transformative outcomes for Indigenous communities. The extraordinary outcomes of an education by Native and non-Native scholar-educators are manifested in the revitalization and use of Indigenous languages, using critical Indigenous theories to guide praxis, engaging in ceremonial practices to sustain communities, protecting what is sacred to us, and maintaining an educational pathway that contributes to Native nation-building for generations to come.

We also call attention to the importance of reconceptualizing Indigenous education that is inclusive of being in solidarity with diverse communities who have experienced and witnessed long-standing injustices. It is vital that scholar-educators join efforts in countering anti-Indigenous, anti-Black, anti-Immigration, and anti-LGBQT challenges occurring across the United States and the world. We must remain diligent in creating opportunities for teaching and learning in relation to and with diverse communities who are also working to engage a decolonial education.

Finally, we close this book by offering our prayers for all who have been impacted by COVID-19. We find it critical that we continue to center love and care in a moment of increased concern for the well-being of communities as we respond to a global pandemic. We believe there is strength and answers in our Indigenous prayers, medicines, and prophecies—the legacies of our Indigenous knowledges.

REFERENCES

Archibald, J. A. (2008). *Indigenous story work: Educating the heart, mind, body, and spirit.* University of British Colombia Press.

Archibald, J. Q., & Garcia, J. T. (in press). The struggles and triumphs of Indigenous teacher education in Canada and the United States. In C. Gist & T. Bristol (Eds.), *Handbook of research on teachers of color and Indigenous teachers.* American Education Research Association.

Beaulieu, D., & Figueira, A. (Eds.). (2006). *The power of native teachers: Language and culture in the classroom.* The Center for Indian Education, Arizona State University.

Beaulieu, D., Figueira, A., & Viri, D. (2005). Indigenous teacher education: Research-based model. *Australian Association for Research in Education 2005 conference papers.* http://www.aare.edu.au/05pap/abs05.htm

Demmert, W. G., Jr., & Towner, J. C. (2002). *Improving academic performance among Native American students: A review of research literature.* Western Washington University.

Garcia, J. (2020). Critical Indigenous pedagogies of resistance: The call for critical Indigenous educators. In S. Steinberg & B. Down (Eds.), *The SAGE handbook of critical pedagogies* (pp. 574–586). Routledge.

Hermes, M., & Kawaiʻaeʻa, K. (2014). Revitalizing indigenous languages through indigenous immersion education. *Journal of Immersion and Content-Based Language Education, 2*(2), 303–322. https://doi.org/10.1075/jicb.2.2.10her

Indian Nations at Risk Task Force. (1991). *Indian nations at risk: An educational strategy for action.* U.S. Department of Education. https://www2.ed.gov/rschstat/research/pubs/oieresearch/research/natatrisk/report.pdf

Kanaʻiaupuni, S. M., & Kawaiʻaeʻa, K. (2008). E Lauhoe mai nā waʻa: Toward a Hawaiian Indigenous Education Teaching Framework. *Hūlili: Multidisciplinary Research on Hawaiian Well-Being, 5*(1), 67–90. http://www.kamehamehapublishing.org/hulili_5/

Kawaiʻaeʻa, K. (2008). Hoʻi hou i ke kumu: Teachers as nation builders. In M. K. P. Ah Nee- Benham (Ed.), *Indigenous educational models for contemporary practice: In our mother's voice* (Vol. II; pp. 40–45). Routledge.

Kawaiʻaeʻa, K., Holt, R., Yazzie-Mintz, T., Garcia, J., Shirley, V., & Carpluk, A. (2019, October 8–12). Lifting our voices for native teacher education: Creating a native professional educators network (NPEN) [Conference workshop]. National Indian Education Association 50th Convention, Minneapolis, MN, United States. https://www.niea.org/.

Kimura, L. (2010). Aia Iā Kākou Nā Hāʺina—The answers are within us: Language rights in tandem with language survival. In C. Galla, S. Oberly, G. Romero, M. Sam, & O. Zepeda (Eds.), *American Indian language development institute: Thirty year tradition of speaking from our heart* (pp. 41–51). http://aildi.arizona.edu/sites/default/files/aildi-30-year-book-10-aia-ia-kakou-na-ha'ina-the-answers-are-within-us.pdf

Little, M. E., & McCarty, T. L. (2006). Language planning challenges and prospects in Native American communities and schools. *Education Policy Research Unit and Language Policy Research Unit.* http://nepc.colorado.edu/publication/

language-planning-challenges-and-prospects-native-american-communities
-and-schools

McCarty, T. L., & Snell, A. W. (2011). *The role of native languages and cultures in American Indian, Alaska Native, and Native Hawaiian student achievement.* Arizona State University.

Shirley, V. (2017). Indigenous social justice pedagogy: Teaching into the risks and cultivating the heart. *Critical Questions in Education, 8*(2), 163–177.

Valenzuela, A. (2017). *Grow your own educator programs: A review of the literature with an emphasis on equity-based approaches.* https://files.eric.ed.gov/fulltext/ED582731.pdf

ABOUT THE EDITORS

Jeremy Garcia is an associate professor of Indigenous education and is co-founding director of the Indigenous Teacher Education Program (ITEP) at the University of Arizona. He is a member of the Hopi/Tewa tribes of Arizona and is of the Hospoawungwa (Roadrunner) clan. Prior to joining the University of Arizona, he was an assistant professor in the School of Education and an endowed professor of the Electa Quinney Institute for American Indian Education at the University of Wisconsin–Milwaukee. Grounded in critical Indigenous research methodologies, his research focuses on decolonization, critical Indigenous curriculum and pedagogy, Indigenous teacher education, and critical and culturally sustaining family and community engagement within Indigenous education.

Valerie Shirley is an associate professor of Indigenous education and co-founding director of the Indigenous Teacher Education Program (ITEP) at the University of Arizona. ITEP's mission is to increase the number of Indigenous teachers serving Indigenous students, schools, and communities. She is a member of the Diné Nation, which continues to shape her research and pedagogical interests. The focus areas of her research are within critical Indigenous pedagogy, social justice pedagogy, youth empowerment, curriculum development, teacher education, and Indigenous education.

Hollie Anderson Kulago is Diné and a mother of two. She is currently an associate professor of education in the Department of Curriculum and

Instruction at Penn State University. Her research focuses on Indigenous teacher education, decolonizing and Indigenous pedagogy, and family–community–school relationships.

ABOUT THE CONTRIBUTORS

Nahrin Aziz is the early childhood education degree program lead at Northwest Indian College. She received her undergraduate degree at UC Berkeley and served as a Teach for America (TFA) corps member in New Orleans, LA. Nahrin received a Master of Education in instructional leadership at UW Seattle and served as an officer for the student organization, Educators for Social Justice. Nahrin also currently serves as a mentor to TFA corps members of color and a scholarship reviewer for UC Berkeley's Cal Alumni Association Leadership Award. Her special interests include ending the education debt for students of diverse cultural backgrounds.

Andrea Box, who comes from Opata and Mayan heritage, has been a high school English teacher for the past 23 years. She has taught Native American literature, multicultural literature, creative writing, International Baccalaureate Theory of Knowledge, senior English, sophomore English, and freshman English. She is a passionate advocate and activist for getting Native American literature, histories, stories, and leaders, as well as other marginalized groups and their stories, into public school curricula. She continues to incorporate and interweave current national and international Indigenous issues and celebrations into her daily lessons, no matter what subject she is teaching.

Cinda Burd-Ironmaker is an enrolled member of the Blackfeet Nation. As a community organizer and advocate for social justice in Indian country, her focus is to inspire, motivate, and empower Native communities through education, advocacy, and civic/political engagement. She is well-known in

Indigenizing Education, pages 303–310
Copyright © 2022 by Information Age Publishing
All rights of reproduction in any form reserved.

Montana for helping individuals and communities by researching, finding resources, and supporting partners in meeting their goals for confronting social and individual challenges. Cinda is also a passionate advocate for the preservation of Native American languages and culture. She has served as a Native American liaison for Montana Senator Jon Tester and is currently a Montana Ambassador.

Ac'araek Lolly Carpluk (aka Lenora Carpluk) is Yup'ik from the Asa'carsarmiut Tribe in Mountain Village, Alaska. Her parents are the late Cunic'uar Johnny and Yungersaq Mary Ann Sheppard. She is the mother of three children and one grandchild. As an Indigenous educator, her Yugtun values and teachings have anchored her in all areas of education, with a special focus on nurturing the identity and cultural knowledge and practices of Indigenous students pursuing a teaching degree and providing culturally based professional development for current educators. She is currently researching national Indigenous teacher education models.

Kari A. B. Chew is a citizen of the Chickasaw Nation and assistant professor of Indigenous education in the Department of Educational Leadership and Policy Studies at the University of Oklahoma. She earned a doctorate in Indigenous language education and linguistics from the University of Arizona in 2016 and completed a postdoctoral fellowship with the NEȾOLṈEW̱ "one mind, one people" Indigenous Language Partnership at the University of Victoria in 2020. Her research focuses on Indigenous language education, Indigenous language curriculum, and the role of technology in Indigenous language education. She works closely with the Chickasaw Nation on language education projects.

Michelle Cooke is senior staff writer for Chickasaw Press and a Chickasaw Citizen. She has worked for the Chickasaw Nation since 2007, where her focus has been writing about, teaching, and researching Chickasaw history and culture. She is the author of *Protecting Our People: Chickasaw Law Enforcement in Indian Territory*, published by Chickasaw Press in 2019. Her work has also appeared in *The Journal of Chickasaw History and Culture*, *Chokma: Chickasaw Magazine*, and the Chickasaw Basic Language workbook series. She studied English at Texas Woman's University in Denton, Texas, and holds a master's degree in that subject.

Eric Cox is medically retired from the U.S. Army. Eric attended the University of Montevallo–Massachusetts where he studied Communications Broadcasting. While in his senior year, Eric's brother passed away. Eric then returned to the Blackfeet Indian Reservation where he attended Blackfeet Community College and graduated with an Associates of Arts in Piikani (Blackfeet) studies. Eric used this time to learn more about his Blackfeet culture and language. He was the lead on technical aspects of the Piikani Digital Storywork project, where his work on the production of "Full Circle" helped to build a "model" for other storytellers using digital means to collect stories.

Somi'mana, also **Ada Joseph Curtis**, is a dedicated educator with 30+ years of classroom experience at the Pre-K and primary levels. She and her husband live in Songoopavi Village on the Hopi reservation. They have one daughter and two sons. Recently retired (May 2021), and due to COVID-19, she closed her teaching career instructing online from home, an experience she never imagined in her wildest dreams. Hopilavayi is of importance to her, and she has assisted in planning and teaching in summer language programs for the youth. Her dream is to hear more Hopilavayi among her people both young and old.

Siwivensi, also **Bernita Duwahoyeoma** received her bachelor's degree from Fort Lewis College in Durango, Colorado in 1972. After attending summer language institutes sponsored by the Hopi Tribe in partnership with the University of Arizona, she applied her credits to earn a master's degree in reading, language, and culture from the University of Arizona in 2010. Siwivensi was a certified classroom teacher for 48 years, teaching Hopilavayi and culture towards the end. She continues to work with Hopilavayi and is a member of the Hopi Transition Team currently working on the Hopi Education Code for a unified Hopi School System.

Anpao Duta Flying Earth (Lakota, Dakota, Ojibwe, Akimel O'odham) is the co-founder of the Native American Community Academy (NACA) and executive director of the NACA Inspired Schools Network (NISN), a network that assists communities in implementing structures of Indigenous education. He's a Pahara Next Gen fellow, a Pahara-Aspen fellow, as well as a W. K. Kellogg Foundation Community Leadership Network fellow. Duta grew up on Standing Rock Reservation and resides in Albuquerque, NM. He graduated from Cornell University with a BA in Government and earned a Master in Business Administration as a Woodrow Wilson Fellow at the University of New Mexico.

Brad Hall is a Blackfeet educator, historian, and researcher who was raised on the Blackfeet Indian Reservation. Brad is a graduate of Montana State University with a bachelor's in history, master's in education, and doctorate in educational leadership. Brad has been a teacher and a higher education professional. Currently, he serves as the tribal outreach specialist for the University of Montana and serves all eight tribal communities in Montana. Brad works to enhance culturally based programing in PreK–20+ education. His presentations and publications involving research culturally based pedagogies promote best practices in tribal, educational, and other community leaders around Indian country.

Tsiehente Herne, Bear Clan of Akwesasne, is a mother of two and was recently engaged. She's a fluent Mohawk speaker and writer and teaches language through art. She's the director of the Title VI program at Salmon River Central School. She is a founding member of Konon:kwe Council, a circle of Mohawk women working to reconstruct the power of their origins through education, empowerment, and trauma-informed approaches. Tsiehente weaves an impeccable matrilineal thread in all her work and upholds the language in all her kinship societies. She's a tributary to the Iakionhehkwen life ways and upholds Haudenosaunee philosophies and self-determination regarding women and girls. Tsiehente graduated from Algonquin College in Ottawa and as a distinguished scholar of the arts from Elmira College.

Dr. renée holt is Diné from the *Tse'naha'bithni* clan and enrolled with the Nez Perce tribe. A mother of three, her work is grounded in Diné *K'é* and *Nimiipuuneewit himyuuweet* frameworks that are land-based and culturally sustaining. Her research interests center on restorative justice as a means towards healing and wellness and she serves as faculty at Northwest Indian College using Indigenous storywork as methodology, and the principles of relationality, respect, reciprocity, responsibility, and redistribution for her work and research in community. With a background in Native teacher education and working with public-school teachers and administrators on and near reservations, she works in her home community on the Nez Perce Reservation.

Monica A. Ka'imipono Kaiwi, a 37-year veteran teacher, currently serves as the English Department Head at Kamehameha Schools—Kapālama. For 32 years, she has practiced culture-based education, using a comparative approach to the integration of indigenous literature (Native Hawaiian) into traditional ELA curriculum; and for the past 16 years, she has taught AP Literature and Composition with Native Hawaiian literature/pedagogy as a comparative foundation. She holds a Master of Arts in English [focused on Hawaiian literature] from the University of Auckland, New Zealand (2001) and a Bachelor of Arts in English from Biola University, California (1983).

Dr. Walter Kahumoku III is currently the executive assistant to the chancellor at UH West O'ahu and the co-director of the Doctorate in Education in professional educational practice. A former school administrator, writing specialist, high school teacher, and director of forensics, Dr. Kahumoku has dedicated his work to improving the well-being of Hawaiian learners through education. His publications and presentations advocate for cultural, linguistic, and Indigenous approaches that advance relevant, rigorous, relationship-based, and responsibility-focused leading, teaching, and learning. As a former classroom teacher and administrator, he is called upon for his knowledge of curriculum development, instructional strategies, assessment, professional development, community integration, educational policy, and educational systems transformation that improve the ways in which native students are educated.

Ataugg'araq Grant Kashatok, (1963–2021; Yup'ik) served as a principal in the Yup'ik homelands for 13 years, after working as a village health aide, teacher's aide, high school teacher, and obtaining bachelor's and master's degrees in education. Grant was a dedicated and beloved son, brother, husband, uncle, father, proud papa (grandad), and coach, and he shared his passion for Yuuyaraq (the way of the human being), Yup'ik language, subsistence and dancing, academic achievement, reading, and basketball with many. Grant's insights on Indigenous education and climate change appear in *Everyday Antiracism: Getting Real About Race in School, Phi Delta Kappan,* and many news pieces and documentaries.

Keiki Kawai'ae'a is associate professor and a Native Hawaiian educator whose passion for revitalizing the Hawaiian language has guided her family and profession journey for over 40 years of Hawaiian-medium education to reestablish and renormalize Hawaiian as a medium of education P–25 (cradle–college–work–community). Dr. Kawai'ae'a currently serves as the director of Ka Haka 'Ula o Ke'elikōlani College of Hawaiian Language at the University of Hawai'i Hilo campus. Her contributions include developing Hawaiian medium programs/schools, Native teacher education, Indigenous accreditation, and Hawaiian educational frameworks, curriculum, and instruction.

Danielle Lansing (Diné) is a faculty member in early childhood education at the Southwestern Indian Polytechnic Institute. She holds a Bachelor of Science in elementary education from the University of New Mexico and a master's degree in early childhood risk and prevention from Harvard University. Additionally, Danielle earned her doctorate in education administration and supervision from Arizona State University. She has dedicated her career to serving Native children and families. Danielle's research interests include Indigenous research methodologies that amplify tribal college and university perspectives within teacher education. Danielle works and lives in Albuquerque, New Mexico with her husband and son.

Tiffany S. Lee (Diné/Oglala Lakota) is a professor and chair of Native American studies at the University of New Mexico. Her research examines educational and culturally based outcomes of Indigenous language immersion schools, Native youth perspectives on language reclamation, and socio-culturally centered education. Her work is published in journals, such as the *Journal of Language, Identity, and Education* and *of American Indian Education*; and in books, such as *Diné Perspectives: Revitalizing and Reclaiming Navajo Thought*. She is a former secondary social studies and language arts teacher. She is currently working with colleagues to open a Diné language nest in Albuquerque and to prepare Diné language immersion educators.

Vibeka Mitchell graduated from the University of New Mexico with a Bachelor of Science in family studies and minor in Native American studies. She has dedicated her career to serving Head Start centers with the Youth Development Incorporated (YDI). Vibeka has been employed as a lead teacher and center specialist at the Southwestern Indian Polytechnic Institute's (SIPI) Early Childhood Learning Center. She has mentored numerous SIPI students and collaborates with the early childhood education program to provide innovative programming for the Albuquerque community. Vibeka is an enrolled member of the Navajo Nation and calls Naschitti, New Mexico home.

Qötsahonmana, also **Sheilah E. Nicholas**, is from Songoopavi Village, Second Mesa, Arizona. A professor in the Department of Teaching, Learning, and Sociocultural Studies, College of Education, she teaches courses in Indigenous culture-based education, language and culture, oral traditions, and teacher research. Her work in Indigenous language revitalization and reclamation efforts is as an instructor for the American Indian Language Development Institute and instructor-consultant for the Indigenous Language Institute in Santa Fe, New Mexico. She is the University of Arizona co-principal investigator of a Spencer-funded, multi-university national study, Indigenous-Language Immersion and Native American Student Achievement, Investigating Indigenous Immersion as an Innovative Education Practice.

Timothy San Pedro is an associate professor of multicultural and equity studies at Ohio State University. He is Filipino-American and grew up on the Flathead Indian Reservation in Western Montana. His experiences there led him to focus his scholarship on the intricate link between motivation, engagement, and identity construction to curricula and pedagogical practices that re-center content and conversations upon Indigenous histories, perspectives, and literacies. San Pedro is an inaugural Gates Millennium scholar, Cultivating New Voices Among Scholars of Color fellow, Ford fellow, Concha Delgado Gaitan Council of Anthropology in Education Presidential fellow, and a Spencer Postdoctoral fellow.

Christine Stanton is an associate professor of education at Montana State University. She is a White woman who grew up near the Wind River Reservation and whose family has farmed for generations on Blackfeet homelands. Despite this proximity, Christine did not begin truly learning about Indigenous experiences until graduate school and her work in schools on and bordering the Wind River. Christine is grateful to mentors who have taught her about the importance of (re)Indigenizing education, especially those from Wind River and Blackfeet communities. Her current work focuses on advancing anti-colonial, social justice education through community-centered teaching, learning, and research.

Samuel Tenakhongva is a proud member of the Hopi tribe from the village of Sitsomovi (Flower Mound). Raised on the Hopi reservation, he is highly involved with his cultural activities and responsibilities including the protection and preservation of Hopi culture and customs. This has led him to being involved in advocating for tribal rights, repatriation of cultural items, and providing community education to build cultural knowledge and understanding. In support of this passion, he also is an elementary teacher on the reservation where he has taught multiple grade levels in all subject areas, along with helping students develop their computer and technology skills. Prior to becoming a teacher, Sam served as the marketing/special events manager for the Hopi Education Endowment Fund. He also served a 3-year term on the board of directors for the Arizona Humanities Council. Sam holds degrees from the University of Arizona with a Bachelor of Fine Arts in visual communications and from Northern Arizona University with a bachelor's in elementary education with a bilingual and multicultural endorsement, and a Master of Education in educational technology.

My name is **Cynthia Wilson**; my Indian name, Oomagelees, from my maternal side of the family. My father's is Culaxten, James H. Wilson, from Lummi and my mother is Roberta Hunt Wilson. I have worked in the education field for many years; I enjoy working with learners of all ages. I am fortunate I learned our language and our way of life. I received my master's degree from Grand Canyon University. I will continue my journey in education; my philosophy is to help our children know who they are and to strengthen the educational experiences. Hy'sh'qe.

Leisy Wyman is a professor of teaching, learning, and sociocultural studies at the University of Arizona. Since the 1990s, when she taught high school in the Yup'ik region of Alaska, her work has focused on intergenerational dialogue and learning, youth language, literacies and development, Indigenous research methodologies, Indigenous education, and language policy and planning. Her work appears in articles, chapters, and books including *Kipnirmiut Tiganrita Igmirtitlrit = Qipnermiut Tegganrita Egmirtellrit = The Legacy of the Kipnuk Elders; Everyday Antiracism: Getting Real About Race in School; Youth Culture, Language Endangerment, and Linguistic Survivance;* and *Indigenous Youth and Multilingualism: Language Identity, Ideology, and Practice in Dynamic Cultural Worlds.*

ABOUT THE ARTIST

Mavasta Bryant Honyouti is Hopi from the village of Hotevilla. He is of the Is'wungwa (Coyote) clan. He lives on the ancestral homelands of the Hopi with his wife and children. A graduate of the Center for Indian Education at Arizona State University, he has been teaching in tribally controlled schools for over 15 years. He is currently a junior high social studies teacher serving the Hopi and Diné youth. Mavasta is a critical Indigenous educator whose work is grounded in sustaining Indigenous values and engaging youth in becoming caretakers and protectors of their communities. He is co-author of the chapter, "Indigenous Teachers: At the Cross-Roads of Applying Indigenous Research Methodologies" (Garcia, Tenakhongva, & Honyouti; 2019, Taylor & Francis). Mavasta is an award-winning artist whose work can be seen at numerous museum exhibits and art shows throughout the country. Mavasta uniquely combines contemporary techniques fused with a traditional approach in his wood carvings. His work can be found at https://mhonyouti.com/